First Amendment

First Amendment

Laura E. Little
James G. Schmidt Professor of Law
Temple University School of Law

Wolters Kluwer

Published by Wolters Kluwer in New York.

Wolters Kluwer Legal & Regulatory U.S. serves customers worldwide with CCH, Aspen Publishers, and Kluwer Law International products. (www.WKLegaledu.com)

Cover images: Nella / Shutterstock; oersin / iStock

To contact Customer Service, e-mail customer.service@wolterskluwer.com, call 1-800-234-1660, fax 1-800-901-9075, or mail correspondence to:

Wolters Kluwer
Attn: Order Department
PO Box 990
Frederick, MD 21705

Printed in the United States of America.

1 2 3 4 5 6 7 8 9 0

ISBN 978-1-5438-2117-8

Library of Congress Cataloging-in-Publication Data

Names: Little, Laura E., 1957- author.
Title: First Amendment / Laura E. Little, James G. Schmidt Professor of
   Law, Temple University School of Law.
Description: New York : Wolters Kluwer, [2021] | Series: Examples and
   explanations | Includes index.
Identifiers: LCCN 2020056308 | ISBN 9781543821178 (paperback) | ISBN
   9781543822298 (ebook)
Subjects: LCSH: United States. Constitution. 1st Amendment. | Freedom of
   expression — United States. | Freedom of religion — United States. |
   Freedom of association — United States.
Classification: LCC KF4558 1st . L58 2021 | DDC 342.7308/5 — dc23
LC record available at https://lccn.loc.gov/2020056308

About Wolters Kluwer Legal & Regulatory U.S.

Wolters Kluwer Legal & Regulatory U.S. delivers expert content and solutions in the areas of law, corporate compliance, health compliance, reimbursement, and legal education. Its practical solutions help customers successfully navigate the demands of a changing environment to drive their daily activities, enhance decision quality and inspire confident outcomes.

Serving customers worldwide, its legal and regulatory portfolio includes products under the Aspen Publishers, CCH Incorporated, Kluwer Law International, ftwilliam.com and MediRegs names. They are regarded as exceptional and trusted resources for general legal and practice-specific knowledge, compliance and risk management, dynamic workflow solutions, and expert commentary.

About Wolters Kluwer Legal & Regulatory U.S.

For Rich, Cate, and Graham
. . . and for the legions of students who have taught me over the years

Summary of Contents

PART I. FREEDOM OF COMMUNICATION

PART II. RELIGION

Contents

Acknowledgments

I gratefully acknowledge the extraordinary production help of Erica Maier and the excellent research assistance of Tyler Friedman, Jeremy Gradwohl, Katie Klodowski, Jonah Levinson, Arbenita Misini, Caitlin O'Malley, Joseph Salaman, Heather Swadley, and Laura Wojcik. I am indebted to the insights and suggestions of the anonymous reviewers for the manuscript to this book, whose suggestions I happily (and humbly) adopted and integrated into the ultimate product. Finally, I tip my hat to other legal academic colleagues who gave suggestions, including Professors Craig Green and Steven Green.

Acknowledgments

Introduction

Congress shall make no law respecting an establishment of religion, or prohibiting the free exercise thereof; or abridging the freedom of speech, or of
the press; or the right of the people peaceably to assemble, or to petition the
Government for a redress of grievances.

As with many parts of the U.S. Constitution, the language of the First
Amendment does not mean precisely what it says. Nor does it have the
impact that it suggests. First, it does not just bind Congress, but acts as a
control on all of government. Also—its seemingly absolute words suggest
that it precludes all limits on the protected activities. But the Amendment
does no such thing. Rather, the doctrines developed to give effect to the
Amendment are nuanced and qualified, belying the simplicity of its words.
The brevity of the First Amendment is also misleading (its words represent
only a small fraction of the Constitution's text). For such a brief admoni-
tion, the First Amendment has impressive impact on government, culture,
society, and everyday life. The length of this book stands as a testament
to the complexity of First Amendment case law. Also, the words focusing on "speech, or of the press" suggest that the First Amendment applies
only to oral or printed communication, but the amendment also applies
to non-verbal, symbolic expressions such as flag burning. Finally, the First
Amendment's text suggests that all speech is of equal value, deserving equal
protection. Yet a dominant theme in First Amendment case law highlights
the importance of political speech, which in the Supreme Court's opinion
serves as an essential handmaiden to effective democratic self-government.

By contrast, other forms of speech receive no protection, as is the case with obscenity or deceptive commercial speech.

Perhaps even more than other areas of constitutional law, the First Amendment is the victim of the U.S. Supreme Court's indecision, politicization, and inconsistency. The doctrines are unstable and contradictory. Moreover, the body of First Amendment law is comprised of parallel strands that are either redundant or inconsistent. A particular fact pattern logically may be resolved using several of the strands, but the Court has never clarified why it uses one strand rather than another in the cases that come before it. Perhaps it simply depends on how the advocates pitch a particular case—with the Supreme Court taking its cues from the arguments in the parties' briefs.

All of these qualities combine to make this a challenging subject. As frustrating and baffling as these qualities are, study of the First Amendment holds many rewards. Its centrality to our system of government and our definition as a people renders it extraordinarily important. Indeed, its place at the beginning of the Bill of Rights is no mistake.

This book not only explains the subtleties of each First Amendment doctrine, but also situates the doctrines within the overall scheme of First Amendment case law. As you begin a new topic in class, read the accompanying portion of this book. This will give you an overview of the area and a preliminary sense of its "moving parts." Most importantly, be an active reader. In reading the examples in the book, try to resolve them yourself before reading the explanation. After you read the actual cases, consider them in light of the doctrinal descriptions in this book. How do the cases compare? Do they have a direct logical relationship with the doctrines? How do they fit within the overall framework described in this book? Could the case have been easily resolved with another strand of doctrine? If so, is there any apparent reason why the Court did not rely on that strand of doctrine?

Although the multitude of doctrinal strands for analyzing a particular fact pattern can be daunting, this quality is actually an opportunity for creative thinking, rich legal analysis, and strategic lawyering. To assist you in reaping these benefits, Chapter 17 and Chapter 21 of this book provide a strategy for choosing the most apt strand or strands of doctrine for analyzing a particular fact pattern.

A. FIRST AMENDMENT VALUES

Given the complexities and internal contradictions among First Amendment cases, you will likely encounter difficulties making a judgment about the proper analysis and proper disposition of First Amendment issues.

Identifying and charting the values motivating the Amendment are enormously helpful to these tasks, providing "tie-breakers" when a dispute presents compelling arguments on opposite sides of an issue. This is true for navigating through case law concerning both major portions of the Amendment: freedom of communication and religion issues. At the same time, you should be mindful of the criticisms leveled against using these values to answer difficult speech and religion issues. Appreciating these criticisms serves to elevate your understanding of the subtle challenges posed by these issues. As you proceed through the different First Amendment subjects presented in the volume, you will find it helpful (1) to watch how courts use the values in developing rationales for decisions and (2) to evaluate whether the rationales are valid given the criticisms of using the values in First Amendment jurisprudence.

I. Freedom of Communication Values

a. The Major Values

The most frequently touted value animating strong protection for freedom of communication is the need to promote effective democratic government. In order to ensure that citizens knowledgeably participate in elections and other aspects of government, they must have access to an extensive trove of information, available only when communication is unhindered. Moreover, citizens' ability to monitor official action and criticize government is an important check on corruption. Staffed by human beings with basic self-preservation instincts, government cannot be expected to evenhandedly censor its critics. Accordingly, any attempt at censorship raises important concerns about protecting the essential role of the citizenry in the functioning of government. These concerns highlight an instrumental and utilitarian view of the First Amendment, focusing on the benefits the Amendment provides to the society that it serves.

This instrumental and utilitarian view of freedom of communication focuses on what good the freedom can achieve. But one can also take the position freedom of communication is an end in itself; it is something to be protected because it is essential to human dignity and the basic human impulse to express oneself. Aligned with the concept of individual dignity is the theory that free communication fosters the value of self-realization. Exposure to a wide range of ideas allows individuals to explore the possible alternatives for how to live their lives to ensure their own well-being and the well-being of others. One can argue that the result promotes personal growth, self-sufficiency, and autonomy. This angle on the First Amendment could be described as "nonconsequential," since it focuses on properties intrinsic to the free expression, rather than its consequences.

A related communication value is truth-seeking. Without a vigorous market place of ideas, the argument goes, individuals cannot fully explore possible points of view. Nor can we know whether false ideas can be exposed and countered. Only through free debate, speech, and counter-speech can pernicious ideas be fully identified and understood.

One can observe that the self-realization and truth-seeking values justify protecting a broader range of speech than would be protected if the only focus of free speech principles were to ensure a functioning democracy. Focus on democratic values leads to particular concern with protecting political speech. By contrast, focus on self-realization and truth-seeking not only concerns political speech, but also emphasizes communicating about other phenomena such as science and art—without regard to whether the phenomena make a political message or not.

Finally, some argue that freedom of communication promotes a basic value in society: tolerance. This argument starts with the premise that we do not have the First Amendment to protect speech that we favor. Such speech does not need protection. Rather, the First Amendment's main function is to protect unfavored speech. In so doing, the First Amendment cases force self-restraint among the government and general population, encouraging them to develop their capacity to control negative reactions to unpleasant speech. According to this theory, protecting unpopular speech is an act of tolerance, and such tolerance serves as a model that models and encourages more tolerance. The end result, this theory maintains, is that citizens learn to better navigate a conflict-infused society.

b. Critiques of the Freedom of Communication Values

Several critiques of developing a First Amendment approach based on these values focus on contemporary social and technical realities. Critics of relying on the self-government value note that its asserted importance assumes that individual citizens have the capacity, time, and interest to make independent personal decisions. That assumption, the argument goes, ignores many voters' tendency to turn off their critical faculties, and even become alienated, in the face of mass media, social media, and big government. Some argue that theories based on the self-government value overemphasize speech on political topics, while ignoring other categories of speech such as speech about philosophy, literature, and the arts that also contribute to thoughtful democratic engagement.

In a similar vein, critics attack the premise that a marketplace of ideas promotes the truth-seeking value. The marketplace of ideas theory necessarily assumes that those who consume communications are critical thinking, rational decision makers. This assumption ignores that humans rely in some measure on emotions and instincts in making decisions. Critics maintain that—in this era of false speech, sophisticated opinion leaders who dominate and manipulate the media, individuals' tendency to consume one-sided social media, and demagogues—the notion of a robust and honest exchange of speech and counter-speech is illusory. The argument continues that, even assuming that truth can ultimately emerge in contemporary society, the process of debate is time-consuming. This luxury of time is not always available, particularly in the context of elections, social unrest, and immediate threats to safety. Finally are those who challenge the underlying notion that objective truth even exists, thus viewing as foolhardy the notion that the truth-seeking value provides a useful guide for navigating free speech challenges.

Those who challenge reliance on the self-realization value in the free speech context largely emphasize the value of other modes of self-determination and self-realization. Other forms of conduct, such as creation of music or refinement of athletic skill, may equally contribute to these goals. Yet the heightened constitutional protection that speech enjoys is usually not extended to these activities.

A common response to the value of promoting tolerance acknowledges that it reflects the honorable goal shaping society's intellectual character for the better. Critics wonder, however, whether allowing disparaging speech to flourish really has the potential of promoting tolerance. Does there really exist a strong causal link between tolerating hateful, ugly speech and tolerating diversity and differences among members of society?

2. Values Animating the Religion Clauses

A notable tension exists between the clause of the First Amendment protecting free exercise of religion and the establishment clause, which precludes government from favoring any particular religion, from preferring religion over non-religion, and from otherwise providing government support for religion. The tension arises because government can violate one of these clauses when it acts to aggressively enforce the other clause. Recognizing this tension, the Supreme Court of the United States has noted the difficulty of charting a neutral path, observing that since the two clauses are cast in absolute terms, they will inevitably clash. So, for example, if the government provides services to a church in order to ensure that the church can fulfill its religious mission, the government risks violating the establishment clause. By contrast, if schools prohibit all student prayer on school property in order to avoid promoting religion, the schools may violate the free exercise clause. The values underlying the two clauses also reflect this tension.

This clash in values is most clearly reflected when one focuses on the notion that the free exercise clause provides special protection for religion because religion is inherently desirable. The problem with government promoting this value, of course, is that the establishment clause inhibits direct government assistance to promote religion. A deeper explanation for the free exercise clause arises from the position that religion is a kind of personal autonomy that the liberal state should protect. Religion is directly tied to an individual's vision of what is good, and individuals should be as free as possible to form their own vision and their own plans for life. The function of government is to establish rules to ensure that individuals can pursue their visions without infringement by others or by government itself.

While the value of protecting religion underlies the establishment clause and the free exercise clause alike, the establishment clause is also motivated by values not relevant to the free exercise clause. For example, the Framers of the establishment clause were concerned that government connection with religion would interfere with church affairs and corrupt church operation. They were worried that the corruption would go in the other direction as well—with religious irrationality invading government. Additionally, the Framers believed that separating church and state would discourage government from showing preference for one religion over another and would promote religious pluralism. Religious pluralism, they thought, would in turn prevent religious factions from becoming powerful enough to oppress other factions.

Critics point out that the need for the establishment clause is diminished in current U.S. society. At the time that the First Amendment was drafted and ratified, some forces in government did promote and engage in the establishment of religion by favoring particular denominations. This suggests to some critics that the establishment clause was indeed necessary at the time of ratification, but that these establishments were long ago eliminated—at least by the time of the Fourteenth Amendment's adoption (1868). Some go further and suggest that some support for fighting of government establishment of religion arose from hostility to the *particular* denominations favored. Accepting the view that government establishment of religion has substantially diminished or disappeared today, one might argue that the establishment clause has now outlasted its purpose and that the free exercise clause alone is adequate to protect against any attempt to infringe on the freedom of adherents to denominations that may be disfavored by forces in society.

Other criticisms of the religion clauses largely focus on the untenable dilemma posed by tension between the free exercise and establishment clauses as well as the difficulties of defining religion. Chapter 18 reviews these problems in detail, and Chapters 19 to 21 illustrate how the problems play out in the context of specific cases.

B. EMPHASIS ON FREEDOM OF COMMUNICATION

A look at the Table of Contents of this book reveals emphasis on freedom of communication over other aspects of the First Amendment. This emphasis mirrors the Supreme Court's focus on freedom of communications as contrasted with other parts of the amendment. First Amendment courses in law school — and First Amendment casebooks — reflect this prominence of materials concerning the amendment's provisions about communication freedoms. For these reasons, this book also highlights freedom of communication matters.

Despite both official and unofficial emphasis on freedom of communication, you should remember as you proceed through this volume that all parts of the First Amendment now apply to both the state and the federal government. You may recall from your introduction to Constitutional Law that the U.S. Supreme Court made clear in *Barron v. Baltimore*, 32 U.S. 243 (1833), that the Bill of Rights applied only against federal government actions. Yet almost a century later, in *Gitlow v. New York*, 268 U.S. 652 (1925), the Supreme Court asserted that freedom of speech and the press "are among the fundamental personal rights and 'liberties' protected by the due process clause of the Fourteenth Amendment from impairment by the States." *Id.* at 630. The rest of the First Amendment followed, with the U.S. Supreme Court ruling that both the free exercise clause and the establishment clause were made applicable to the states through the Fourteenth Amendment due process clause. *Everson v. Board of Education*, 330 U.S. 1 (1947) (incorporating the establishment clause); *Cantwell v. Connecticut*, 310 U.S. 296 (1940) (incorporating the free exercise clause).

PART I

Freedom of
Communication

The speech and press clause is the major part of the beginning of the First Amendment. The freedom of association concept, however, is considered closely linked with the speech and press clause. Together they make up the freedom of communication protections of the First Amendment. That said, the freedom of speech portion of the First Amendment is not only often deemed the most important protection, but has also attracted most of the U.S. Supreme Court's energy in the First Amendment area.

CHAPTER 1

The Distinction Between Content-Based and Content-Neutral Regulations

A. THE GENERAL CONCEPT

A content-based restriction on speech is triggered by the substance or content of the message that is conveyed. A content-neutral regulation of speech is unrelated to the speech content. The courts are particularly suspicious of content-based restrictions because they are a form of censorship and carry the appearance that the government is attempting to take particular subject matters out of the marketplace of ideas. Accordingly, once a court labels a restriction as content based, the court will evaluate the restriction with strict scrutiny. Examples of content-based restrictions are those that are aimed at a particular subject and those with restrictions resulting from the speaker's identity. A particularly suspicious content-based restriction is viewpoint based: that is, a restriction targeted at one side of debate. So, for example, assume that a public school banned all speakers in the school who discussed current events. This appears to be a content-based restriction. If the ban were more fine-tuned, targeting only speakers who criticize the President, then the restriction would be viewpoint based as well. Courts generally apply strict scrutiny to viewpoint-based restrictions with particular vigor.

Under the strict scrutiny test, the government must show that the regulation serves a compelling state interest. In addition, the government must provide that it has narrowly tailored the restriction to serve that interest.

If the restriction is content neutral, the restriction is still subject to First Amendment concerns. Although courts take a more relaxed approach to content-neutral regulations than content-based regulations that are generally subject to strict scrutiny, courts still subject content-neutral restrictions to intermediate scrutiny. Specifically, they find that a government regulation can be constitutional if the regulation

1. is narrowly tailored to serve "a significant government interest;"
2. is justified "without reference to the content of the regulated speech;" and
3. leaves open "ample alternative avenues for communication of the information."

Ward v. Rock Against Racism, 491 U.S. 781, 791 (1989) (quoting *Clark v. Community for Creative Non-Violence*, 468 U.S. 288, 293 (1984)).

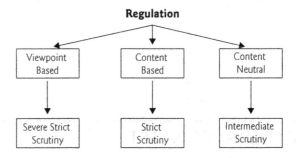

Figure 1-1

Example 1-1:

City #1 institutes a ban on all marches down the city's main artery during rush hour. City #1 maintains that the reason for its ban is to avoid disrupting traffic during a time of day when traffic is already congested. City #2 institutes a ban on all marches down the city's main artery on the topic of "Black Lives Matter." City #2 maintains that the reason for its ban is to avoid disrupting traffic and that Black Lives Matter marches can become highly disruptive. Both cities maintain that their bans are content neutral. Are both cities correct?

Explanation:

Only City #1 is correct. Its ban makes no reference to the subject of the march and it proffers an explanation for the ban that applies to all marches at a particular time. For that reason, the ban is content neutral. City #2's ban focuses on marches concerning a specific subject and is therefore content based. City #2's explanation for the ban may be relevant to evaluating whether the ban can satisfy strict scrutiny, but does not qualify for making the ban content neutral.

I. The Distinction Between Content-Based and Content-Neutral Regulations

Note that although a content neutral restriction may not be motivated by a desire to censor a particular message, the restriction can still infringe communication freedoms. Take for example City #1's ban: the city may not be motivated to censor any message, but refusing to allow marches during rush hour may deprive marchers the opportunity to communicate their message most effectively and to the greatest number of people. This type of effect is considered in determining whether a content–neutral restriction is constitutional.

* * *

Example 1-1 is a relatively easy case for distinguishing between content-neutral and content-based restrictions. Determining how to characterize a restriction, however, is not always simple. In *Reed v. Town of Gilbert*, the Court described the framework for determining whether a government's regulation of speech is a content-based law that "target[s] speech based on its communicative content, or a content-neutral "time, place, or manner" restriction. 576 U.S. 155 (2015). The *Reed* Court described the content-based test as a "commonsense" determination: a government regulation of speech is content based if "on its face [it] draws distinctions based on the message a speaker conveys." *Id.* at 163 (internal quotations omitted). In the "second step" of the *Reed* test, a facially neutral regulation will also be classified as content based if it "cannot be justified without reference to the content of the regulated speech" or if it "was adopted by the government because of disagreement with the message [the speech] conveys." *Id.* (internal quotations omitted). One notable aspect of the *Reed* test is the Court's suggestion that the government's motive for passing the regulation is not relevant. In the *Reed* Court's words: "A law that is content based on its face is subject to strict scrutiny regardless of the government's benign motive, content-neutral justification, or lack of 'animus toward the ideas contained' in the regulated speech." *Id.* at 2228 (quoting *Cincinnati v. Discovery Network, Inc.*, 507 U.S. 410, 429 (1993)). In other words, a law that is content based on its face will not be viewed as content neutral even if the government did not wish to censor any particular message.

How broadly should *Reed*'s holding be construed? The answer to this question requires an understanding of an earlier case, *Renton v. Playtime Theatres, Inc.* In *Renton*, the Court suggested that a facially content-based restriction will be deemed content neutral if it serves a permissible content-neutral purpose. 475 U.S. 41 (1986). The *Renton* Court rejected a First Amendment attack on an ordinance prohibiting motion picture theaters from locating within 1,000 feet of any residential zone, dwelling, church, park, or school. *Id.* at 43. Because the ordinance applied only to theaters featuring sexually explicit films, it appeared content based. *Id.* at 47. Nonetheless, the Court treated the law as content neutral because the government designed the law to control the effects of the theaters on matters such as crime rather than to restrict speech. *Id.* Indeed, the Court held that the Renton ordinance was "consistent with [their] definition of content neutral speech regulations" because it was "justified without reference to the content of the regulated speech." 475 U.S. at 48. The approach that the *Renton* Court outlined is called the "secondary effects" doctrine: the government's regulation focuses on the secondary effects of speech and not the speech's content. The end of this chapter explores the secondary effects doctrine in greater depth.

Reed suggested a different role for evaluating the function or purpose of a speech restriction than *Renton*. Specifically, the *Reed* Court described the ways in which a regulation can be content based as follows: "Some facial distinctions based on a message are obvious, defining regulated speech by its particular subject matter, . . . others are more subtle, defining regulated speech by its *function or purpose*." *Reed*, 576 U.S. 163-164 (emphasis added). The *Reed* Court went on to explain that BOTH of these distinctions are content based and are thus subject to strict scrutiny. Moreover, the *Reed* Court's statement that governmental motive is not relevant to the analysis is in tension with the *Renton* Court's statement that the government's desire to regulate the secondary effects of speech (rather than the speech's content) can render the regulation content neutral.

As a consequence of *Reed*'s unclear approach to this issue, questions have arisen as to whether — contrary to the suggestion in *Renton* — a regulation that discriminates against speech based solely on its purpose or function can still be considered content neutral. Lower courts have taken different approaches to the question. Some courts have treated this "function or purpose" language as a binding part of *Reed*'s holding, while others have dismissed this language and distinguished a speaker's purpose from the communicative content of their speech. This split is difficult to resolve because *Reed* did not disparage or overrule *Renton*.

For illustration of the lower court confusion over the importance of "function or purpose" language, consider the following two Examples. In *Working America., Inc. v. City of Bloomington*, 142 F. Supp. 3d 823 (D. Minn. 2015), the court invalidated a licensing scheme directed at door-to-door solicitation. The scheme imposed significant restrictions on the door-to-door activity depending on the function and purpose of the solicitation. For that reason, the court struck down the scheme using the following reasoning:

> [Under the challenged scheme], speech that has the function or purpose of generating money or property on behalf of a person, organization, or cause is [subject to permitting restrictions], while speech that lacks such purpose is not . . . [as] in *Reed*, the need to obtain a permit depends entirely on the communicative content of the message. If the purpose of the speaker is merely to raise awareness for an issue or to collect signatures for a proposed ballot initiative, a permit is not required. However, once the individual asks for a

donation, the purpose or function of the speech has changed and a permit is now required.

Id.

This reasoning contrasts with the court's opinion in *March v. Mills*, 867 F.3d 46 (1st Cir. 2017), which concerned a state statute creating a "bubble zone" against certain communication outside health care facilities. The statute at issue allowed regulation of communication made with intent to "jeopardize the health of persons receiving health services within the building; or . . . [t]o interfere with the safe and effective delivery of those services within the building." *Id.* at 51. Surely this regulation targets the function or purpose of the communication. But the court upheld the statute, focusing instead on the statute's lack of reference to the content of the communication regulated. Citing this reason, the *March* court concluded that the regulation was content neutral, even under the authority of *Reed*. For further consideration of a statute similar to that in *March*, see Example 1-5 below.

Example 1-2:

Citing "aesthetic concerns," a city passes an ordinance that regulates permissible signage. The measure imposed size limitations on any "sign" that is visible from a public right-of-way in the city. The ordinance, however, exempted any "flag or emblem of any nation, organization of nations, state, city, or any religious organization," and any "works of art that in no way identify or specifically relate to a product or service." A local radio station places a large billboard protesting the city government's use of eminent domain outside of its studio in a location visible from a nearby interstate highway. The radio station would like to enjoin the city from enforcing the ordinance against their billboard, arguing that the ordinance is an impermissible content-based regulation.

Explanation:

The sign ordinance is unconstitutional. The ordinance is content based because it draws distinctions, on its face, based on the signs' content. The city has not demonstrated that the ordinance passes strict scrutiny because it has provided no compelling analytical connection between the distinctions made and the aesthetic purpose of the ordinance. Even assuming that "aesthetic concerns" qualify as a compelling purpose, the details of the regulation (including its distinctions among different signs) must *serve* that compelling purpose.

Example 1-3:

A city ordinance regulates mobile advertising displays on motor vehicles operating on city streets. The city does not define the word "advertise" in the ordinance in reference to the content promoted, and state courts interpreted the word broadly to apply to both commercial and non-commercial content promotion.

The term "advertise" in the ordinance is not limited to calling the public's attention to a product or a business. The definition of "advertise" is more general: "to make something known and to announce publicly, especially by a printed notice or a broadcast." Thus, although the subject matter of the banned notice may be commercial, it is not necessarily so. The ordinance makes clear that messages endorsing a political candidate, a social cause, or a religious belief would also fall within the term "advertise." Citing safety concerns, the legislative history for the ordinance stated that—after evaluating data related to traffic accidents—the city council determined that mobile advertising signs create a significant risk of distracting drivers.

The operator of a video billboard truck would like to enjoin the city from enforcing the statute, arguing that the ordinance is an impermissible content-based regulation because it applies only to advertisements.

Explanation:

The ordinance is likely constitutional, and the operator of the video billboard truck will not receive the requested injunction. First, the ordinance appears content neutral. The ordinance is not limited to calling the public's attention to a product or a business but covers all likely topics of mobile advertising displays. For this reason, the ordinance does not appear to discriminate based on content. Accordingly, the test of evaluating the constitutionality of the ordinance is intermediate scrutiny. The ordinance serves the significant purpose of avoiding traffic accidents and is narrowly tailored to the type of advertisements that have been shown to distract drivers. Because the ordinance does not prohibit all advertisements, it allows for ample alternative options for communication.

Example 1-4:

Responding to complaints about litter and unsightliness in its historic district, a village enacted a scheme that governs the placement and operation of unattended collection boxes. No box that "accepts personal property items to be used by the operator for distribution, resale, or recycling," may operate on any city block on which over half of the buildings have been designated as historic by the town's city council.

A non-profit that distributes donated clothing would like to place a collection box on one of these blocks and seeks to challenge the regulation as an impermissible content-based regulation.

Explanation:

The ordinance is constitutional. It appears content neutral. Although the ordinance focuses on the function of the collection boxes, it does not differentiate based upon the mission of the organization sponsoring the box. It applies broadly to all collection bins for personal property, regardless of whether they are operated for a charitable or for-profit purpose. Moreover, the ordinance does not differentiate among drop-off boxes based on: (1) the non-expressive (functional) aspect of the boxes or (2) anything written on the boxes or other aspects of the boxes' attempt to express a message.

Intermediate scrutiny applies. The concern with maintaining the historic character of the district is a substantial governmental purpose. Because the restriction is confined to historic areas, it is narrowly tailored. Many other places in the city exist for placing the boxes. For this reason, the ordinance also satisfies the "ample alternative avenues for communication of the information" prong of intermediate scrutiny.

* * *

In *Hill v. Colorado*, the U.S. Supreme Court upheld as content neutral a criminal statute prohibiting any person from knowingly approaching within eight feet of persons near a health care facility without the persons consent "for the purpose of passing a leaflet or handbill to, displaying a sign to, or engaging in oral protest, education, or counseling with such other person . . . ." 530 U.S. 703 (2000). Consider the following Example in light of *Hill* and the U.S. Supreme Court's 2015 sign case, *Reed v. Town of Gilbert*, which was discussed above.

Example 1-5:

A state statute bars a person from making noise that "can be heard within a building" when, following an order from law enforcement to cease the noisemaking, the noise is made with the intent to either disrupt the safe and effective operation of health services within the building or jeopardize the persons receiving health services.

An anti-abortion activist would like to organize a protest outside of a reproductive health clinic and seeks to enjoin the enforcement of the statute, arguing that it is impermissible content-based regulation.

17

Explanation:

Based on the *Renton* decision, the statute is arguably content neutral because the disruptive intent requirement in the measure does not discriminate based on the "communicative content" of the speech. Yet, as explained above, this emphasis on intent appeared discredited in the *Reed* opinion when the Court explained how a statute can be content based as follows: "Some facial distinctions based on a message are obvious, defining regulated speech by its particular subject matter, ... others are more subtle, defining regulated speech by its *function or purpose*." *Reed*, 576 U.S at 163-164 (emphasis added). This language makes clear that regulation of speech based on its function or purpose is content based and thus subject to strict scrutiny. *But see March v. Mills*, 867 F.3d 46 (1st Cir. 2017) (discussed earlier in this chapter).

If one ignores this language from *Reed* and focuses only on whether the regulation explicitly targets speech on particular topics, one could conceivably conclude that the state statute in this Example is content neutral. Indeed, *Reed* held that the town's sign measure in that case was content based because the restriction "depend[ed] entirely on the communicative content of the sign." *Id.* at 164. Yet even with this narrow focus on the rule of *Reed* (which would allow one to ignore the state statute's focus on the function and purpose of the regulated speech), one might still reason that this statute's regulation does have a content-based quality. Because the statute's restriction confines its scope to particular locations—outside buildings where health care services occur—one might infer that the restriction targets certain types of speech that one expects would be communicated outside a health care facility. On the other hand, the statute appears content neutral to the extent that it would not treat a protest outside of a hospital differently depending on whether it was carried out by hospital staff calling for higher wages, opponents of abortion rights, or property owners protesting the hospital's effects on nearby real estate values.

Although the ultimate determination of whether the state statute is content based is uncertain, the statute had several qualities that arguably tip the balance in favor of determining that it was content neutral: (1) *Reed's* apparent refusal to criticize *Renton*, (2) the statute's restricted scope (allowing alternative avenues for speech), and (3) the statute's equal treatment of all kinds of loud activity outside medical facilities. Another factor favoring a content-neutral characterization is the statute's similarity to the statute upheld in *Hill v. Colorado*, 530 U.S. 703 (2000). Weakening the strength of this factor, however, is the fact that it predates the *Reed* decision. Nonetheless, no language in *Reed* directly diminishes the precedential value of *Hill v. Colorado*.

Focusing on all these factors, one might conclude that the statute is constitutional if it satisfies intermediate scrutiny. Because human health and life hang in the balance, protection of the welfare of those receiving medical treatment is the type of purpose that easily earns the label "significant." Given that other places to protest exist and the statute does not discriminate among types of protests, the statute would pass intermediate scrutiny.

Example 1-6:

Seeking to protect the sanctity and residential privacy of its citizens, a state passes a law that bans robocalls made without the called individual's consent for the purpose of "soliciting political support for a candidate or cause" or "for the purpose of marketing consumer goods."

A political consulting firm would like to use automated dialer machines to place robocalls to voters ahead of an election. The firm therefore challenges the statute as impermissible content-based regulation.

Explanation:

The law is content-based because it applies only to calls with consumer or political messages and not to calls for other purposes. The law is unconstitutional because it does not pass strict scrutiny. The proffered reason for the law—protecting the sanctity and residential privacy of citizens—could possibly be characterized as compelling, but the reason does not explain why the law singles out consumer and political calls only. Other types of calls are likely to be equally invasive. Making matters worse, First Amendment jurisprudence reflects a special solicitude for political speech, since it is considered an important handmaiden to democracy. Because political messages may educate the voting public, courts are likely to scrutinize the law especially closely.

The United States Supreme Court decided a case similar to this Example in *Barr v. American Association of Political Consultants*, 140 S.Ct. 2335 (2020). In that case, the Court held that a portion of the Telephone Consumer Protection Act violated the First Amendment because it was content based and did not survive strict scrutiny. The plaintiffs in the case were political organizations who wished to make robocalls on political subjects. The Act prevented nearly all robocalls, but provided an exemption for government debt collection. The Court stated that a law favoring speech made for collecting government debt over political speech is "as content based as it gets," and invalidated this exemption in the Act. In arguing that the Act was content neutral, the government had argued that the law made distinctions based on the identity of the speaker rather than on what the speaker said. Rejecting this argument, the *American Association of Political Consultants* Court said that a law could still be content based if the distinction made in the law is based on the speaker's identity.

Example 1-7:

A town passes an ordinance aimed at curbing panhandling in its downtown historic district. The ordinance prohibits an individual from making an "oral request for an immediate donation of money." The ordinance does not apply to signs requesting immediate donations of money, nor does it apply to oral requests for donations of money at a later time.

A local non-profit that relies upon the solicitation of donations in the downtown historic district challenges the town's ordinance, arguing that it is impermissible content-based regulation.

Explanation:

The law does not restrict speech based on the ideas it conveys. Nor does the law restrict speech because the government disapproves its message. Nonetheless the ordinance is content based because it draws distinctions based on the communicative content of someone's message. The Constitution does not distinguish between content regulation and subject-matter regulation. First Amendment jurisprudence therefore requires a compelling justification. Although concern with the character of an historical district may be a substantial state interest, it does not rise to the level of compelling — the standard needed to uphold this content-based law. For that reason, the local non-profit's constitutional challenge is likely to prevail.

Example 1-8:

A state restricts ballot provisions by imposing a single-subject rule: No ballot referendum may include multiple subjects, and any ballot referendum that does must list each subject separately on the ballot to be voted upon separately by voters. The rule is designed to avoid voter confusion.

A political advocacy group seeks to place an initiative on the ballot that asks the voters to approve an amendment to the state's constitution that would simultaneously impose term limits on justices of the state supreme court and require that all laws apply equally to members of all of the state's governmental branches. The state's board of ballots, applying the single-subject rule, split the initiative into two, such that voters would have to vote on each question separately. The political advocacy group would like to challenge the single-subject rule, arguing that it is impermissible.

Explanation:

Governments have substantial latitude in determining what appears on a ballot. This single-subject rule in this Example, however, presents a particularly easy case because the rule is content neutral. Although its application requires enforcement authorities to evaluate the content of the message on the ballot — raising concerns with official intermeddling — the rule applies to all petition initiatives no matter the topic discussed or message conveyed. The purpose of avoiding voter confusion is a substantial state interest. Because the rule regulates only the form of ballots and does not prohibit multiple single-subject initiatives, it allows ample opportunities for communicating different initiatives.

B. TIME, PLACE, AND MANNER RESTRICTIONS

The government can regulate speech indirectly by imposing limits that are not concerned with the content of speech, but affect the circumstances under which expression takes place. These restrictions are content neutral and are called "time, place, and manner restrictions." Time, place, and manner restrictions are often used by the government to regulate the use of government property for speech purposes.

Time, place, and manner restrictions are, by nature, content neutral because they are not focused on the identity or the subject or message of the speech. Rather, these restrictions focus on the circumstances under which the speech is delivered. Yet because time, place, and manner restrictions can have the effect of limiting expression and restricting the audience for expression, the law carefully evaluates whether the restrictions are appropriately limited and are truly intended to regulate only on the time, place, and manner in which the communication occurs. In order to be constitutional, the regulation must also be narrowly tailored to serve a significant state interest and must leave open ample alternative channels for communication. (It should be noted, however, that these constitutional time, place, and manner requirements do not apply to the government when the government is the speaker).

Example I-9:

A city passed a regulation limiting the volume that music could be played in the music pavilion of a public park. The city intended the regulation to minimize disturbance to those living around the park and those visiting the park to relax, and not to listen to the music. Pointing to case law holding that music is "speech" for the purpose of the First Amendment, plaintiffs alleged this regulation violates First Amendment principles.

Explanation:

The plaintiffs are correct that music can be viewed as speech, but that does not necessarily mean that the regulation violates the First Amendment. In *Ward v. Rock Against Racism*, the Supreme Court recognized music as a mode of communication covered by the First Amendment and upheld the regulation of sound volume, even in the face of a costly requirement in the regulation that musicians must use sophisticated amplifiers and a sound technician provided by the city. 41 U.S. 781 (1989). The Court found that the regulation did not regulate on the basis of content and left ample alternative means of communication, since the regulation allowed full access to the music pavilion, but merely controlled the volume allowed. *Id.* Limitations on the volume of music in the music pavilion in this Example appear to satisfy a substantial state interest, to allow music to occur (thereby ensuring a means of communication), and regulate without regard to the content of the music.

Example 1-10:

The state fair committee in a U.S. state instituted a rule providing that anyone seeking to distribute or sell "merchandise" (including printed material) must obtain a license and perform activities in a fixed location. Under the rule, representatives of the organization could stroll the fair grounds and orally reach out to patrons, but all sales, fund solicitation, and distribution had to occur at a fixed, designated location on the fair grounds. The state fair committee decided that the rule was necessary to ensure the ease of pedestrian traffic flow through the most congested areas of the fair grounds. Representatives of a religious organization challenged the rule as a violation of their First Amendment rights of free expression.

Explanation:

The challenge will not be successful. In *Heffron v. International Society for Krishna Consciousness*, the U.S. Supreme Court described a rule similar to the one in this Example as a proper time, place, and manner restriction. 452 U.S. 641 (1981). The Court observed that the rule provided ample opportunity for alternative communication, particularly since the members of the organization could engage in face-to-face discussion while circulating with those attending the fair or speaking from a fixed location. Moreover, the rule in *Heffron* (like the rule in this Example) was not geared to the content of communication: it applied to all organizations that distributed literature while walking around the fairgrounds. Moreover, the Court determined that the rule was justified by the substantial state interest of ensuring ease of traffic flow—particularly in the case of emergency. That would also be the case with the present Example.

Example 1-11:

A state passed a statute prohibiting all convicted child sex offenders in the state from using any social media. A convicted sex offender filed suit arguing that the statute violated his First Amendment right. The state defended by arguing that the statute is a constitutional time, place, and manner restriction. Is the state correct?

Explanation:

Although preventing child sex abuse is easily classified as a significant — even compelling — state interest, the state is incorrect in suggesting that this is a proper time, place, and manner restriction because it is not neutral: it targets a specific speaker. As the Supreme Court stated in *Barr v. American Association of Political Consultants*, 140 S.Ct. 2336 (2020), a law can be content based if the law makes distinctions based on the speaker's identity.

Moreover, one might reasonably argue that this prohibition does not leave open sufficient alternative avenues for expression. As the U.S. Supreme Court stated in a case challenging a similar statute:

> Social media allows users to gain access to information and communicate with one another about it on any subject that might come to mind. By prohibiting sex offenders from using those websites, [the statute,] with one broad stroke[,] bars access to what for many are the principal sources for knowing current events, checking ads for employment, speaking and listening in the modern public square, and otherwise exploring the vast realms of human thought and knowledge. These websites can provide perhaps the most powerful mechanisms available to a private citizen to make his or her voice heard.

Packingham v. North Carolina, 137 S. Ct. 1730, 1737 (2017).

C. SECONDARY EFFECTS

As observed earlier in this chapter, the U.S. Supreme Court has stated that First Amendment analysis does not require strict scrutiny when government imposes restrictions that appear to be content based so long as the government's real motivation for the restriction is to suppress the secondary effects of a particular kind of speech. The challenge with this secondary effect principle is determining which effects qualify as secondary effects and which are deemed to regulate the content of speech. Courts will uphold speech restrictions when they fear that the speech will cause harm through noncommunicative effects. The secondary effect doctrine had its genesis in

Renton v. Playtime Theatres, Inc., in which the Supreme Court rejected a First Amendment attack on an ordinance prohibiting theaters featuring sexually explicit films from locating close to certain buildings. 475 U.S. 41 (1986). The Court treated the law as content neutral because—in the Court's judgment—the law was motivated by the desire to control the secondary effects of the theaters on matters such as crime rather than by the desire to restrict speech. *Id.*

As explained earlier, the current status of the secondary effect doctrine is not certain. Language in the U.S. Supreme Court's decision in *Renton* suggests that the government's motive should not be relevant to decide whether a regulation is content based and subject to strict scrutiny. 475 U.S. at 62. *Reed* also cast doubt on whether the doctrine has broad application beyond the zoning context. Nonetheless, lower courts still invoke the doctrine with some regularity and it is important to have some understanding of its parameters.

Example 1-12:

A city ordinance banned news racks on public sidewalks if the news racks contained newspapers with more than 85 percent advertising materials. The city maintains that the purpose of the ordinance is to avoid clutter on sidewalks and litter in the streets. For that reason, the city argues that the ordinance is content neutral and is designed only to address the secondary effects of the advertising circulars.

Explanation:

The city's argument is unpersuasive. Advertising circulars in news racks do not pose more a threat to clutter and litter than other types of publications distributed in news racks. For this reason, the ordinance appears to be content based and the secondary effect doctrine is inapplicable. *See* City of Cincinnati v. Discovery Network, 507 U.S. 410 (1993).

Example 1-13:

A state university instituted a policy banning speech on campus that had the effect of offending students or the tendency to persuade students to break the law. A lawsuit challenges the policy as a violation of the First Amendment. The university argues that it is merely attempting to regulate the secondary effects of speech and not the content of the speech. Is the university likely to prevail in this defense?

Explanation:

The university is not likely to prevail and the court will likely strike down the policy. The tendency of speech to offend people does not amount to a secondary effect allowing speech regulation, even if the speech prompts offense. Similarly, the ability of speech to inspire criminality at some unspecified time in the future does not alone render a regulation exempt from the First Amendment. The emotive power of these two types of speech is not secondary to its content. Instead, it is the content of the speech that persuades or offends the listener. Accordingly, an attempt to stifle these types of communications is content-based regulation, and not secondary effect regulation. *See R.A.V. v. City of Saint Paul,* 505 U.S. 377 (1992).

Brandenburg v. Ohio, sets out the circumstances under which the First Amendment allows the law to suppress speech that incites others to engage in illegality. 395 U.S. 444 (1969). The circumstances here do not satisfy the *Brandenburg* test, which is explored in detail in Chapter 6.

CHAPTER 2

Overbreadth and Vagueness

Consider a law that might offend you. In the First Amendment context, the law might seek to prevent you from posting a sign on your lawn that protests your township's attempt to cut down old growth trees on public lands. Perhaps the law's text provides: "It shall be unlawful to display signs on any property, visible from the road, that concern matters other than the sale of the property."

In the context of your desire to post the protest sign, you believe this prohibition is unconstitutional particularly because your message pertains to a matter of public concern. Your challenge to this law is likely an "as applied" challenge. What does that mean? Your concern focuses on how the law prevents you from expressing your particular message on a matter of public concern and that is how you would likely frame your lawsuit. From this point of view, the law as applied to your situation is unconstitutional.

The other possible approach would be for you to claim that the law is unconstitutional as a general matter. This would be a challenge attacking the law "on its face," an approach that is typically less successful than an "as applied" challenge. An "on its face" or "facial" challenge is a frontal attack on the constitutional judgment and wording of the lawmakers who drafted the law. Facial challenges are bolder and sometimes seen to invite judicial overreach. Why? Because facial challenges suggest that the lawmakers were especially reckless in framing the reach of a law, so as to create a prohibition that is unconstitutional when applied to a substantial number of cases. Moreover, because facial challenges reach beyond the plaintiff's particular circumstances, the plaintiff bringing the facial challenge is engaging in a usually unfavored litigation approach (particularly among federal courts): The "party seeks to vindicate not only his own rights, but those of others who may also be adversely impacted by the statute in question." *City of Chicago v. Morales*, 527 U.S. 41, 55 n.22 (1999). As explained further below, allowing plaintiffs to do this is unusual in federal litigation because it does not follow the usual standing requirements governing plaintiffs.

By contrast, an as-applied challenge may rest on the premise that a law-making body cannot predict the future or foresee every possible application of a general law. Hence, the First Amendment challenge may simply suggest that unforeseen circumstances reveal that the law—as applied to a narrow set of facts—regulates constitutionally protected speech and that the regulation directly injures the plaintiffs.

Facial challenges represent a broader attack on a statute than as-applied challenges. Specifically, a facial challenge attacks the full scope of the statute's reach and not merely the effect of the statute on the facts of the particular case. That said, a statute that does not survive a facial challenge could conceivably have survived an as-applied challenge had the plaintiff originally framed the lawsuit as an as-applied challenge. This would occur if the facts and circumstances that gave rise to the as-applied challenge could properly be regulated or prohibited consistently with the First Amendment. The opposite is also true: a statute that survives a facial challenge may be unconstitutional as applied to a particular situation.

More to the point of First Amendment doctrine: A facial challenge often suggests that, as a general matter, a law is so broad that it prohibits a wide-range of expression that the freedom of speech protects. Specifically, the law may inspire a speaker to "abstain from protected speech" to avoid the risk and expense of litigating whether particular expressions are constitutionally protected. *Virginia v. Hicks*, 539 U.S. 113, 119 (2003). Such a law is "overbroad." Similarly, traditional authority supports the notion that a facial

Relationship Between Facial and "As Applied"
Challenges

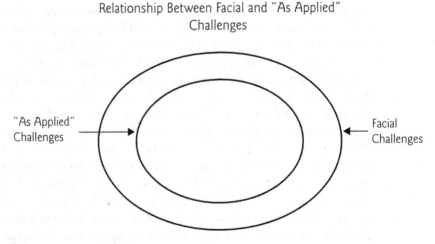

"As Applied"
Challenges

Facial
Challenges

Figure 2-1

challenge can suggest that the law is so unclear and lacking in standards that people forebear from constitutionally protected expression to avoid litigation or other problems.[1] This approach argues that the law is void for vagueness. Both overbreadth and vagueness provide First Amendment theories for attacking a law, and both are concerned with preserving "an uninhibited marketplace of ideas" by avoiding the "chilling effect" of a law on protected speech. Id. Both doctrines provide a mechanism allowing citizens an early opportunity to litigate a law's constitutionality so that they do not need to forebear from expression out of cautious fear of punishment or other negative legal consequences, even though the expression may be constitutionally protected. Likewise, the doctrines help to prevent against the risks of arbitrary or biased enforcement of an overbroad or vague law motivated by official disapproval with the viewpoint expressed in a communication.

Both the overbreadth and vagueness theories are more closely aligned with facial challenges than with as-applied challenges. That said, the line between facial and as-applied challenges is often fuzzy. This often results because the plaintiff's litigation approach is not clear, the court opinion disposing of the case is ambiguous regarding the nature of a law's infirmity, or both. As the U.S. Supreme Court observed in *Citizens United v. Federal Election Commission*: "the distinction between facial and as-applied challenges is not so well defined that it has some automatic effect or that it . . . always . . . control[s] . . . [the] disposition in every case." 558 U.S. 310, 331 (2009).

A. OVERBREADTH

First Amendment doctrine allows government officials to restrict lesser-valued expression (e.g., commercial speech and expression that deserves no protection at all, for example, obscenity). The overbreadth doctrine does not challenge this notion, but nonetheless empowers courts to strike down statutes that may permissibly regulate some expression, but are also so broad that they could prohibit constitutionally protected expression. An early decision addressing this concept is *Gooding v. Wilson*, in which the Supreme Court held that an overly broad statute justifies a constitutional challenge from someone whose speech might have been rightfully restricted under a

---

1. But see *Holder v. Humanitarian Law Project*, 561 U.S. 1, 18-19 (2010), in which the Supreme Court suggested that under modern law, vagueness challenges must generally be as-applied challenges rather than facial challenges: "We consider whether a statute is vague as applied to the particular facts at issue, for '[a] plaintiff who engages in some conduct that is clearly proscribed cannot complain of the vagueness of the law as applied to the conduct of others.'" Id. at 18-19 (quoting *Hoffman Estates v. Flipside, Hoffman Estates, Inc.*, 455 U.S. 489, 495 (1982)). While the U.S. Supreme Court has shown a preference for as-applied challenges in many contexts, it is not entirely clear, however, whether this language was meant to establish that one could never use the vagueness doctrine in making facial challenges to a law.

"narrowly and precisely drawn statute." 405 U.S. 518, 520 (1972). Thus, from its inception, the doctrine made clear that the statute need not be unconstitutional as applied to a particular defendant. Instead, the salient issue is whether the statute would be constitutional if applied to anyone, including parties other than the defendant.

From this perspective, the overbreadth doctrine is unique to First Amendment jurisprudence. To put this another way, the overbreadth doctrine is unusual because it does not require the traditional showing in federal litigation that the plaintiff has "standing" to bring a challenge and to ask the court to provide a remedy for a wrong done.

Take, for example, a situation when an individual wishes to raise a challenge based on the Fourth Amendment requirement that a government official must have probable cause before conducting a search. "Probable cause" requires a showing that a crime has been committed, is in the process of being committed, or will be committed. Assume further that a state law authorizes officials to conduct a search upon the lesser showing that they have only a "reasonable suspicion" that a crime has occurred, is occurring, or will occur. A plaintiff who was subject to a search wishes to challenge this state law lowering the standard to "reasonable suspicion." Yet—in the plaintiff's case—the officials actually had probable cause to make the search. In that event, the plaintiff may not proceed with the challenge because the plaintiff lacks standing to assert the Fourth Amendment claim.

By contrast, consider a situation when a plaintiff has a business selling only obscene merchandise. Assume that a state law prohibits the selling of any merchandise that depicts sexually explicit subjects under any circumstances. As explained in Chapter 8, the First Amendment case law adheres to a specific standard of defining something as "obscene" and makes clear that obscene speech is outside First Amendment protection. Sexually explicit speech, however, is not necessarily obscene and can be subject to at least some First Amendment protection. Can the plaintiff who sells only obscene merchandise properly challenge the state law? Yes, the plaintiff can bring an overbreadth challenge, even though the plaintiff would be deemed to lack standing to assert a claim based on a theory other than the First Amendment.

Substantial criticism targets this quality of the doctrine. Critics argue, for example, that allowing a plaintiff to assert the rights of others inappropriately requires abstract decision-making, inviting a court to speculate about the real-life consequences of its ruling. As such, the practice is contrary to settled rules governing judicial review, which hold that adjudication should be confined to resolving the particular problem between the particular parties before the court.[2]

---

2. See, e.g., ALEXANDER BICKEL, THE LEAST DANGEROUS BRANCH 115-116 (1962). On the other hand, some scholars suggest that lower federal court decisions rarely affect anyone outside of the particular parties to the litigation. See generally Richard H. Fallon, Making Sense of Overbreadth, 100 Yale L.J. 853 (1991).

2. Overbreadth and Vagueness

The Court's justification for this departure from the ordinary constraints on judicial decision-making was the "transcendent value to all society" of free speech, which warrants attacks on overbroad statutes without regard to whether the application of the statute to a particular defendant would be constitutional. Id. at 521.[3] As stated above, the doctrine also diminishes the improper chilling effect of flawed laws and protects against inappropriate official use of laws to stifle unpopular, yet protected, speech.

How do you determine whether a statute is overbroad? The *Gooding* Court looked to dictionary definitions, statutory construction principles, and common law interpretations of the statutory words in question. For a particularly egregious statute, one might also identify a generic or widely framed term that could include a substantial class of protected speech.

Example 2-1:

Damian Defendant, an anti-war protester, used racial slurs and death threats against a police officer who was attempting to control a protest in an army building. Damian was arrested and found guilty of using "opprobrious words and abusive language tending to cause a breach of the peace" in violation of a State A statute.

According to standard American dictionary definitions, the term "opprobrious" means "conveying or intended to convey disgrace" and "abusive" includes "harsh insulting language." WEBSTER'S THIRD NEW INTERNATIONAL DICTIONARY. Prior cases in State A defined the phrase "breach of the peace" to encompass "all violations of the public peace, order, or decorum." Despite these sweeping definitions, the prosecution claimed that the statute was narrowly drawn such that it was applicable only to a well-defined, constitutionally unprotected class of speech—specifically, fighting words.

Is the statute under which Danny was been convicted constitutional, or is it overbroad?

Explanation:

Danny is correct: the statute is overbroad. The facts in this Example mirror the facts of *Gooding*, in which the U.S. Supreme Court affirmed a decision to strike down a state law regulating "fighting words," a category of speech outside First Amendment protection. The Court determined that the terms "breach of the peace," "opprobrious," and "abusive" carried meanings determined by dictionary and common law that were far broader than the definition of "fighting words." In the *Gooding* Court's view, the statutory

---

3. Commentators have observed that this deviation from the normal rules of judicial decision-making rarely if ever appears outside the First Amendment context. *See generally* John F. Decker, *Overbreadth Outside the First Amendment*, 34 N.M. L. Rev. 53 (2004).

prohibition covered speech that was constitutionally protected. (Chapter 7 in this volume discusses the parameters of the fighting words doctrine. The point here is simply that the *Gooding* Court looked to court decisions and a non-legal dictionary to evaluate how a reasonable speaker might interpret the words of the statute.)

* * *

In *Broadrick v. Oklahoma*, 413 U.S. 601 (1973), the Court limited the reach of the overbreadth doctrine. Observing that laws could be overbroad because they deter protected speech, the *Broadrick* Court further ruled that "there comes a point" when resolving whether a statute prohibits protected speech is "at best a prediction [, which] cannot, with confidence, justify invalidating a statute on its face and so prohibiting a state from regulating conduct that is admittedly within its power to proscribe." *Id.* at 615. The Court therefore concluded that in order to find a statute invalid, its overbreadth "must not only be real, but substantial as well." *Id.*

In the subsequent case of *Members of City Council v. Taxpayers for Vincent*, 466 U.S. 789 (1984), the Court elaborated on this standard, explaining that to establish "substantial overbreadth," it is insufficient that "one can conceive of some impermissible applications of the statute." *Id.* at 800. Rather, a facial overbreadth challenge can succeed only when there exists "a realistic danger that the statute itself will significantly compromise recognized First Amendment protections of parties not before the Court." *Id.* at 801.

Example 2-2:

A federal statute makes it illegal to encourage or induce an undocumented immigrant to remain in the United States for the purposes of financial gain. This law allows felony prosecutions of such persons if the encourager knows or recklessly disregards the illegality of the immigrant's entry or residence in the United States.

Amanda is an immigration consultant who assists clients in securing legal permanent resident status and labor certification. After the immigrant residency program expired, Amanda continued to encourage her clients to stay in the country and to apply for labor certification—telling them they were likely to receie it. She also continued to accept payment from these clients on a retainer basis.

Amanda has now been charged under the federal statute. She argues that it is overbroad because it might criminalize lawful advocacy undertaken by private individuals, immigration lawyers, and immigrant rights groups. For example, lawyers often encourage their clients not to leave the country while attempting to adjust or normalize their status.

Is Amanda correct that the statute is overbroad?

Explanation:

Amanda is correct that the statute may be overbroad. Although the government may legally regulate speech that induces or encourages others to break the law, this statute could proscribe speech protected by the First Amendment. For example, the statute could apply to protected activity such as protests and public debates that express support for immigrants. Presumably the statute might also apply to private conversations between family members as well. In addition, it is generally an appropriate task for immigration attorneys to strategize ways to maximize their clients' chances for achieving a particular goal. Depending on the circumstances, these attorneys may be acting in accordance with established professional norms by suggesting that clients stay in the country while adjusting their statuses. These Examples illustrate that one can imagine diverse scenarios in which the statute outlaws protected speech. Both the number and diversity of scenarios one can imagine where the statute touches speech protected by the First Amendment support the conclusion that the statute meets the *Broadrick* standard for substantial overbreadth.

Example 2-3:

Douglas is an animal rights activist. He broke into a farm that bred and sold minks. In the process, Douglas "freed" approximately 2,000 minks and vandalized the farm. He was charged under a federal statute that prohibited "damaging any real or personal property through conduct made with the purpose of damaging or interfering with the operations of an animal enterprise." Douglas argues that the statute is overbroad because the dictionary definition of "property" includes lost profits, which could be damaged by lawful protest and advocacy. Is Douglas correct that the statute is overbroad because it might criminalize lawful protest that results in lost profits, or is the statute constitutional because one could read it as targeting only individuals who commit unlawful destruction of property?

Explanation:

The statute is likely not substantially overbroad. At least one case has interpreted a statute like this not to apply to purely economic harm resulting from lawful conduct. *See United States v. Johnson*, 875 F.3d 360, 364 (7th Cir. 2017). Given that the terms "real or personal property" are generally understood not to include intangibles like lost profit, the statute does not appear to prohibit lawful advocacy that merely affects the profitability of farms. The terms "real or personal property" thus restrict the statute's reach, arguably limiting the prohibition to conduct that is generally not protected by the First Amendment and preventing the statute from prohibiting protected speech. Indeed, a substantial portion of the cases in which the statute would apply would involve vandalism, which is not constitutionally protected expression.

Given the limitation of the terms "real or personal property," the statute is not likely to have substantial regulatory effect on protected speech and thus does not run into problems under the *Broadrick* test.

Example 2-4:

A state statute requires "adult-oriented" establishments to register with the state and limits the types of entertainment that they can present. For example, the statute specifies the covering that an exotic dancer must have on his or her body. Failure to register and comply with the entertainment limits subjects the business owner to criminal prosecution. The statute is supported by evidence that such establishments are associated with increased crime, the spread of sexually transmitted diseases, lowered property values, and other public welfare issues. In addition, the statute provides the following definition of adult-oriented establishments:

> Establishments that are devoted to providing sexually explicit entertainment. Such entertainment includes any exhibition of any adult-oriented motion picture, live performance, display or dance of any type that has as a principal or predominant theme, emphasis, or portion of such performance that contains one of the following:
>
> [i]   any actual or simulated performance of specified sexual activities;
> [ii] exhibition and viewing of specified anatomical areas;
> [iii] removal of articles of clothing or appearing unclothed;
> [iv] nude or partially nude modeling; or
> [vi] any other personal service with sexual content that is offered to customers.

The owner of Della's Den brings a First Amendment challenge to this statute, arguing that it is overbroad. The owner of Della's alleges that nearly any type of establishment could qualify as an "adult-oriented" establishment and could therefore be subject to the law's licensing and punishment scheme. Is the owner correct that the words "adult-oriented establishment" are unconstitutionally overbroad?

Explanation:

The owner of Della's Den is likely incorrect: The definition of "adult-oriented" establishment is quite specific and narrowed to a set of sexually explicit types of entertainment. As you will see in Chapter 8 below addressing indecent and obscene expression, lawmakers have significant latitude in regulating in this area. This is particularly true where (as in this Example) the proffered reason for the regulation is not the content of the expression, but the secondary effects of the expression (i.e., sexually transmitted diseases, lowered property values, and other public welfare issues). The particular statute here appears framed in a way that its scope complies with the restrictions of First Amendment doctrines. *See Entertainment Productions, Inc. v. Shelby Cty.*, 588 F.3d 372, 376 (6th Cir. 2009).

B. VAGUENESS

An unconstitutionally vague law is so unclear that people "of common intelligence must necessarily guess at its meaning." *Connally v. General Construction Co.*, 269 U.S. 385, 391 (1926). Although closely related, the vagueness and overbreadth doctrines do not overlap completely. Sometimes a law can be overbroad, but not vague—and vice versa. Take a situation where a statute says that "all speech and other communication that is not protected by the First Amendment" is prohibited in an airport. By definition, this statute is not overbroad because it does not regulate protected speech. The statute may still be vague since a reasonable person may not know what is and what is not protected by the First Amendment.[4] By contrast, consider a statute that prohibits selling merchandise in which "human genitalia are pictured in a black and white or color photograph." This statute is likely not vague because it clearly describes what the statute prohibits. The statute is overbroad, however, because some photographs of human genitalia fall within First Amendment protection. Although circumstances exist that implicate only one of the doctrines, both doctrines often serve to successfully attack a statute as unconstitutional under the First Amendment.

Example 2-5:

Michael gets into a fight over the phone with his neighbor and uses the words "asshole" and "shit" against the man in the conversation. He has been charged with using profane language during the call under a State B statute that provides: "If any person shall curse or abuse anyone, or use vulgar, profane, threatening or indecent language over any telephone in this State, he shall be guilty of a misdemeanor." Courts have provided no narrowing construction of this statute in State B courts. Michael had defended the charges saying that the statute is both overbroad and overly vague. Will Michael succeed in his defense?

---

4. *See* ERWIN CHEMERINSKY, CONSTITUTIONAL LAW: PRINCIPLES AND POLICIES, 1032-1033 (6th ed. 2019), for further elaboration on this hypothetical.

Explanation:

Yes, the law is likely both overbroad and vague. Consider the following case, which helps evaluate Michael's position. In *Walker v. Dillard*, 523 F.2d 3, 4 (4th Cir.), *cert. denied*, 423 U.S. 906 (1975), the Fourth Circuit considered a vagueness and overbreadth challenge to an identical statute. The court of appeals avoided ruling on the vagueness challenge, choosing instead to decide the case on overbreadth grounds. Although the court recognized the state's legitimate interest in preventing obscene threats, it found that nearly every word of the statute was subject to overly broad interpretations. The Fourth Circuit found that no narrowing constructions of the statute had been applied to date and therefore reasoned that each of the terms "threatening," "vulgar," "profane," and "indecent" could be construed so broadly as to encompass protected speech. Because the act was not narrowly tailored, the court held it was unconstitutional under the *Broadrick* standards. *See also Johnson v. Quattlebaum*, 664 F. App'x 290 (4th Cir. 2016) (holding that a South Carolina statute prohibiting use of obscene or profane language within hearing distance of a schoolhouse or church was not overbroad when prior decisions limited its application to constitutionally unprotected "fighting words").

What would be the argument on vagueness grounds? Certainly, one could reasonably argue that the words "threatening," "vulgar," "profane," and "indecent" were not self-defining. Individuals have different sensibilities when it comes to evaluating whether these words match a particular statement made in a particular situation. One might argue that no consensus exists as to the meaning of these terms. For that reason, a person of ordinary intelligence might need to guess whether Michael's statement is covered by one of the terms. These arguments suggest that the State B law is unconstitutionally vague.

* * *

Vague laws have many defects. To begin, they fail to provide fair notice to citizens regarding the scope of a prohibition. This concern with fairness shows that the vagueness doctrine is analytically connected to the due process clauses of the Fifth and Fourteenth Amendments, both of which are designed to ensure that the government provides adequate notice of what the law prohibits and what it allows. When the government fails to give that notice, it is deemed to be acting unfairly.

As mentioned at the beginning of the chapter, the vagueness doctrine, like the overbreadth doctrine, diminish the improper chilling effect of flawed laws and protect against inappropriate official use of laws to stifle unpopular speech. Selective prosecution can flourish in the context of vague statutes: Officials have greater latitude to pick and choose whom they would like to punish when the law is unclear. Here is a related defect: Vague laws lack specific standards and thus give little or no guidance to law enforcement personnel as they try to identify illegal conduct. Finally, the stakes are particularly high in the First Amendment area. As the U.S. Supreme Court stated in *NAACP v. Button*, 371 U.S. 415 (1963), the First Amendment's protection for free expression is "delicate and vulnerable, as well as supremely precious in our society . . . . Because First Amendment freedoms need breathing space to survive, government may regulate in the area only with narrow specificity." *Id.* at 433.

Despite the challenges that vague laws present to First Amendment protections, no decisive test exists for testing whether a law is unconstitutionally vague. Obviously, the more specific the law, the more likely it will survive a challenge under the vagueness doctrine. That said, the doctrine stands as a powerful tool for attacking a statute in First Amendment litigation. The question whether a regulation is too vague can be hard to pin down and — as suggested in Example 2-5 above — can give way to an overbreadth analysis. Often the question whether a regulation is unconstitutionally vague is tied to the specific First Amendment context in which it arises. If the restriction on communication closely tracks away from the precise prohibitions laid out in existing First Amendment doctrine, the restriction is more likely to avoid a vagueness attack. This is illustrated in Example 2-6.

Example 2-6:

"Crisis Pregnancy Center" is a for-profit, commercial establishment that offers limited pregnancy-related services with a stated goal of ending all abortions. The Center routinely advertises more services than it actually provides. The Center does not advertise its commitment to ending abortions, and its advertisements are worded in such as way that those who desire abortions may conclude that the Center offers that medical procedure.

The city in which the Center is located passes an ordinance prohibiting limited service pregnancy centers "from making false or misleading statements to the public about pregnancy-related services the centers offer or perform." In the legislative history, the City Council members noted that these centers often provide indigent women with false information about their pregnancy-related options, in addition to providing misleading information about the services that they provide.

Is this statute unconstitutionally vague, or are its prohibitions sufficiently clear?

Explanation:

The ordinance is not unconstitutionally vague: The prohibitions in the ordinance are confined to regulating false or misleading statements and the Center is a commercial establishment. Significantly, the legislative history to the ordinance suggests that the prohibition is not a pretext for regulating speech on the basis of its truthful content. Under the First Amendment case law governing commercial speech (covered in Chapter 9 below), the U.S. Supreme Court has made clear that lawmakers have wide latitude in regulating false and misleading statements made in the context of commercial speech. The ordinance is clearly confined to this subject matter: The statutory language proscribes only "false or misleading statements," and the legislative history of the ordinance suggests that the prohibition is not a pretext for regulating speech on the basis of its truthful content. Because the speech restriction closely tracks existing First Amendment doctrine, it will likely withstand a vagueness challenge. *See First Resort, Inc. v. Herrera*, 860 F.3d 1263 (9th Cir. 2017), *cert. denied*, 108 S. Ct. 2709 (2018). Note, however, that the U.S. Supreme Court has held that a law similar to this was compelled speech in violation of the First Amendment. *National Institute of Family and Life Advocates v. Becerra*, 138 S. Ct. 2361 (2018). Chapter 5 of this volume discusses *Becerra* in greater detail.

* * *

Political Speech

Core to the First Amendment is the notion that the United States needs to preserve robust debate about political matters. Indeed, some thinkers believe that protecting political speech is the sole purpose of the First Amendment and the source of its power.[1] U.S. Supreme Court cases often echo a sense of the privileged status of political speech in analyzing a broad array of protected expression. This tendency to elevate the importance of protecting political speech is tied to a key value animating the First Amendment: promoting democratic self-government. For that reason, you will observe an apparently privileged view of political speech, which from time to time becomes plain in the case law covered in this volume.

The view that political speech is special, however, is not a formal part of the actual rules applied in First Amendment cases. In First Amendment doctrine, political speech shares the same status as many other types of speech that the Court treats as high value speech. The U.S. Supreme Court has at times made of a point of highlighting this: we "have never suggested that expression about philosophical, social, artistic, economic, literary, or ethical matters—to take a nonexhaustive list of labels—is not entitled to full First Amendment protection." *Abood v. Detroit Board of Education*, 431 U.S. 209, 231 (1977). This approach

---

1. *See, e.g.*, ALEXANDER MEIKLEJOHN, FREE SPEECH AND ITS RELATION TO SELF-GOVERNMENT (Harper Brothers Pub. 1948). Meiklejohn was a pioneering political theorist who found support for the Constitution's freedom of speech protections solely on the basis of democratic theory. According to Meiklejohn, the First Amendment does not protect speech on private matters, which he argued should be governed only by the Constitution's due process protections. Although his focus on a political theory foundation for the free speech guarantees has been enormously influential, Meiklejohn's argument about private speech has not carried the day.

to speech that doctrine treats as on par with political speech is contrasted with lower value speech such as speech that incites violence, defamation, and child pornography, discussed in chapters 7, 8, and 10 of this volume. The point here is that political speech is treated doctrinally the same as other high value speech: when a regulation of these types of speech is content-based, the regulation is subject to strict scrutiny. Yet one also gleans from the case law a sense that the Court is hyper-vigilant of protecting political speech given its value for a functioning democracy. See, e.g., Meyer v. Grant, 486 U.S. 414, 422 (1988) (stating that for "interactive communication concerning political change . . . First Amendment protection is at its zenith). In other words, regulation of political speech does not appear to get a unique standard of scrutiny, but one can often discern "a thumb on the scale" in favor of protecting it.[2]

Although issues of political speech appear throughout this volume, this chapter has two angles on the topic not covered elsewhere. First, the chapter wrestles with the difficult question of what precisely amounts to political speech (as opposed to mere conduct that occurs in a political setting). The chapter ends with a discussion of a unique area of First Amendment law that turns on the political context in which it arises: the status of money as a mode of expression in political campaigns.

A. DEFINING POLITICAL SPEECH

The analytical connection between political speech and democracy is helpful for resolving particularly troublesome freedom of communication issues, such as hate speech. Nonetheless, a definitional problem exists: How do we define what qualifies as political speech? With a little imagination, can't anything be defined as political speech?

In Buckley v. American Constitutional Law Foundation, 525 U.S. 182 (1999), the Supreme Court emphasized the concept of "core political speech," which the Court defined as "interactive communication concerning political change." 525 U.S. 182, 186 (1999). The Buckley Court derived this language from Meyer v. Grant, 486 U.S. 414 (1988), in which the Supreme Court had ruled

---

2. There does, however, remain confusion in the lower court on the precise level of scrutiny the Supreme Court has mandated for political speech regulation. The Court has used a variety of terms in defining this level of evaluating the wisdom of a regulation, using the words "exacting scrutiny" and scrutiny "at its zenith" to establish the required standard. McIntyre v. Ohio Board of Elections, 514 U.S. 334, 347 (1995); Meyer, 486 U.S. at 425. If First Amendment protection is at its "zenith" for interactive communication concerning political change, does that mean that exacting or strict scrutiny is less deferential? More deferential? The same? See R. George Wright, A Hard Look at Exacting Scrutiny, 85 UMKC L. Rev. 207, 210 (2016) (noting confusion among lower courts as to whether exacting scrutiny is more demanding than strict scrutiny).

that courts should use heightened First Amendment scrutiny when evaluating regulations on ballot-initiative petitions. The Supreme Court used an alternative approach, however, in *McIntyre v. Ohio Board of Elections*, 514 U.S. 334 (1995), stating that political speech encompassed "[d]iscussion of public issues and debate on the qualifications of candidates . . . ." *Id.* at 346.[3] This second definition is more specific than the first. One may find it difficult to identify the parameters of "interactive communication concerning political change." Nonetheless, lower courts confronting First Amendment issues directly relating to the political process appear to prefer the term "core political speech," another term without self-evident meaning but nonetheless associated with *Buckley v. American Constitutional Law Foundation* and *Meyer v. Grant*.

The concept of core political speech is particularly important in cases involving regulation of non-verbal conduct associated with political activity — such as signature-gathering as well as collecting and submitting voter registration forms. These "political activity" cases are distinct from disputes that concern only regulation of political speech per se, but they do focus on interactive communication during the political process. As in *Meyer*, *McIntyre*, and *Buckley*, constitutional concern is heightened when the regulation burdens interactive communication in this context. If that occurs, these cases make clear that the regulation is subject to exacting scrutiny. If this type of communication or something analogous are not present, the court applies rational-basis review to the regulation so long as the regulation does not pose a "severe burden" on the fundamental rights to vote or to associate with one another politically. *Burdick v. Takushi*, 504 U.S. 428, 434 (1992), explained that when a state election law provision imposes only "'reasonable, nondiscriminatory restrictions' upon the First and Fourteenth Amendment rights of voters, 'the State's important regulatory interests are generally sufficient to justify' the restrictions." *Id.* at 434 (quoting *Anderson v. Celebrezze*, 460 U.S. 780, 788 (1983)).

The distinction that courts make between regulations of core political speech and non-communicative conduct is important to the disposition of cases, but the distinction is not always obvious or easy to understand. Patterns in the cases do emerge, but the results can be baffling. For example, courts are reluctant to disaggregate from core political speech activities such as petition circulation and canvassing. These involve advocacy about a candidate or a point of view. On the other hand, courts have been less willing to deem voter registration activities to be core political speech. Courts that have found that voter registration is not core political speech have therefore disaggregated voter registration into its communicative and non-communicative

---

3. The *McIntyre* Court stated in full: "Discussion of public issues and debate on the qualifications of candidates are integral to the operation of the system of government established by our Constitution. The First Amendment affords the broadest protection to such political expression in order 'to assure the unfettered interchange of ideas for the bringing about of political and social changes desired by the people.'" *Id.* at 346.

components. Once the courts finish making this distinction, they apply rational-basis review to those regulations for which courts characterize as non-communicative conduct.

The apparent bottom line is the following: a restriction that touches communicative interactions is core political speech and a restriction that is categorized as non-communicative interactions is not. That said, the lower court decisions do not sort easily into the communicative/ non-communicative categories. For example, a speech regulation pertaining to the process of encouraging people to register to vote, such as requiring persons who participate in the process to be residents of the locale where the voting will take place, would be subject to heightened scrutiny. See, e.g., League of Women Voters v. Hargett, 400 F. Supp. 3d 706 (M.D. Tenn. 2019) (analyzing process requirements for those who participate in registration drives). Registration itself appears neutral. Yet if more voters empirically means that one party over another will receive more support in an election, a registration issue can easily take on an idea-laden (i.e., communicative) component. By contrast, requiring the person who physically collects and delivers the voter registration to the state to be a resident is more tied to practical concerns and may be subject only to rational-basis review. See, e.g., Voting for America, Inc. v. Steen, 732 F.3d 382 (5th Cir. 2013). Like the regulations placed on encouraging people to register, this regulation also limits the pool of available participants, but courts have decided that it does not directly proscribe the "interactive communication" aspect of voter registration activities and thus does not merit anything other than rational basis review.

Needless to say, courts are reluctant to wrestle with and tinker with the political process and the guiding legal doctrine can be vague and contradictory. The best one can do in resolving a dispute in light of this ambiguity between the communicative and non-communicative categories is (1) to note the ambiguity, (2) to point out the arguments on both sides, and (3) to make a choice between the categories backed up by reasoned analysis about how much the restriction affects the exchange of ideas. Recently, the courts are less willing to evaluate the effect of a restriction on which a political or ideological group gets the upper hand in an election, but focus instead on whether the restriction is tied to an apparently neutral purpose such as avoiding fraud. Consider the following two examples:

Example 3-1:

A state statute requires that signatures on political nomination petitions must be witnessed by a state resident of voting age. A local activist challenges this regulation as an impermissible burden on her core political speech. The state counters that the regulation was not burdensome and should be subject only to rational-basis review because it does not proscribe any communication regarding the petition's content. In the state's view, the regulation implicates only signature-gathering logistics. Is the statute constitutional? What level of scrutiny should the court use to evaluate this question: rational basis or exacting scrutiny?

Explanation:

Strong arguments exist that a court should use exacting scrutiny and the regulation is likely unconstitutional. The process of petitioning for signatures for a nomination often involves advocacy and expression of political preferences. As such, the process easily categorizes as communicative. For that reason, a court is unlikely to disaggregate the expressive component of the activity from the conduct itself. Accordingly, a court is likely to invoke exacting scrutiny. (To support this conclusion, a court might also note that petitioning activity is generally associated with the U.S. Supreme Court exacting scrutiny case of *Meyer v. Grant*, 486 U.S. 414 (1988)).

This then leads to the question of whether the restriction survives exacting scrutiny. Even assuming that the restriction serves an overriding and compelling state purpose, such as preventing voter fraud, a court has good reason to hold that the regulation is not narrowly tailored to serve that interest. For example, the state could use a less restrictive approach than the residency requirement, such as conditioning receipt of the petition on the circulator's agreement to comply with civil and criminal subpoenas. *See Libertarian Party of Virginia v. Judd*, 718 F.3d 308 (4th Cir. 2013).

Example 3-2:

A state allows registered voters to be poll watchers in their local voting precinct. Under this state authorization, individuals may monitor their polling place on Election Day to ensure that the precinct captains are following the state's election laws. The state does not, however, allow individuals to serve as a poll watcher for a polling place that is not in the precinct where they vote. Adriana lives in Township A, but works in Township B. Adriana would like to serve as a poll watcher in Township B during her lunch break from work there.

Can the state validly enforce the poll-watching restriction against her? What standard of review should a court use in evaluating this question? Specifically, may the court use a rational-basis standard of review by disaggregating the act of ensuring the polls are fraud-free from any communicative aspects of participating in the election process?

Explanation:

This is a close case, particularly if Adriana has a political interest in being present at the polls so as to promote her personal political agenda. In that event, the court should use exacting scrutiny to evaluate the restriction. Nonetheless, the court in *Republican Party of Pennsylvania v. Cortés*, 218 F. Supp. 3d 396 (E.D. Pa. 2016), determined that poll watching, a state-sanctioned observance of polling locations, is not core political speech. The court ruled that a poll watcher performs only a state function of regulating the electoral process. The court reasoned that, by observing and reporting polling site misconduct, poll watchers neither "facilitate[] public discussion of a political issue nor advocate[] for a particular candidate, issue, or viewpoint." *Id.* at 415. According to this characterization, poll watchers are carrying out a state ministerial function through their conduct and nothing more.

B. MONEY AS A MODE OF FACILITATING EXPRESSION IN POLITICAL CAMPAIGNS

In one often quoted passage, the Supreme Court has trumpeted the following: "[T]he First Amendment 'has its fullest and most urgent application' to speech uttered during a campaign for political office." *Eu v. San Francisco County Democratic Central Committee*, 489 U.S. 214, 223 (1989), quoting *Monitor Patriot Co. v. Roy*, 401 U.S. 265, 272 (1971). Hence the close connection between spending money in a campaign and the First Amendment's protection of political speech. This connection has profound importance, since financing of election campaigns is a keystone to ultimate success in obtaining public office in the United States. Unsurprisingly, through its First Amendment campaign finance rulings, the U.S. Supreme Court has deeply influenced today's political landscape.

The Court has decided a number of important campaign finance cases since 1976. By far the most influential cases have been *Buckley v. Valeo*, 424 U.S. 1 (1976), and *Citizens United v. Federal Election Comm'n*, 558 U.S. 310 (2010). Both cases treat spending money in a political campaign as a constitutionally significant mode of facilitating political speech.

Buckley v. Valeo concerned a challenge to provisions of the Federal Election Campaign Act of 1971, which established a restriction on the amount of money a person or group can give in contribution to a political campaign and set a cap on expenditures. Among the Act's more salient provisions were the following limitations on contributions: (1) a person could only contribute $1,000 to any single candidate per election; (2) a political committee could contribute only $5,000 to a political candidate; and (3) each contributor was limited to $25,000 per year. The Act also focused on overall expenditures: (1) independent expenditures by individuals and groups "relative to a clearly identified candidate" were limited to $1,000 a year; and (2) candidates were limited to contributions to campaigns from personal funds or funds from immediate family. *Buckley*, 424 U.S. at 7. The Act also established (1) limitations on campaign spending by candidates for various federal offices and spending for national conventions by political parties, (2) public disclosure requirements, (3) a system of public funding for presidential campaigns, and (4) an administrative entity, the Federal Election Commission, to administer and enforce this legislation. Challengers to the law were candidates for office, political parties, and various groups with political interests. They alleged that the Act violated both the First Amendment's freedom of speech and freedom of association clauses.

The driving force behind the Federal Election Campaign Act was avoiding actual political corruption — or the appearance of such corruption. The idea here is that the large expenditures and contributions to a particular candidate sometimes occur as a *quid pro quo* for political favors that will come after a candidate wins an election.

Most importantly, the Court determined that courts must use exacting scrutiny to evaluate the expenditure and contribution limits. The Court rejected the notion that spending money was pure conduct without qualities essential to communication (and thus outside First Amendment protection). The Court observed that virtually all means of communication in society requires spending money and proceeded on the tacit assumption that the contributions are intrinsically tied to the expression of political speech.

To structure its analysis, the Court distinguished between expenditure and contribution limits. The Court was harsher on the expenditure limits, concluding that that these "represent[ed] substantial rather than merely theoretical restrictions on the quantity and diversity of political speech." *Id.* at 19. As for contribution limits, the Court reasoned that limiting monetary amounts a person may donate to a candidate or campaign organization does not significantly restrain the person from communicating political views, since it allows "the symbolic expression of support evidenced by a contribution but does not in any way infringe the contributor's freedom to discuss candidates and issues." *Id.* at 20-21.

Turning to the corruption rationale, the Court also found this rationale more compelling for controlling contribution limits than for expenditure limits. The Court reasoned that restrictions on the amount that a person or group could contribute to a candidate were justified to prevent "the actuality and appearance of corruption resulting from large individual financial contributions . . . ." *Id.* at 26. The notion here is that the larger contributions increase the risk of an actual or perceived *quid pro quo* arrangement between individual contributors and politicians. The Court did not find the same level of risk for expenditure limits and rejected the notion that the First Amendment allows the government to restrict expenditures of one group so as to equalize political influence.

3. Political Speech

It is important to note that—in *Buckley v. Valeo* and in later cases—the Court did not hold that money is speech or even that money is a mode of expression. By way of analogy, consider a law banning spending more than $50 on a private education or the assistance of counsel. This law would violate constitutional provisions protecting an individual's right to pursue these things, but not because money is a mode of education or lawyering. Rather, to quote Justice Breyer:

> On the one hand, a decision to contribute money to a campaign is a matter of First Amendment concern—not because money is speech (it is not); but because it *enables* speech. Through contributions the contributor associates himself with the candidate's cause, helps the candidate communicate a political message with which the contributor agrees, and helps the candidate win by attracting the votes of similarly minded voters. . . . Both political association and political communication are at stake.

Nixon v. Shrink Missouri Government PAC, 528 U.S. 377, 400 (2000) (Breyer, J. concurring) (citing *Buckley v. Valeo*).

Buckley v. Valeo enormously changed political campaigning by invalidating expenditure limits; the decision caused an upsurge in campaign costs and in flourishing political action committees. The Court further solidified this trend in *Citizens United v. Federal Election Comm'n*, 558 U.S. 310, 318-366 (2010).

In *Citizens United*, the Court confronted the question of corporate campaign contributions and found them without problem and protected by the First Amendment. The Court determined that regulatory restrictions on campaign contributions should be limited to *quid pro quo* bribery. According to the Court: "That speakers may have influence over or access to elected officials does not mean that those officials are corrupt. . . . [T]he appearance of influence or access will not cause the electorate to lose faith in this democracy." *Id.* at 314. The Court took a deferential—perhaps favorable—approach to corporate contributions, stating that restrictions on corporate expenditures silenced "the voices that best represent the most significant segments of the economy," depriving citizens of "information, knowledge and opinion vital" to economic function. *Id.* at 354 (quoting *McConnell v. Federal Election Comm'n*, 540 U.S. 93 (2003), and *United States v. Congress of Industrial Orgs.*, 335 U.S. 106 (1948)).

Example 3-3:

You have been asked to prepare a short memo presenting arguments on both sides pertaining to following question: "Was the *Citizens United* Court correct in stating that muzzling the ability of corporations to express political preference through campaign contributions would have a negative effect on full and robust political debate?" What are the major points your memo would present?

Explanation:

Legions of pages exist analyzing this question: *Citizens United* is a controversial decision and many arguments exist as to the wisdom of the decision. Here is a sampling of some of the arguments in favor of or against the proposition presented in this Example.

Selected arguments in favor of the stated proposition:

*Corporations are an important force in society, which directly affect the economic vitality of the United States. This in turn has a dramatic impact on the citizens of the United States. Corporations should therefore have the ability for full participation in debate about public and economic policy.

*Corporations enjoy resources that allow them to research and to develop well-reasoned positions on policy decision. To prevent corporations from expressing their positions would be to censor an important, informed contribution to political debate.

*The United States is based on a system of capitalism, of which corporations are an important component. This system is based on the notion that the greatest good arises from an efficient and rational allocation of resources and corporations are particularly well-suited to promote that goal. For this reason, all citizens benefit from allowing corporations full access to public debate.

Selected arguments against the stated proposition:

*The structure and theory behind corporations is profit-maximization. Whether or not one agrees with the notion that this profit motive ultimately serves the interests of all, the immediate effect of the strong profit incentive is not to ensure that corporate decision making on particular issues primarily serves the greater public interest. For that reason, corporations are not entitled to an unfettered, privileged voice of political discourse, which their economic strength allows them.

*One cannot expect the original drafters of the First Amendment to have anticipated the current economic conditions and corporate structure. But few debate that the drafters were deeply concerned with avoiding government attempts to silence voices of the weak and to enhance the powerful's influence. Giving corporations the enhanced power that their economic strength allows them in the campaign financing sphere is contrary to the basic premise of the First Amendment.

*Consider two uncontroversial principles: (1) the First Amendment is designed to encourage uninhibited political debate; and (2) if political contributions are speech for the purpose of the First Amendment, corporations are allowed to "speak louder" than most other participants in democracy because they have greater economic resources to contribute to campaigns. The result of these two principles is to consolidate political power in the hands of corporations at the expense of broader political participation.

3. Political Speech

*Under the corporate structure of U.S. state and federal law, a handful of officers and directors make the primary decisions over corporate policy. Limited legal mechanisms exist for the owners of a corporation to question or evaluate the officers' and directors' decisions. This includes decisions about campaign contributions. As a consequence, the out-sized ability of a corporation to participate in the political process arguably results in the political success of certain candidates to fall to the decision–making powers of a few privileged individuals.

* * *

Although the Court has determined that *Citizens United* protects the speech of corporations and labor union, the scope of *Buckley v. Valeo* and *Citizens United* has not otherwise been clarified. Nonetheless, lower courts have had the occasion to apply them in diverse contexts, including those well outside the corporate setting. *See, e.g., Human Life of Washington Inc. v. Brumsickle,* 624 F.3d 990, 995 (9th Cir. 2010) (evaluating campaign expenditure limitations affecting a group opposing a ballot initiative focused on whether terminally ill residents could self-administer lethal medication prescribed by a physician); *Lodge No. 5 of Fraternal Order of Police ex rel. McNesby v. City of Philadelphia,* 763 F.3d 358, 360-361 (3d Cir. 2014) (evaluating restriction preventing members of a police department from making contributions to their union's political action committee).

4

Prior Restraints

Courts often brand prior restraints on speech as the most inimical of all speech regulations. Some thinkers also observe that outlawing prior restraints was the driving force behind the framing and ratification of the First Amendment. While this primary focus on prohibiting prior restraints may have been a particularly salient observation at an earlier time when courts tolerated after-the-fact punishment of offensive speech and found no constitutional problems with this punishment, such is not the case now that subsequent punishments are mostly held unconstitutional. Even though much First Amendment litigation today concerns evaluating the legality of subsequent punishment for speech, the rule against prior restraints remains important as well. The rule against prior restraints on speech remains firmly entrenched in First Amendment doctrine and the prohibition still triggers vigorous negative responses from courts. Thus, when confronting a licensing scheme, a prescreening requirement, or an injunction that touches on communication, you should be alert to the potential for a prior restraint violation.

A precise definition of a prior restraint is difficult to articulate. Perhaps the most straightforward approach describes a prior restraint as a judicial order or other governmental mechanism that stops speech from taking place. The judicial order may come in the form of an injunction (violation of which is subject to contempt). Other governmental mechanisms could include licensing or permitting schemes, which require that the government issues a license or permit before speech occurs. This chapter considers the proper definition of a prior restraint in detail below. In the meantime, consider the following Examples.

Example 4-1:

The President of the United States learned of the impending publication of a book with personal details about his family. He filed a lawsuit asking the court to enjoin the publication and distribution of the book. The book's author maintains that this is a prior restraint. Is the author correct?

Explanation:

Yes, the author is correct. The President is asking the court to issue an order before a communication has occurred. The order operates to prevent the communication from occurring. If the prior restraint issues, the author could proceed with the publication, but would do so only upon threat of being held in civil or criminal contempt of the prior restraint.

Example 4-2:

A book about the President has been published and distributed containing facts about the President's personal life. The President files suit against the author, seeking damages against the author for invading the President's privacy rights. The book's author maintains that this action could result in a prior restraint because damages would discourage the author and others from writing and publishing similar books about the President in the future. Is the author correct that a damage judgment amounts to a prior restraint?

Explanation:

No, the author is not correct that a damage judgment would amount to a prior restraint. Under the author's approach to defining a prior restraint, all laws outlawing or imposing consequences for speech would amount to a prior restraint. Although the author accurately points out that the damages might operate to deter future speech, the damages are not specific to the future speech. The determination whether to engage in the future speech is in the hands of the speakers, who would not be speaking under threat of contempt.

Many say that prior restraints are theoretically subject to a higher presumption of unconstitutionality than a content-based subsequent punishment of speech. Indeed, the U.S. Supreme Court in the 1970s stated that "prior restraints on speech and publication are the most serious and least tolerable infringement on First Amendment rights." *Nebraska Press Ass'n v. Stuart,*

427 U.S. 539, 559 (1976). First Amendment scholars agree. The gist of their concern is this: When the only consequence of offensive speech is subsequent punishment, the idea imbedded in the speech has had the chance to be expressed, heard, and considered. The marketplace of ideas and vigorous debate cannot operate if—as is the case with a prior restraint—the restraint prevents an idea from being uttered. Moreover, the consequences of the speech have played out in real life and no need exists to speculate about the impact of the words and thoughts uttered. The following statement by First Amendment scholar Thomas Emerson provides further elaboration on the evils of prior restraint:

> A system of prior restraint is in many ways more inhibiting than a system of subsequent punishment: It is likely to bring under government scrutiny a far wider range of expression; it shuts off communication before it takes place; suppression by a stroke of the pen is more likely to be applied than suppression through a criminal process; the procedures do not require attention to the safeguards of the criminal process; the system allows less opportunity for public appraisal and criticism; the dynamics of the system drive toward excesses, as the history of censorship shows.

Thomas Emerson, THE SYSTEM OF FREEDOM OF EXPRESSION 50 (1970).

Despite these criticisms of prior restraints, the question remains as to whether a preclearance system may actually serve the needs of controversial speakers better than a system imposing punishment after speech has occurred. Consider this question in light of the following Example.

Example 4-3:

A newspaper in a major city publishes extensive investigative articles about local, prominent personalities who engage in potentially unethical behavior. The public generally regards the investigative exposés to reflect the best in good journalism and to perform an important public service. On several occasions, however, targets of exposés have sued the newspaper for defamation. The targets have been successful in establishing the requisite standards for both substantial compensatory damage and punitive damages. Because the punitive damages are calculated by reference to the net worth of the newspaper, the penalties have nearly brought the newspaper to bankruptcy. If given a choice, might the newspaper prefer a prior restraint system where they could have submitted their draft articles for preclearance by a government administrative entity? The government entity could then opine about whether the articles were defamatory. When considering this question, assume that a ruling by the administrative entity that an article was "defamation free" would immunize the newspaper from defamation liability in any subsequent lawsuit.

Explanation:

This Example presents a difficult policy question as well as a difficult strategic choice for the newspaper. On the one hand, a preclearance system has its advantages. Whenever a proposed publication was cleared, the newspaper would publish with the assurance that it would not be exposed to crippling liability. A certain freedom flows from that assurance, and that freedom could encourage more aggressive journalism that exposes the truth. The possibility of a damage verdict that could bankrupt the newspaper could have a powerful chilling effect — perhaps more than a preclearance system. The newspaper might be apt to engage in self-censorship, knowing that juries are unpredictable in using their power to set damages.

On the other hand, the preclearance system would present several downsides for the newspaper. First, the preclearance system would be — in effect — a government censorship system. Such a system would slow the speed of publishing important news. Furthermore, it could protect rights under defamation law at the expense of free press rights under the First Amendment. Preclearance would likely also disadvantage compliant news outlets as compared to those news outlets that do not use the system and are able to publish a story without waiting for approval. The procedural protections for such a system may be minimal, even less than the protections of a civil litigation system where a defamation action would be litigated. Also, public knowledge that the articles were precleared by government officials might render the news less credible and powerful. If the articles have been through a government filter, surely they might not be regarded as the WHOLE naked truth and NOTHING BUT the truth.

Another important legal consideration is the identity of the decision maker in the two systems. In the preclearance system, the decision makers would be government officials, possibly including judges who might support a "don't publish" decision with an injunction. Only judges entertain injunction actions, and a violation of an injunction can carry serious consequences, including judicially designed criminal punishment. By contrast, an after-the-fact defamation lawsuit might be heard by a jury. A jury might be more sympathetic to the newspaper and its mission (and less sympathetic to the prominent, entitled elite in a community). Moreover, since the jury would be engaged in one-shot decision making with no personal consequences, the jury might be less inclined to be overprotective of the target of the speech. In a government preclearance system, those responsible for issuing a ruling might be more likely to act conservatively so as not to jeopardize their jobs or significantly harm the target of the speech. Such conservative decisions may tilt toward suppressing speech with the potential to damage the reputations of powerful people in the community or burden the courts. Under those circumstances, a preclearance system may lead to broader speech suppression than the First Amendment permits.

Accordingly, a controversial speaker would not likely have a clear preference for either a prior restraint censorship system or an after-the-fact civil or criminal punishment system. The answer may depend on local factors that could vary from case to case and from jurisdiction to jurisdiction.

A. WHAT IS A PRIOR RESTRAINT?

When a regulation suppresses the communication of speech *before* it is uttered, you should consider the possibility that it is a prior restraint. A law is classified as a prior restraint if it prevents speech protected by the First Amendment. Thus, a law prohibiting communication of obscenity is not a prior restraint because obscenity is not protected by the First Amendment. In addition, a before-the-fact restriction on speech is a prior restraint if it suppresses speech "before an adequate determination that it is unprotected by the First Amendment." *Pittsburgh Press Co. v. Pittsburgh Commission on Human Relations*, 413 U.S. 376, 390 (1973).

The precise contemporary definition of a prior restraint under contemporary law is elusive. Perhaps the most useful comes from *Alexander v. United States*, 509 U.S. 544 (1993), which explained that the phrase "prior restraint" describes "administrative and judicial orders *forbidding* certain communications when issued in advance of the time that such communications are to occur." *Id.* at 550 (citation omitted).

Two significant problems with prior restraints are (1) the manner in which punishment can be imposed for a violation and (2) the collateral bar rule. Prior restraints usually come in the form of a judicial order enjoining speech. When injunctions are violated, penalties can be imposed more swiftly and without the same safeguards that the criminal justice system requires for a violation of a statute. Moreover, the collateral bar rule precludes a person who disobeys a judicially ordered prior restraint from raising arguments about its invalidity as a defense in contempt proceedings. By contrast, arguments that a statute is invalid may be raised as a defense to prosecution for its violation.

No one can doubt that the label "prior restraint" carries stark consequences. As a result, the U.S. Supreme Court has several times gone out of its way *not* to label a restriction as a prior restraint. For example, in one case, the Court held that an order stopping newspapers from placing help wanted ads based on gender (e.g., "Jobs-Male Interest") was not a prior restraint. Why? The Court said that order did not suppress arguably protected speech because it targeted conduct, not speech. *Pittsburgh Press Co.* at 390. Significantly, the Court emphasized that the requirement was imposed by administrative fiat (not court order) and that a violation of an administrative decision would not be punishable by contempt. *Id.* at 390 n.14.

Another case in which the Supreme Court refused to place the "prior restraint" label on an order preemptively restricting speech (before it occurred) was *Madsen v. Women's Health Center*, 512 U.S. 753 (1994). In *Madsen*, the Supreme Court held that a judicial order restricting speech in a buffer zone around the entrance of an abortion clinic was not a prior restraint, even though the order prevented speech from occurring. A violation of the court order would expose the speaker to the harsh consequences of a contempt proceeding (unlike the *Pittsburgh Press* case discussed immediately above). Why then was the buffer zone order not a prior restraint? No obvious answer presents itself. One can conclude that past obstructions of entrance into a medical facility provide a sufficient basis for suppressing speech, but that explains why the order is properly in place, not why it is not a prior restraint. Such is the confusing nature of First Amendment case law.

Example 4-4:

A man was convicted of charges stemming from his business of distributing obscene pornography to retail stores. The action against him included criminal charges alleging obscenity violations as well as violations of the federal Racketeer Influenced and Corrupt Organizations Act (RICO) stemming from the widespread distribution of the obscenity. Pursuant to RICO, the district court held a forfeiture hearing, after which the man was ordered to forfeit all of the assets and proceeds derived from operating his adult entertainment business. The man challenged the RICO forfeiture order as an unconstitutional prior restraint due to the fact that it stood as an obstacle to expressing himself in the future through the conduct of his adult entertainment business.

Explanation:

The forfeiture order is not a prior restraint on speech. In similar circumstances, the U.S. Supreme Court held that the forfeiture order amounted to after-the-fact criminal punishment rather than a forward-looking prior restraint. *Alexander* at 549-550. The *Alexander* majority reasoned that the forfeiture order did not impede the petitioner's expression—if the petitioner wanted to, he could continue to operate an adult entertainment business notwithstanding the order. Moreover, the case was distinguishable from other earlier obscenity, prior restraint jurisprudence because the RICO statute is one of general applicability, "oblivious to the expressive or nonexpressive nature of the assets forfeited." Id. at 551. To hold otherwise "would undermine the time-honored distinction between barring speech in the future and penalizing past speech . . . to such a degree that it would be impossible to determine with any certainty whether a particular measure is a prior restraint or not." *Id.* at 553-554.

Example 4-5:

A group of black employees sue their employer for racially discriminatory practices. After hearing that the employees' counsel had contacted former employees in an attempt to pool a group of plaintiffs to bolster its class certification, the employer sought and obtained an injunction barring employees' counsel from soliciting former employees to join the action. Specifically, the order prevented communicating "directly or indirectly, orally or in writing" with "any actual or potential class member not a formal party" of the case with the purpose of solicitation. The plaintiffs' counsel challenged the order as a prior restraint on speech.

Explanation:

The counsel is correct that the order is a prior restraint on speech. The purpose of the order is to prevent speech from happening. While it is true that ethical rules governing lawyers prohibit certain types of solicitations, those rules are enforced through after-the-fact punishment. As a prior restraint, the order embodies an immediate and irreversible sanction that can be imposed in contempt proceedings with lesser procedural protections than criminal or disciplinary proceedings. During the contempt proceedings, the collateral bar rule will prevent alleged violators from arguing that the prior restraint is unconstitutional or otherwise invalid. Moreover, the counsel's speech to potential class members could happen in a variety of contexts, including those that do not fall within the categories of solicitation conduct proscribed by the ethical rules. *Bernard v. Gulf Oil Co.*, 619 F.2d 459, 467-470 (5th Cir. 1980).

Example 4-6:

The Federal Trade Commission (FTC) promulgates rules that proscribe certain telemarketing conduct. Specifically, the rules prohibit (1) calls placed to people on a "do-not-call list;" (2) calls made during certain times of the day; and (3) "abandoned calls" where a consumer is not transferred to a sale representative within two seconds of the consumer's greeting. The rules further provide that organizations that make calls that do not comply with these proscriptions may be fined. A group of non-profit organizations that employ telemarketers' challenged the rules, arguing that they act as a prior restraint on speech.

Explanation:

The FTC telemarketer rules do not impose a prior restraint, but rather comprise "typical subsequent punishment." *National Federation of the Blind v. FTC*, 303 F. Supp. 2d 707, 723 (D. Md. 2004). The FTC regulatory scheme does not require that the telemarketers obtain permits before placing calls. Moreover, the FTC views the telemarketers' violation of the rules to occur *only after* the proscribed call is placed.

Example 4-7:

At a state university, a female student-athlete reported to her coach that she was raped by a male student-athlete. The coach directed her not to speak about the incident to anybody whom she had not yet already told about it. The student argued that the coach imposed an impermissible prior restraint on her free speech by telling her to not report the incident to others.

Explanation:

Many courts—including the U.S. Supreme Court in *Alexander*—have recognized that informal orders by an administrator such as a coach at a state university could amount to a prior restraint. Nonetheless, the coach's statement in this situation is probably not a prior restraint. Even if the coach's statement coerced the female student-athlete into remaining quiet about the rape allegations, the coach's directive was more like a restriction that would subject the student to subsequent punishment than a prior restraint. This is because the coach did not require the female student-athlete to seek the coach's permission before speaking, and the coach did not reserve the right to screen or censor any of the student-athlete's statements on the subject. *See Kesterson v. Kent State University*, 345 F. Supp. 3d 855 (N.D. Ohio 2018), *appeal denied*, No. 19-3080, 2019 U.S. App. LEXIS 9217 (6th Cir. Mar. 27, 2019).

Example 4-8:

Congress passes a comprehensive regulatory scheme that expands the FBI's ability to subpoena subscriber data from Internet service providers in order to fight cyberterrorism. The regulations permit the FBI to send a nondisclosure order to the recipient of such a subpoena that restricts their ability to discuss the subpoena publicly. The orders provide that the recipient may discuss neither the content nor the existence of the order with "anyone else," including attorneys and management within the Internet service provider itself. A social networking website regularly receives FBI subpoenas for subscriber information and would like to inform the public of the scope and breadth of the FBI's investigatory patterns. As such, the website challenges the subpoena gag order as an impermissible prior restraint.

Explanation:

Although the subpoena gag order is technically a prior restraint, it is not prohibited. Courts that have considered similar issues stress that such gag orders are permissible when they are narrowly drawn, and the repressed speech is generated for the government and not intended for public fora. This gag order meets that standard. *See, e.g., John Doe, Inc. v. Mukasey*, 549 F.3d 861 (2d Cir. 2008).

B. NATIONAL SECURITY THREATS

Near v. Minnesota ex rel. Olson, 283 U.S. 697 (1931), was one of the first cases to clarify that the rule against prior restraints is not absolute. In *Near*, the Court stated:

> No one would question but that a government might prevent actual obstruction to its recruiting service or the publication of the sailing dates of transports or the number and location of troops. On similar grounds, the primary requirements of decency may be enforced against obscene publications. The security of the community life may be protected against incitements to acts of violence and the overthrow by force of orderly government.

Id. at 716.

The national security exception mentioned in *Near*, however, has limits. Most notably in *New York Times Co. v. United States*, 403 U.S. 713 (1971) (the "Pentagon Papers case"), the Court overturned an injunction against the publication of stolen classified government documents pertaining to an ongoing military conflict. In so holding, the Court established a high bar that the government must clear in order to justify a prior restraint on communications that might threaten national security. That said, the Court subsequently allowed an injunction against a CIA agent who planned to write a book about the agency in violation of his contractual obligation to obtain preclearance from the agency. *Snepp v. United States*, 444 U.S. 507 (1980).

C. PRIOR UNLAWFUL CONDUCT

In *Pittsburgh Press Co.* the Supreme Court upheld an injunction that prohibited a local newspaper from unlawfully printing job postings that discriminated against potential applicants on the basis of sex. The Court reasoned that the injunction did not "endanger arguably protected speech," as the newspaper's advertisements had already been deemed unlawful commercial speech, validly proscribed under the Pittsburgh ordinance barring sex-designated jobs in classified advertising. *Id.* at 390. Importantly, the injunction came after the advertisement practices had been deemed unlawful. The Court emphasized: "The special vice of a prior restraint is that communication will be suppressed . . . *before* an adequate determination that it is unprotected by the First Amendment." *Id.* (emphasis added). Moreover, the Court need not "speculate as to the [chilling] effect of publication" because the order was based on a "continuing course of repetitive conduct." *Id.*

Example 4-9:

A domestic abuse victim sought and obtained a protection order against her ex-husband, with whom she had two minor children. The order provided, among other child custody restrictions, that the father (1) may not go within 120 feet of the mother's house; and (2) may not contact the mother or their minor children "whether in person, with or through other persons, by telephone, letter, electronic means, or in any other way." After the ex-husband violated the terms of the order several times, a court extended the order for 50 years. The ex-husband would like the court to vacate the order and argues that it is an impermissible prior restraint.

Explanation:

Although the order is properly characterized as a prior restraint, it is likely permissible because it appears content-neutral (not dependent on what matters the respondent sought to communicate to the victim or her children) and is primarily based on the respondent's past violence. Moreover, the father is not prevented from expressing his ideas, just not to the particular audience specified in the order. *T.C.B. v. Bergstrom (In re Rew)*, 845 N.W.2d 764, 776 (Minn. 2014).

Example 4-10:

A manager repeatedly directed racial slurs at Latino employees of a rental car facility. The employees brought a state employment discrimination action against the manager. After a jury found that this constituted unlawful employment discrimination, the court granted an injunction preventing the manager from making further racially discriminatory statements. The injunction permanently barred "any future use" of "any derogatory racial or ethnic epithets directed at, or descriptive of Hispanic/Latino employees."

The injunction included examples of epithets that were proscribed and limited the scope of its prohibition to statements made in the workplace. The manager challenges the injunction as an impermissible prior restraint on speech.

Explanation:

The injunction is likely a permissible prior restraint. Because the order was issued after the defendant's conduct had already been determined to be unlawful employment discrimination, the order simply precluded the manager from continuing his unlawful activity. *Aguilar v. Avis Rent A Car System, Inc.*, 980 P.2d 846, 858 (Cal. 1999).

Example 4-11:

A computer hacker obtained a copy of computer code that movie distributors put in DVDs to prevent them from being copied. The hacker created a decryption code that allowed individuals to copy protected DVDs and posted it on a website. The movie distributors sued under trade secrets law and prevailed. The court then issued an injunction that prevented the hacker from distributing the anti-piracy code, or any information derived from it, on the web or elsewhere. The hacker challenges the injunction as an improper prior restraint.

Explanation:

The injunction is likely permissible because it is content-neutral on its face, and it was based on the hacker's prior unlawful conduct. Moreover, the case concerned a private plaintiff's attempt to protect its property rights and not the government's attempt to censor speech. *DVD Copy Control Ass'n, Inc. v. Bunner*, 75 P.3d 1, 17-18 (Cal. 2003).

Special rules related to prior restraints arise in the context of the news media. In particular, courts sometimes issue gag orders to the parties, lawyers, and jurors in a case in an attempt to prevent them from speaking to the media and others. The purpose of these orders is generally to ensure that the trial proceedings are fair and not tainted by publicity. A gag order is effectively a prior restraint on speech. Nonetheless, if done properly and in compliance with detailed factors outlined in *Nebraska Press Associates v. Stuart*, 427 U.S. 539 (1976), gag orders are consistent with the Constitution. These issues pertaining to the news media are discussed further in Chapter 15 of this book.

CHAPTER 5

Compelled Speech

A logical corollary of the First Amendment's protection of the right to speak is the right not to speak.[1] What does this mean? Many examples spring to mind. First, speakers' messages can be affected by speech that they are forced to accommodate. Alternatively, the government may force speech that interferes with speakers' messages. Also, there are circumstances when citizens are compelled to spend money to support a viewpoint with which they do not care to support (such as paying government mandated union dues). These are not the only ways to divide up the cases in the compelled speech area, but they provide a workable structure for understanding.

Indeed, compelled speech is one of the most diverse, developing, and sprawling topics in the area of the First Amendment. This chapter addresses the subject from multiple angles, with an eye toward categorizing the subject areas as cleanly and comprehensively as possible. As you will see, the general principle against compelled speech is deeply rooted, but the various categories are only loosely related and require different analyses. All topics discussed in this chapter are evolving concepts under the umbrella of compelled speech: (1) compulsion to endorse specific positions as a condition for some benefit; (2) compulsion in professional speech and forced disclosure; (3) compulsion to make commercial disclosures; (4) compulsion to subsidize speech; and (5) compulsion to disclose one's identity.

---

1. *Riley v. Nat'l Fed'n of the Blind of N.C., Inc.*, 487 U.S. 781, 796-797 (1988) (stating that the "First Amendment guarantees 'freedom of speech,' a term necessarily comprising the decision of both what to say and what not to say.")

5. Compelled Speech

These five categories are not a universally followed taxonomy. Nonetheless, the categories provide a coherent framework for evaluating landmark U.S. Supreme Court opinions on compelled speech. Although this chapter covers diverse material, it presents one overarching question: At what point does a government regulation that compels speech become problematic and thus subject to heightened First Amendment scrutiny?

A. COMPULSION TO ADOPT SPECIFIC POSITIONS

1. Compulsion or Pressure to Communicate Specific Content

One of the first cases to take up the issue of whether government may compel an individual to communicate an ideological message was *West Virginia State Board of Education v. Barnette*, 319 U.S. 624 (1943), in which the U.S. Supreme Court held unconstitutional the West Virginia Board of Education's policy of forcing students to salute the flag and recite the Pledge of Allegiance. In so doing, the Court stated: "If there is any fixed star in our constitutional constellation, it is that no official, high or petty, can prescribe what shall be orthodox in politics, nationalism, religion, or other matters of opinion or force citizens to confess by word or act their faith therein." Id. at 642. The Court further applied this prohibition against government requirements that citizens communicate an ideological position in *Wooley v. Maynard*, 430 U.S. 705 (1977). In *Wooley*, the Court upheld the First Amendment right of a Jehovah's Witness couple to refuse to display the New Hampshire motto "Live Free or Die," on their state-issued car license plate. The Court stated: "A system which secures the right to proselytize religious, political, and ideological causes must also guarantee the concomitant right to decline to foster such concepts. The right to speak and the right to refrain from speaking are complementary components of the broader concept of 'individual freedom of mind.'" Id. at 714.

Example 5-1:

Every September, local public school teachers are required to sign statements professing their faith in the competence of the school's administrators. The signed statements are displayed on bulletin boards in the front halls of the various school buildings where teachers work. Teachers who refuse to sign the statement are dismissed from their jobs. Is this requirement constitutional?

Explanation:

The requirement violates the First Amendment. The requirement clashes with both the teachings of *Barnette* and *Wooley* by improperly requiring teachers to profess an orthodox attitude toward school administrators. Adding to this constitutional problem, this requirement resembles *Wooley's license plate compulsion* by imposing on teachers the role of being a "billboard" for a message that is not their own. This is an easy case.

Example 5-2:

A prison inmate witnessed a fight between prison guards and another prisoner's violation of the prison's regulations. A prison guard pressured the inmate to sign a statement including (1) a false account of the fight between the guards and (2) inculpatory information about the other prisoner. Not wanting to "snitch," the prison inmate declines, and the prison guards placed him under more restrictive supervision for six months. The guards explicitly said that the punishment resulted from the inmate's refusal to sign the statement.

The inmate has consulted a lawyer about pursuing a First Amendment claim based on his punishment for rejecting compelled speech. The lawyer explains that many legal obstacles stand in the way of a prisoner bringing any civil rights suit. The lawyer further explains that the First Amendment claim, standing alone, is a strong one. If it were possible to overcome other obstacles to bringing any civil rights suit, the lawyer takes the view that the prisoner's treatment violated his First Amendment right to be free from compelled speech. Is the lawyer's interpretation of the First Amendment correct?

Explanation:

The lawyer's interpretation of the First Amendment is likely correct. As described more fully in Chapter 13 below, the prisoner did not enjoy the full First Amendment rights afforded to the general public because of his incarceration. Nonetheless, in a case similar to this Example, the Court of Appeals for the Second Circuit ruled that the First Amendment protects prisoners from retaliation for refusing to speak to the government. *Burns v. Martuscello*, 890 F.3d 77, 87, 90 (2d Cir. 2018). The *Burns* court recognized the "extreme risk that attends the act of snitching in the prison context," as a "jailhouse snitch is imprisoned alongside the very individuals that pose the greatest risk to her safety, creating a unique burden on the liberty interests of the individual inmate." *Id.* at 91. The court determined that the prison could not impose punishments — such as more restrictive confinement — for declining to provide inculpatory information. However, it might constitutionally refuse to provide a benefit, such as reducing charges in exchange for cooperation.

One should note, however, that the prisoner's situation may be unique in the compelled speech area. Consider analogous situations when pressure similar to what the prisoner experienced would be viewed as constitutional. For example, subpoenas pressure people into providing inculpatory information about others under threat of being held in contempt (and possibly incarceration or other punishment). Our judicial system views such pressure appropriate and constitutional. Similarly, a prosecutor can offer reduced charges to a defendant if the defendant reveals inculpatory information about others — with the threat of charges or extra punishment against the defendant hanging in the balance.

* * *

One must note that the First Amendment allows the government to compel speech under certain circumstances: the protection against speech compulsion is not absolute. Consider the following Example.

Example 5-3:

Jamie is a juvenile defendant who was convicted of sexual assault. As part of his sentencing conditions, the judge orders him to write an apology letter to the victim that is approved by the state's parole and probation office. Jamie seeks to overturn the sentencing condition as an impermissible compulsion of speech. Is Jamie correct that forcing him to write an apology letter as part of his punishment violates his First Amendment rights?

Explanation:

Although Jamie is correct that the forced apology letter did compel his speech, he will likely not win his First Amendment claim. As with most First Amendment claims, courts confronting a compelled speech claim sometimes evaluate the reasons for the compulsion and the context in which it takes place. In *State v. K.H.-H.*, 374 P.3d 1141 (Wash. 2016) (en banc), the Washington Supreme Court upheld a sentencing order such as the one here, ruling that Jamie, by virtue of his conviction, had diminished First Amendment rights. Turning to analysis akin to intermediate scrutiny applied in some other First Amendment contexts, the court evaluated whether "sentence conditions that implicate free speech rights [are] narrowly tailored to serve an important government interest and [are] reasonably necessary to achieving that interest." *Id.* at 1143. In so holding, the Court noted that juvenile courts enjoy wide latitude and discretion when imposing sentences.

As rehabilitation is a guiding principle behind juvenile punishment, the Washington Supreme Court concluded that the apology letter requirement served an important state purpose: It forced the defendant to appreciate and accept responsibility for his harmful actions.

One can explain this result in large part by reference to criminal sentencing rules and procedures. In the criminal sentencing context, First Amendment rules are different from the rules applicable outside that context. For example, probation conditions can limit a person's association with political extremists or a person's viewing of pornography that is not obscene and is therefore usually protected under First Amendment law. Although these conditions may be unconstitutional under standard First Amendment rules, they are lawful and enforceable within the context of criminal sentencing.

* * *

2. Compulsion to Alter a Speaker's Message

Note that the government did not require the speakers to change the content of their speech in either *Barnette* or *Wooley*. It simply required individuals to say or display a message. In another category of cases, the Supreme Court has held that the government may not compel a speaker to change the particular message a speaker is making. So, for example, in *Hurley v. Irish-American Gay, Lesbian, and Bisexual Group of Boston*, 515 U.S. 557 (1995), the U.S. Supreme Court reversed a state court ruling requiring organizers of an annual St. Patrick's Day parade to include an organization of gay, lesbian, and bisexual Irish-Americans. The *Hurley* Court determined that the organizers were entitled to "speak[ ] on one subject while remaining silent on the other." Id. at 574. By forcing organizers to include the group—which would march under a banner identifying its constituents as openly gay, lesbian, and bisexual people of Irish descent—the government interfered with the organizers' right to remain silent about homosexuality and bisexuality within the Irish-American community.

3. Compulsory Conditions

In contrast to *Hurley*, the Court has held that under some circumstances the government may condition funding on the requirement that a speaker make a particular statement or take a communicative action. For example, the government may condition education funding on the requirement that school officials allow government representatives to speak on school property. In *Rumsfeld v. Forum for Academic Institutional Rights, Inc.*, 547 U.S. 47 (2006), an association of law schools unsuccessfully challenged a federal law conditioning certain federal funds on campus access for military recruiters. The law schools opposed the condition because they considered the military's "Don't Ask, Don't Tell" policy for homosexual recruits to be discriminatory. The *Rumsfeld* Court reasoned that the condition did not violate the First Amendment because the schools remained free "to express whatever views they may have on the military's congressionally mandated employment policy, all the while retaining eligibility for federal funds." *Id.* at 60. Importantly, the Court also ruled that the government could have directly required schools to provide equal access to military recruiters, even without attaching the requirement to a grant of federal funds.

Example 5-4:

Congress passed a regulation granting funds to organizations that provided foreign aid to countries facing high incidences of infectious diseases, such as HIV/AIDS and malaria. To receive the funding, an organization must comply with two conditions: (1) The organization may not use the funding to "promote or advocate the legalization of prostitution or sex trafficking, and (2) the organization must adopt a policy that explicitly opposes prostitution and sex trafficking."

A non-governmental aid organization whose mission is to combat the spread of HIV/AIDS in developing countries challenges the regulation, arguing that both conditions impermissibly burden its First Amendment exercise of free speech. Is the organization correct?

Explanation:

The organization is correct under existing U.S. Supreme Court precedent. In *Agency for International Development v. Alliance for Open Society International*, 570 U.S. 205 (2013), the Court held that the government violates the First Amendment when it requires — as a condition of federal funding — that organizations adopt a policy expressing opposition to human trafficking and prostitution. The regulation in *Alliance for Open Society* mirrored that provided in this Example. The *Alliance for Open Society* ruling balanced two principles in sharp tension: (1) The federal government may impose conditions upon funding recipients that burden their exercise of First Amendment rights; and (2) the government may not take action that outright denies "a benefit to a person on a basis that infringes his constitutionally protected . . . freedom of speech, even if he has no entitlement to that belief." *Id.* at 214 (quoting *Rumsfeld*, 547 U.S. at 59). In navigating this distinction, the Court drew the line "between conditions that define the limits of the government spending program — those that specify the activities Congress wants to subsidize — and conditions that seek to leverage funding to regulate speech outside the contours of the program itself." *Id.* at 214-215. When the funding comes with conditions that regulate speech outside of the scope of the program, the funding scheme violates the First Amendment. The Court made clear that "Congress cannot recast a condition on funding as a mere definition of its program in every case, lest the First Amendment be reduced to a simple semantic exercise." *Id.* Courts make their own judgment on whether a congressionally imposed condition actually regulates speech that falls in the contours of a program.[2]

The *Alliance for Open Society* Court relied on several cases in making this distinction. *See, e.g., FCC v. League of Women Voters of California*, 468 U.S. 364 (1984) (overturning a federal funding condition that barred recipient broadcast television and radio stations from all editorializing, even when done with private funds); *Regan v. Taxation with Representation of Washington*, 461 U.S. 540 (1983) (upholding the ban on non-profit organizations receiving 501(c)(3) tax exemptions from spending money on lobbying).

Indeed, another case, *Rust v. Sullivan*, 500 U.S. 173 (1991), clearly illustrates the distinction between compelled speech which is and is not permissibly conditioned on funding. In *Rust*, the Court upheld a federal funding condition that barred health care providers from using funds for programs that included abortion as a family planning method. (The Court made clear that federal grantees could not be barred from using *any and all* funds to promote abortions, but only those funds the federal government allocated to them.) The Court tracked this logic in *Agency for International Development*, making it clear that the government may conditionally bar an organization from using allocated funds to promote prostitution and sex trafficking, but the organization as a whole, private funds included, could not be compelled to take that position.

One can also distinguish *Agency for International Development* from the earlier *Rumsfeld* decision in two significant ways: (1) the *Rumsfeld* regulation regarding military recruiters did not require schools to actually endorse the "Don't Ask, Don't Tell" policy; and (2) the *Rumsfeld* regulation arguably operated as a restriction on conduct only, since the schools had only to provide equal access to military recruiters in order to comply with the condition.

Despite these distinctions, compelled conditions cases are difficult to square with one another. As Dean Erwin Chemerinsky suggests, the cases may simply turn on whether members of the Supreme Court approve or disapprove of the particular compelled condition at issue in the case. ERWIN CHEMERINSKY, CONSTITUTIONAL LAW: PRINCIPLES AND POLICIES 1071 (6th ed. 2019).

---

2. In a subsequent decision in the case, the U.S. Supreme Court held that First Amendment protections did not apply to the foreign affiliates of the plaintiff in the case, Alliance for an Open Society International. *Agency for International Development, et al. v. Alliance for Open Society International*, No. 19-177 (U.S. June 29, 2020).

B. PROFESSIONAL SPEECH COMPULSIONS

Many professionals rely heavily on oral and written language in practicing their trade: lawyers, psychologists, teachers, and physicians . . . just to name a few. From a First Amendment point of view, one would think that the content of these various communications is protected. Professionals presumably need freedom in their communications so that they can effectively navigate the challenges of mastering complex subjects, counsel their clients on sensitive subjects, explain the subtleties of the judgments, and debate the wisdom of various courses of action.

But the matter is not properly resolved simply by concluding that regulation should never touch professionals' communications made in their professional capacity. One must remember that professionals are often subject to significant government regulation. This regulation comes in a variety of forms, such as licensing requirements, requirements regarding professional malpractice liability insurance, and advertising regulations. Few dispute the general validity of professional regulation, given the profound responsibilities that professionals hold toward those they serve.

Dispute arises, however, over those regulations that focus on the content of professionals' communications with their clients and others. As one scholar has noted, "[s]ometimes, such regulation aligns with professional insights, but sometimes it contradicts them." Claudia Haupt, *Professional Speech*, 125 YALE L.J. 1150, 1150 (2015-2016). Given the potential clash between the regulations of professionals, matters of social controversy, and the First Amendment, the U.S. Supreme Court has become involved in the area.

One of the most significant cases is *National Institute of Family & Life Advocates (NIFLA) v. Becerra*, 138 S. Ct. 2361 (2018), in which the Supreme Court held that California's posted notice requirements for crisis pregnancy centers violated the First Amendment. The challenged law provided that: (1) licensed clinics had to notify patients that California provided free or low-cost services—including abortions—and provide a phone number to call for information; and (2) unlicensed clinics had to notify patients that California had not licensed them to provide medical services. The *Becerra* Court struck down these disclosure requirements under the First Amendment, holding that they impermissibly compelled the speech of the crisis pregnancy centers.

One of the important issues that arose in the challenge to California's disclosure requirements was the appropriate standard of constitutional scrutiny to use when evaluating government compulsions of "professional speech." California proposed a theory—embraced by the lower court in the cases—that the Supreme Court should hold that restrictions of professional speech require only intermediate scrutiny. The *Becerra* Court declined the opportunity, concluding as follows:

5. Compelled Speech

> In sum, neither California nor the Ninth Circuit has identified a persuasive reason for treating professional speech as a unique category that is exempt from ordinary First Amendment principles. We do not foreclose the possibility that some such reason exists. We need not do so because the licensed notice cannot survive even intermediate scrutiny.

Id. at 2375.

Having declined to take the opportunity to recognize a unique category for professional speech, the Court analyzed the case in light of standard First Amendment analysis. Applying this standard analysis, the Court reasoned that a regulation that compels a professional to say something specific is content-based, and thus presumptively unconstitutional and subject to strict scrutiny. The Court further determined that the regulation did not fit into one of two previously recognized exceptions: (1) a restriction that merely "require[s] professionals to disclose factual, noncontroversial information in their 'commercial speech'" about the services they provide in a manner that is not unduly burdensome; or (2) a regulation of professional conduct that only "incidentally involves speech." *Id.* at 2372. Concluding that the law in *Becerra* did not fall into either exception and thus should be analyzed simply as a content-based regulation of speech, the Court turned to the question of whether the notice requirements passed strict scrutiny. The Court found the notice requirements failed strict scrutiny because they were not narrowly tailored to achieve California's stated interest of "providing low-income women with information about state-sponsored services." *Id.* at 2375. The *Becerra* Court determined the notice requirement was "wildly underinclusive" because it only applied to clinics whose *primary* purpose was the provision of family planning or pregnancy related services. *Id.* at 2367. It did not apply to other clinics which provided those services as a supplement to their primary purpose. The Court also determined that the state could use less intrusive means to serve its goals, such as a public information campaign.

An important observation about *Becerra*'s holding is its tension with the Court's abortion decision in *Planned Parenthood v. Casey,* 505 U.S. 833 (1992). *Becerra* held that the government cannot require pregnancy crisis centers to inform patients about the availability of low-cost abortions. Yet *Casey* held that the government can require doctors who perform abortions to "inform the woman of the nature of the procedure, the health risks of the abortion and of childbirth, and the 'probable gestational age of the unborn child.'" *Id.* at 881. Moreover, in other relatively recent abortion decisions, the U.S. Supreme Court has stated that a state may legitimately act with intent to encourage childbirth rather than abortion. *Casey* and other Supreme Court abortion opinions did not fully reckon with the First Amendment implications of their holdings. The *Casey* plurality's First Amendment analysis appeared only in one paragraph, stating simply that the informed consent statute implicated a "physician's First Amendment rights not to speak . . . but only as part of the practice of medicine, subject to reasonable licensing and regulation by the State." Id. at 884.

At oral argument in Becerra, Justice Breyer's line of questioning addressed this asymmetry regarding Casey, stating "what is sauce for the goose is sauce for the gander." Transcript of Oral Argument at 11, National Institute of Family & Life Advocates v. Becerra, 138 S. Ct. 2361 (2018). Justice Breyer also stressed this point in his dissent: "If a State can lawfully require a doctor to tell a woman seeking an abortion about adoption services, why should it not be able, as here, to require a medical counselor to tell a woman seeking prenatal care or other reproductive healthcare about childbirth and abortion services?" Becerra, 138 S. Ct. at 2385 (Breyer, J., dissenting).

The majority distinguished the Becerra notice requirement from the Casey informed-consent statute, contending that the latter is an example of conduct regulation that incidentally burdens speech since it occurs attendant to a medical procedure. On the other hand, the Becerra notice requirement compelled speech regardless of whether it accompanied a medical procedure.

Example 5-5:

A state enacts a statute requiring that a physician who performs abortions obtain informed consent from the woman before performing the procedure. To do so, the physician must show the woman an ultrasound image of her fetus and describe to her, in the physician's own words, the fetus's anatomical attributes, including whether its organs have developed and whether the woman is pregnant with twins.

A group of physicians challenge the statute as an unconstitutional burden on their First Amendment right to free speech. Will they prevail?

Explanation:

At least one lower court case following Becerra supports the conclusion that the physicians will not prevail. In EMW Women's Surgical Center, P.S.C. v. Beshear, 920 F.3d 421 (6th Cir. 2019), cert. denied, 140 S. Ct. 655 (2019), the Court upheld informed consent requirements identical to those in this Example as valid regulations of medical care that "incidentally burden speech." Id. at 428 (quoting Becerra, 138 S. Ct. at 2373). In light of this characterization, the EMW Women's Surgical Center case reasoned that the informed consent statute should be evaluated by a lower standard of scrutiny if it "(1) relate[d] to a medical procedure; (2) [was] truthful and not misleading; and (3) [was] relevant to the patient's decision whether to undertake the procedure, which may include, in the abortion context, information relevant to the woman's health risks, as well as the impact on the unborn life." *Id.* at 428-429. The *EMW Women's Surgical Center* majority easily concluded that the informed consent statute satisfied those conditions and upheld the law.

One might reasonably argue that the *EMW Women's Surgical Center* court's approach is inconsistent with the U.S. Supreme Court's *Becerra* decision in terms of its characterization of restrictions of conduct incidentally affecting speech. In *Becerra*, the Court determined that the two requirements— (1) notifying women that California provides free or low-cost services, including abortions, and provide them with a phone number to call; and (2) notifying women that California has not authorized unlicensed clinics to provide medical services—were *not* regulations of conduct with incidental effects on speech. In *EMW Women's Surgical* Center, the court determined the requirements: (1) that physicians show women considering abortion an ultrasound image of the fetus; and (2) that physicians describe the anatomical features of the fetus—*were* regulations of conduct incidentally affecting speech. Thus, the *Becerra* regulations failed strict scrutiny and were struck, while the *EMW Women's Surgical Center* regulations were not subject to strict scrutiny and survived. Although the regulations in the latter case did not mandate specific content and were explicitly tied to the practice of medicine—unlike those in *Becerra*—in both cases the regulations clearly prescribed the specific messages that medical providers must deliver. One could also point out that the *EMW Women's Surgical Center* requirements did not necessarily serve a medical purpose endorsed by consensus of the medical community—a factor deemed important to upholding regulations in a more recent U.S. Supreme Court abortion decision. *See Gonzales v. Carhart,* 550 U.S. 124, 176 (2007). At bottom, however, it is far from clear precisely what the Supreme Court meant by the terms "incidentially affects speech" in *Becerra*. As a consequence, the safest route is to look for analogies with the regulation in *Becerra* in deciding whether a regulation of professional speech runs into constitutional problems.

Example 5-6:

A state enacts an informed consent statute that governs what physicians must disclose to a patient before inducing a medical abortion with pills. For these procedures, the physician must inform the woman of the availability of an abortion reversal drug that she may take if she changes her mind. The statute requires a physician to tell the woman that if she would like this reversal drug to work, "time is of the essence" in making that decision: Her delay might prevent the reversal drug from working. The statute does not, however, require the physician to disclose that medical professional organizations have not endorsed the drug because its efficacy has not been proven with empirical studies.

A physician challenges the ordinance as a burden on her First Amendment right to free speech. Will she prevail?

Explanation:

The law is likely unconstitutional, and the physician will likely prevail. First, the informed consent statute requires that the physician communicate precisely specified information. This suggests that the statute regulates the content of the physician's speech, and not simply the physician's conduct which may have an incidental effect on speech. One may therefore argue that the statute is subject to strict scrutiny. Under that standard, the state would have difficulty arguing that disclosing the existence of a drug that is not medically accepted serves a compelling state interest.

Even if a court were to conclude that the statute regulates conduct and is thus entitled to a lower standard of scrutiny, the statute runs into constitutional difficulty. First, the law forces physicians to give their patients unsound and unproven medical advice, the type of requirement that is not approved by even the most conservative U.S. Supreme Court abortion decisions. Moreover, the mandated message has a misleading quality, since the medical evidence deems the treatment potentially ineffectual. *See American Medical Association v. Stenehjem*, 412 F. Supp. 3d 1134 (D.N.D. 2019).

* * *

Becerra and the informed consent cases grapple with compelled speech for health care professionals. The professional speech question also arises in other contexts. In this regard, consider the following Example.

Example 5-7:

The National Labor Relations Board (NLRB) promulgated a rule that requires employers to post notices for its employees of upcoming union elections. The mandated notice displays the NLRB seal on all four corners and reads "THIS IS AN OFFICIAL GOVERNMENT NOTICE" in large font at the top of the page. Each notice must also include the date and time of the upcoming election as well as a list of employee rights for labor union elections that the NLRB has promulgated.

A group of employers file suit, challenging the rule as impermissibly compelling their speech in violation of their First Amendment rights. Will they prevail?

Explanation:

The chances are good that the employers will prevail, but the outcome is not certain. In a case that proceeded *Becerra*, the U.S. District Court for the District of Columbia upheld the NLRB requirement described in this Example. *Chamber of Commerce of the United States of America v. NLRB*, 118 F. Supp. 3d 171 (D.D.C. 2015). The *Chamber of Commerce* court rejected the employers' challenge because the notices were clearly marked as government speech, given the presence of the government insignias and required text "THIS IS AN OFFICIAL GOVERNMENT NOTICE." The court determined that compelling employers to post the notices did not interfere with their ability to communicate their own messages. *See also Rumsfeld*, 547 U.S. 47 (holding that grant of federal education funds conditioned on access to military recruiters did not violate schools' First Amendment rights because schools were free to criticize the military's "Don't Ask, Don't Tell" policy while remaining eligible for funding). Moreover, the court ruled that the notice-posting requirement did not "dictate what they may or may not say about the notice, the petition, or the representation election process." 118 F. Supp. at 194. In the court's view, the posting requirement did not impede "an employer's ability to convey its own pre-election message to counteract what it sees as disagreeable government speech." *Id. See also National Association of Manufacturers v. Perez*, 103 F. Supp. 3d 7 (D.D.C. 2015) (upholding an NLRB rule that required an employer, as a condition of receiving a federal contract, to post a workplace notice informing its employees of their rights under the National Labor Relations Act.)

Despite this precedent and reasoning, the question arises whether *Becerra* would change the result of this Example. The NLRB posting requirement does not easily fall into the two exceptions to strict scrutiny mentioned in *Becerra*: the requirement is not easily characterized as commercial speech and appears to regulate the employer's speech alone as opposed to an employer's conduct. Nor do they seem to compel communication of truthful health or safety information as protected by the holding in *EMW Women's Surgical Center* (discussed in Example 5-6, above).

Yet one can come to a different conclusion by focusing on context. Hostility to abortion rights may have influenced the First Amendment ruling in *Becerra*. The organized labor context raises a whole set of separate policy issues that may influence the First Amendment analysis. *See, e.g., Janus v. AFSCME, Council 31*, 138 S. Ct. 2448 (2018) (holding that state law requiring public employees to subsidize a union violates the free speech rights of non-members by compelling them to subsidize private speech on matters of substantial public concern). Understanding of the forces behind these separate contexts is important, but predicting their effect is always dubious without specific information.

C. COMPULSION TO MAKE COMMERCIAL DISCLOSURES

In an important case that predated *Becerra*, the U.S. Supreme Court wrestled with the issue of commercial disclosures, an issue that was covered by subsequent U.S. Supreme Court cases. In *Zauderer v. Office of Disciplinary Counsel of Supreme Court of Ohio*, 471 U.S. 626 (1985), the Court ruled that the First Amendment protects truthful advertisements, but allows government to punish deceptive advertising, including misleading advertising occurring because of omission. Interestingly, *Zauderer* concerns attorney speech, and in that way could be characterized as a professional speech case. It has now been generalized, however, as a commercial speech case. *Zauderer* still continues to govern the constitutionality of required disclosures in commercial speech today, although it must be understood in light of *Becerra*. Under *Zauderer*, the government may compel disclosure in commercial speech when the disclosure is (1) purely factual, (2) non-controversial, and (3) not unjustified or unduly burdensome. *Becerra*, 138 S. Ct. at 2372 (interpreting *Zauderer*, 471 U.S. at 651).

How did *Becerra* modify the reach and meaning of *Zauderer*? To begin, *Becerra* stressed that to fall within *Zauderer*, the commercial disclosure must actually relate to the service or product the speaker provides and must be aimed to "remedy a harm that is potentially real[,] not purely hypothetical." *Becerra*, 138 S. Ct. at 2377. More specifically, *Becerra* clarified the *Zauderer* "noncontroversial" element. After *Zauderer* and *Becerra*, courts find compelled, truthful speech to be impermissibly controversial when it requires an entity "to convey a message fundamentally at odds with its mission." *CTIA—The Wireless Association v. City of Berkeley*, 928 F.3d 832, 845 (9th Cir. 2019), cert. denied, 140 S. Ct. 658 (2019).

In evaluating the current reach of *Zauderer*, consider these Examples presenting the interaction between the generic commercial disclosure context covered by *Zauderer* and more controversial contexts modified by *Becerra*.

Example 5-8:

Concerned with obesity and diabetes rates, a city enacts an ordinance that requires soda manufacturers to affix a warning label to their products. The label reads: "WARNING: The City has determined that drinking beverages with added sugar(s) contributes to obesity, diabetes, and tooth decay." The label must cover 20 percent of the soda can or bottle label and must be enclosed in a sold rectangular box. An organization of soda manufacturers filed a lawsuit challenging this regulation. The parties presented conflicting testimony: The city provided examples of tobacco and prescription drug warnings that similarly comprised 20 percent of the entire labels, but the defendant soda industry organization introduced expert testimony that a warning label comprising of 10 percent of the label would be sufficient to accomplish the city's stated goal of avoiding obesity, diabetes, and tooth decay.

The soda industry organization moves for summary judgment dismissal, arguing that the warning label requirement is "unduly burdensome" under *Zauderer*. Should the court grant the motion for summary judgment?

Explanation:

The answer is maybe. The *Zauderer* test, as modified in *Becerra*, requires a court adjudicating such a summary judgment motion to first evaluate whether this compelled disclosure in commercial speech is "(1) purely factual, (2) non-controversial, and (3) not unjustified or unduly burdensome." *Becerra*, 138 S. Ct. at 2372 (interpreting *Zauderer*, 471 U.S. at 651).

The court in this Example could focus on any of these factors, but the most obvious conflict point is the "unduly burdensome" prong of analysis. It seems relatively clear that the disclosure is factual and concerns an uncontroversial link between high sugar intake and health effects. Significant arguments, however, surround the question whether this regulation is unduly burdensome.

The unduly burdensome analysis is inherently subjective. Some questions to consider here are: Would a more restrained wording accomplish the warning purpose? Is the warning sufficiently justified? To answer these questions, one might first note that the required label is large, particularly when one considers that beverage labels are generally larger than cigarette labels. Could a smaller label accomplish the same purpose? Perhaps a smaller warning with eye-catching qualities might still be sufficient to draw attention to it yet intrude less on the rest of the label. Even simply adding a bright color-contrasting border to a smaller warning might be sufficient.

As illustrated here, the unduly burdensome evaluation requires a significant amount of subjective judgment. The answers to such questions are not always obvious. A well-reasoned argument—such as good faith balancing—is sometimes the best one can do. In this case, one can reasonably argue that a smaller warning using other techniques might accomplish the same result. For that reason, one might conclude that the warning requirement is unduly burdensome because one could draw attention to the health hazards of sugary drinks with a lighter intervention. *See American. Beverage Association v. City and County of San Francisco*, 916 F.3d 749 (9th Cir. 2019).

Example 5-9:

A city enacts an ordinance requiring cell phone retailers to display the following message, either on an 8.5″ × 11″ poster or smaller handbills, prominently at retail locations:

> To assure safety, the Federal Government requires that cell phones meet radio-frequency (RF) exposure guidelines. If you carry or use your phone in a pants or shirt pocket or tucked into a bra when the phone is ON and connected to a wireless network, you may exceed the federal guidelines for exposure to RF radiation. Refer to the instructions in your phone or user manual for information about how to use your phone safely.

Assume that the statement is factually true and that the Federal Communications Commission (FCC) has required that cell phones include a similar warning in their operating manuals. Nonetheless, no proof exists that RF radiation is dangerous, and the FCC includes the message out of an abundance of caution that future research would reveal health risks.

A group of cell phone retailers challenge the city's ordinance as an impermissible compelled disclosure because the warnings are either untruthful, controversial, or unduly burdensome under *Zauderer*. Will the cell phone retailers likely prevail in their challenge?

Explanation:

This is a close case, although existing case law suggests that the retailers will likely not prevail in challenging the required disclosure under *Zauderer*. *See CTIA—The Wireless Association v. City of Berkeley*, 928 F.3d 832 (9th Cir. 2019). Looking to the first *Zauderer* prong, the retailers could argue that the disclosure is untruthful because it omits neutral facts about the dangers of RF radiation. However, the *CTIA* court determined that the compelled warning merely relayed the FCC's position on RF radiation. *Id.* at 846. Furthermore, since the ordinance did not prohibit retailers from providing supplemental information about the safety of RF radiation, retailers could easily address any potentially misleading effect. Therefore, the compelled disclosure was truthful.

The disclosure satisfies the second *Zauderer* prong as uncontroversial. In *CTIA*, the court determined that since the statement was factually accurate, and the retailers never disputed the potential dangers of RF radiation as a general matter, the disclosure was not controversial. *Id.* at 848.

The disclosure is not unduly burdensome because it requires retailers to post only a single 8.5″ × 11″ notice, or an even smaller handout. Also, as previously discussed, retailers are free to supplement the mandatory disclosures with their own information. Therefore, all three elements of the *Zauderer* test are satisfied, and the compelled speech is constitutional.

5. Compelled Speech

Alternatively, the retailers could argue that *Zauderer* does not apply at all because the compelled disclosure is not commercial speech. Since the retailers are engaged only in the business of promoting and selling cell phones, the disclosure about RF radiation and phone safety is beyond the scope of their business. Nonetheless, the *CTIA* court rejected this argument because *Zauderer* applies to "purely factual and uncontroversial disclosures about commercial products." *Id.* at 848 (quoting *Becerra* at 2376). Cell phones are certainly commercial products, and since the disclosure was deemed factual and uncontroversial, *Zauderer* should apply.

D. COMPULSION TO SUBSIDIZE SPEECH

The U.S. Supreme Court has recognized that compelled private subsidies for government speech are consistent with the First Amendment. Take for example *Johanns v. Livestock Marketing Association*, 544 U.S. 550 (2005), where the Court held that beef ranchers could be compelled to pay fees for federally mandated beef promotional campaigns, including the classic "Beef, It's What's For Dinner" commercials.

Similarly, in *Board of Regents v. Southworth*, 529 U.S. 217 (2000), the Court upheld a public university's requirement of mandatory student activity fees. The university's goal in distributing the funds was to promote diversity. To that end, the university paid attention to content in distributing the funds, but did so in a viewpoint-neutral manner.

By contrast, a government regulation that compels an individual to subsidize speech is only presumptively constitutional if the funding is distributed in a content-based manner to private speakers. Indeed, the Court has recognized several instances in which compelled subsidies to private organizations violated the First Amendment. *See, e.g., Elrod v. Burns*, 427 U.S. 347 (1976) (evaluating compelled contributions to political parties); *Keller v. State Bar of California*, 496 U.S. 1 (1990) (evaluating compelled payments to state bars used for political purposes); *Janus v. AFSCME*, 138 S. Ct. 2448 (2018) (evaluating compelled payments to unions, including when used for nonpolitical purposes).

Janus is generally considered the key recent case in this area, although as in so many First Amendment contexts, one wonders whether the politics of the case and the emotions surrounding public labor union issues may restrict the reach of its holding. *Janus* overruled *Abood v. Detroit Board of Education*, 431 U.S. 209 (1977), which upheld a law compelling an individual to pay union "agency fees" to fund collective bargaining. Agency fees are levied against non-members in bargaining units and are calculated to cover only the costs of collective bargaining, and not political activity. In *Janus*, a public sector employee who chose not to join his representative union challenged a state law requiring non-union public employees to pay an agency fee. The Court held that the compelled subsidy violated the First Amendment because it impermissibly required employees to subsidize speech that they might not endorse. Although the agency fees were not used for political activity, the Court accepted Janus' argument that he was compelled to support the union's aggressive collective bargaining strategy despite a state budget crisis. *Janus* left many questions unanswered and its precise scope is uncertain. For example, is it relevant outside of the public employee context? Consider the following Example.

Example 5-10:

A state requires that attorneys join a private bar association in order to qualify to practice law in the state. The private bar association charges mandatory yearly dues to fund the organization's operations. An attorney who opposes the bar association's political positions would like to challenge the requirement that she pay mandatory dues each year, arguing that it violates her First Amendment rights.

Will her challenge succeed?

Explanation:

The chances are good that the attorney's challenge will succeed. The issue here is whether a state may require a lawyer to pay mandatory bar dues to a private bar organization under the First Amendment. In *Keller v. State Bar of California*, 496 U.S. 1 (1990), the U.S. Supreme Court held that attorneys have a First Amendment right to refrain from subsidizing a bar association's politically ideological activities. The subsequent *Janus* decision reinforces this view, calling into question whether the First Amendment would allow mandatory bar dues at all.

Janus suggests that attorneys may not be compelled to either subsidize the non-ideological activities of private bar organizations or to become members of a private bar organization that takes positions with which they disagree. Interestingly, *Janus* mentioned that the problem could also be cast in terms of the First Amendment's freedom of association guarantees: Although a state may impede free association by requiring non-members to accept union representation in collective bargaining, the compelled association may not be stretched so far as to require non-members to subsidize the union. *Janus*, 138 S. Ct. at 2478. This characterization is common in this context.

Although *Janus*'s scope is unclear, it likely applies to lawyers because courts have long tolerated regulations restricting their associational freedoms. The Supreme Court has generally recognized that states have more leeway to curtail the First Amendment rights of attorneys. *See e.g., Gentile v. State*

Bar of Nevada, 501 U.S. 1030, 1036 (1991) (reasoning that lawyers may be constitutionally prohibited from speech that can prejudice ongoing litigation). That said, the challenge to the mandatory bar dues for non-political and non-ideological purposes may prevail, as it is closest to the facts in *Janus*. Cf. *Fleck v. Wetch*, 937 F.3d 1112 (8th Cir. 2019), *cert. denied*, 140 S. Ct. 1294 (2020).

Example 5-11:

A state authorizes a labor union as the exclusive representative for collective bargaining for employment contracts for state-sponsored childcare providers. Under the regulation, the state will negotiate only with the labor union, not with any individual childcare providers.

Simon is an employee for a state-sponsored childcare provider and objects to many of the union's policies. He would like to challenge the state's authorization of the union as his exclusive representative, claiming that authorization violates his First Amendment rights.

Explanation:

Recent precedent suggests that Simon will not win this challenge to the union's exclusive bargaining arrangement with the state. *Mentele v. Inslee*, 916 F.3d 783 (9th Cir. 2019). The foundation for this decision lies partially in the freedom of association component of the unionization issue. Freedom of association is not specifically mentioned in the First Amendment, but has been inferred from other aspects of the Amendment's explicit protections. Freedom of association analysis often blends with that of freedom of expression. *See* Chapter 16 for further information on freedom of association.

The *Mentele* decision rests in part on an earlier U.S. Supreme Court case, *Minnesota State Board for Community Colleges v. Knight*, 465 U.S. 271 (1984). *Knight* upheld a Minnesota law providing the following: If state employees have selected an exclusive representative for mandatory labor bargaining — concerning wages, hours, and working conditions — the employer state agency may only "meet and confer" with that representative for bargaining on non-mandatory subjects. *Knight* held that the mandatory, restricted "meet and confer" sessions did not violate the First Amendment associational rights of employees who disagreed with the policies of their exclusive representative group. Relevant to the compelled speech doctrine, the *Knight* Court held that the arrangement did not infringe associational freedoms of these employees: The employees had no First Amendment right to an audience with the government on policymaking issues, and the employees were free to form their own advocacy groups.

Without mentioning *Knight*, *Janus* (in dicta) purported to allow states to authorize a union to bargain collectively and exclusively on behalf of a group of state employees. The majority opinion, however, left the door open for other challenges to exclusive employment-based associational requirements:

> It is also not disputed that the State may require that a union serve as exclusive bargaining agent for its employees — itself a significant impingement on associational freedoms that would not be tolerated in other contexts. We simply draw the line at allowing the government to go further still and require all employees to support the union irrespective of whether they share its views.

Janus, 138 S. Ct. at 2478.

Does *Janus* support the conclusion that exclusive union representation is impermissibly compelled association under the First Amendment? *Janus* did not overrule *Knight*, as *Janus* endorsed "a bright line distinction between allowing exclusive representation and mandating the payment of agency fees." *Mentele*, 916 F.3d. at 791. Further, the underlying logic of *Knight* is covered by *Janus*'s statement that exclusive bargaining arrangements "in no way restrain[ ] . . . freedom to associate or not to associate with whom [employees] please, including the exclusive representative." *Id.* at 789 (quoting *Knight* at 288). *See also Bierman v. Dayton*, 900 F.3d 570 (8th Cir. 2018), *cert. denied*, 139 S. Ct. 2043 (2019) (rejecting the argument that exclusive bargaining representation violates First Amendment rights); *Reisman v. Associated Faculties of Univ. of Maine*, 356 F. Supp. 3d 173 (D. Me. 2018), *aff'd*, 939 F.3d 409 (1st Cir. 2019) (same).

E. COMPULSION TO DISCLOSE IDENTITY

When you hear a controversial message, do you often wonder who is making the message? From knowledge of the speaker's identity, you might determine their motives, biases, access to information, and the like. All of these factors may be important to your perception of the message. But does that mean that the government should require individuals delivering a message to disclose their identity? People may have many reasons for wanting to speak anonymously, with fear of economic or physical retribution being high on the list. This is the dilemma of compelled disclosure of speaker identity.

The First Amendment exists, in part, to protect controversial viewpoints so that they might provoke reasoned debate and enrich civil discourse. From the speaker's point of view, dramatic consequences may follow from being forced to add one's name to the communication and the logical approach might likely be for a speaker required to disclose identity to choose instead to avoid communicating at all. And of course that impulse does not add more important knowledge into public discourse. The tension arises because disclosure of the speaker's identity serves the listener's point of view: more information enables more reasoned evaluation of whether a viewpoint is accurate and worthy of respect. With knowledge of the speaker's identity, listeners may filter out inaccurate or bad faith viewpoints, improving the quality of discourse.

In a series of cases, the U.S. Supreme Court has fairly consistently chosen to protect speakers' choices to conceal their identity and has struck down laws requiring speakers to disclose their identity. The Court treads especially carefully when the speech at issue is political, ruling as to encourage speech and reduce incentives for self-censorship.

The watershed case in this area is *Talley v. California*, 362 U.S. 60 (1960), in which the Court held unconstitutional a Los Angeles ordinance that prohibited the distribution of any handbill in the city unless it contained the name and address of the person who prepared, distributed, or sponsored it. The Court determined that government should not compel speakers to identify themselves because that would "deter . . . peaceful discussions of public matters of importance." *Id.* at 65. In so ruling, the Court accepted the importance of anonymous speech to human progress.

Following the Court's decision in *Talley*, the right to anonymity established in that case has remained in First Amendment jurisprudence. Nonetheless, the Court did not review the right to anonymous speech for three decades, until *McIntyre v. Ohio Elections Commission*, 514 U.S. 334 (1995). In the time between the *Talley* and *McIntyre* decisions, the Court upheld identity disclosure laws regarding financial contributors to political campaigns. *See, e.g., Buckley v. Valeo*, 424 U.S. 1 (1976) (upholding identity disclosure requirements for financial contributors to both official political campaigns and independent advocacy groups for the election or defeat of a candidate). Guiding decision making in this area during the time between *Talley* and *McIntyre* were two other cases that touched on freedom of association: *NAACP v. Alabama*, 357 U.S. 449 (1958), and *Brown v. Socialist Workers '74 Campaign Committee*, 459 U.S. 87 (1982). In these two cases, the Court had established that some disclosure requirements would be unconstitutional as applied if a speaker was vulnerable to harassment, threats, loss of employment, and the like.

In *McIntyre*, the Court considered a challenge to an election law that prohibited individuals from circulating anonymous leaflets in connection with political campaigns. Importantly, the Court determined that because the state statute impacted political speech, it should apply strict scrutiny. The Court held that the state statute failed strict scrutiny because it was not narrowly tailored to support the compelling interest in preventing fraud and libel. Since the statute applied regardless of whether leaflets were distributed months in advance or on election night, it extended to communications that did not present "a substantial risk of libel." *McIntyre*, 514 U.S. at

352. McIntyre is further discussed in Chapter 3 above in connection with the definition of "core political speech."

Example 5-12:

A state has a ballot-initiative process with three requirements: (1) ballot-initiative circulators must be registered voters; (2) circulators must wear a name badge while seeking signatures; and (3) the sponsor of the initiative must report each circulator's name, address and pay. Are these requirements constitutional?

Explanation:

This scheme is unconstitutional. To begin, the scheme restricts political speech—a fact that raises the stakes on its judicial scrutiny of its constitutional validity. Indeed, the facts of this Example are based substantially on *Buckley v. American Constitutional Law Foundation*, 525 U.S. 182 (1999), which is discussed in Chapter 3 above in connection with constitutional regulation of core political speech in the political process.

The *Buckley* Court spoke to the question of the value of anonymity in the political process. Invoking *McIntrye*, the *Buckley* Court reasoned that the anonymity issue is significantly more important when circulating petitions than other political activities. Why? Circulating petitions necessarily implicates matters of public concern because it requires advocates to seek political support directly from citizens. Since this goes to the heart of political debate, regulations that deter participation are inherently suspect. Moreover, the identity disclosure requirements for circulators—such as name badges and employment information—do not further the state's interest in political transparency. A general disclosure of financial sponsors and their contributions is sufficient to achieve the state's purpose. *Id.* at 203-204.

Example 5-13:

A city passes an ordinance prohibiting the use of masks, hoods, or other items in public places by any person 18 years or older when worn for the purpose of disguising or concealing one's identity. The penalty for violating the ordinance is high. The city passed the ordinance to prevent violence and assist law enforcement in capturing criminals. Members of the Ku Klux Klan seek to have the ordinance invalidated because it criminalizes their desire to present their ideas in public while wearing a mask, and therefore violates their right to freedom of anonymous expression under the First Amendment. Will they succeed with their challenge?

Explanation:

The lower courts are conflicted on this question, and the politicization of mask-wearing during the COVID-19 pandemic throws uncertainty into the equation. On one hand is *American KKK v. City of Goshen*, 50 F. Supp. 2d 835 (N.D. Ind. 1999), which held that the ordinance violates the First Amendment by prohibiting members from communicating anonymously. The court agreed that the ordinance violated the First Amendment because it prevented individuals, such as the American KKK members, from being able to express themselves anonymously. Citing the U.S. Supreme Court's decision in *McIntyre*, the court determined that the ordinance stifled public speech touching on issues of public concern, was content-based, and did not pass strict scrutiny. On the other hand, the U.S. Court of Appeals for the Second Circuit held that such an ordinance was constitutional in *Church of the American Knights of the KKK v. Kerik*, 356 F.3d 197, 206-207 (2d Cir. 2004).

In arguing that it is constitutional, one can point out that the ordinance has a limited reach. It does not require individuals to disclose their names to the government or anyone else. It is not limited to masks alone and includes hoods and other items that can be used to conceal one's identity. For this reason, it does not necessarily target a particular mode of head or face gear associated with a particular group. Nor does the ordinance target the expressive qualities of the gear, and includes a specific intent requirement that the item be worn for the purpose of disguising or concealing one's identity. Therefore, face coverings worn for medical, safety, and religious purposes appear exempt. Additionally, to the extent that those who want to wear these items are motivated by a desire to express a message, they can find many alternative ways to do so, such as posting messages online, calling people on the phone, and distributing pamphlets in the mail. For these reasons, one could argue that the prohibition is narrowly drawn.

On the other hand, such an ordinance might be unconstitutional because it fails judicial scrutiny. In *American KKK*, the Northern District of Indiana was unpersuaded that a prohibition of face coverings would reduce crime. The court considered testimony that Ku Klux Klan members often demonstrate without hoods and masks, and that no clear proof existed that anonymity led to increased violence at rallies. 50 F. Supp. 2d at 843. Furthermore, the court determined that even if the link between masks and crime could be proven, the ordinance was not narrowly tailored. Given the context, a prohibition of face coverings would lead members of the Klan to self-censor, implicating the dilemma of anonymity in First Amendment jurisprudence.

Example 5-14:

A state allows citizens to challenge its laws by referendum. The first step in this process is to circulate petitions soliciting signatures along with printed names and addresses. A small number of signatures are required to place the referendum on the general ballot. The petitions must include the names and addresses of the signers. The election authorities in the state then verify that all signatories are registered voters. The Sunshine Law in the state requires the election authorities to disclose the petitions, with names and addresses, if a private person makes a proper request for disclosure.

Victoria challenges this referendum process as unconstitutional. She argues that if the First Amendment protects the right to leaflet anonymously, the First Amendment should also protect the right to endorse a petition anonymously. Is she correct?

Explanation:

According to the U.S. Supreme Court, Victoria is probably not correct. In *Doe v. Reed*, 561 U.S. 186 (2010), the Court held that disclosure of referendum petitions (with addresses and signatures) would not violate First Amendment. The *Reed* Court used an ambiguous level of scrutiny characteristic of political process cases (see Chapter 3 above). The Court stated that this regulation should be subject to "exacting scrutiny," a phrase that suggests strict scrutiny. But in describing the actual requirements, the Court used the language of intermediate scrutiny: the Court stated that in order to be constitutional, the regulation must be justified by a "sufficiently important government interest" and must have a "substantial" relationship with that interest. *Id.* at 196. The plaintiffs argued that the law is particularly troublesome because the petitions could make their way onto the Internet and the signatures and addresses on the petitions could be easily matched with phone numbers and the like. The *Reed* Court was not persuaded by this argument, but limited its holding to the specific facts of this case.

Incitement of Illegal Activity

The question of how much society may suppress speech inciting others to engage in illegal activities presents two important policy questions about the delicate balance of a flourishing democracy:

(1) How much importance should society place on maintaining social control?
(2) How much should this concern outweigh the need to ensure free expression?

These two concerns fight against each other and require weighing one against the other. This weighing process is often particularly sensitive because the content of speech intended to incite illegal action frequently concerns highly valued speech regarding political matters. In this context, stakes rise because advocacy of law violations is a potent vehicle for expressing a political message. The process of exploring this important clash has—in large part—formed the foundation for First Amendment jurisprudence governing speech and assembly today. For that reason, the history of the law's evolution in this area is especially important.

A. DEVELOPMENT OF THE DOCTRINE

Over many decades—starting around the time of the World War I—the U.S. Supreme Court experimented with several different approaches for deciding when, if ever, the government may restrict speech that appears to incite illegality. One impetus for the development of First Amendment law at this time was the Espionage Act of 1917, which made it a crime to "make or convey false reports or false statements with intent to interfere" with a war effort, to "obstruct the recruiting or enlistment" of military members, or to "cause or attempt to cause insubordination, disloyalty, mutiny, or refusal of duty, in the military or naval forces." Prosecutors and courts generally interpreted this language broadly, making possible aggressive prosecutions of individuals disagreeing with the war effort.

A contrasting interpretation of the Act during this time appeared in the opinion of Judge Learned Hand in *Masses Publishing Co. v. Patten*, 244 F. 535 (S.D.N.Y.), *rev'd*, 246 F. 24 (2d Cir. 1917). Judge Hand read the Act narrowly, concluding that it criminalized only writings or oral speech that constituted "direct incitement to violent resistance" to the law. *Id.* at 540. Making clear his speech-protecting approach to the Act, Judge Hand refused to broadly interpret its use of the word "cause" and explained that such an interpretation would run counter to "the normal assumption of democratic government that the suppression of hostile criticism does not turn upon the justice of its substance or the decency and propriety of its temper." *Id.*

Although Judge Hand's opinion later became a source of admiration, it was not well embraced at the time. The U.S. Court of Appeals for the Second Circuit reversed the decision, and soon thereafter, the U.S. Supreme Court adopted a formulation that provided a broad reading of the Espionage Act. This formulation came in the famous words of Justice Holmes, stating that the question to be asked in evaluating the constitutionality of a prosecution is whether the allegedly dangerous "words used are used in such circumstances and are of such a nature as to create a clear and present danger of that they will bring about the substantive evils that Congress has a right to prevent." *Schenck v. United States*, 249 U.S. 47, 52 (1919).

The words "clear" and "present" suggest concern with probability that harm will occur as well as with whether the harm is likely to occur soon. The Court added, however, that the inquiry should include questions of proximity and degree—presumably referring to whether the danger is grave and whether it is close in time and space as well. This test focused on the actual context in which speech occurs, evaluating the possible consequences of the challenged advocacy.

Although the clear and present standard may appear difficult for authorities to satisfy, courts did not necessarily apply the standard with rigor. For example, the U.S. Supreme Court upheld convictions under the federal Espionage Act of individuals' anti-war advocacy that was unlikely to have significant effect. Instead, the Court merely focused on the *tendency* of the advocacy to cause harm. *Frohwerk v. United States*, 249 U.S. 204 (1919); *Debs v. United States*, 249 U.S. 211 (1919). As Justice Holmes stated in *Schenk*: "If the act (speaking, or circulating a paper,) its tendency and the intent with which it is done are the same, we perceive no ground for saying that success alone warrants making the act a crime." 249 U.S. at 52.

Justice Holmes quickly evolved in his thinking, however. Dissenting in *Abrams v. United States*, 250 U.S. 616 (1919), Justice Holmes shrouded his clear-and-present-danger approach with a speech-protecting philosophy. He stated that even though the desire to suppress dissenting opinions is an understandable human inclination:

> [W]e should be eternally vigilant against attempts to check the expression of opinions that we loathe and believe to be fraught with death, unless they so imminently threaten immediate interference with the lawful and pressing purposes of the law that an immediate check is required to save the country.

Id. at 630.

It took some time, however, before the majority of the U.S. Supreme Court embraced this view toward regulation of incitement to violence. In fact, the Court swung even further toward restricting dissenting speech in *Gitlow v. New York*, 268 U.S. 652 (1925). The defendant in that case was prosecuted under an anarchy statute that prohibited advocacy of the overthrow of the government by force and violence. In upholding the prosecution, the Supreme Court invoked one of the most deferential tests in constitutional law, asking only if the legislature that passed the statute acted reasonably. Specifically, the Court ruled that the legislature could reasonably determine that it was appropriate to authorize suppression of "threatened danger in its incipiency." Id. at 669. This language contrasts starkly with Justice Holmes' dissent in *Abrams*: indeed, the *Gitlow* language gives license to authorities to punish advocacy before the circumstances suggest that words would inspire immediate grave danger.

The next memorable statement in this important line of decisions came in the concurring opinion of Justice Brandeis in *Whitney v. California*, 274 U.S. 357 (1927). Rejecting *Gitlow's* deferential, "reasonableness" approach to legislatures, Justice Brandeis stated that repression of speech should occur only in an emergency when grave danger is near:

> Whenever the fundamental rights of free speech and assembly are alleged to have been invaded, it must remain open to a defendant to present the issue whether there actually did exist at the time a clear danger, whether the danger, if any, was imminent, and whether the evil apprehended was one so substantial as to justify the stringent restriction interposed by the Legislature. The legislative declaration, like the fact that the statute was passed and was sustained by the highest court of the State, creates merely a rebuttable presumption that these conditions have been satisfied.

Id. at 378-379.

Justice Brandeis's position failed to persuade the Court majority in the next major decision in this area: *Dennis v. United States*, 341 U.S. 494 (1951). Writing at the time of strong anti-Communist fervor during the McCarthy era, the Supreme Court upheld a federal law prohibiting conspiracy to advocate the overthrow of the government by force and violence. For the Court, the "inflammable nature of world conditions" justified finding that the existence of a conspiracy—without a showing of imminence and the like—was alone sufficient to justify suppression.

B. THE *BRANDENBURG* TEST

Although the Court later narrowed the broad approach in *Dennis*, it was not until 1969 that the Court settled on an approach that placed greater emphasis on the importance of showing incitement that is tied to actual danger. Favoring speech protection over social control, the Court announced the test in *Brandenburg v. Ohio*, 395 U.S. 444 (1969). The *Brandenburg* test has taken firm hold in First Amendment jurisprudence and appears to remain the currently prevailing general test.

According to the *Brandenburg* Court, the government may forbid "advocacy of the use of force or of law violation [only where] advocacy is directed to inciting or producing imminent lawless action and is likely to incite or produce such action." Id. at 447. In applying this test, the formal analysis requires evaluation of the following three components:

(1) imminent harm;
(2) a likelihood that the speech will produce illegal action; and
(3) the intent to cause the imminent illegality.

Translated these three concerns boil down to the following:

(1) concern with time (imminence = soon);
(2) concern with probability; and
(3) intent to make harm occur.

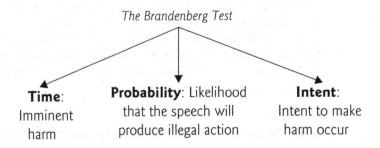

Speech that Incites Illegality

The Brandenberg Test

Time: Imminent harm

Probability: Likelihood that the speech will produce illegal action

Intent: Intent to make harm occur

Figure 6-1

Please take note of how these three concerns manifested in subsequent cases.

Imminence Lacking: The Court veered close to the three-part *Brandenburg* test in two subsequent cases, paying specific attention to imminence. In *Hess v. Indiana*, 414 U.S. 105 (1973), the Court held unconstitutional the disorderly conduct conviction of an individual who yelled "We'll take to the fucking street later," after police had cleared a demonstration off the street. The *Hess* Court found the imminence (timing) component of the *Brandenburg* test lacking in this declaration, concluding that "at worst, it amounted to nothing more than advocacy of illegal action at some indefinite future time." *Id.* at 108. *Hess* shows how context dependent the imminent requirement is: "later" could mean in a few minutes or "later" could mean in a reasonably close time in the indefinite future, depending on the context.

Likelihood Lacking: The Court also found the *Brandenburg* test was not satisfied in *NAACP v. Claiborne Hardware Co.*, 458 U.S. 886 (1982), a case concerning the NAACP's boycott of white-owned businesses alleged to be racially discriminatory. In a public speech, a NAACP official had stated: "If we catch any of you going in any of them racist stores, we're gonna break your damn neck." The Supreme Court found this statement constitutionally protected, since it amounted to no more than "mere advocacy of the use of force or violence . . . ." *Id.* at 927. The *Hess* case demonstrates that evaluating whether communication calls for mere advocacy (rather than an impassioned call to action) is an important component of the First Amendment inquiry. Again, evaluating this question requires considering the entire context in which the statement is made. Moreover, language in the case law suggests that a significant probability must exist that the illegality truly threatens harm. Advocating a victimless crime would not be sufficient.

Intent Lacking: In any context, intent can be one of the hardest concepts to show under standards of legal proof. The easiest mode of proof is a confession. Confessions on intent to prove harm are difficult to obtain in any situation, but particularly challenging in the context of intent to incite illegal activity. The proof is generally circumstantial, emanating from the spirit of words stated in public or gleaned from the gist of private statements.

Example 6-1:

A candidate for high office is running for election. The candidate is highly controversial and has frequently encountered violence in campaign rallies. Often the violence has come from supporters of the candidate reacting to those who protest against the candidate. A group of protestors attended a campaign rally in order to show their disapproval of the candidate. The candidate spoke for about 30 minutes during which the protestors boisterously ridiculed the candidate's speech. Five times during his speech, the candidate responded to the commotion, saying: "Do whatever—I mean

WHATEVER—you can to get 'em out of here without delay.'" Law enforcement authorities eventually ushered the protestors out of the rally. Members of the audience pushed, shoved, and assaulted the protesters as law enforcement escorted them out of the room. Several of the protestors suffered significant injuries from the crowd. The protestors want the candidate punished for unlawful incitement to inflict violence. The authorities would like your opinion on whether they can pursue this case consistently with First Amendment protections.

Explanation:

The authorities would likely be acting consistently with the First Amendment if they chose to pursue charges. Applying the *Brandenburg* test, one sees that the candidate alluded to violence in the phrase "do what you can." This phrase suggests that the candidate is calling for all means—including violent means—of getting the protestors away from the rally. Saying the phrase "do whatever you can" five times suggests intent that violent means may be necessary to getting the protestors out of the rally and that such means are appropriate. "Without delay" would likely establish the imminence requirement. Does it make a difference that the address focused on the crowd, not the law enforcement authorities, who attacked the protestors? Probably not. The candidate did not designate who should "do what you can." Nonetheless, all of the elements of the *Brandenburg* test seem established. Cf. *Nwanguma v. Trump*, 903 F.3d 604, 606-610 (6th Cir. 2018).

Example 6-1 touches all the *Brandenburg* categories, thus making it likely that the candidate could not raise a successful First Amendment defense to an action against the candidate for inciting violence. This conclusion is buttressed by the facts: violence occurred soon thereafter. Imminence (close timing) is present given the "without delay" statement and its repeat several times. Likelihood is captured by the fact that violence occurred and that it had occurred at campaign events in the past under similar circumstances. Even without this eventuality, words like "do what you can" certainly help to satisfy the likelihood prong of the analysis. Finally there is intent. Repeated statements of "do what you can" support the conclusion that the candidate was focused on getting others to take action that may be "over the line" of legality.

Example 6-2:

The defendant was a member of a group dedicated to fighting law enforcement authority. He posted on his social media page the following message: "I WAS HARASSED BY THE LOCAL POLICE WHO INSISTED THAT THEY SHOULD SEARCH MY HOUSE. I DID NOT CONSENT. They said they would be going to the magistrate to get the warrants. THESE POLICE

DON'T NEED WARRANTS TO GET INTO MY HOUSE, THEY WILL NEED BODY BAGS NEXT TIME. THIS EXPERIENCE SHOWS WHY WE NEED TO START KILLING WITH LOVE THOSE WHO VIOLATE OUR CIVIL RIGHTS OF SOCIETY. PICK UP YOUR ARMS NOW!"

One week after this post became public, a person arrived at the police station aggressively demanding to see the chief of the police about unauthorized searches. When the police refused the person access to the chief, the protestor became louder and more belligerent. Refusing to answer commands that he leave, the police arrested him and took him into custody. At the time of the arrest, this individual was not armed and—upon questioning—never mentioned the social media post.

The authorities then sought to arrest the defendant who posted this message on social media, claiming that the post amounts to an illegal incitement of violence—not protected by the First Amendment. Are they correct?

Explanation:

This is a close case. The post definitely refers to illegal violence. It seems also to be intended to encourage others to engage in such violence. The wrinkle emerges, however, from *Brandenburg's* imminence requirement. Searching the post for temporal references, one finds a single reference: "PICK UP YOUR ARMS NOW!" On one hand, the reference to "now" suggests immediacy. On the other hand, the phrase has a classic, almost trite, ring to it. From one point of view, the reference to "now" suggests importance, not timing. The triteness of the reference also suggests generality and not a specific need for urgency. The difficulty of settling on a proper interpretation reveals that applying the *Brandenburg* test requires a deep understanding of the nuances of the English language and culture as well as the dynamics of a particular situation.

The fact that one person appeared at the police station a week later to demand to speak to the head of police about illegal searches suggests that the posting may have been reasonably interpreted as a call to lawlessness. The causation, however, is not definite, since the person did not mention the post.

One wonders whether the social media context diminishes the possibility for liability here because social media is often associated with hyperbolic statements. For that reason, courts might take into account that readers of a posting may discount what appears to be an immediate call for violence. So far, however, that perception has not profoundly influenced social media cases such as this. The one court to have addressed a posting similar to this concluded, under similar circumstances, that the posting was not protected by the First Amendment under the *Brandenburg* test: *State v. Taupier*, No. K10KCR170338626S, 2018 WL 2946202, at *1-6 (Conn. Super. Ct. May 23, 2018), *aff'd on other grounds, State v. Taupier*, No. AC 42115, 2020 Conn. App. LEXIS 175 (Conn. App. Ct. June 9, 2020).

Example 6-3:

A high school student, David, was an avid player of the video game called "High School Basketball," which features the killing of a basketball team by a student using six guns during a high school game. David showed up at a live high school basketball game with six guns and shot the players on the court in the same way and with the same shot angles, language, and flourish as the shooter used in the video game. David's parents filed suit against the company that produced and maintained the "High School Basketball" video games, which the parents alleged desensitized their son to violence and provided a road map for his crime. Is the *Brandenburg* test satisfied by these facts?

Explanation:

No, these facts do not satisfy the *Brandenburg* test. The speech did not constitute an incitement to imminent violence. There is no showing that the video game companies intended to inspire violent actions in consumers as required by the *Brandenburg* test. Nor did the video game amount to an *imminent* threat of violence. Even if the parent's theory is correct that the game glorified and slowly desensitized their son to violence, the game amounted to a mere depiction of violence, not advocacy of violence. No intent to inspire violence emerges from these facts. *See James v. Meow Media, Inc.*, 300 F.3d 683, 687-698 (6th Cir. 2002).

Example 6-4:

Assume that you are clerking for a U.S. Supreme Court justice who has asked you to give your opinion on the function of requiring the following three showings when the government wishes to regulate speech that incites illegality: imminence, likelihood, and intent.

Explanation:

Here is a discussion of the wisdom of requiring these three showings:

Imminence: The imminence requirement makes it more likely that government restriction of speech is necessary to ensure that harm does not occur. The value of avoiding regulation of speech is to increase the likelihood that speech will be expressed, will be considered by others, and will spur the expression of possible counter-speech. In a situation in which "lawless action" is soon to occur as a result of speech, the chance is diminished that counter-speech and debate will successfully serve to diffuse a tense situation and prevent lawless action actually occurring.

6. Incitement of Illegal Activity

Likelihood: As with imminence, the likelihood requirement ensures that the intrusion on freedom of expression is indeed justified and necessary. A required showing of likelihood also guarantees a high risk that the speech to be regulated will produce harm that flows from the illegality. Likelihood can also be linked to express statements that incite violence: the more explicit the incitement, the more probable that the harm will occur. This is in turn connected with intent.

Intent: Because intent is difficult to prove, intent functions to circumscribe the opportunities to stifle speech. As such, the requirement serves to make it more likely that speech is expressed. Requiring intent protects against punishing an individual for making a mere mistake in how they choose to express themselves. Fear of making a mistake can create a chilling effect: a speaker may forbear from engaging in protective speech in order to avoid possible punishment.

Intent is also relevant to causation. Sometimes speech can have unintended consequences, harm that was not predictable when uttered. It is fairer to impose punishment when a speaker intended to cause the harm. Without the intent requirement, the specter of punishment will not be less likely to have a deterrent effect on communication that causes someone harm. The intent requirement protects songwriters, singers, authors, the producers of video games, and similar creative persons, whose work may sometimes be the impetus for unintended harm. In some instances, the harm that occurs is quite remote from the expression and thus is an unlikely consequence of the expression that would be difficult to foresee.

* * *

One can see an exception to *Brandenburg*'s speech-protecting approach in the Supreme Court's decision in *Holder v. Humanitarian Law Project*, 561 U.S.1 (2010). *Holder* presented one of the many issues confronting the United States after the 9/11 attacks for which the task of combatting terrorism challenged the country's commitment to important civil liberties. At issue in *Holder* was a federal law that prohibits providing "material assistance" to a "foreign terrorist organization." The statute defines material assistance to include such activities as "training" and "expert advice or assistance." Upholding the law, the Court did not use *Brandenburg* as the standard for assessing constitutionality. Rather, the Court focused on how the law confined its prohibitions to forbidding speech communicated in concert with a foreign terrorist organization. Moreover, the Court concluded that Congress did not intend to "suppress ideas or opinions," but rather focused only on material support, which the Court conceded "most often does not take the form of speech at all." Finally, the Court concluded that the statute's prohibitions were necessary to further an objective of the highest order: fighting terrorism.

Example 6-4:

Five individuals were convicted of conspiracy to provide material support and to provide actual material support to a foreign terrorist organization in violation of the same statute at issue in Holder, 18 U.S.C. § 2339B(a)(1). The individuals ran a charitable organization, which touted its mission as providing humanitarian aid to a radical minority group that had been denied essential privileges of citizenship in a country outside the United States. The foundation acted as the fundraising arm for the radical minority group's goal of conducting violent activities. The organization raised money for the radical minority group by holding nationwide fundraising events, conferences, and seminars. These various events featured songs, performances, and skits glorifying the foreign minority group. The organization openly supported the radical minority group up until the time the minority group became designated as a terrorist organization for the purposes of 18 U.S.C. § 2339B(a)(1). After that point, the organization continued to engage in fundraising activities, but was more circumspect in its approach. Evidence documents that the foundation forwarded the minority group large sums of money after each event—both before and after the minority group's designation as a terrorist organization. May the United States, consistent with Holder, constitutionally pursue prosecution of the foundation under 18 U.S.C. § 2339B(a)(1)?

Explanation:

Yes, under prevailing law, the prosecution may constitutionally pursue prosecution of the foundation under 18 U.S.C. § 2339B(a)(1). The activities during the fundraising events clearly fall into the category of speech or expressive conduct. Brandenburg would not authorize prosecution of the group for the events that occurred because no evidence satisfied the imminence requirement. But Holder held that Congress has the ability to criminalize speech that provides material support to designated terrorists—thus possibly placing a case like this in a separate category from the usual Brandenburg scenario.

The foundation continued the promotional events for the purpose of fundraising for the minority group even after the group had been designated as a terrorist organization. The foundation's forward of money to the minority group after each of these expressive events shows that the foundation held the events with the intent to support the group. The success of the foundation in collecting and forwarding large sums of money leads one easily to conclude that the foundation was providing "expert" assistance to the radical minority group. See United States v. El-Mezain, 664 F.3d 467, 536-539 (5th Cir. 2011).

* * *

6. Incitement of Illegal Activity

The relationship between *Holder* and *Brandenburg* is difficult to pin down. Did *Holder* change the direction of the law governing speech that could incite violence? After all, the history of the First Amendment (and constitutional law generally) in this area show that the constitutional doctrine changes — sometimes quite radically — to accommodate concerns about unrest and threats to the security of the United States. From this point of view, *Holder* could be viewed as a signal of the changed direction. That theory, however, has yet to be confirmed. More likely, *Holder* creates an exception to *Brandenburg* or is an aberration — both reactions created by the gravity of 9/11 and deference to Congress's firm and specific response.

Dangerous and Offensive Speech: Fighting Words, Hate and Disparaging Speech, and True Threats

Closely related to speech that incites illegality is speech that is deemed dangerous because it amounts to "fighting words" or true threats. Speech that offends—such as hate speech and disparaging speech—are more distant cousins of speech that incites illegality. The U.S. Supreme Court has defined "fighting words" as those words that "by their very utterance inflict injury or tend to incite an immediate breach of the peace." *Chaplinsky v. State of New Hampshire,* 315 U.S. 568, 572 (1942). Indeed, one might easily argue that communications characterized as fighting words fall under the same umbrella as communications one might conclude are incitements to illegality. Nonetheless, the U.S. Supreme Court continues to refer to "fighting words" as a separate category of unprotected speech, emphasizing that the fighting words doctrine generally focuses on the potential reaction of the recipient of speech. Analytically, true threats are similar to fighting words in that both categories of speech are considered low value speech. A primary focus of the true threats doctrine, however, is on the intent of the speaker: specifically, true threats cases often turn on whether the speaker intended to inspire fear in the recipient of speech.

Hate speech and disparaging speech are separate from true threats and fighting words. Sometimes hate and disparaging speech can have the same effect on the recipient of speech as fighting words, but that is not always the case. The focus on litigation about hate and disparaging speech is whether government can constitutionally prevent hate speech because it denigrates disadvantaged citizens in ways that damage them psychologically or promote hatred and discrimination against them. Unlike true threats and fighting words, hate speech is treated as high value speech. In other words, under current law, one can generally offend without legal consequence, but one's speech can be regulated when it becomes fighting words, a true threat, or some other type of lower value or unprotected speech (such as obscenity and commercial speech).

A. FIGHTING WORDS

In *Chaplinsky v. State of New Hampshire*, 315 U.S. 568 (1942), a Jehovah's Witness—Walter Chaplinsky—distributed religious material on the streets of Rochester, N.Y. Citizens complained that Chaplinsky denounced other religions as "rackets." A traffic officer warned Chaplinsky that the crowd that was listening to him was getting restless. The officer started to escort him to the police station. On the way to the station, they encountered another official who had heard that a riot was underway. At that point, Chaplinsky told the official: "You are a God damned racketeer and a damned Fascist and the whole government of Rochester are Fascists or agents of Fascists . . . ." *Id.* at 569 (internal quotations omitted). Given the world events unfolding at the time of this cases (early 1940s), calling someone a Fascist was deeply provocative.

Chaplinsky was prosecuted under a statute prohibiting use of insulting language.[1] In upholding the conviction, the U.S. Supreme Court observed that the statute was confined to language that the speaker intended to invite a breach of the peace on behalf of the audience. In the Court's view, the statute covered fighting words, which the Court described as words that "by their very utterance inflict injury or tend to incite an immediate breach of the peace." *Id.* at 572. In holding these words outside of First Amendment protection, the Court reasoned that the words were not an "essential part of any exposition of ideas, and are of such slight social value as a step to truth that any benefit that may be derived from them is clearly outweighed by the social interest in order and morality." *Id.*

This language is broad: indeed broad enough to prohibit most of what is now called hate speech. Nonetheless, subsequent decisions have restricted its reach. *Chaplinsky* is the only fighting words conviction ever upheld by the U.S. Supreme Court. For example, in *Gooding v. Wilson*, 405 U.S. 518 (1972), the Court refused to uphold a conviction under a statute that provided any person using "opprobrious words or abusive language, tending to cause a breach of the peace . . . shall be guilty of a misdemeanor." *Id.* at 519. The defendant had said the following to a police officer during an anti-war

---

1. The statute provided: "No person shall address any offensive, derisive or annoying word to any other person who is lawfully in any street or other public place, nor call him by any offensive or derisive name, nor make any noise or exclamation in his presence and hearing with intent to deride, offend or annoy him, or to prevent him from pursuing his lawful business or occupation." *Id.* at 569.

demonstration: "White son of a bitch, I'll kill you," "[y]ou son of a bitch, I'll choke you to death, " and "[y]ou son of a bitch, if you ever put your hands on me again, I'll cut you all to pieces." *Id.* at 534. Holding that the statute was overbroad, the Court held that the terms opprobrious, abusive, and breach of the peace extended beyond fighting words. Moreover, state courts had held the statute prohibited expression that inspired violence at some later time. The *Gooding* Court explained that the fighting words doctrine is limited to attempts to incite an *immediate* violent reaction.

Reinforcing the view that the fighting words doctrine has minimal use is a line of cases that the U.S. Supreme Court decided in the wake of *Chaplinsky*. These cases presented a related doctrine focused on whether government can punish a speaker for causing a disruption because the speaker's audience responds in a hostile manner to a speaker's ideas. Known as the hostile audience doctrine, this approach has not been used by the U.S. Supreme Court to uphold a conviction since 1951.

Example 7-1:

Priscilla called a supermarket and stated she was coming in for a money transfer from the customer service desk. Frieda, an assistant store manager, told her the desk had closed and the transaction would not be able to be processed. Priscilla stated she "didn't really give a shit" and then swore further at Frieda before terminating the call. A few minutes later, Priscilla arrived at the supermarket and began filling out a money transfer form even though no lights were illuminated at the customer service desk. Frieda confronted Priscilla. Priscilla responded by calling Frieda a "fat ugly bitch," and a "cunt." During their encounter, Priscilla also said "fuck you, you're not a manager." Frieda remained professional in her demeanor and told Priscilla to "have a good night." This caused Priscilla to leave.

Priscilla was convicted of violating a state statute that allowed prosecution for those who utter fighting words. She appealed, arguing that she did not say any fighting words. Is Priscilla correct that the words she said were not fighting words?

Explanation:

Priscilla is likely correct. The reason for this is not the words she spoke, which were in fact quite offensive. Rather, it was the circumstances in which she spoke the words that prevented them from having the tendency to inspiring the situation to become violent. *See R.A.V. v. St. Paul*, 505 U.S. 377, 432 (1992) (Stevens, J., concurring) (stating that the status of an utterance as "fighting words is determined in part by their context"); *Lewis v. New Orleans*, 415 U.S. 130, 135 (1974) (Powell, J., concurring) (stating that "words may or may not be 'fighting words,' depending upon the circumstances of their utterance"); *Hammond v. Adkisson*, 536 F.2d 237, 239 (8th Cir. 1976) (explaining that First Amendment requires "determination that the words were used *'under such circumstances'* that they were likely to arouse to immediate and *violent* anger the person to whom the words were addressed"). In connection with this, courts also consider the demographics of the individuals involved and distinguish between the average citizen and those targets of an utterance who are in a position that carries with it an expectation of exercising a greater degree of restraint. *Lewis v. New Orleans*, 415 U.S. at 135.

Part of the decision on fighting words may also turn on the tone and manner of delivery of the challenged utterance. As the Court stated in *Chaplinsky*, words that are profane, obscene, or otherwise threatening might not be fighting words if uttered with a "disarming smile." *Chaplinsky v. New Hampshire*, 315 U.S. at 573.

Applying these principles to the facts of this Example, one might first note that the expletives that Priscilla spoke were not only vulgar and demeaning, but were targeted at Frieda's gender. These characterizations militate in favor of branding the utterances to be fighting words. But as with many situations implicating the First Amendment, one must remember that simply because a statement is wrong, offensive, and in bad taste, that does not mean it should be illegal (much less criminal). *See Cohen v. California*, 403 U.S. 15 (1971) (refusing to uphold a conviction for breach of the peace based on wearing a jacket with the anti-war inscription "Fuck the Draft" in a courthouse).

Most other aspects of the circumstances in this Example, however, suggest that Priscilla's statements did not amount to fighting words. One can best undertake the fighting words inquiry from the perspective of a neutral onlooker as well as from the perspectives of the speaker of the abusive words and the target. From these various perspectives, one might first note that Priscilla's phone call to the supermarket suggested that Priscilla was frustrated by her inability to get the services that she wanted. After the original abusive phone call, Frieda reasonably would have been aware of the possibility that Priscilla would treat her to a similar barrage of insults when Priscilla arrived at the store and began to fill out the money transfer paperwork. As such, Frieda would likely have been prepared to try to diffuse the situation. Frieda's assistant manager title put her in a position of authority that required handling potentially confrontational customer service matters. Frieda's approach to the circumstances suggested that she would remain professional in her demeanor and would not resort to violence in handling the circumstances.

Logic would suggest to Priscilla or an observer that, as a person in a role of some power in the situation, Frieda could easily call authorities to diffuse the confrontation if she were unable to deescalate the tensions herself without violence occurring. This interpretation was played out in Frieda's final statement to Priscilla: "Have a good evening"—a statement that politely disposed of interaction without violent reaction. Taken together these facts would have suggested to Priscilla that Frieda was acting in a professional role requiring her to handle customer service matters and that Frieda would not react with violence.

Finally, the question arises how a court might properly take into account that both individuals involved in the confrontation were women. Suppose the court was under the impression that women are less likely to be spurred to violence than men. Would this be a consideration in determining whether the words amounted to fighting words? Considerations of this kind are certainly invited by case law stating that the demographics of the participants are relevant to the fighting words determination. But how do we know that assumptions about the connection between the demographics and propensity for violence are rooted in fact?

Under facts similar to those in this Example, the court in *State v. Baccala*, 163 A.3d 1 (Conn. 2017), also determined that the words uttered did not amount to fighting words.

* * *

In addition to its failure to use the fighting words doctrine to uphold a conviction since the *Chaplinsky* decision itself, the U.S. Court has much more recently made the following statement that is in tension with the doctrine. Noting that one function of free speech is to "invite dispute," the Court reiterated that "[i]t may indeed best serve its high purpose when it induces a condition of unrest, creates dissatisfaction with conditions as they are, or even stirs people to anger." *Texas v. Johnson*, 491 U.S. 397, 408-409 (1989). The Court has nevertheless continued to refer to fighting words as a category of lower value speech. As used in the lower courts, the doctrine appears limited to one-on-one communication between speaker and recipient, and likely applies only when an immediate reaction is possible. This largely confines the doctrine's relevance to in-person interactions, arguably limiting its application to social media communication.

B. HATE AND DISPARAGING SPEECH

A series of cases have been litigated with the vision of trying to ensure that vicious or disparaging statements and demonstrations about specific groups could be deemed outside First Amendment protection. Perhaps the strongest case in support of regulating this type of speech is *Beauharnais v. Illinois*, 343 U.S. 250 (1952). In *Beauharnais*, the Court appeared to accept the notion of group defamation, stating that the state could punish certain types of utterances "directed a defined group . . . ." *Id.* at 258. Although *Beauharnais* has not been overruled, it is no longer used as precedent and some declare that the decision is no longer good law. *See, e.g.*, *American Booksellers Ass'n v. Hudnut*, 771 F.2d 323 (7th Cir. 1985). One reason for this position is that *Beauharnais* was premised on the view that defamation is unprotected by the First Amendment, even when the defamation consists of opinions that damage reputation (but cannot be proven as true or false), or of reputation-damaging statements that are in fact true, but were inspired by bad motives. As illustrated in Chapter 10, the U.S. Supreme Court's later defamation precedents, such as *New York Times v. Sullivan*, 376 U.S. 254 (1964), and *Garrison v. Louisiana*, 379 U.S. 64 (1964), undermine this premise. Nonetheless, despite questions about its continuing validity, *Beauharnais* remains the most direct support for regulating hate and disparaging speech.

The Supreme Court has never defined hate speech, and the difficulty of settling on a finite definition is perhaps one reason why the Court is reluctant to allow government to regulate it under the First Amendment. For a working definition, the statute at issue in *Beauharnais* provides a starting point: communications that "portray depravity, criminality, unchastity, or lack of virtue of a class of citizens, of any race, color, creed, or religion [exposing citizens] to contempt, derision, or obloquy." A more updated definition might include antagonistic or dehumanizing statements about groups of individuals, such as those identified by gender, ethnicity, class, race, color, religion, or sexual orientation

A related line of cases also address derogatory speech, which may or may not qualify as hate speech cases. Although the cases dealing with regulation of disparaging speech and hate speech have two different tracks, the two lines of cases often focus on defamation of an entire demographic group and share other qualities. The U.S. Supreme Court has neither defined nor recognized a separate label "disparaging speech." To some extent, one might regard disparaging speech as a potentially less antagonistic, virulent form of hate speech, which often inflicts harm, but does not necessarily contain a vicious or spiteful message focused on a specific person or groups of persons. Because the disparaging speech cases are handled differently from what are generally regarded as hate speech cases, it is useful to regard them separately. This subsection begins with a discussion of hate speech, which has become a more prominent area of First Amendment law (at least in the lower courts) than the cases addressing speech that is merely disparaging.

I. Hate Speech

For a time, courts experimented with using the fighting words doctrine to allow regulation of hate speech directed at a group, but that too proved nonviable. The U.S. Supreme Court made this clear in *R.A.V. v. City of St. Paul*, 505 U.S. 377 (1992), which concerned an ordinance that prohibited the display of a symbol that one knows or has reason to know "arouses anger, alarm or resentment in others on the basis of race, color, creed, religion or gender . . . ." *Id.* at 380. The state supreme court had interpreted the statute as limited to fighting words and other speech not protected by the First Amendment. Overturning the conviction of a white man who burned a cross on a black family's lawn, the U.S. Supreme Court held the statute unconstitutional. A main reason for this determination lay in the state law's discrimination among which groups are protected against expressions of hate. The statute targeted specific groups (defined by reference to race, religion, or gender), but did not include expressions of hate against other groups, such as those defined by sexual orientation or political identity. Accordingly, the majority concluded that the state statute discriminated on the basis of content.

Example 7-2:

A group dedicated to racial justice was targeted by those who opposed its views. Members of the group had to confront a small group of protesters on the street outside of their homes every morning. The protesters' main message was that racism is not a problem in U.S. society, and that the racial justice group is opportunistically exploiting a problem attributed to other causes. The few protesters who appeared every morning held signs and passed out leaflets that bore the message that racism is not a problem in our society and that any white person who is dedicated to the cause of fighting what they call "racism" is betraying their own white race in favor other races. In response to these protests, a municipality passed an ordinance that stated: "Those who protest in favor of the message that racism is not a problem in society are punishable by a fine of no more than $500 and/or 3 months imprisonment." Is this ordinance constitutional?

Explanation:

The ordinance is not constitutional. To begin, the ordinance regulates on the basis of content and viewpoint. No facts show that the ordinance would pass strict scrutiny. More specifically, *R.A.V.* makes clear that a law prohibiting hateful speech against a single group is constitutionally suspect because it regulates on the basis of content. The terms "racism" and "race" are hard to define precisely, but they decidedly do not include groups such as those defined by political affiliation, union membership, sexual orientation, and the like. As such, the ordinance suffers from being over-specific about its target—thus suggesting that the government that passed the ordinance was trying to quell expression regarding one particular point of view bearing on a matter of public and political concern. Even assuming that the ordinance did not run into problems under *R.A.V.* by targeting just one category of speech, the ordinance would be unconstitutional anyway. Why?

The ordinance prohibits fully protected speech on the basis of content without a showing that it is narrowly tailored to serve a compelling interest.

* * *

Although *R.A.V.* made clear that the First Amendment would not tolerate singling out a particular group for protection from hate speech, this practice has been tolerated for the purpose of defining specialized crimes and enhanced punishments in some instances. It would seem that at least some of the laws are tolerated because they are part of the practice of protecting everyone from violent crime motivated by the target group's membership. In that regard, consider the following Example.

Example 7-3:

After viewing a movie in which a white man gratuitously attacked a black man, a black defendant who had viewed the movie asked a group of other black men whether they wanted to "move on" some white people. When a white youth walked by, the black defendant said: "There goes a white boy; go get him." As a consequence the white youth suffered a severe beating. Because the victim was selected on the basis of race, the defendant received an enhanced punishment for the crime. Arguing that the enhanced punishment violated the First Amendment, the defendant maintained that the punishment resulted from mere thoughts and ideas that arguably motivated his actions. Is the defendant correct that the enhanced punishment is unconstitutional?

Explanation:

The defendant is not correct. In a case presenting similar facts, the U.S. Supreme Court upheld the practice of using racial motivation to enhance a sentence. *Wisconsin v. Mitchell*, 508 U.S. 476 (1993). According to the *Mitchell* Court, facts such as those in this Example are unlike *R.A.V.* because the enhancement was aimed at conduct and not expression. The Court also noted that the motivation was appropriately used to enhance punishment because it increased the risk of inspiring retaliation, causing significant emotional harms, and provoking community unrest.

* * *

Following *R.A.V.*, the U.S. Supreme Court revisited the issue of criminalizing cross burning in *Virginia v. Black*, 538 U.S. 343 (2003). The statute in *Virginia v. Black* banned cross burning "with an intent to intimidate" a person or group of persons.

Virginia v. Black is notable for its treatment of two different sets of facts. In one set, the defendant Black burned a cross at a Ku Klux Klan rally held on farmland with the permission of the landowner. Black was convicted at a trial in which the jury was instructed that burning a cross was prima facie evidence of intent to intimidate. In other words, the prosecution did not need to provide direct proof of intent to intimidate; the mere act of cross burning created a presumption that the defendant possessed the requisite intent. By contrast, in the second set of facts, two other defendants attempted to burn a cross on the yard of defendant's next-door African-American neighbor. At trial, the court instructed the jury that the state prosecutor must prove that "the defendant intended to commit cross burning," that "the defendant did a direct act toward the commission of the cross burning," and that "the defendant had the intent of intimidating any person or group of persons."

The Court treated the two sets of facts differently. As for the first, the Court held that treating any cross burning as prima facie evidence of intent to intimidate (as was the case under Virginia law) is unconstitutional. With respect to the second set of facts, the Court agreed that a state could prosecute an act of cross burning carried out with the intent to intimidate. In order to satisfy this standard, the Court stated that the First Amendment permits a state to ban "true threats," which encompasses those statements where the speaker means to communicate a serious expression of an intent to commit an act of unlawful violence to a particular individual or group of individuals. That said, the Court held that the Constitution requires that the prosecution must present specific proof of an intent to intimidate and that the prima facie presumption of intent is inconsistent with First Amendment requirements. Applying this approach to the second set of facts, the Court concluded that the dispute required more fact finding—as the circumstances were such that evidence may exist to prove that the attempt at cross burning on the lawn of a private family may have occurred with intent to intimidate.

Virginia v. Black is often thought of in connection with regulating hate speech and with R.A.V. These connections are understandable because both Virginia v. Black and R.A.V. dealt with cross burning, which is a symbol of embrace of white supremacy. It is important to understand, however, that the Supreme Court disposed of two cases on the basis of very different theories. R.A.V. turned on how the statute unconstitutionally singled out specific targets of racism for protection and not others. The statute in R.A.V. failed because it was over-specific in its target. The Supreme Court handled Virginia v. Black as a threats case, which turned on whether there existed actual proof of intent to intimidate. One of the joined cases in Virginia v. Black failed because of an unconstitutional presumption of an intent to intimidate; the other joined case was remanded because the circumstances were such that proof of intent to intimidate might be established.

Example 7-4:

A governmentally owned and operated transportation authority earns extra revenue by selling advertising space on its trains and buses. The authority vets prospective ads for offensive or inappropriate content and applies a standard prohibiting "[a]dvertising that tends to disparage or ridicule any person or group of persons on the basis of race, religious belief, age, sex, alienage, national origin, sickness or disability."

A pro-Israel advocacy group submitted an ad highlighting the friendship between a prominent Muslim leader and Adolf Hitler. The ad also alleges that the Quran promotes hatred of Jews and calls on the U.S. government to cease sending aid to "Islamic countries." The transportation authority rejects the advertisement for violating its anti-hate standard. In response, the advocacy group sued the transportation authority to enjoin enforcement of the anti-hate standard, arguing that the standard constitutes improper content-based discrimination. How should the court decide this lawsuit under *R.A.V.*? Would the Court reach the same result on the basis of *Virginia v. Black*? How might the analysis differ between the two cases?

Explanation:

The transportation authority's standard is unconstitutional under *R.A.V.* A main defect of the statute in that case is that it singled out particular groups for protection. As such, the statute was content-based. As a content-based regulation, the statute in that case could not survive strict scrutiny because its prohibition drew a distinction among expressions of hate that protected only some groups without sufficient justification. The standard in this Example suffers from the same defect, since the standard would apparently allow advertisements on the basis of such categories as political affiliation or union membership.

The transportation authority's standard is also unconstitutional under *Virginia v. Black*. Although the prohibition in *Virginia v. Black* singled out a particular symbol of hate, the Court determined that, upon proof of intent, the prohibition could be constitutional because the symbolic action — the burning of a cross — was capable of serving as a threat of an act of violence. Here the standard makes mention neither of an intent to commit violence nor of symbols that carry that message.

An interesting and important issue that neither *R.A.V.* nor *Virginia v. Black* reckoned with directly is the following: Is it a constitutional problem that a prohibition covers disparaging speech but not favorable speech about protected groups? Isn't such a distinction based on differences in viewpoint? From that point of view, the standard in this Example is not viewpoint neutral. If that is the case, should not a court evaluate whether the viewpoint distinction is valid under a strict scrutiny standard?

Both *R.A.V.* and *Virginia v. Black* contained language suggesting that the Court may have been sympathetic to singling out hateful speech for regulation, given its hurtful impact, but was not willing to constitutionalize that inclination. The Court in both cases avoided directly addressing the issue of whether hate speech could be classified as unprotected speech or whether a distinction based on positive versus negative speech in this context could pass strict scrutiny. In both cases, the Court found other means of analyzing the problems raised in the statute. This is typical of hate speech cases, in which courts often use less charged theories for striking down a statute, such as vagueness and overbreadth.

For a case holding that a standard similar to the one in this Example represented unconstitutional viewpoint discrimination because of the standard's sole focus on derogatory (rather than positive) speech, *see American Freedom Defense Initiative v. SEPTA*, 92 F. Supp. 3d 314 (E.D. Pa 2015).

Hate speech is a highly emotional, charged issue. For some it seems like an easy call—i.e., of course something so hurtful is not constitutionally protected speech! For others it is more difficult—i.e., of course the message is abhorrent, but hate speech is very tied to a political message and we place the highest value on political messages! The U.S. has a radically different approach to the issue than many other countries—some even call the U.S. an "outlier" on this issue. The U.S. approach is attributable in part to the strength of the free speech value, but also attributable to the diminished (although growing) value given to human dignity in U.S. constitutional jurisprudence. A rich and thoughtful literature on hate speech exists. One way to navigate this extremely sensitive, complex issue to read arguments on both sides of the question whether hate speech should be constitutionally protected. *See, e.g.,* Rebecca L. Brown, *The Harm Principle and Free Speech,* 89 S. Cal. L. Rev. 953 (2016); Mari J. Matsuda, *Public Response to Racist Speech: Considering the Victim's Story,* 87 Mich. L. Rev. 2320, 2364 (1989); Robert C. Post, *Racist Speech, Democracy, and the First Amendment,* 32 Wm. Mary L. Rev. 267 (1991); James Weinstein, *Hate Speech Bans, Democracy, and Political Legitimacy,* 32 Const. Comment. 527, 534 (2017).

2. Disparaging Speech

Hate speech is sometimes described as disparaging speech. As such, the distinction between what some regard as two categories of cases, hate speech and disparaging speech cases, is blurry. Nonetheless, the two categories are usefully separated for the purpose of understanding and analysis. Hate speech is largely confined to speech with a vicious or spiteful message focused on a specific person or groups of persons. Disparaging speech, on the other hand, is not necessarily confined to hateful messages or messages targeted at specific people.

An important recent disparaging speech case arose from a provision in the federal statute, the Lanham Act, which regulates the regulation of trademarks. The Act contains a provision barring a trademark that "may disparage . . . persons, living or dead, institutions, beliefs, or national symbols, or bring them into contempt or disrepute." *Matal v. Tam,* 137 S. Ct. 1744, 1753 (2017).

In *Matal v. Tam,* the U.S. Supreme Court held this Lanham Act provision violated the free speech clause of the First Amendment. The case arose from an attempt by Simon Tam, the lead singer of a musical group called "The Slants," to register the group's name with the trademark office. Tam chose that name in order to "reclaim" and "take ownership" of stereotypes regarding people of Asian ethnicity. *Id.* at 1754. In refusing to register that name, the Trademark Office had observed that numerous dictionaries defined "slants" as a derogatory term.

The *Matal* court rejected the arguments that the government put forward to defend the disparagement provision in the Act, holding that: (1) trademarks are not government speech; (2) trademarks are not a form of government subsidy; and (3) the government-program doctrine is not the proper vehicle for testing the provision. In the process of rejecting these defenses, the Court made clear its aversion to government regulations that suppress speech that the government views as offensive or disturbing. Specifically, the Court stated that attempts to prevent speech that "express[es] ideas that offend . . .strikes at the heart of the First Amendment." *Id.* at 1764. The Court added that "the proudest boast of our free speech jurisprudence is that we protect the freedom to express 'the thought that we hate.'" *Id.*

Example 7-5:

In a case preceding *Matal,* the Court of Appeals for the Federal Circuit ruled that the Trademark Office properly rejected a trademark suggesting that a particular religious group spread terrorism in the United States. The trademark specifically mentioned the name of the religion. Would the case be decided differently after *Matal?*

Explanation:

The case presenting these facts was *In re Geller,* 751 F.3d 1355 (Fed. Cir. 2014). The case would likely be decided differently after *Matal.* The Federal Circuit in that case noted that the proposed trademark suggested that the particular religion was violent, when in fact it had a peaceful message. Accordingly, the *Geller* court approved the Trademark Office's refusal to register, concluding that the trademark violated the disparagement provision, struck down in *Matal.*

* * *

Following *Matal*, the U.S. Supreme Court invalidated yet another provision of the Lanham Act, which prohibited immoral or scandalous trademarks. *Iancu v. Brunetti*, 139 S. Ct. 2294 (2019). The case had arisen when an artist and entrepreneur, Erik Brunetti, founded a clothing line for which he wanted to use the trademark FUCT. *Id.* at 2297. While the name was intended to be pronounced as four letters, many read it as a word sounding like a well-known profanity. *Id.* The Trademark Office refused to register the mark because it was vulgar.

In striking down this provision of the trademark law, the *Iancu* Court relied on *Matal* in concluding that because the prohibition on immoral and scandalous trademarks was unconstitutionally viewpoint-based, the prohibition was unconstitutional. *Id.* at 2299. Specifically, the Court applied this viewpoint test to the bar against immoral or scandalous trademarks. Pointing to dictionary definitions of *immoral* as "inconsistent with rectitude, purity, or good morals" and *scandalous* as "giv[es] offense to the conscience or moral feelings," the Court reasoned that these and other definitions make clear that the trademark provision "distinguishes between two opposed sets of ideas: those aligned with conventional moral standards and those hostile to them; those inducing societal nods of approval and those provoking offense and condemnation." *Id.* at 2299-2300.

In criticizing this discrimination against negative messages, the Court made an intriguing observation that the statute seemed to disfavor negative messages, and to favor positive ones: 'Love rules'? 'Always be good'? Registration follows. 'Hate rules'? 'Always be cruel'? Registration does not follow. *Id.* This language gestures at a question left open in the cross-burning cases, *R.A.V.* and *Virginia v. Black*: Does the government engage in viewpoint discrimination every time its regulation distinguishes between positive speech and negative speech? A direct answer is yet to come from the U.S. Supreme Court.

Example 7-6:

Conor was offended by the trademarked name of a restaurant in his town called "Goats on a Roof." The sign for the restaurant featured goats eating grass and other vegetation that was grown on a roof. He believed that the trademark was demeaning to goats and denigrated the value that humans place on the respect, dignity, and worth of animals.

He therefore filed a petition to cancel the trademark under a provision in the trademark law allowing such petitions to be granted when the petitioner has a personal stake in the outcome in the case because the petitioner was personally damaged by the trademark.

Leaving aside the question of whether Conor had experienced legally cognizable personal damage from the mark (he did not), evaluate whether the *Matal* and *Iancu* cases foreclose the merits of Conor's claim.

Explanation:

EXPLANATION

Both *Matal* and *Iancu* foreclose the claim. Conor's theory implicates both the "disparagement" standard struck down in *Matal* and the "scandalous" standard struck down in *Iancu*. Granting the petition would violate the First Amendment principles applied in those cases. For a case with similar facts, *see Bank v. Al Johnson's Swedish Restaurant & Butik, Inc.*, 795 F. App'x 822 (Fed. Cir. 2019).

C. TRUE THREATS

As one can see from *Virginia v. Black*, the true threat approach seems to have carried the day in analyzing when the First Amendment allows government to regulate hate speech, turning a hate speech problem into the question of whether an utterance amounts to a true threat. This enhances the importance of the cases exploring the contours of what constitutes a true threat. *Virginia v. Black* made clear that a true threat must put the target of the threat in fear of violence. Although the case established that the speakers must make the threat with the intent to intimidate, the *Virginia v. Black* opinion also stated that speakers need not actually intend to carry out the threat. This raises the question of precisely what state of mind a speaker must possess in order for the government to punish the speaker.

The most direct guidance we have on this question arose in the context of a case of statutory, not constitutional, interpretation. Interpreting a federal criminal statute, the U.S. Supreme Court addressed requirements regarding the mental state to establish a true threat in *Elonis v. United States*, 135 S. Ct. 2001 (2015). In that case, the defendant (Elonis) wrote threats to his ex-wife and others in the form of rap lyrics posted to his Facebook page. Elonis was convicted of violating a federal law making it a crime to transmit in interstate commerce "any communication containing any threat . . . to injure the person of another." 18 U.S.C. § 875(c).

In overturning Elonis's conviction, the Court observed that the jury instructions in the case focused on how his posts would be understood by a reasonable person. According to the Court, the "reasonable person" standard is a familiar feature of civil liability in tort law but is inconsistent with "the conventional requirement for criminal conduct—awareness of some wrongdoing." *Elonis*, 135 S. Ct. at 2011. The Court reasoned that "[h]aving liability turn on whether a reasonable person regards the communication as a threat—regardless of what the defendant thinks—reduces culpability on the all-important element of the crime to negligence." *Id.* (internal quotation marks omitted). The Court added that we have long been reluctant to infer that a negligence standard was intended in criminal statutes.

At the end of the *Elonis* opinion the Court emphasized that it decided the case on statutory grounds, and therefore did not need to reach any First Amendment questions. Indeed, lower courts are struggling to settle on the issue whether the First Amendment requires a greater standard than negligence. *Elonis*, however, is the closest Supreme Court guidance we have on the issue at the present time.

Example 7-7:

Over a heated political discussion at Thanksgiving dinner, 19-year-old Johnny told his Uncle Bob (from whom he differs politically), "I don't care if the President of the United States presents me with the Medal of Honor. If I see him, I'm shooting him." Uncle Bob, who wanted to teach Johnny a lesson, called authorities. Johnny was ultimately convicted of knowingly and willfully making a threat to injure or to kill the President in violation of federal law. Did Johnny's statement amount to a true threat that falls outside First Amendment protection?

Explanation:

The statement likely does not amount to a true threat, and therefore Johnny's conviction violated his First Amendment rights. To begin with, the circumstances when Johnny made the statement do not suggest that he intended to inspire fear or that he truly planned to shoot the President. This was a simply a family spat at a holiday dinner.

As for the precise words spoken, the U.S. Supreme Court's decision in *Watts v. United States*, 394 U.S. 705 (1969), is instructive. In *Watts*, a young man attending a public rally opposing the draft stated: "If they ever make me carry a rifle, the first man I want to get in my sights is [the President]. They are not going to make me kill my black brothers." *Id.* at 706. The jury found that he had violated a federal statute making it a felony to knowingly and willfully threaten the life of the President, but the U.S. Supreme Court overturned the conviction. Noting that it would interpret the federal statute against the background of First Amendment constraints, the *Watts* Court held that, taken in context, the statement was simply political hyperbole. Such comments, the Court suggested, are covered by the national commitment to uninhibited and sometimes vituperative political debate.

One can easily characterize the words of Johnny's Thanksgiving statement as similar political hyperbole. Although Uncle Bob believed that Johnny should not get away with saying such disrespectful things about the President, nothing suggests that Uncle Bob believed that Johnny would do such a thing or that Johnny wanted his statement to suggest he intended to kill the President. Finally, one could support the conclusion that the conviction should not be upheld by pointing to *Elonis's* rejection of the reasonable person standard and adoption of a more subjective standard for evaluating the alleged threat (remembering, of course, that *Elonis* is a statutory and not a constitutional decision).

Example 7-8:

A group of physicians provided reproductive health services that included abortions. An anti-abortion group created "Guilty" and "Wanted" posters identifying the addresses and photographs of several of the physicians. In three prior incidents, a "Wanted"-type poster identifying a specific doctor who provided abortion services was circulated, and the doctor named on the poster was killed. The anti-abortion activists and the physicians knew of this. Charges were brought against the activists for threatening force against the doctors. The statute criminalized those who make a threat of force in connection with abortion-related activities. Under that statute, it is a crime to make a "threat of force," defined as a circumstance under which a reasonable person would foresee that a statement would be interpreted by those to whom the maker communicates as a serious expression of intent to harm. The activists were convicted under the statute and argue that the conviction is unconstitutional under the First Amendment. Will the activists succeed with this argument?

Explanation:

The answer here is probably yes, the activists will succeed with the argument. In a similar case preceding both *Elonis* and *Virginia v. Black*, the U.S. Court of Appeals for the Ninth Circuit concluded that the statements made were a true threat and upheld the convictions. *Planned Parenthood v. American Coalition of Life Activists*, 290 F.3d 1058 (9th Cir. 2002). Yet *Virginia v. Black* emphasizes actual proof of intent to put individuals in fear of their safety and the *Elonis* decision makes clear (in a statutory, not constitutional, interpretation context) that the reasonable person standard is not appropriate for a criminal prosecution focused on expression. In a decision after the *American Coalition of Life Activists* case and *Virginia v. Black*, the Court of Appeals for the Ninth Circuit recognized that the U.S. Supreme Court had changed the law in *Virginia v. Black*. The court of appeals stated that "speech may be deemed unprotected by the First Amendment as a 'true threat' only upon proof that the speaker subjectively intended the speech as a threat." *United States v. Stewart*, 420 F. 3d 1007, 1017 (9th Cir. 2005). This reasoning appears consistent with the U.S. Supreme Court decision in *Elonis*, which was decided subsequent to the court of appeals decision in *Stewart*.

Interestingly, however, the facts in this Example suggest that the proof may have been sufficient to satisfy the standards of both *Elonis* and *Virginia v. Black*. The facts make plain that the three earlier killings based on previous "Wanted" posters of physicians who perform abortions were well publicized and known to the activists and the physicians, who were the target of the activists' posters in this Example. As such, the "Wanted" posters took on a power of symbolism akin to the act of cross burning. Thus, both the activists and the doctors likely held the subjective understanding that the posters were a threat. The problem with this argument, however, is that— in a criminal case — courts are loathe to uphold a conviction based on a statute with words that are unconstitutional. Those statutory words guided the deliberations of guilt and to conclude after-the-fact that the evidence was sufficient, despite the defect in the statute, would arguably take away the function of the fact finder. (This is true, of course, unless a reviewing court were to determine that the improper standard in the statute was harmless error.)

Sexually Oriented Speech: Obscenity, Indecency, and Profanity

On one hand, analyzing constitutional questions about the justifying intrusive regulation of sexually explicit speech may seem an easy task. This type of speech is not necessarily essential to the functioning of a working democracy. And for many, sexually explicit speech has nothing to contribute to science or culture. Some believe that it deeply harms the moral fabric of society and encourages intolerance of women and other groups in society by promoting degrading and dehumanizing visions of other humans. A robust debate nonetheless exists about whether some sexually explicit speech may be an important part of artistic expression. And would you not agree that acceptance of sexually oriented speech promotes personal autonomy and tolerance? Then one encounters the question of where to draw the line between acceptable and inacceptable. How do decision makers decide what material is sufficiently unsavory as to merit curtailing whatever individual or collective merits the material may have? These questions pose the central dilemmas for analyzing regulations of sexually oriented speech.

First Amendment limitations on the regulation of sexually orientated speech fall within several categories. Some of the categories include unprotected speech: specifically, obscenity and child pornography. Although the Court has made clear that obscene speech is not protected by the First Amendment, it has struggled to pin down a precise definition of obscene. Child pornography is associated with obscenity because it is sexually oriented and is unprotected. But child pornography retains its unprotected status even if it does not fall within the definition of obscenity. Next is the areas of profanity and indecency. These areas concern words and expressive conduct that often touch on sexual topics but do not amount to obscenity.

Although they are not necessarily "low value" speech, government often can regulate them more than other types of high value speech. Finally, within the context of these areas, governments have used a variety of techniques for regulating—the most prominent being licensing schemes and zoning.

This chapter also contains discussion of attempts to regulate violent speech. This case law is relevant to the other material in this chapter because (1) it discusses the concept of unprotected speech and (2) it often concerns statutes that rely on the Supreme Court's obscenity precedent.

A. OBSCENITY

The U.S. Supreme Court attempted again and again—starting in the late 1950s—to provide a useful test for determining what counts as "obscene" speech so as to place it outside First Amendment protection. In 1973, the Court settled on a test that still prevails today, no matter how workable or unworkable it might seem. Announcing the test in *Miller v. California*, 413 U.S. 15 (1973), the Supreme Court set forth the following guidelines for a trier of fact to determine if the sexual content of speech renders it obscene:

> (a) whether "the average person, applying contemporary community standards" would find that the work, taken as a whole, appeals to the prurient interest;
> (b) whether the work depicts or describes, in a patently offensive way, sexual conduct specifically defined by the applicable state law; and
> (c) whether the work, taken as a whole, lacks serious literary, artistic, political, or scientific value.

Id. at 24.

Example 8-1:

Sally is the publisher of a magazine that features sexually explicit material. So far, she has distributed her magazine by hard copy in only one city. She is evaluating what the magazine's legal exposure is if she starts to publish it—in hard copy—for distribution throughout the United States. The primary place of circulation of the magazine is in a state with a permissive attitude toward sexually explicit material.

Sally worries, however, about publishing and circulating the magazine nationwide because it will be accessible in jurisdictions that are less tolerant of sexually explicit material than others. Specifically, she wonders which community standard will be applied? What standard will be used to evaluate the "prurient interest," "patently offensive," and "serious literary, artistic, political or scientific value" components of the *Miller* test? Will the applicable community standard come from the place where the legal action is brought, the place where she produces the magazine, the most restrictive community in the nation, or some other jurisdiction? Please advise her on this question and any other advice that you glean from the case law.

Explanation:

Sally asks a difficult question, but some guidance exists. The available U.S. Supreme Court case law on the matter suggests that the standard for evaluating "prurient interest" and "patently offensive" will come from the local jurisdiction in which legal action is brought. *Miller* itself stated that the "people of Maine or Mississippi" need not tolerate depictions that might be tolerable in Las Vegas or New York City. *Id.* at 32. A year later in *Hamling v. United States,* 418 U.S. 87 (1974), the Court ruled that local standards should govern federal obscenity prosecutions and that the question of evaluating community standards is a jury issue. Since juries must generally be drawn from a cross section of a community where legal proceedings are brought, that ruling usually ensures that the standard applied will be local.

For Sally, the worrisome observation about this language is that the nationwide publication of the magazine might subject her to legal liability in one of the most conservative jurisdictions that can access it. Not only are the standards for "prurient interest" and "patently offensive" in these jurisdictions more difficult to avoid, but the authorities may be more motivated (or funded) to pursue rigorous enforcement proceedings against her.

This, of course, opens up greater legal exposure. If she wants to avoid legal liability, should the most conservative jurisdiction's preferences and sensibilities dictate how Sally pitches her publication for all jurisdictions? Should she publish different versions of the publication? If a lawsuit is filed in an actively prosecuting, conservative jurisdiction, would that jurisdiction include in its liability judgment consideration of the version of the magazine that is circulated in the few, most permissive jurisdictions?

In *Pope v. Illinois,* 481 U.S. 497 (1987), the Supreme Court added an important qualification that may influence Sally's decision. According to *Pope,* the standard for determining the third component of the *Miller* test (i.e., whether the work, taken as a whole, lacks serious literary, artistic, political, or scientific value) is the reasonable person standard, not the local community standard. Specifically, the *Pope* Court stated that:

> Just as the ideas a work represents need not obtain majority approval to merit protection, neither . . . does the value of work vary from community to community based on the degree of local acceptance it has won. The proper inquiry is not whether an ordinary member of any given community would find

serious [value in the material], but whether a reasonable person would find such value in the material, taken as a whole.

Id. at 500-501.

This guidance from *Pope* may suggest to Sally that she will be working within a greater "comfort zone" in distributing hard copies of her magazine nationwide, since the "reasonable person" likely has a more permissive approach to defining value than the most conservative citizens in the United States who may happen to be fact finders in legal actions against her. (Of course, one always wonders whether a jury instruction on the reasonable person standard actually inspires anyone (including those with strident conservative views) to question whether their views could be anything but the views held by reasonable people.) *Pope* is also useful to Sally in making content decisions about her magazines. If she has a choice between (1) content that evokes literature, art, politics, or science in some meaningful way and (2) content that does not mention these matters, she may want to veer toward using the first category of material. To the extent that the content evokes literature, art, politics, or science, it is more likely to suggest that it meets the reasonable person's conception of value.

Example 8-2:

Assume the same facts as in Example 8-1, but now also assume that Sally wants to know about her legal exposure if she decides to publish on the Internet. What advice would you give her on how this might enhance or restrict her legal exposure?

Explanation:

One can easily say that publishing on the Internet is likely to increase her legal troubles. But again, this is a complicated question without a clear bottom line. The U.S. Supreme Court has often dodged questions regarding the impact of the Internet on constitutional questions, but it has provided at least some guidance in the First Amendment area.

The first glimmer of guidance regarding First Amendment standards in an era of developing technologies did not come in an Internet case at all. Rather, the Supreme Court ventured into questions about First Amendment standards governing developing technologies in a case regarding accessing "dial-a-porn" recordings by telephone. In *Sable Communications v. FCC*, 492 U.S. 115 (1989), the Court evaluated the constitutionality of § 223(b) of the Communications Act of 1934, which prohibited "indecent as well as obscene interstate commercial telephone messages." *Id.* at 117. The Court upheld the Act, reasoning that the First Amendment erects "no constitutional barrier to the ban on obscene dial-a-porn recordings" and ruled that the act did not contravene *Miller's* community standard requirement. *Id.* at 124-125.

On the question of which community standard should apply for those who provide services to many different communities, the Court simply stated that Congress was entitled to enact laws to prohibit the distribution of obscene materials, even if this meant that service providers were "forced to incur some cost in developing and implementing a system of screening the locale of incoming calls . . . ." *Id.* at 125. The Court therefore suggested that the local community standard, and not a nationwide standard, applied.

In a subsequent 2002 case, the Court evaluated a similar question in the context of a federal statute regulating Internet material deemed harmful to minors. In *Ashcroft v. ACLU*, 535 U.S. 564 (2002), a majority of the justices determined that the statute's endorsement of the community standards approach did not render the statute unconstitutionally overbroad. The justices, however, were split on whether to endorse that standard in the Internet context, with some justices arguing that a nationwide standard was more appropriate for Internet communications.

For Sally, a clear answer does not exist to her Internet question. Certainly, a risk exists that she might be subject to the most restrictive approach to obscenity that exists in the United States. It bears noting, however, that some lower courts have indeed started to apply a nationwide standard in the Internet context, although lower court approaches are not uniform.[1]

Discussion of community versus nationwide standards does not, however, fully answer the issue that Sally presents. She must also consider the consequences of viewers outside of the United States viewing her magazine. Different nations across the world have varying approaches to speech regulation. The U.S. is well known for being extremely speech protective, possibly an outlier by contrast with the rest of the world (particularly on the subject of hate speech). Other jurisdictions — such as Canada — have much more stringent restrictions on obscenity, restrictions that courts have upheld in light of their own country's constitutions. *See, e.g., R. v. Butler*, [1992] 1 S.C.R. 452 (Can.) (upholding statutory restrictions on obscenity).

Some countries have acted proactively in attempting to enforce their more restrictive foreign standard for regulating speech on U.S. entities than would be tolerated by the First Amendment scrutiny of regulations under U.S. law. Yet other obstacles remain for enforcing the standards of another country against an entity situated in the United States. Would the foreign country have regulatory authority or personal jurisdiction over an entity situated in the United States? Even assuming that the country does have personal jurisdiction, does it have proper power to enforce its laws against

---

1. *Compare United States v. Kilbride*, 584 F.3d 1240 (9th Cir. 2009) (embracing a national rather than local community standard), with *United States v. Little*, 365 F. App'x 159 (11th Cir. 2010) (declaring that *Miller's* local community standard governs Internet material).

the U.S.-based entity? Moreover, if its courts or regulatory body has entered judgment against the U.S. entity, would the country be able to enforce the foreign judgment against the entity?

Precedent exists for non-U.S. countries attempting to enforce decisions against an offshore U.S. entity, but practical and legal obstacles exist. For example, the U.S. Congress has enacted a statute bearing the catchy name "the SPEECH act," which is designed to allow enforcement of foreign judgments in U.S. courts only when the First Amendment (and related statutory protections) would have allowed the judgment to be rendered in a U.S. court. *See* 28 U.S.C. §§ 4101-4105 (2020). For an introduction to the effect of actions by other countries against U.S. players in light of the First Amendment as well as the U.S. Congress's First-Amendment-protecting legislative reaction in the form of SPEECH Act, *see, e.g.,* Laura E. Little, *Internet Defamation, Freedom of Expression, the Lesson of Private International Law for the United States,* 14 EUROPEAN YEARBOOK OF PRIVATE INTERNATIONAL LAW 181 (2012/2013) (European Institute of Comparative Law, University of Lausanne, Switzerland) (discussing the challenges of Internet regulation of speech in light of the different approaches to freedom of communication among the world's nations). For a thoughtful consideration of the balance between freedom of expression and constitutional protection against degrading and dehumanizing speech, *see, e.g.,* R. v. Butler, [1992] 1 S.C.R. 452 (Can.) (evaluating constitutionality of Canada's criminal prohibitions of obscene speech).

Example 8-3:

Sally understands that special considerations pertain to publishing sexually explicit material that may involve minors, but she is unfamiliar with the details. For the purpose of giving her advice, assume the same facts as Examples 8-1 and 8-2. But now Sally has asked you about her legal exposure if she includes sexually explicit pictures that include children engaged in sex acts in her magazine. Please advise her on her exposure of liability if she does so.

Explanation:

The involvement of minors in Sally's publication adds important caution to your advice. Even if she has no moral compunction against using minors in her material, many legal factors suggest that she should avoid doing this.

The U.S. Supreme Court has made clear that protecting children from potential sexual exploitation is a compelling state interest that justifies an even broader regulation of child pornography than is authorized under the Miller standard. The Court first ventured into this territory in *New York v. Ferber,* 458 U.S. 747 (1982). In the context of evaluating a New York law regulating material in which a child under 16 was depicted in a sex act, the Court emphasized that using children in such materials is harmful to the children's emotional, physiological, and mental health. Importantly, the Court made clear that the concern with protecting children justified regulating child pornography material that does not meet the definition of obscene.

Subsequently, in the Child Pornography Prevention Act of 1996 (the "Virtual Child Porn Act"), Congress expanded federal laws barring child pornography to include not only images of actual children engaging in explicit sexual conduct but also "any visual depiction, including any photograph, film, video, picture, or computer or computer-generated image or picture." The U.S. Supreme Court, however, struck down two provisions of the law outlawing visual materials that "appear to be a minor" or "conveys the impression" that a minor was involved. *Ashcroft v. Freedom of Speech Coalition*, 535 U.S. 234 (2002). The *Freedom of Speech Coalition* Court determined that these provisions were overbroad, emphasizing that the First Amendment required more precise formations of the restrictions. (The parts of the Virtual Child Porn Act banning images using real minors had not been challenged.)

In reaching its holding, the *Freedom of Speech Coalition* Court distinguished the Virtual Child Porn Act from the statute at issue in *Ferber*, which focused on the production of the child pornography and the consequent injury to the individual children involved. That injury included not only trauma inflicted in having children participate in sexual acts, but also the harm inflicted by publication. The Court explained that "as a permanent record of a child's abuse, the continued circulation [of the material produced] would harm the child who had participated. . . [by causing] new injury to the child's reputation and emotional well-being" each time the material is published. *Id.* at 249. The Court reasoned that these injuries are not threatened by the creation and publication of visual materials created without the participation of an actual child.

(At the behest of activists, legislatures and opinion leaders have now begun to use the term "child sexual abuse material" or CSAM rather than "child pornography." The U.S. Supreme Court, however, has yet to adopt this terminology.)

Ferber and *Free Speech Coalition* suggest that Sally could work hard to restrain her presentations to those that comply with existing law, but she should know that the restrictions are challenging to navigate. U.S. case law has not been particularly sensitive to material containing edgy, somewhat sexualized, materials in any context—much less materials pertaining to children. Sally must remember as well that child sexual abuse material can in fact meet the definition of obscenity and thus be unprotected speech. Interestingly, other countries have taken approaches to these issues that are different than in the U.S., pursuing a more searching view of the propriety of controlling sexual depictions that touch on minors. *See, e.g., R. v. Sharpe*, [2001] 1 S.R.C. 45 (Can.) (construing a federal statute as narrowly proscribing child pornography to exclude personally created depictions that were not created for commercial consumption).

Should Sally decide to proceed with publishing the material, she must tread carefully and might reasonably decide to avoid any use of minors in her magazine at all so as to simplify her creative process and marketing strategies.

Example 8-4:

Assume that Dalia Defendant created and distributed child pornography that depicted images of minor females. The images were created by a digital process known as "morphing." Essentially, the pictures consisted of a minor's head superimposed over the heads of images of nude and partially nude adult females engaged in sexually explicit conduct. All of the images could be said to be pornographic, but not all of the images would necessarily meet the Miller definition of obscene. Would a prosecution of Dalia for creating and distributing these images be consistent with the U.S. Supreme Court's child pornography precedent?

Explanation:

The answer to this question may depend on how whether the minors' heads that appear in the images resemble actual children. If they do resemble actual children, then Dalia's prosecution is more likely to be constitutional.

The analysis of the Ashcroft v. Free Speech Coalition turned on the lack of harm to an actual child arising from virtual images. If, however, the image is recognizable as the face of an actual child then the distribution of the image could inflict physiological, reputational, and emotional harm on the child. Ferber relied in part on this concern in holding that government could regulate child pornography consistently with the First Amendment, even if the pornography was not obscene.

One should note that the lower courts that have addressed this issue regarding the constitutionality of child pornography prosecutions involving "morphing" have varied in their approaches to resolving the question. Compare United States v. Hotaling, 634 F.3d 725 (2d Cir. 2011) (holding that prosecution was consistent with the First Amendment because a minor's face was is recognizable in the pictures), with People v. Gerber, 126 Cal. Rptr. 3d 688 (Cal. Ct. App. 2011) (holding that child pornography prosecution was unconstitutional because altered materials created by morphing are closer to virtual child pornography than actual child pornography and the creation process does not necessarily involve the sexual exploitation of a child).

* * *

It is important to note a significant distinction in the area pertaining to sexualized material and children. The terms "child pornography" or "child sexual abuse material" pertain to material made using minors (or at least appearing as though they use minors). Concern with avoiding harm to individual children as well as creating a permanent depiction of the abuse animate these cases. A separate line of cases is concerned with protecting children from being able to access sexual material, a problem that the Internet has exacerbated. The Court took on this latter concern in *Ashcroft v. American Civil Liberties Union*, 535 U.S. 564 (2002). This case involved an evaluation of Congress's Child Online Protection Act (COPA), which prohibited any person from "knowingly and with knowledge of the character of the material, in interstate or foreign commerce by means of the World Wide Web, making any communication for commercial purposes that is available to any minor and that includes any material that is harmful to minors." *Id.* at 569. COPA hewed close to the three-part *Miller* test.

The *Ashcroft v. American Civil Liberties Union* Court was impressed that the COPA's scope was limited: it applied to a limited scope of material, restricted to depictions of sexual acts that are patently offensive to minors and lacked any serious literary, artistic, political, or scientific values for minors. In a subsequent decision, however, the U.S. Supreme Court held that COPA was likely unconstitutional because it burdened the First Amendment rights of adults by preventing them from accessing protected material. *Ashcroft v. American Civil Liberties Union*, 542 U.S. 564 (2004). Lower courts ultimately followed suit, holding that COPA was unconstitutional.

B. USE OF OBSCENITY JURISPRUDENCE IN EVALUATING VIOLENT SPEECH

Violent speech sometimes overlaps with obscene speech. But sometimes not: violence is depicted in many formats that lack sexual content. Nonetheless, those who wish to restrict violent speech in society have taken guidance from the *Miller* test. Whether you believe the *Miller* case is persuasive and effective or not, *Miller* took on the difficult task of articulating a test for identifying when unsavory, disfavored speech is entitled to constitutional protection and developed an approach to evaluating constitutionality that courts adhere to faithfully.

Taking a lead from *Miller*, legislatures in the United States relied on its three-part test for creating restrictions on violent speech. The legislatures' track record, however, has not been particularly successful.

The U.S. Supreme Court evaluated the U.S. Congress's attempt to regulate violent speech in *United States v. Stevens*, 559 U.S. 460 (2010). Congress had criminalized the commercial creation, sale, or possession of certain depictions of animal cruelty. (Importantly, the statute addressed only portrayals of animal cruelty, not the acts themselves.) The statute made illegal any visual or auditory depiction of a living animal being maimed, mutilated, tortured, wounded, or killed, but removed from its scope any depictions with "serious religious, political, scientific, educational, journalistic, historical, or artistic value." The defendant, Stevens, was convicted under the statute for selling videos of dogfighting.

The Supreme Court found the statute invalid under the First Amendment. The Court noted the few categories of speech for which an absolute speech prohibition was permitted, including obscenity. Animal cruelty, the Court determined, was not one of those categories and should not be added to that list. The Court held the statute unconstitutional, however, because it was overbroad. According to the Court, the statute was not restricted to conduct directed at animal cruelty and could apply to activity such as the humane slaughtering of a cow.

Stevens is particularly significant for its explanation for refusing to identify a new category of speech as unprotected. Specifically, the Court described unprotected categories of speech "as being 'of such slight social value as a step to truth that any benefit that may be derived from them [was] clearly outweighed by the social interest in order and morality'" Id. at 470 (quoting *R.A.V. v. St. Paul*, 505 U.S. 377 (1992)). The Court emphasized, however, that this description did not articulate a test to determine whether categories of speech were outside the scope of the First Amendment. Reluctant to develop such a test or to expand the list of unprotected speech, the Court simply reasoned that because animal cruelty was not a historically unprotected category of speech, it should not be considered outside the scope of the First Amendment.

Example 8-5:

After the *Stevens* decision, Congress amended the animal crush video statute. The statute defines an "animal crush video" as "any photograph, motion-picture film, video or digital recording, or electronic image" that

> (1) depicts actual conduct in which 1 or more living non-human mammals, birds, reptiles, or amphibians is intentionally crushed, burned, drowned, suffocated, impaled, or otherwise subjected to serious bodily injury . . . including conduct that, if committed against a person, [would violate certain other federal statutes]; and
> (2) is obscene.

Specifically exempted from the statutory prohibitions is any visual depiction of "customary and normal veterinary or agricultural husbandry practices," "the slaughter of animals for food," or "hunting, trapping, or fishing."

Is this statute constitutional?

Explanation:

It appears as though the statute is not constitutional. Addressing this revised version of the statute, the Court of Appeals for the Fifth Circuit in *United States v. Richards*, 755 F.3d 269 (5th Cir. 2014), *cert. denied*, 575 U.S. 95 (2015), ruled that the statute violated the First Amendment. Noting that the prohibition was confined to "obscene" videos, the court of appeals observed that the governing *Miller* test applies only to material regarding sexual conduct and has not been expanded. Deciding that animal crush videos generally do not portray sexual conduct, the *Richards* court ruled that the expression prohibited in the statute did not fall into an unprotected category. For that reason, the *Richards* court treated the statute as a content-based restriction on protected speech, and thus evaluated the statute under the strict scrutiny standard.

The *Richards* court concluded that the statute served a compelling state interest because it was grounded not only in society's interest in avoiding animal suffering resulting from cruelty, but also in concern with preventing degradation of social morals. Nonetheless, the court determined, the statute was not narrowly tailored to this interest. According to the court, Congress's general approach with the statute was to "dry up the market" for animal crush videos, and in so doing Congress intended to include the statute prohibitions that were not limited to acts of illegal animal cruelty.

* * *

The U.S. Supreme Court continued *Stevens*'s approach to evaluating the constitutionality of attempts to restrict depictions of violence in *Brown v. Entertainment Merchants*, 564 U.S. 786 (2011). In that case, the Court evaluated a California statute attempting to control the sale of violent video games to minors. The law traced the *Miller* factors, delimiting its scope to patently offensive depictions of violence that lacked redeeming social value and violated community standards.

Example 8-6:

Assume that a state legislature is concerned with minors having access to various forms of entertainment that do not necessarily violate the *Miller* test, but are sufficiently violent as to raise concern about whether to protect minors from exposure to them. The state legislature therefore passed a law that prevented minors from purchasing a picture, photograph, drawing, or video representation of the human body that

(1) predominately appeals to the shameful or morbid interest of minors in violence;
(2) is patently offensive to prevailing standards in the adult community as whole with respect to what is suitable material for minors; and

(3) is without redeeming social importance to minors under contemporary community standards.

Is this statute constitutional?

Explanation:

No, the current state of the law suggests that the statute is not constitutional. As explained above, the Court reaffirmed the inclination to disallow regulation of violent speech in *United States v. Stevens*, and then again applied this inclination in *Brown v. Entertainment Merchants*. The statute in *Brown* was similar to the statute in this Example. Refusing to uphold the restriction on violent expression, Justice Scalia, writing for the *Brown* majority, highlighted many classic depictions of violence depicted and revered in main stream culture: an apple poisoning Snow White, the wicked witch baking children in the oven, Odysseus blinding a cyclops with a stake in the eye, and Piggy murdered by other children in *Lord of the Flies*. Yet in an earlier case regarding sexually explicit materials presented to minors, the Supreme Court upheld a similar regulation, concluding that a less protective version of the *Miller* standard was a constitutionally appropriate approach to regulating minors' access to these materials. Dissenting in the video game case—*Brown*—Justice Breyer had a poignant point to make using *Ginsburg* as a foil:

> [T]oday the Court makes clear that a State cannot prohibit the sale to minors of the most interactive violent video games. But what sense does it make to forbid selling to a 13-year-old boy a magazine with an image of a nude woman, while protecting a sale to that 13-year-old of an interactive video game in which he actively, but virtually, binds and gags the woman, then tortures and kills her? What kind of First Amendment would permit the government to protect children by restricting sales of that extremely violent video game *only* when the woman—bound, gagged, tortured, and killed—is also topless?

Id. at 857.

Both Justice Scalia and Breyer had important points, no? If the question is—"what is the current state of the law?"—the answer is, Justice Scalia's version. Even if the attempt to protect minors carefully traces the *Miller* test, the law of the land is that violence is not a topic for which the First Amendment makes a significant exception.

C. PROFANITY AND INDECENCY

U.S. culture presents us with material that is off color and capable of offending but does not satisfy the *Miller* test. Does the First Amendment allow any regulation of that material? The short answer is yes; the long answer is more complicated. To begin, one might find helpful an attempt to segregate this category of offensive speech between profanity and indecency. The case law does not sort neatly into these two categories. One might easily evaluate the restrictions together, although one should also be sensitive to the fact-specific nature of each U.S. Supreme Court statement of the applicable legal rule. The Supreme Court's approach has not been clearly consistent along a particular pro-First Amendment protection line. Thus, the specifics of each case and context require careful attention. Case law on profanity appears first below.

As an initial matter, the Court in *Chaplinsky v. New Hampshire*, 315 U.S. 568 (1942), suggested in dicta that the lewd and the profane were within the categories of unprotected speech. Courts wondered thereafter about the scope of that statement. An answer came in a case directly confronting profane speech in a political speech context: *Cohen v. California*, 403 U.S. 15 (1971). The defendant in that case, Cohen, was convicted for being in a courtroom with a jacket that said "Fuck the Draft" on its back. Reversing the conviction, the Court stated "[w]e cannot indulge the facile assumption that one can forbid particular words without also running a substantial risk of suppressing ideas in the process. . . . [G]overnments might soon seize upon the censorship of particular words as a convenient guise for banning the expression of unpopular views." *Id.* at 26.

The next, and more important, case in this area was *FCC v. Pacifica Foundation*, 438 U.S. 726 (1978). *Pacifica* concerned comedian George Carlin's famous monologue, "Filthy Words." Carlin gave a list of words that he stated you would not be able to say on public airwaves and repeated them over and over again. A New York radio station owned by Pacifica later broadcast Carlin's monologue. Evaluating a complaint about this broadcast, the Federal Communications Commission (FCC) found a violation of rules regarding broadcasting offensive language during a time when children may be listening. (A parent had complained that he had heard the broadcast while driving with his teenage son.) Pacifica explained that the monologue had been played during a program about contemporary society's attitude toward language and that immediately before the broadcast began there had been a warning about language which could be regarded as offensive. Nonetheless, since the broadcast occurred during hours when young people may be listening, the FCC issued a declaratory order that Pacifica had opened itself up for administrative sanctions. On appeal of the FCC decision, the U.S. Supreme Court agreed.

The *Pacifica* Court acknowledged the potential for the FCC's strict decisions to encourage broadcasters to censor themselves, but also stated that the potentially offensive references lie at the periphery of First Amendment concerns. The Court made clear that offensiveness to society is not alone a sufficient reason for suppressing speech, but concern with protection of minors during hours when they may be listening was enough to convince the Court to uphold the FCC decision that fines could be imposed.

Example 8-7:

Frasier, an untenured state college instructor, received a warning against using profane language in class. (Frasier's students range from 17 to 25 years old). Frasier continued to do so—using the words fuck and shit, even sometimes directing these words at the students in the class. As a result of his actions, Frasier was fired. He sued the state college and is now arguing that his First Amendment rights had been violated. Does Frasier have a valid First Amendment challenge?

Explanation:

Several factors suggest that the First Amendment would support sanctioning Frasier. As a teacher of some students below the age of majority, the standard for regulation of Frasier's speech is higher than others who teach young adults. As students in a class for which they are enrolled for academic credit, the audience was captive: in fact, they even paid tuition to be that captive audience. That makes this an even stronger case for First Amendment concern than in *Pacifica*, a circumstance where the listener could easily switch to another channel without repercussions. In this Example, an element of compulsion is present: if the student wants credit, the student must listen.

The language of *Pacifica* and many other U.S. Supreme Court cases suggest that Frasier will not prevail. For college professors who do not work for a state entity, a substantial obstacle would exist to pushing the First Amendment claim, since no state action is present. But Frasier does not work for a private entity. He works for a state entity and thus can properly claim that the First Amendment applies because the actions of his school are "state actions." While this fact helps him in one way, it hurts him from another perspective. As an employee of a state school, Frasier is a government employer. As explained in Chapter 13 below, the speech rights of government employees are dramatically circumscribed. *See, e.g., Buchanan v. Alexander,* 919 F.3d 847 (5th Cir. 2019) (relying on government-employee precedents restricting speech rights in determining that a higher education professor did not have a successful First Amendment challenge to her firing for discussing sex and using profane language).

Finally, Frazier's chances of success are further diminished because some of his students are minors. Case law makes clear that the First Amendment protection has a lighter touch when it comes to regulation of speech directed at minors—particularly those in an educational setting where the students are a captive audience component.

* * *

The U.S. Supreme Court revisited FCC indecency rules in 2010 and 2012. Although the agency had begun to take the position that it would not punish so-called fleeting expletives, it backed off that position. The FCC took the position that the word "fuck" and depictions of nudity were sufficiently sexual as to merit punishment, even if their appearance in a broadcast was fleeting. After two rounds in the U.S. Supreme Court, this new FCC approach to fleeting indecency did not survive. The Court, nonetheless, struck it down on narrow grounds. According to the Supreme Court, the FCC failed to give sufficient notice of its position to the broadcast media because it did not give the media adequate warning that "fleeting expletives and momentary nudity could be found actionably indecent." FCC v. Fox Television Stations, Inc., 567 U.S. 239, 258 (2012).

As for the continuing vitality of U.S. Supreme Court's approach in Pacifica, one should note that it does not appear to have had broad influence. The case has been distinguished in the context of similar indecency scenarios such as those involving indecency or phone sex. One might reasonably conclude therefore that the case is unique and that future cases are unlikely to fall within its criteria.

D. LICENSING AND ZONING

Litigating obscenity and indecency issues is expensive. Other methods of addressing the issue thus emerged with the appeal of cheaper regulatory alternatives, particularly for cash-strapped local governments. Most prominently, licensing systems and zoning requirements became attractive as (arguably) side-door means of regulating this type of speech. Neither method escaped the notice of those concerned with freedom of expression.

Challenges to licensing schemes emerged in the 1960s. A leading case, Freedman v. Maryland, 380 U.S. 51 (1964), set forth three default procedural safeguards for an administrative licensing system with the potential to censor speech. First, the decision of whether to prohibit the speech must be made within a "specified brief period" during which the status quo is maintained. Next, the government must have the burden of initiating judicial review of the speech. According to Freedman, this meant that the government censoring board must "either issue a license or go to court to restrain" the expression. The Freeman Court added that government must bear the burden of proving that the expression can be regulated. Finally, the Court described the licensing system as a mode of prior restraint and stated that the government's prompt judicial review process was required "to minimize the deterrent effect of an interim and possibly erroneous denial of a license." Id. at 58-59.

The Court has nonetheless arguably lessened the procedural require-
ments for some types of licensing systems in recent years. First, in *FW/PBS,
Inc. v. City of Dallas*, 493 U.S. 215, 229 (1990), while holding a municipality's sexually oriented business licensing scheme unconstitutional, Justice
O'Connor's majority opinion mentioned that only two of the *Freedman*
Court's safeguards were necessary for systems that issue permits (which the
Court distinguished from censorship boards): (1) any restraint on speech
may last only for a specified brief period of time during which the status quo must be maintained, and (2) the applicant must be guaranteed to
have expeditious access to judicial review. The Supreme Court later in City
of *Littleton v. Z.J. Gifts D-4, LLC*, 541 U.S. 774, 780-781 (2004), clarified that
prompt judicial determination on the merits (not just procedural matters)
must be guaranteed as well.

Example 8-8:

A city enacts a statute that requires individuals to obtain a license before
operating an adult entertainment business. The license administrators were
given 40 days to decide whether to issue the license and could deny the
license on eight enumerated grounds. An applicant may seek review of a
license denial through normal state court procedures, although the statute does not mandate a deadline by which a judicial determination must
be made

Darien applied for a license, which was denied. He would like to challenge the statute, arguing that the statute fails to guarantee sufficiently expeditious judicial review. All agree that his claim is justiciable, but the question
is whether he has a valid First Amendment challenge. Does Darien have a
viable First Amendment challenge?

Explanation:

No, under U.S. Supreme Court case *Littleton v. Z.J. Gifts*, Darien most likely does
not have a viable First Amendment claim. The statutory structure and judicial review process provided in this fact pattern sets forth the same process
deemed acceptable in *Littleton v. Z.J. Gifts*. The statute specifies a process that
appears to allow for full judicial review, along with specifically articulated
guidelines for evaluating validity of the application. Darien appears to be
out of luck in his challenge.

* * *

Under the umbrella of protecting neighborhoods from the derogat-
ing or unsavory influence of those who are attracted to sexual establishments (for example, prostitutes and their patrons), local governments have
also used zoning laws to restrict businesses offering obscene or indecent

8. Sexually Oriented Speech

entertainment options. Even for offerings that may not satisfy the *Miller* standard for obscenity, the Court has been inclined to reduce First Amendment protections. So, for example, in *Young v. American Mini Theatres, Inc.*, 427 U.S. 50 (1976), the opinion of the Court states "there is surely a less vital interest in the uninhibited exhibition of material that is on the borderline between pornography and artistic expression than in the free dissemination of ideas of social and political significance . . . ." *Id.* at 61.

The Court has shown a similar low regard for nude dancing and has upheld strict regulations of establishments that offer that entertainment. *See, e.g.*, *City of Erie v. Pap's A.M.*, 529 U.S. 277 (2000); *Barnes v. Glen Theatres*, 501 U.S. 560 (1991). These cases evaluate restrictions in light of the diminished value of sexual speech directly, explicitly or implicitly acknowledging that the restrictions are content-based. Other cases, such as *City of Renton v. Playtime Theatres, Inc.*, 475 U.S. 41 (1986), evaluate the restrictions in light of the secondary effects of the adult establishment on crime, property values, and the like. More discussion of the secondary effects doctrine appears in Chapter 1.

Commercial Speech

After a series of cases grappling with the question of whether the First Amendment governed commercial speech, the U.S. Supreme Court unequivocally extended First Amendment protection to that category of expression. Citing consumers' interest in the free flow of commercial information, the Court also celebrated societal benefits from commercial speech: "So long as we preserve a predominantly free enterprise economy, the allocation of our resources in large measure will be made through numerous private economic decisions. It is a matter of public interest that those decisions, in the aggregate, be intelligent and well informed." *Virginia State Board of Pharmacy v. Virginia Citizens Consumer Council, Inc.*, 425 U.S. 748, 765 (1976).

As an introduction to various arguments about individual and collective interests in framing arguments at play during commercial speech disputes, consider the following Examples.

Example 9-1:

Cereal Corp. manufactures and distributes various types of breakfast cereal, including a whole wheat variety with a very high sugar content, called "Whole Wheat Pizazz." Cereal Corp. has sponsored a series of television infomercials in which it trumpets Whole Wheat Pizazz as "one of the healthiest choices in breakfast cereal." The infomercials detail the importance of consuming high-fiber foods to maintain human health. State A takes the position that this infomercial is a misleading advertisement that should be removed from the airwaves. Cereal Corp. argues that the infomercials are educating the public about the importance of high-fiber foods. What type of arguments regarding commercial speech regulation might these two parties make?

Explanation:

Cereal Corp. might argue that it should be allowed full latitude in running the infomercials because it is providing a public educational service and providing a constitutionally protected opinion about its view of nutrition generally and the value of its cereal more specifically. State A would likely argue that the infomercials are designed solely to serve Cereal Company's own economic interest. The State will also likely assert that the claims about the nutritional value of "Whole Wheat Pizazz" are false and misleading and therefore justify full regulation, including suppression, of the infomercials. As will become clear below, the presence of an economic motive helps to steer a communication toward the commercial speech characterization and allegations of false and misleading representations support identifying the communication as unprotected speech.

Example 9-2:

State B has imposed special, high taxes on magazines that specialize in testing and rating household products. A magazine entitled "HOUSEHOLD PRODUCT REVIEW" is challenging the tax as a violation of the First Amendment. Although the magazine appears to provide a neutral evaluation of a random assortment of products, close study shows that the magazine features many of the products that are manufactured and distributed by the magazine's wholly owned subsidiary. Study of the magazines reveals no indications that the testing of these products is rigged or the information provided is false, but the descriptive articles in the magazine highlight the usefulness and safety of the particular products manufactured by the subsidiary.

State B has filed a motion for summary judgment, asking the court to dismiss the tax challenge. You have been asked to outline arguments on both sides of the motion, including arguments for why the tax threatens First Amendment values and arguments for why the tax is constitutional. What types of arguments would you include?

Explanation:

You might start by outlining what is likely the basis of State B's position: this magazine serves the economic interest of a close affiliate of the magazine and, as such, has the earmarks of commercial speech. State B might also argue that, even though the magazine's presentations appear neutral and accurate, the failure of the magazine to disclose this economic self-interest is misleading.

State B may also argue that the magazine is over-claiming its entitlement to constitutional protection. Constitutional protection is not triggered every time public policy concerns suggest that a particular government regulation is imprudent. Standard constitutional analysis maintains that the U.S. Constitution should be used sparingly and that it is unwise to constitution-alize every matter of public concern. State B may further argue that, when it comes to commercial activity, the Constitution tolerates extensive economic regulation, and one would think the same applies to commercial speech such as advertisements. Indeed, constitutional jurisprudence regards commercial speech as having lesser value than other forms of communication.

The countervailing arguments supporting the magazine are more numerous and possibly more persuasive. You might start articulating these counterarguments from the point of view of household purchasers of consumer products who wish to be educated about what products exist and where to get them. In addition, the household purchasers will usually want to identify the best product that they can obtain at certain prices. They would like answers to questions such as "which product is the best deal?" "what features does each product have?" and "what product features are worth the extra cost?" The desire for this type of information, an economist may argue, helps to ensure that resources in the local, national, and international economies are allocated as rationally and efficiently as possible.

One cannot necessarily expect a profit-maximizing product producer to disclose all unfavorable information about a product and about its connections with other business entities. Magazines such as HOUSEHOLD PRODUCT REVIEW serve to bring unfavorable qualities to light, foster debate about the merits of products, and may ultimately inspire improvements in the product. You might also argue that this disclosure of unfavorable information might provide incentive to other producers to develop alternative products that better serve the consumers and inspire the competition on which the U.S. economic system thrives. Thus, the individual consumer is not the only beneficiary of the free flow of commercial information: the entire society benefits as well.

An especially important advantage for the society at large is full disclosure of information about the safety of a product that restrictions on commercial speech might hinder. Moreover, when an entity such as HOUSEHOLD PRODUCT REVIEW enjoys full latitude to disclose information about the safety of a product, this may encourage producers to rebut any statements made regarding the safety of a product, thus inspiring debate that may guide consumers closer to truth about safety concerns.

Finally, information about product price, safety, and quality implicates matters that relate to the political process. Information about these issues helps to shed light on political debates concerning such topics as foreign trade, inflation, domestic infrastructure, the growth of administrative agencies that regulate product manufacturing, and the environmental impact of certain products. In this way, commercial speech is a key component to informing speech that the First Amendment favors: political speech.

* * *

Several reasons support placing commercial speech on a lower rung of protection than other forms of speech. One approach is to focus on some of the values animating the First Amendment as a general matter. (The Introduction to this volume provides an overview of these values.) In analyzing these values, some say that commercial speech is not as essential to self-government as other matters key to a functioning democracy, such as expressions of political ideology. Others argue that the search for commercial truth will occur even without stringent constitutional protection for commercial speech. This argument relies on the strength of the profit motive to ensure that those who participate in the market will contradict unfavorable commercial statements about their products or services. Cf. R. H. Coase, *Advertising and Free Speech*, 6 J. LEGAL STUDIES 1 (1977) (advocating that the marketplace of ideas should be regulated with the same level of government interference as the economic marketplace). Some also argue that the autonomy justification for the First Amendment does not support protecting commercial speech. This argument points out that most commercial speech comes from business entities that lack the human capacity to exercise free will and self-actualization. *See, e.g.,* Thomas Jackson & John Jeffries, *Commercial Speech: Economic Due Process and the First Amendment*, 64 VA. L. REV. 1 (1979) (stating that the First Amendment value of protecting speaker autonomy "stops short of a seller hawking his wares").

Another approach to justifying lesser protection for commercial speech draws on common sense and intuition. Many thinkers point out that commercial speech is particularly hardy and does not whither in the face of hostility or government regulation. As explained by Martin Redish, *The Value of Free Speech*, 130 U. PA. L. REV. 591 (1982), little risk emerges that "commercial magazines and newspapers will cease publication for fear of the government regulation, because they are in business for profit" and that indeed even communications focusing on only on politics and ideas could provide a problem. Even communications focusing solely on politics and ideas are interested in profit: they are worried about commercial viability. Finally are those who point to general human instincts in arguing that citizens simply do not cherish commercial speech in the same way that they cherish other types of expression. *See* DANIEL A. FARBER, THE FIRST AMENDMENT (5th ed. 2019) (observing that "few would send their children to war to defend the right of pharmacies to advertise the prices of prescription drugs. Few . . . would consider a ban on price advertising to be a human rights violation . . . .").

A. DEFINING COMMERCIAL SPEECH

The Court in *Virginia State Board of Pharmacy* stated that commercial speech does not include all speech that is produced for profit and is confined to speech that proposes a commercial transaction. *Virginia State Board of Pharmacy* reinforced that the First Amendment protects economically motivated speech: "[t]he interests of the contestants in a labor dispute are primarily economic, but it has long been settled that both the employee and the employer are protected by the First Amendment when they express themselves on the merits of the dispute in order to influence its outcome." 425 U.S. at 762 The Supreme Court has at times appeared to expand commercial speech to include communication tied to economic interests of a speaker or the speaker's audience, yet the Court has also continued to maintain the position that economic motivation does not disqualify speech from full constitutional protection. For example, in Citizens United v. Federal Election Commission, 558 U.S. 310 (2010), the Court made clear that some economically motivated speech qualifies for full speech protection. (Chapter 3 includes an extensive discussion of Citizens United.) Thus, the Court has taken two positions on the question of constitutional protection for speech imbued with economic motivation that are in tension with one another. Although the Court has provided some additional guidance on this matter — as explored in the Example below — the Court has more recently resisted further definition of commercial speech, writing only in generalities. See, e.g., Sorrell v. IMS Health, Inc., 564 U.S. 552, 567 (2011) (stating that "a great deal of vital expression" deserving of full protection under the First Amendment "results from economic motive . . . ."). Accordingly, the Virginia State Board of Pharmacy opinion appears to provide a safe definition to use as a starting point for analysis, with the caveat that — as reflected in the Example below — the matter can be more complicated.

Example 9-3:

A condom manufacturer distributed what it termed "informational pamphlets" that bore the titles "Condoms and Human Sexuality" and "Plain Talk about Venereal Disease." The first pamphlet described condom use as well as the manufacturer's products. The second explained condoms' disease prevention capabilities and stated on the last page that the pamphlet was a public service of the manufacturer. The manufacturer's product brand name also appeared on this last page. Are these pamphlets commercial speech?

Explanation:

Yes, the pamphlets are commercial speech. In Bolger v. Youngs Drug Products Corp., 463 U.S. 60, 66 (1983), the Court held that pamphlets such as those described in this Example were indeed commercial speech. Invoking the Virginia State Board of Pharmacy definition of commercial speech, the Bolger Court stated that the pamphlets were more than mere proposals "to engage in commercial transactions." Id. Although advertising was a clear purpose of the pamphlets, that alone did not make them commercial speech. The manufacturer's economic motive for mailing the pamphlets and the pamphlets' mention of specific products also did not make the pamphlets commercial speech. The Court concluded, however, that, taken together, these three factors did render the pamphlets commercial speech. The Court noted that the pamphlets' discussion of issues of public concern that did not relate to the manufacturer's economic motives did not insulate the pamphlets from the commercial speech characterization.

* * *

The *Bolger* case discussed in Example 9-3 provides three factors to consider in evaluating whether a communication is commercial speech: (1) the communication is an advertisement; (2) the communication mentions a specific product; and (3) the speaker had an economic motivation to make the communication. The precise relationship among the three factors is unclear. For example, if two of the factors are strong, can a communication still be commercial speech if the third factor is missing? *Bolger* does appear to establish, however, that any communication that satisfies all three factors is commercial speech.

Example 9-4:

A chain of grocery stores—known as "Food Bazaar"—agreed to buy a page in a special issue of a sports magazine dedicated to celebrating the career of a baseball player. The page featured a photograph of the ball player as well as a graphic featuring the player's jersey number. The name of Food Bazaar as well as the brand logo appeared at the bottom of the page, with the words: "Specialists in Foods Enjoyed by All Sports Figures." At the top of the page, appeared the words "Food Bazaar Stores Celebrate a Brilliant Career!" Does this page that appeared in the magazine qualify as commercial speech?

Explanation:

Yes, the page is commercial speech. The mention of Food Bazaar—a commercial entity not connected to the sports world—twice on the page suggests that the chain wished to engage in a commercial transaction with the magazine readers, particularly because Food Bazaar is a commercial food retailer that has no obvious connection to the sports world or to the particular athlete being celebrated. Moreover, each one of the *Bolger* factors is arguably satisfied: (1) the appearance of Food Bazaar's name twice on the page as well as the chain's logo support the characterization of the page as an advertisement; (2) the reference to "foods enjoyed by all sports figures" alludes to food, which qualifies as a specific category of products (albeit not a "specific product" as that term was used in *Bolger*); and (3) Food Bazaar's lack of general involvement in the sports world as well as the strong representation of its brand on the page support the conclusion that the merchandiser had an economic motivation for purchasing and designing the page. Cf. *Jordan v. Jewel Food Stores, Inc.*, 743 F.3d. 509 (2014).

B. THE GENERAL TEST OF EVALUATING COMMERCIAL SPEECH REGULATIONS

Mindful of the balance of values at play with commercial speech, the U.S. Supreme Court has expounded on First Amendment protection for commercial speech announced in *Virginia State Board of Pharmacy*. In *Central Hudson Gas & Electric Corp. v. Public Service Commission of New York*, 447 U.S. 557, 558-572 (1980), the Court articulated a test for commercial speech, which largely prevails today.

Making clear that commercial speech does not merit full First Amendment protection, the *Central Hudson* Court nonetheless took a pragmatic view toward protecting commercial speech from unwarranted regulation. The Court stated that, even if advertising communicated an incomplete version of the relevant facts, the First Amendment presumes that some accurate information is better than no information at all.

The test that the *Central Hudson* Court articulated for evaluating whether a regulation of commercial speech is constitutional has four steps, to be followed in order:

1. *Illegality or misleading representations*: A court must determine whether the expression at issue is protected by the First Amendment. For commercial speech to come within that provision, the speech at least must concern lawful activity and not be misleading.
2. *Substantial government interest*: The court should ask whether the asserted governmental interest is substantial.
3. *Regulation direct advances interest*: If the answer to both of these previous inquiries is yes, then the court must determine whether the regulation directly advances the governmental interest asserted.
4. *No more extensive than necessary*: If the regulation directly advances the governmental interest asserted, then the regulation may be upheld so long as it is not more extensive than is necessary to serve that interest.

To survive this test and justify a regulation, the government must show EITHER that the advertisement is illegal or misleading (element 1) OR satisfies elements 2-4. If the advertisement is illegal or misleading, it is not protected by the First Amendment at all. If it does not satisfy that first element, then the First Amendment protects the advertisement, but the

9. Commercial Speech

Central Hudson Test

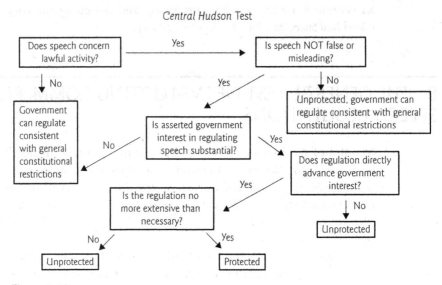

Figure 9-1*

government can comply with First Amendment restrictions by satisfying elements 2-4.

The regulation in *Central Hudson* was a ban on an electric utility's promotional advertising. The state's reason for the ban was concern that the advertising would increase demand and thereby undermine the need for fuel conservation. The ban stumbled at the last step of the *Central Hudson* four-part test. The Court accepted the connection between advertising and demand but concluded that the state could satisfy its conservation goal through less restrictive means of regulation.

A number of cases have come to the Supreme Court regarding illegality, or false and deceptive advertisements. Several involved circumstances in which the commercial entity was required to make a disclosure as a corrective for the wrongdoing and several have concerned action brought by the Federal Trade Commission. The Court has not, however, resolved many cases concerning an outright ban on advertising. In one such case, *Pittsburgh Press Co. v. Pittsburgh Commission on Human Relations*, 413 U.S. 376 (1973), the Court upheld a city Human Relations Commission's decision that a newspaper violated a city ordinance by running help-wanted ads in columns labeled "Jobs-Female Interest," "Jobs-Male Interest," and "Male-Female."

---

* Note regarding Figure 9-1: As explained later in this chapter, the U.S. Supreme Court has in subsequent decisions arguably changed the way in which the last step of the *Central Hudson* test is applied: shifting from evaluating whether the regulation provides the least restrictive means for achieving the government's goal in regulating the speech to evaluating whether the regulation is narrowly tailored to achieving that goal.

Despite the dearth of case law on the first step of the *Central Hudson* test, the Court has held that the First Amendment does not protect advertisements that bear the inherent risk of deception. The Court has found this risk present in upholding laws prohibiting professional organizations from practicing under a trade name. Recognizing that risk of deception that is present when lawyers solicit prospective clients in person, the Court has restricted that solicitation. The Court has reached an opposite conclusion on the laws restricting the ability of accountants to solicit prospective clients, noting that accountants are not "trained in the art of persuasion." *Edenfield v. Fane*, 507 U.S. 761, 775 (1993).

As the four-part test plays out in the case law, advertisements that are not false, deceptive, or promotions of illegal products tend to fail (if they do fail) the *Central Hudson* test on the basis of the third and/or fourth steps. Consider the following Example.

Example 9-5:

A group of licensed pharmacies which specialized in drug compounding prepared promotional materials that they wished to distribute by mail and at medical conferences. The goal of these promotional materials was to inform patients and physicians of the use and effectiveness of specific compounded drugs. Nevertheless, the pharmacies were concerned that they would be prosecuted under the Food and Drug Administration Modernization Act of 1997 (FDAMA). The FDAMA exempted certain drugs from the drug approval requirements of the Food and Drug Administration (FDA) so long as they abided by several restrictions. These restrictions included refraining from the advertisement or promotion of those drugs. The government maintained that this restriction was justified because it was supported by three substantial interests: (1) maintaining the integrity of the FDA's new drug approval process, (2) ensuring that individual patients who cannot use commercially available products approved by the FDA have access to effective pharmaceuticals, and (3) maintaining a proper balance between those two competing interests. The pharmacies challenged FDAMA, arguing that it constituted an unconstitutional restriction on the right to engage in commercial speech. Are they correct?

Explanation:

The pharmacists are correct: they have a valid First Amendment claim. This case exclusively concerns advertising and therefore is governed by the *Central Hudson* test. In *Thompson v. Western States Medical Center*, 535 U.S. 357 (2002), the Supreme Court evaluated circumstances similar to this case and ruled that the restriction did not pass that test. Because the restricted advertisements did not concern misleading information or promotion of unlawful activity, the government could not successfully defend the advertising prohibition under the first prong of *Central Hudson*. Although the government had proffered three interests that the prohibition was designed to serve, the Court scrutinized those interests and concluded that the government did not prove that the challenged regulation directly served those interests and failed to establish that the regulation was not "more extensive than necessary" to serve these interests.

Example 9-6:

Assume that you are a lawyer working for the Federal Trade Commission (FTC). FTC investigators have determined that a manufacturer of a fruit drink, Wonder Juice, made representations about the health effects of its product in advertisements that are unsubstantiated. The advertisements stated that Wonder Juice helped to address problems with heart disease, cancer, and erectile dysfunction.

The FTC is considering what type of corrective action to impose on the manufacturer to ensure that its representations are adequately substantiated, and has sought your advice. Specifically, the FTC decision makers are considering whether to issue an order requiring the manufacturer to undertake one or more randomized and controlled human clinical trials (RCTs) to test where human experience supports the claimed health benefits.

Evaluate whether the proposed action satisfies the *Central Hudson* test.

Explanation:

Applying the *Central Hudson* elements, one could argue that the advertisement's claims of health benefits made possible by Wonder Juice are sufficiently extravagant that they could be characterized as misleading given that the manufacturer had not substantiated the claims. The facts as stated in this Example, however, are sufficiently sketchy that this is only a tentative conclusion. It is therefore appropriate to include elements 2-4 in your analysis.

Element 2, requiring that the governmental interest is substantial, is satisfied. The Supreme Court has made clear that the governmental "interest in ensuring the accuracy of commercial information in the marketplace is substantial." *Edenfield v. Fane*, 507 U.S. 761, 769, (1993). The requirement of using the RCT procedure would be designed to ensure the accuracy of the information in the advertisements. Element 3, requiring that the restriction advance the governmental interest directly, is also satisfied in the likely event that the FTC can establish that experts in relevant fields use the RCT procedure as a means of testing the health benefits of various products.

9. Commercial Speech

Your advice on the number of RCT procedures to require, however, would be more complicated. Element 4 requires that the regulation imposed be no more extensive than necessary. In a case similar to this one, the U.S. Court of Appeals for the District of Columbia Circuit held that requiring "some" use of the RCT procedure satisfied this test, but that requiring two separate RCT studies was too extensive. *POM Wonderful, LLC v. FTC*, 777 F.3d 478 (2015). Accordingly, you would be prudent to advise the FTC decision makers to limit the order to one RCT study.

* * *

Recent Supreme Court cases sometimes invoke the fourth prong of the *Central Hudson* test (asking whether the "regulation is not more extensive than necessary") by using an analysis that appears to evaluate whether the regulation is the least restrictive means of achieving the goal. In contrast with the Supreme Court's recent articulation of the fourth prong of *Central Hudson* (whether the "regulation is not more extensive than necessary"), the Court has in the past sometimes looked instead to evaluating whether the regulation is "narrowly tailored to achieve the government's goal." Indeed, the Court in one case specifically repudiated the "least restrictive means" standard—calling it too strict for scrutinizing commercial speech—and instead endorsed the "narrowly tailored to achieve the government's goal" standard. *See Board of Trustees of the State University of N.Y. v. Fox*, 492 U.S. 469 (1989). The Court has been inconsistent about whether this change is permanent, producing a confusing array of opinions on the matter. *See, e.g., Liquormart, Inc. v. Rhode Island*, 517 U.S. 484, 507 (1996) (referring to the "not more restrictive than necessary" standard as though it should evaluate whether the government is using the least restrictive means to achieve its goal, but also evaluating whether a regulation of commercial speech establishes a "reasonable fit" between the abridgment of speech and the goal of the regulation. The preponderance of cases after *Fox*, however, have used the "narrowly tailored" language.

At bottom, however, one wonders how often the different wording can make a difference in the ultimate result in the case. The goal of switching to the narrowly tailored wording was to widen the possibility for upholding a regulation. But does the change in wording effectively make that shift? Is there really a meaningful practical distinction between a narrowly tailored requirement and the least restrictive alternative requirement? One is hard pressed to come up with a realistic scenario in which a regulation would not be the least restrictive option, but would be narrowly tailored. One point is certain: the Court has been signaling that the lower courts should approach regulations of commercial speech with a greater presumption of constitutionality than may have initially been thought.

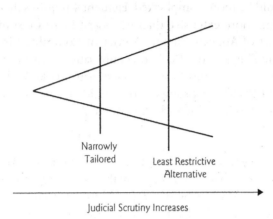

Standard for Commercial Speech

Figure 9-2

C. REGULATING COMMERCIAL SPEECH TO ADDRESS OTHER GOVERNMENT GOALS

Starting in the 1980s, the Court decided cases regarding regulations of speech promoting socially disapproved (although not illegal) activities and concluded that this commercial speech did not enjoy the same protections as commercial speech in other contexts. This led some to wonder whether the Supreme Court was creating an exception to First Amendment protection for promoting undesirable activities—a so-called "vice exception" to the commercial speech doctrine. During this period, the Court upheld outright prohibition on advertising for gambling, casinos, and lotteries. But the Court later switched its position when it came to alcohol advertisements, and issued an opinion rejecting any suggestion that legislatures should be given broader latitude to regulate speech that promotes socially harmful activities. *Rubin v. Coors Brewing Co.*, 514 U.S. 476 (1995).

Example 9-7:

After the U.S. Supreme Court handed down *Rubin v. Coors Brewing Co.*, a group of broadcasters decided they would challenge a law that placed certain restrictions on broadcast advertising of lotteries and casino gambling. The broadcasters from one state wished to advertise over the radio in states where casino gambling was legal. The Federal Communications Commission, however, prohibited this for two reasons: (1) to diminish the social costs of gambling; and (2) to avoid the risk that neighboring states would receive these broadcasts even though such gambling was illegal or severely restricted in those states.

The broadcasters filed suit, arguing that the federal regulation violated their First Amendment speech rights. Does the government satisfy each step of the *Central Hudson* test? If not, which step or steps does the government fail to establish?

Explanation:

No, the government will not prevail, and the broadcasters will win their First Amendment challenge. In *Greater New Orleans Broadcasting Association, Inc. v. United States*, 527 U.S. 173 (1999), the Court considered a regulation similar to the regulation in this Example and found it unconstitutional under the *Central Hudson* test. The Federal Communications Commission asserted that the regulations were designed to serve two interests: reducing the social costs of gambling and assisting states in restricting gambling within their own borders. The Court accepted that these interests could be considered substantial for the purpose of the *Central Hudson* test.

The *Greater New Orleans Broadcasting* Court nonetheless found the regulations unconstitutional under the third and fourth steps of the test. As for the third step—whether the regulation directly advances the government interest—the Court emphasized that the government needed to show that "the harms it recites are real and that its restriction will in fact alleviate them to a material degree." *Id.* at 188 (internal quotation marks omitted). The Court concluded that the government failed to do so.

In applying the fourth element of the *Central Hudson* evaluation, whether the test restriction is no more extensive than necessary, the Court reiterated the change in approach articulated by the *Fox* case:

> The fourth part of the test complements the direct-advancement inquiry of the third, asking whether the speech restriction is not more extensive than necessary to serve the interests that support it. The Government is not required to employ the least restrictive means conceivable, but it must demonstrate narrow tailoring of the challenged regulation to the asserted interest—a fit that is not necessarily perfect, but reasonable; that represents not necessarily the single best disposition but one whose scope is in proportion to the interest served.

Id. (internal quotations omitted). Applying this test, the Court concluded that the government did not successfully connect casino broadcast advertising with casino gambling and compulsive gambling. Given that the Court's motive for switching to the narrowly tailoring standard was to lower the scrutiny of commercial speech regulations, the *Greater New Orleans Broadcasting* would surely have struck down the regulation using a least restrictive means approach.

* * *

9. Commercial Speech

Cases before *Rubin v. Coors Brewing Co.* and *Greater New Orleans Broadcasting* suggested that a substantial government interest in discouraging behaviors deemed injurious to public health and morals could justify restrictions on speech advertising as opportunity to indulge in those behaviors. The Court in *Greater New Orleans Broadcasting* explicitly rejected this concept, reasoning that government's power to regulate particular conduct does not necessarily include the power to regulate speech about that conduct. What does this mean for government regulations of advertisements for other types of potentially harmful behaviors, which government may attempt to regulate? Consider the following Example.

Example 9-8:

A state decides to regulate smokeless tobacco advertising at a time when no federal regulation of the product existed. Seeking to protect children from seeing smokeless tobacco advertisements, the state passed a law prohibiting any outdoor advertising of smokeless tobacco within 1,000 feet of a school or playground. The smokeless tobacco manufacturers challenged this law as a violation of the First Amendment. Are they correct that the state law is unconstitutional?

Explanation:

Yes, the smokeless manufacturers are correct. The U.S. Supreme Court evaluated a state law similar to this in *Lorillard Tobacco Co. v. Reilly*, 533 U.S. 525 (2001), holding that the outside advertising regulation of smokeless tobacco was unconstitutional. The parties did not contest that the first two steps of the *Central Hudson* were satisfied: the advertising was not false or misleading and preventing minors from using smokeless tobacco is an important and substantial goal. The Court also concluded that that the state had adequately documented the conclusion that the advertising restriction directly and materially advanced the goal of preventing underage smokeless tobacco use. A majority of the justices concluded, however, that regulations were not sufficiently narrowly tailored to satisfy the government interest. For example, the restrictions were not calibrated to the specific characteristics of different geographical areas, some of which were configured in such a way as to prevent any advertising at all if the advertisers complied with the 1,000-feet specification. Likewise, the Court concluded that the restriction on all signs of any size was ill-suited to the government's purpose of targeting signs visible to children. For these reasons, the Court held the advertising restrictions unconstitutional.

* * *

9. Commercial Speech

In striking down the smokeless tobacco restrictions in *Lorillard*, the Supreme Court stated the following:

> We must consider that tobacco retailers and manufacturers have an interest in conveying truthful information about their products to adults, and adults have a corresponding interest in receiving truthful information about [these] products. In a case involving indecent speech on the Internet we explained that "the governmental interest in protecting children from harmful materials . . . does not justify an unnecessarily broad suppression of speech addressed to adults."

Id. at 564. This language is reminiscent of the point made in *Greater New Orleans Broadcasting* that disentangled a government's legitimate and substantial interest in discouraging certain conduct from the constitutionality of restrictions of advertisements concerning that conduct. This approach may have ramifications for other specialized commercial speech areas of First Amendment doctrine, including regulation of advertising regarding the service of lawyers, accountants, and other professionals as well as abortion and contraceptives.

CHAPTER 10

Defamation and Related Torts

Under common law, plaintiffs enjoyed generous options when harmed by false statements about them. They could succeed in recovering damages without showing that the false statements were made deliberately or negligently. Available damages were also quite favorable. The result, of course, was that speakers who wrote or spoke unfavorably about anyone did so at their potential peril.

Prior to the last century, the relation of these defamation rules to the Constitution received little attention. Significant historical controversy did arise, however, from the Sedition Act of 1798. The Sedition Act made it a crime to print "false, scandalous, and malicious writing" about the government. The Federalist Party used the Act against its opponents, who in turn pushed back, arguing that the Act violated the First Amendment. Although the U.S. Supreme Court never ruled on the constitutionality of the Sedition Act, the general sense in the country was the Act violated the spirit of the new Constitution and Bill of Rights. Once the Federalist Party lost the White House, the Act no longer served as a weapon in political wars. As Justice Brennan once declared: "Although the Sedition Act was never tested in this Court, the attack upon its validity has carried the day in the court of history." *New York Times v. Sullivan*, 376 U.S. 254, 276 (1964).

For the next 150 years or so, the notion that First Amendment principles restricted the reach of defamation laws fell into disfavor. The generally accepted view was that defamation was not within the purview of the free speech protections: defamatory speech was unprotected. As a consequence, states had full latitude to regulate defamation claims as they wished. Defamation was generally defined then, as it is now, to include a communication by the defendant: (1) that tends to blacken the reputation of the plaintiff in the community; (2) that is "of and concerning" the plaintiff; and (3) that was published to at least one party other than the plaintiff and the defendant. In large part, however, the specific details about the conduct of defamation litigation were quite plaintiff-friendly. Significantly, the standard of care attached to the traditional defamation standard was the ordinary negligence standard of a reasonable person acting with reasonable care, no matter the circumstances or the identity of the plaintiff.

Matters changed dramatically, however, in 1964. Perhaps more than any other area of First Amendment law, current principles governing the First Amendment's relationship with defamation and other torts have their genesis in a constitutional thunderbolt issued by the United States Supreme Court in *New York Times v. Sullivan*. The decision was very much a creature of its times. The case focused on an advertisement in the *New York Times* stating that non-violent civil rights demonstrations against segregation in the South were encountering a "wave of terror" from officials there. The plaintiff in the case, L.B. Sullivan, was not named in the advertisement, but claimed that its description of police conduct negatively reflected on him as the administrator of the Montgomery Alabama police. As such, the dispute was not only an outgrowth of the civil rights movement in the 1960s, but was also evidence of efforts by Southern officials to use state defamation law to discourage northern newspapers from covering attempts to quell civil rights demonstrations.

In mapping an entirely new category of First Amendment principles, the *Sullivan* Court proclaimed "a profound national commitment to the principle that debate on public issues should be uninhibited, robust, and wide-open, and that it may well include vehement, caustic, and sometimes unpleasantly sharp attacks on government and public officials." *Id.* at 270. Specifically, *Sullivan* reversed a large judgment against a public official, holding that the First Amendment requires proof of a heightened standard of care in order for a public official to successfully recover for defamation. More precisely, *Sullivan* ruled that the First Amendment prohibits "a public official from recovering damages for a defamatory falsehood relating to his official conduct unless he proves that the statement was made with 'actual malice'—that is, with knowledge that it was false or with reckless disregard of whether it was false or not." *Id.* at 279-280.

The Court has handed down several cases parsing out the various aspects of this holding and expounded on the definitions of a "public official," "defamatory falsehood," and "actual malice." The Court has also expanded the rule and spirit of *Sullivan* to include public figures, limited-purpose public figures, and certain private persons as well. Indeed, most of the current rules governing defamation actions turn on the identity of the plaintiff: public official, public figure, or private person. Finally, the Court has extended *Sullivan* —along with its refinements—into other tort suits, including suits seeking damages for intentional infliction of emotional distress, false light, and disclosing private facts. The rest of this chapter will review each of these matters.

A. DEFAMATION ACTIONS BY PUBLIC OFFICIALS

1. Who Is a Public Official?

A prime motivation behind *Sullivan* was to ensure robust debate regarding the performance of public officials. This highlights the importance of pinning down precisely who is a public official. While the *Sullivan* Court made clear that not every public employee is a public official, the Court declined "to determine how far down into the lower ranks of government employees the 'public official' designation would extend . . . ." Id. at 283 n.23.

The Court took up the task of describing the contours of the public official designation in *Rosenblatt v. Baer*, 383 U.S. 75, 85 (1966), explaining that the label designation applies to "those among the hierarchy of government employees who have, or appear to the public to have, substantial responsibility for or control over the conduct of governmental affairs." Id. at 85. The Court also characterized a public official as one who "would invite public scrutiny and discussion of the person holding it, entirely apart from the scrutiny and discussion occasioned by the particular charges in controversy." Id. at 86 n.13. Likewise, a public official's position "has such apparent importance that the public has an independent interest in the qualifications and performance of the person who holds it, beyond the general public interest in the qualifications and performance of all government employees . . . ." Id. at 86. Helpfully, the *Rosenblatt* Court gave the example of a "night watchman accused of stealing state secrets" as a non-public official for whom "society's interest in protecting reputation" superseded constitutional concerns. Id. at 86 n.13.

Example 10-1:

A Secret Service agent who served as the Special-Agent-in-Charge of the Secret Service detail that protects the President brought a defamation claim against a radio station for its incorrect assertion regarding his sexual orientation. The radio station moved to dismiss the suit, arguing that the Secret Service agent was a public official for the purpose of *Sullivan* and that the agent had not alleged actual malice. The Secret Service agent argued that he was not a public official since he had never been a subject of large-scale public discussion before the radio broadcast. Is the Secret Service agent a public official for the purposes of this defamation case?

Explanation:

Yes, the Secret Service agent is a public official according to the *Sullivan* approach. First, he is a law enforcement officer, an occupation that weighs heavily in favor of his status as a public official, since law enforcement officers generally possess the *Rosenblatt* attribute of "substantial responsibility for or control over the conduct of governmental affairs." And as the special agent in charge of the President's security detail, the plaintiff had to "make judgment calls and split-second decisions" and was "authorized to use whatever force is necessary" to protect the President. This is an important duty in the public interest not only because it is crucial to the government interest and national security, but also because it empowers the Secret Service agent to infringe individual freedom. These are both clearly matters of great concern to the public.

Of course, one might reasonably point out that the agent's sexual orientation is irrelevant to his authority in matters of public concern. That observation, however, does not change the effect of his public official status. Once a court concludes that he holds that status, the *Sullivan* actual malice standard will apply to his defamation suit. *See Buendorf v. National Public Radio, Inc.*, 822 F. Supp. 6 (D.D.C. 1993).

Example 10-2:

A newspaper reported on a contentious child custody dispute between a local assistant prosecutor and his ex-wife. The article included descriptions of claims that the assistant prosecutor had abused the child. The assistant prosecutor brings a claim for defamation against the newspaper. The newspaper moved to dismiss the suit, arguing that the assistant prosecutor was a public official who could not establish actual malice. The assistant prosecutor countered that he is a new hire at the prosecutor's office, only assists in prosecuting minor crimes, has only second chaired a trial once, and has been directed to relay any press inquiries to a supervisor. He also argued that he does not create or direct policy in the office and has no significant input on how the prosecutor's office is run. Is this entry-level prosecutor a public official?

Explanation:

This is a close case, but the chances are good that the assistant prosecutor is a public official. The office he holds carries with it substantial decision-making authority regarding how to litigate particular cases and whether to pursue particular prosecutions. As such, he exercises governmental authority over matters in which the public has substantial interest. The assistant prosecutor's personal conduct may bear on his character and ability to exercise that authority appropriately. For that reason, he accepted some loss of his privacy in taking on the position as an assistant prosecutor. The prosecutor has the power to pursue a process by which an individual ultimately can become labeled a convicted criminal. One might argue that—in exercising that power—the prosecutor has also taken the risk of losing a defamation suit in instances when he is unable to prove that the defendant acted with actual malice.

On the other hand, the assistant prosecutor appears to have limited, if any, access to the media within the context of his duties, which is a factor relevant to whether he is a public official. He has also enjoyed only restricted responsibility in the job (either because of his entry level status or his personal proclivities). These two limitations, however, do not necessarily overshadow the generally accepted characterization of prosecutors—even assistant prosecutors—as public officials. See Mandel v. Boston Phoenix, Inc., 456 F.3d 198 (1st Cir. 2006).

Example 10-3:

In the town of Championville, high school basketball is a highly visible activity to the public and a widespread, cross-section of the community attends the school games. The local newspaper covers each game in detail, and frequently interviews the coach. The public high school team is highly ranked in the state, having won several recent state-wide championships. This has enhanced community pride and may have even increased real estate values in Championville.

The public high school team is coached by a man whose exclusive role in the school is coaching basketball: he does not teach in a classroom or otherwise participate in the school's educational mission. A group of parents told the local newspapers that the coach routinely mistreated his players.

The coach filed a defamation action against the parents' group and the newspaper. The defendants argued that the basketball coach is a public official, a status the coach denies. Is this public high school basketball coach a public official?

Explanation:

Although the answer to this question is not clear cut, the coach is probably not a public official. The coach's duties do not relate to a core government function and are only tangential to the operation of government and to the delivery of essential services to the public. The coach does not wield much power over the implementation of educational policy, which may hold significant public concern for which citizens may have strong theoretical, moral, and ideological differences. Moreover, strong arguments could be made that the coach's decision to take his position did not include his embrace of the possibility that he may be subject to negligently communicated defamation for which he would have no legal recourse.

Countervailing arguments are present, however. The allegation that the coach mistreated high school players is a matter that the public may reasonably find of great concern. The situation would be different if the criticism focused on his judgments about game strategy or the color of the high school team jerseys. To be sure, the coach's team and its performance is an integral part of the social fabric of the community and sparks deep passions and opinions among some community members. Moreover, the keen public interest in the team makes possible the coach's easy access to the media. One could argues that the heightened public interest in a person's job and decision making render it more likely that the person should be deemed an official who holds authority on sensitive matters.

But—at bottom—the coach's role is ancillary to the core educational function of the school—a matter for which the coach has no decision-making authority. From this point of view, he may be even less of a "public official" than a front-line high school classroom teacher—an occupation that many courts have refused to designate as public officials. *McGuire v. Bowlin*, 932 N.W.2d 819, 825 (Minn. 2019) (concluding that a high school basketball coach is not a public official and stating that "basketball is not fundamental to democracy").

* * *

Lower courts are not uniform on whether public school teachers are public officials. The same is true on the question of whether public school principals are public officials. *Compare, e.g., Palmer v. Bennington School District, Inc.*, 615 A.2d 498 (Vt. 1992) (holding principal is a public official), with, e.g., *Beeching v. Levee*, 764 N.E.2d 669 (Ind. Ct. App. 2002) (holding principal is not a public official). *See also Johnson v. Robbinsdale Independent School District No. 281*, 827 F. Supp. 1439, 1442-1443 (D. Minn. 1993) (collecting cases regarding whether school principals are public officials and concluding that "[t]he division among courts appears to be based on differing perspectives concerning whether education is an important aspect of government and the responsibility for and control principals have over public education").

Although the high school basketball coach in Example 10-3 is likely not a public official, his role in the community and access to media may qualify him to be a public figure or limited public figure. These statuses are relevant to whether the defendants in the dispute would get the benefit of the *Sullivan* standard of culpability, a matter discussed later in this chapter.

2. What Is a Defamatory Falsehood?

The *Sullivan* actual malice standard applies in circumstances when the plaintiff alleges to have been defamed by the defendant. In other words, the standard applies in only those instances when the defendant has uttered a false statement of fact about the defendant. According to the U.S. Supreme Court, this requires that the defendant communicated "a statement . . . [that is] provably false . . . ." *Milkovich v. Lorain Journal Co.*, 497 U.S. 1, 20 (1990).

In following this instruction, lower courts sometimes have a devil of a time figuring out what qualifies as a statement that is provably false. To make this determination, a court must conclude that the challenged statement attempts to assert something that appears factual. If, on the other hand, the statement expresses a mere personal opinion, then it is not capable of being proven true or false. Although the Supreme Court has not designated this process as a fact/opinion dichotomy, many lower courts have treated it as such. Despite the confusion over what is a fact and what is an opinion, there appears to be consensus on one point: one cannot avoid defamation liability by simply saying "this is just a matter of my opinion." The question whether something is an opinion protected by the First Amendment is informed by legal principles and is not under the control of the speaker.

The Supreme Court has provided some additional guidance on the issue. For example, the Court has explained that a "rhetorical hyperbole" or a "vigorous epithet" do not qualify as factual assertions. *Greenbelt Cooperative Publishing Ass'n v. Bressler*, 398 U.S. 6, 14 (1970) (concluding that newspaper description of activity as "blackmail" was not a factual assertion). The Supreme Court also commented on the matter in *Hustler v. Falwell*, 485 U.S. 46 (1988), a decision discussed in detail later in this chapter. Evaluating the constitutional implication of a tort action asserting damages arising from a parody, the Court found determinative that the parody at issue in the case could not reasonably have been interpreted as asserting "actual facts about [the plaintiff] or actual events in which [the plaintiff] participated." *Id.* at 57.

Example 10-4:

A teenage boy got into a car accident, totaling the car. In the hours after the accident, the teenager began behaving erratically, started drinking, and ultimately died by suicide. The boy's parents believed that his suicide was the result of a traumatic brain injury that occurred in the accident. The boy's parents wrote an obituary where they described his death as "the result of a fatal car accident." They did not mention the suicide, deciding that they would prefer not to announce that to the general public.

A month later, a columnist in the local newspaper wrote a column expressing the view that it is immoral to "cover up" suicides of young men because that practice assures that the problem will not be properly addressed. Although the columnist never mentioned the teenage boy by name, the columnist quoted his obituary and mentioned that he died from suicide, which was not mentioned in the original obituary (although it was a matter of public record). The parents of the teenage boy sued the columnist for defamation. Was the columnist's suggestion that there was a "cover up" of the boy's suicide an assertion of fact for the purposes of the *Sullivan* standard?

Explanation:

This Example presents a close call. As an initial matter, the question arises whether a report that the parents wished to keep the cause of death private was defamatory. To be defamatory, a statement must tend to blacken their reputation in the community. Is not it an understandable sentiment for parents not to want to disclose that their child died by suicide? Nonetheless, the expression "cover up" is a highly charged term that carries with it the connotations that willful actions were taken to conceal something. The existence of willful actions and the intention to conceal are matters that can be proven as true or false. To the extent that the word "cover up" also suggest that either the circumstances of the death or the parents' subsequent actions were connected with criminal activity, that insinuation would clearly tend to blacken reputations and could also be proven true or false. Assuming these readings of the column are correct, defamation liability could attach if no willful actions were taken to conceal the suicide and no criminal activity was involved.

If, on the other hand, the statement "cover up" is interpreted as opinion or mere hyperbole, then the expression is deemed incapable of being proven as false. In a case with facts similar to the Example, the Supreme Court of Texas concluded that a similar reference in a column was opinion, and not verifiable as true or false. *Dallas Morning News, Inc. v. Tatum*, 554 S.W.3d 614 (Tex. 2018), *reh'g denied*, 2018 Tex. LEXIS 972 (Sept. 28, 2018), *cert. denied*, 139 S. Ct. 1216 (2019). Pointing out that *Milkovich* requires courts to consider the "entire context" in which an offending statement appears, the *Dallas Morning* court said that even when a single statement is verifiable as false, it does not give rise to liability if the "entire context" in which the statement appears reveals that the statement was merely an opinion masquerading as fact. *Id.* at 639. The court reasoned that, given the opinionated thrust of the column in suit, the context made clear that any implied accusation of deception or concealment on the part of the parents was no more than opinion.

Example 10-5:

A singer was arrested in a public restroom for obscene and harassing behavior. A few months later, the singer released a song and music video that referenced the incident. While promoting the song, the singer said in several televised interviews that the police officer who arrested him incited him into the behavior by performing lewd acts himself. The police officer sued the singer for slander. The officer said that the only "act" that he performed during the incident in the restroom was arresting the singer. He alleged that the singer's account of the incident was false. Was the singer's recounting of the arrest during the interviews his opinion of the incident or a statement of verifiable fact?

Explanation:

The statement "perform a lewd act himself" is probably a verifiable fact. Although the words "lewd act" are indistinct and arguably reflect a personal characterization, the words suggest that the officer took definite actions that one could describe in unsavory terms. One could prove whether or not the officer took the action. Accordingly, the statement is capable of being proved false. *See Rodriguez v. Panayiotou*, 314 F.3d 979 (9th Cir. 2002).

3. WHAT CONSTITUTES ACTUAL MALICE?

A public official suing for defamation must show with clear and convincing evidence that the defendant made the statement with actual malice. This standard has nothing to do with the concept of "malice" as it is normally understood. Rather the standard requires that the defendant make a statement with a "high degree of awareness of [its] probable falsity . . . ." *Garrison v. Louisiana*, 379 U.S. 64, 74 (1964). In *St. Amant v. Thompson*, 390 U.S. 727 (1968), the Supreme Court explained that this means that sufficient evidence is required to show that "the defendant in fact entertained serious doubts as to the truth of [her] publication." *Id.* at 731. Proving a defendant's mental awareness of a fact or possible fact imposes a tough burden. But plaintiffs can establish actual malice through a sufficient showing of objective evidence, which is evidence demonstrating that the defendant *should have* known the statement's falsity. This "should have known" evidence can be probative of whether the defendant had actual subjective knowledge of the statement's falsity. Mere negligence in failing to take extra steps to confirm the truth of a statement or failure to follow professional standards (journalistic standards or others) is not enough to establish actual malice.

The *St. Amant* Court offered three examples of scenarios in which actual malice may be properly inferred: (1) "where a story is fabricated by the defendant, is the product of his imagination, or is based wholly on an unverified anonymous telephone call;" (2) "when the publisher's allegations are so inherently improbable that only a reckless man would have put them in circulation;" and (3) "where there are obvious reasons to doubt the veracity of the informant or the accuracy of his reports." *Id.* at 732.

Example 10-6:

A newspaper ran a story that alleged a local judicial candidate bribed a grand jury witness into providing information about an investigation into his opponent. The newspaper, who had endorsed the opponent, relied largely on an interview with a grand jury witness who said that the candidate had engaged in "dirty tricks" and had offered her a job and a trip to Florida in exchange for assistance with the investigation into the incumbent judge. In her interview, the grand jury witness spoke in a hesitant, inaudible, and sometimes unresponsive tone, often looking away from both the reporter and the camera. The newspaper interviewed the candidate about his alleged bribery, and the candidate denied the claims. The candidate provided the newspaper with a videotape of the witness's sister explaining that there had been no bribery or other misconduct. In further investigations, four more people denied the newspaper's claim. There was also credible evidence that the newspaper neither reviewed the videotape, nor tried to contact the witness's sister, nor tried to contact others who may have had knowledge of the events. Does the judicial candidate have sufficient evidence of the newspaper's actual malice?

Explanation:

The judicial candidate may have enough evidence to establish actual malice. If the newspaper were simply careless or unprofessional, that would not be enough to establish actual malice. But the evidence suggests the possibility that the newspaper was skeptical of the truth but avoided further investigation because it wanted to publish the story. That skepticism is still not sufficient to establish clear and convincing evidence of actual malice. Nonetheless, if the newspaper was aware of facts tending to discredit the grand jury witness informant and failed to pursue obvious leads to further establish the informant's veracity, the candidate may have enough to establish actual malice, particularly because the newspaper had a motive to cut corners in order to publish the story: the newspaper had already made known its support for the candidate's opponent. See *Harte-Hanks Communications, Inc. v. Connaughton*, 491 U.S. 657 (1989), in which the Court ruled that similar evidence showing that a speaker purposefully avoided learning the truth may be enough to show actual malice.

Example 10-7:

In the midst of a vicious state senatorial campaign, Carly Candidate approved and aired an advertisement that alleged that Paul Plaintiff, her opponent, had sold reportedly dangerous drugs to children when he was employed by a pharmaceutical company. For confirming this proposition, Carly relied on the research supplied to her by a veteran political operative who was versed in using opposition research. While it was true that Paul had worked for a company that had marketed sleeping aid medications to children, and that the company was publicly criticized for unethical sales tactics, Paul was only involved with the company's diabetes drug division. Carly and Paul had a hostile relationship with one another.

Carly was concerned about the advertisement because she wondered whether it was strategically appropriate to run an advertisement with such a negative, oppositional tone. She decided to test Paul's reaction to the advertisement before airing it. After viewing a copy of the advertisement before it aired, Paul denied the advertisement's allegation and demanded that Carly pull it before putting it on the air. Carly refused and aired the advertisement.

Does Paul have sufficient evidence that Carly acted with actual malice?

Explanation:

This is a close case on whether Paul has sufficient evidence of actual malice. While the evidence reflected that she had doubts about airing the advertisements, Carly's doubts were focused on its negative, attacking tone and did not appear to stem from doubts about its accuracy. The facts do not show that the opposition research the candidate reviewed was so unreliable as to be unworthy of credence and thus her use of the evidence did not establish reckless disregard for the truth. While Carly's animosity toward Paul might be circumstantially probative of a motive to turn a blind eye to the possibility of the falsity of the advertisement, it was insufficient on its own to show actual malice by clear and convincing evidence. Furthermore, Paul's vehement denial of the truth of advertisement after the fact did not put Carly on notice of its falsity, given his combative relationship with Carly and his self-interest in denying the claim. Finally, the high-speed nature of political campaigning helps to explain why Carly may not have made further efforts to confirm the advertisement's veracity. That being said, being in a rush could be relevant to establishing reckless disregard of the truth. Attack ads often contain either blatant "half-truths" or are designed to suggest facts that are false. Given that context, one could argue that Carly should have detected the possibility of a false suggestion and asked follow up questions of the individual who created the ad. But cf. Bertrand v. Mullin, 846 N.W.2d 884 (Iowa 2014) (finding no actual malice under similar circumstances).

B. DEFAMATION ACTIONS BY PUBLIC FIGURES AND LIMITED-PURPOSE PUBLIC FIGURES

The U.S. Supreme Court has extended the approach of New York Times v. Sullivan beyond the context of defamation action by public officials. The Court has applied the *Sullivan* test in defamation actions brought by public figures and limited purpose public figures. This section explores the parameters of these two specifications. The Court has also applied the *Sullivan* approach in other types of tort actions, a matter discussed later in this chapter. In all these new and additional contexts, the Supreme Court has required the actual malice standard.

The Supreme Court extended *Sullivan*'s holding to cases involving public figures who bring defamation actions not long after the *Sullivan* decision. *Curtis Publishing Co. v. Butts*, 388 U.S. 130 (1967). The Court's *Curtis Publishing* decision actually joined together two actions, one brought by the athletic director and former coach at University of Georgia and the other brought by a former Army general who had gained notoriety by virtue of his political activism. Both men had thrust themselves into the public light and gained prominence in separate spheres. The *Curtis* Court not only extended the *Sullivan* holding to public figures like these men, but also embossed on public figure suits all of *Sullivan*'s procedural safeguards, such as requiring the plaintiff to prove actual malice by clear and convincing evidence and requiring the plaintiff to bear the burden of proving the falsity of the defamatory communication.

What *Curtis* left imprecise, however, was the parameters of who is and who is not a public figure. Lower courts have struggled with this issue — with one court even lamenting that finding a precise definition of a public figure "is much like trying to nail a jellyfish to the wall." *Rosanova v. Playboy Enterprises, Inc.*, 411 F. Supp. 440, 443 (S.D. Ga.1976).

The Supreme Court did, however, provide useful guidance on the meaning of "public figure" in *Gertz v. Welch*, 418 U.S. 323 (1974). In *Gertz*, the Court explained that public figures are treated like public officials because they have access to the media and have assumed the risk of additional publicity through their involvement in public affairs. At least one of these two rationales must be implicated in a case in order for the defendant to be treated as a public figure. Otherwise, the *Gertz* Court explained, society has a weightier interest in allowing individuals to vindicate their reputations through defamation claims based on mere negligence, than any interest it has in imposing a more difficult standard of fault for the plaintiff to establish.

According to *Gertz*, individuals who are public figures for all purposes — which the Court dubbed "all-purpose" public figures — must show actual malice in all defamation suits. All-purpose public figures are those who have "assumed roles of special prominence in the affairs of society" and have thus achieved "pervasive fame or notoriety . . . ." *Id.* at 354, 351. Although generally limited only to individuals who have achieved celebrity status, certain types of public figures — such as candidates for elected office and criminal defendants accused of hei-nous crimes — have also been deemed public figures for all purposes.[1] (Note that a candidate for public office who is not currently holding public office is not a public official, but is generally regarded as a public figure).

Gertz also recognized a category of defamation plaintiff that is a pub-lic figure for a limited purpose. Sometimes called "vortex" public figures, limited-purpose public figures are individuals who "have thrust them-selves to the forefront of particular public controversies in order to influ-ence the resolution of the issues involved," and thus "invite attention and comment." Id. at 345. How does the limited-purpose public figure desig-nation work? In those instances when the subject of the defamation relates to what made the person enter the public eye, the actual malice standard of liability applies.

Three post-*Gertz* cases provide guideposts that help narrow and define the limited-purpose public figure category. In *Time, Inc. v. Firestone*, 424 U.S. 448 (1976), the Supreme Court held that a woman did not become a limited-purpose public figure through her participation in a vigor-ously contested divorce because her act of filing for divorce could not be viewed as voluntarily interjecting herself into a public controversy. In *Wolston v. Reader's Digest Association, Inc.*, 443 U.S. 157, 166 (1979), the Court determined that a private figure did not become a limited-purpose public figure by ignoring a grand jury subpoena. Under these circumstances, the private figure was not transformed into a public figure for the pur-poses of media coverage of the grand jury investigation because he was unwillingly injected into the controversy. Finally, in *Hutchinson v. Proxmire*, 443 U.S. 111 (1979), the Court held that a research scientist did not become a limited-purpose public figure by virtue of receiving federal grant funding.

The case law discloses no one set of variables that courts apply in con-sidering whether an individual is a limited-purpose public figure. The most important factors tend to center on (1) whether the plaintiffs voluntarily interjected themselves into a public controversy, (2) the plaintiff's level of involvement in that controversy, and (3) whether the controversy existed before the defamatory speech in question. This latter factor derives from

---

1. *See, e.g., Ray v. Time, Inc.*, 452 F. Supp. 618 (W.D. Tenn. 1976), *aff'd*, 582 F.2d 1280 (6th Cir. 1978) (James Earl Ray, Dr. Martin Luther King's assassin); *Williams v. Pasma*, 656 P.2d 212 (Mont. 1982) (candidate for U.S. Senate); *see also* Rodney A. Smolla, § 2:58. *Examples of Limited Public Figures—Candidates for Public Office*, 1 LAW OF DEFAMATION (2d ed. 2020); Rodney A. Smolla, § 2:90. *Examples of All Purpose Public Figures—Persons Associated with Criminal Activity*, 1 LAW OF DEFAMATION (2d ed. 2020).

concern that the plaintiff should not be boot-strapped into a limited-person public figure status by virtue of a controversy that they did not start. Other factors that courts often consider include the degree of public divisiveness concerning the controversy, the plaintiff's prominence in the controversy, and the extent to which the controversial speech was geographically or institutionally limited to the area in which the plaintiff became known in the public sphere.

Within the limited-purpose public figure determination, courts have expressed uncertainty over whether and when an individual may become an "involuntary" public figure, which is someone who is thrust into the spotlight of a public controversy unwillingly. *Gertz* addressed this scenario specifically: "[I]t may be possible for someone to become a public figure through no purposeful action of his own, but the instances of truly involuntary public figures must be exceedingly rare." *Gertz*, 418 U.S. at 345. It is difficult to evaluate how seriously to take the "involuntary" public figure determination given the extensive discussion in the limited-person public figure cases about whether the plaintiff willfully injected themselves into a controversy.

Example 10-8:

Pierce Plaintiff is an investment banker who has been the best friend of the former President of the United States for a long time. Pierce became well-known among the American public during the time the President was in office. Pierce served as the President's personal financial advisor during the President's time in office and continues to serve in that capacity now. Pierce also became well known for managing the President's re-election campaign. Pierce's relationship with the President was explored in-depth through the news media's coverage of various scandals that the President was involved in during his time in office. Pierce continues to be a "household name" in the United States as a consequence of his entanglement with the President.

In a transaction unrelated to his relationship with the President, Pierce has become enmeshed in a real estate deal that is the subject of a law enforcement investigation. A newspaper ran a story about Pierce's involvement with the real estate deal, and Pierce brought a defamation suit against the newspaper, claiming the story contained false representations of fact. The newspaper argued that Pierce is a public figure and that the actual malice standard applies. Pierce acknowledged that he may be a limited-purpose public figure for matters connected with the President, but argued that he does not hold that status for matters unrelated to his relationship to the President and thus the standard would not apply to the real estate matter that is the subject of his suit. Is Pierce correct?

Explanation:

Pierce is correct that if he is a limited-purpose public figure, that status would not control this lawsuit because the article concerns a matter not connected to the President. Yet it appears that Pierce is an all-purpose public figure, meaning that he must show actual malice for all defamation suits he files on his own behalf. Pierce has achieved lasting fame and notoriety as a result of his relationship with the President, which continues to the present day. Because Pierce played such a visible role in managing the President's re-election campaign and the President's affairs, he voluntarily exposed himself to public scrutiny. As a consequence of his interactions with the President—which continue to the current day—Pierce has enjoyed significant access to the media. Pierce's continued media access is an important factor supporting his current status as an all-purpose public figure. *Rebozo v. Washington Post Co.*, 637 F.2d 375 (5th Cir. 1981). *But see Lawrence v. Moss*, 639 F.2d 634 (10th Cir. 1981), in which the Tenth Circuit held that a "bag man" to Vice President Spiro Agnew who had also served in various government and electioneering roles was a private figure.

Example 10-9:

Mai is a local television reporter, who has won four Emmy awards and is widely known throughout her metropolitan area and in national journalism professional circles. One of her best-known investigative stories concerned the unsolved case of a missing woman. The case has not been solved so the investigation continues. Mai made a series of on-the-air updates about her own investigation of the woman's disappearance. Apparently, the missing woman's husband served as an unnamed source for Mai.

A blogger wrote a commentary about Mai's association with the woman's husband, suggesting that Mai conducted the relationship with the man in an unprofessional manner. The blogger accompanied the commentary with video footage of Mai and Mai's children swimming in the husband's pool. Mai filed a defamation suit against the blogger. The blogger maintained that Mai is an all-purpose public figure. Is the blogger correct?

Explanation:

The blogger may not be correct in asserting that Mai is an all-purpose public figure. She likely lacks the pervasive fame necessary for that status, particularly because she is known only by viewers in her local area who frequently tune into her channel to get their news. Nonetheless, Mai is likely a limited-purpose public figure for the purpose of the investigative story about the missing woman. The blogger's commentary on Mai's relationship with the missing woman's husband is connected with Mai's limited notoriety, which arises in part from Mai's ongoing investigative coverage of the missing woman. As a consequence, Mai will need to establish the actual malice standard for the purpose of the defamation suit relating to the offending blog. *See Jacobson v. CBS Broadcasting, Inc.*, 19 N.E.3d 1165 (Ill. App. 2014).

Example 10-10:

A television talk show host tweeted a photo of a city council meeting in which a white woman named Pamela was seemingly shouting at a Latino boy. The talk show host added a caption to the tweet that suggested Pamela was saying, "You are going to be the first deported" . . . "dirty Mexican!" In truth, Pamela did not say that, and the conversation was apparently civil.

Pamela filed a defamation action against the talk show host. The talk show host claimed that Pamela was a limited-purpose public figure because she frequently attends city council meetings, about as much as eight times in the last four years. When she attended the meetings, she spoke, giving her opinion at those meeting on various matters unconnected with immigration policy. The talk show host also pointed to the interview that Pamela gave to a newspaper regarding the talk show host's tweet. The newspaper had reached out to Pamela in order to report Pamela's side of the story regarding the tweet. In that interview, Pamela defended herself, stating that she did not say the words quoted in the tweet.

Is the talk show host correct that Pamela is a limited-purpose public figure?

Explanation:

The talk show host is likely not correct. Pamela did interject herself into public controversy by speaking occasionally at city council meetings, but she did not do so frequently enough to suggest that she had regular and continuing access to the media or the public at large. The Supreme Court has required that a limited-purpose public figure must maintain such "regular and continuing access . . . ." *Hutchinson*, 443 U.S. at 136. Such access ensures that a person can defend their reputation in the public arena.

To be sure, Pamela did enter the public arena to defend her reputation after the tweet when she gave the newspaper interview. But media access that become available only after the damaging publicity at issue in the defamation case transpires hardly makes someone acquire any public figure status. Pamela did not request the media interview or inject herself into the public domain in order to prompt the interview invitation. The interview occurred only because she became the subject of a stranger's tweet.

Moreover, Pamela's participation as a concerned citizen in a public meeting does not make her a limited-purpose public figure. To conclude otherwise would improperly provide disincentives for citizens to participate in the political process and contribute to community dialogue on matters of public interest. In addition, Pamela's contributions at the city council meetings pertained to different topics than the allegedly defamatory tweet. Neither the substance of her contributions nor the fact that she contributed at all were newsworthy until a stranger tweeted a photo of her with an erroneous caption.

For a case with slightly different facts from this Example that came to the same conclusion on the limited-public figure status, *see La Liberte v. Reid*, No. 19-3574, slip op. at 6, 16, 23-28 (2d Cir. July 15, 2020).

* * *

Many defamation cases present the question whether a business entity can be treated as a public figure or limited-purpose public figure. The Supreme Court has not settled the matter, and the lower courts have not reached a consensus. Most courts, however, treat business entities as "people" for the purpose of deciding whether the actual malice standard applies. *See* Rodney A. Smolla, § 2:98. *Corporate Plaintiffs and the Public Figure/Private Figure Dichotomy — Majority "Particularized" Approach*, 1 LAW OF DEFAMATION (2d ed. 2020). A few courts take this approach for corporations only. Yet another approach, endorsed by the New Jersey Supreme Court, adopts a more nuanced analysis, holding that a small business "like a local 'mom and pop' stationery store, shoemaker, tailor, cleaner, or barber" is not a public figure unless the defamatory speech alleged "criminal fraud, a substantial regulatory violation, or consumer fraud that raises a matter of legitimate public concern." *Turf Lawnmower Repair, Inc. v. Bergen Record Corp.*, 655 A.2d 417, 428 (N.J. 1995).

Example 10-11:

A telemarketing sales agency advertises its services widely and employs 500 employees who place 1,500 calls each week in order to pedal the agency's services. Part of the script used by the employees making the calls describes the agency's business approach, including its cancellation policy. An online business review website ran an article describing the cancellation policy as greedy and draconian. In the sales agency's view, the article included many false facts about the cancellation policy.

The sales agency brings a defamation suit against the business review that runs the website, alleging that the business review made false claims about the agency's subscription cancellation policies. The business review argues that the sales agency is an all-purpose public figure that must establish that the business review acted with actual malice in researching and publishing the online article. Is the business review correct that the sales agency has acquired the status of an all-purpose public figure?

Explanation:

Although the business review is probably wrong in labelling the sales agency an all-purpose public figure, the business review could make a good case that the sales agency is a limited-purpose public figure for the purpose of this lawsuit. This conclusion assumes that the court that makes the status determination adopts the view that an artificial entity, such as the business review, qualifies as a "person" for the purposes of the limited-purpose public figure status.

What has the sales agency done to qualify it as a limited-purpose public figure for the purpose of this lawsuit? It has thrust itself into the public eye through extensive person-to-person advertising. Since the designation would be limited, the alleged defamation would need a subject-matter nexus with the activity that thrust the sales agency into the public sphere. That is satisfied in this case because a main topic in the article was advertising practices, including cancellation policies. *See American Future Systems, Inc. v. Better Business Bureau of Eastern Pennsylvania.*, 923 A.2d 389 (Pa. 2007).

C. DEFAMATION ACTIONS BY PRIVATE PERSONS

The standard of fault generally applicable in defamation actions is ordinary negligence. Federal law, in the form of First Amendment protections, does not usually inject itself into defamation actions, at least for the purpose of private person liability. The "private person" designation is largely a process of elimination: one is deemed a private person in a defamation action if one is not a public official, a public figure, or a limited-purpose public figure. The U.S. Supreme Court, however, has recognized another designation to be added to this list: actions brought by private persons on matters of public concern. The ramifications of this designation are more limited than the other designations: the question whether the case involves a private person on a matter of public concern is relevant only in light of the type of damages sought.

Dun & Bradstreet, Inc. v. Greenmoss Builders, Inc., 472 U.S. 749 (1985), determined that in a suit regarding a private person on a matter of private concern, the plaintiff need not prove malice. The decision suggests, however, that private figures must show actual malice when the alleged defamatory statements touch on a matter of "public concern" when they seek presumed damages or punitive damages. (Presumed damages are those that allow compensation without actual proof of harm on the theory that the damages presumed are the natural result of a tortious act).

As with the definitions of "public officials" and "public figures," the definition of "public concern" remains somewhat elusive. *Dun & Bradstreet* provided a functional approach to the definition, requiring courts to consider the speech's "content, form, and context" in evaluating whether the speech addresses a matter of public concern. *Id.* at 761. This process requires looking at such matters as whether the speech is primarily of interest to the speaker or the speaker's close associates or whether the speech concerns a subject of general interest. Other factors that can be relevant include whether the speaker chooses the subject for the purpose of contributing to public discourse or whether the speaker uses the subject opportunistically as a means to air a private grievance.

Example 10-12:

A commercial pilot's ex-girlfriend—Maria—was angry at the pilot. She therefore sent a letter to his employer stating that the pilot had once used marijuana. Maria also filed a report to this effect with the Federal Aviation Administration (FAA). The pilot filed a defamation claim against Maria. She argued that the letter pertained to a public concern about the safety of air travel. The pilot argued that he need not show that his ex-girlfriend acted with actual malice because Maria's letters to his employer and to the FAA did not address a matter of public concern. Is the pilot's argument likely to succeed?

Explanation:

This is a close case. Surely, air travel safety is a matter of public concern and drug use by pilots is relevant to travel safety. One could argue that the context here, however, is a personal, not public, matter. Only one complaint about the marijuana use was made—and even that complaint pertained to only one instance of marijuana use that did not necessarily occur in connection with air travel. Moreover, the circumstances suggest that Maria was acting out of a desire for revenge against a former boyfriend rather than her interest in contributing to public knowledge on a particular issue. Finally, one might argue that the actual malice requirement does not necessarily apply in instances when unprotected speech is uttered for the purpose of attracting sensational or human interest and only by happenstance turns out to relate to society at large.

Thus, arguments on both sides exist on the "matter of public concern" question. The lower courts do not embrace consistent outcomes on the matter. *Compare Ayala v. Washington*, 679 A.2d 1057 (D.C. 1996) (finding that complaint by one person about a pilot's marijuana use was not a matter of public concern), *with Veilleux v. NBC*, 206 F.3d 92, 134 (1st Cir. 2000) (finding that reports of drug use by a truck driver were matters of public concern), *and Starrett v. Wadley*, 876 F.2d 808, 817 (10th Cir. 1989) (finding that allegation that supervisor in tax assessor's office had an alcohol problem is a matter of public concern).

Example 10-13:

A health care insurance company prepared a newsletter each month that was sent to medical professionals around the county. The newsletter included a diverse assortment of stories regarding recent developments in medical science. Although the insurance company was primarily concerned with profitability by minimizing medical claims, the newsletter had the more general goal of fostering good relationships with medical professionals and explaining reasons behind the company's decisions to allow or to deny insurance coverage for certain procedures and other medical expenses.

One of the insurance company's newsletters reported on information that questioned the efficacy of a particular prosthetic jaw and stated that the device had not been sufficiently tested. At the time of the newsletter, the device had been used on thousands of patients.

The prosthetic jaw manufacturer claimed the report was false and filed a defamation suit against the insurance company. The manufacturer argued that the insurance company's newsletter was commercial speech and did not touch a matter of public concern. Is the manufacturer correct that the newsletter did not pertain to a matter of public concern?

Explanation:

The manufacturer is not likely to win this argument. The insurance company's report touched on a matter of public concern because there was legitimate public interest in the utility of the manufacturer's implants, as thousands of people had already received similar jaw implants. In addition, both medical professionals and patients have an interest in learning the reasons behind denial of insurance coverage for medical procedures. The reality of the insurance company's profit motive does not undermine the public implications of the information included in the newsletter, particularly because the insurance company's newsletter is motivated by the general desire to promote communication and to ensure good will with medical professionals. In addition, the insurance bulletins are likely widely referred to by a variety of medical personnel in discussions among themselves as well as in discussions with patients. Thus, the challenged report had broader public implications than a simple business dispute between the insurance company and the manufacturer. *See TMJ Implants, Inc. v. Aetna, Inc.*, 498 F.3d 1175 (10th Cir. 2007).

It bears noting that in defamation litigation between business entities that compete with each other, commercial speech doctrines may enter the analysis or even displace the relevance of public figure status and the actual malice determination. *See, e.g., U.S. Health Care, Inc. v. Blue Cross of Greater*

Philadelphia, 898 F.2d 914 (1990). Chapter 9 of this volume cover commercial speech doctrines.

D. ACTUAL MALICE IN OTHER TORT ACTIONS

In a number of instances, the U.S. Supreme Court has applied First Amendment principles in tort cases outside of defamation. The most common contexts are actions seeking recovery for intentional infliction of emotional distress. The Court has also used First Amendment standards in the context of torts implicating privacy issues, including false light claims as well as claims based on disclosure of private information (sometimes framed as invasion of privacy claims or intrusion on seclusion claims). Within the context of intentional infliction of emotional distress and false light claims, the Court has imposed the *Sullivan* actual malice standard—since these claims often involve allegations of false speech. Actual malice is generally not relevant to claims concerning disclosure of private information, which usually concern the disclosure of true, private information. This section discusses these three types of tort claims.

The Supreme Court has also applied First Amendment principles in the context of fraud actions. Chapter 14 of this volume discussed this matter in connection with the Court's decision in *Illinois ex rel. Madigan v. Telemarketing Associates, Inc.,* 538 U.S. 600 (2003).

1. Intentional Infliction of Emotional Distress

In *Hustler v. Falwell,* 485 U.S. 46 (1988), the Court held that the First Amendment immunizes speakers from state-law intentional infliction of emotional distress (IIED) claims brought by public officials or public figures where the speakers' statements are either non-factual or factual but not made with actual malice. The particular communication in *Hustler* was a parody of a liquor advertisement that featured a public figure. Citing the historical and cultural importance of parody, the *Hustler* Court noted that the intentional infliction of emotional distress cause of action calls for a determination that the challenged communication is outrageous. According to the Court, the outrageousness standard is inherently subjective and would improperly invite fact finders to impose liability for communications that they regarded were in bad taste or otherwise not to their personal liking.

The Court reinforced *Hustler* in *Snyder v. Phelps*, 562 U.S. 443 (2011), a case involving a picketing group in the vicinity of a military funeral. The group carried signs with sayings such as "Thank God for Dead Soldiers" and "God hates the USA" for tolerating homosexuality. The deceased's father brought an IIED action against the picketing group, but the Court held that the signs were constitutionally protected because they addressed a political matter of public concern.

The meaning of the holding in *Snyder v. Phelps* is somewhat uncertain. Most courts have interpreted *Snyder* as extending *Hustler* to require private figures to show actual malice to prevail on an IIED claim when the harmful speech touches on a matter of public concern. That reading is supported by the *Snyder* Court's explanation that any First Amendment protection of the funeral protests depended "largely on whether that speech is of public or private concern." Id. at 451. One should be careful in applying this fixed rule, however, because the Court also cautioned that the *Snyder* holding was "narrow," and that "the reach of our opinion here is limited by the particular facts before us." Id. at 460.

Lower courts after *Snyder* and *Hustler* have largely required private-figure plaintiffs in IIED claims to show that the harmful speech was not speech on a matter of public concern. This approach brings IIED case law into conformity with First Amendment case law on defamation. One problem, however, is that the First Amendment defamation case law focuses on actual malice. The Court's reference to actual malice in *Hustler* seemed misplaced in the IIED context. Actual malice operates by reference to statements that can be shown to be true or false. Yet IIED cases often concern either opinions (which cannot be shown to be true or false) or indisputably true statements that are claimed outrageous because civil behavior suggests that they should not be shared with others.

Example 10-14:

Elsabe pens a letter to her local radio station expressing her disgust with the station's decision to air a nationally syndicated radio program hosted by Jacques Shock, which she claims is vulgar and misogynistic. A production assistant at her local radio station obtained a copy of Elsabe's letter and forwarded it to Jacques.

Jacques read and ridiculed Elsabe's letter on the air, making several derogatory comments about Elsabe and the letter. He provides enough detail about Elsabe that listeners are able to determine her identity. Jacques encouraged his listeners to call Elsabe at publicly listed phone numbers and "make her life a living hell."

Elsabe brought an intentional infliction of emotional distress claim arising from Jacques' reading of the letter, his derogatory comments about her, and his inducement of his listeners' harassment of her. Is Elsabe likely to prevail in her claim?

Explanation:

Elsabe is likely to prevail on the harassment portion of her complaint because Jacques' urging fans to harass Elsabe did not implicate a matter of public concern. The remaining portions of her complaint regarding the letter and derogatory comments are a closer call. The question whether Jacques' show should air—which Elsabe's letter addressed—is a matter that the public may be interested in debating. Jacques' ridicule of the letter on the air contributed to that debate. Thus, under the authority of *Snyder*, the reading of the letter and the ridicule of the letter are likely protected by the First Amendment. *See State v. Carpenter*, 171 P.3d 41 (Alaska 2007).

Example 10-15:

During a nightly newscast, a television station broadcasts a high-speed police chase that ends in the suspect dying by suicide. The suspect's wife brings a claim for intentional infliction of emotional distress on behalf of her daughter over the station's failure to edit or to use broadcast delay to censor the suicide. The station moves to dismiss the suit, arguing that the broadcast of the police chase was protected speech on a matter of public concern. Should the court dismiss the suit?

Explanation:

The court should dismiss the suit because the video did portray a matter of public concern. The public has an interest in learning about crime and public safety threats. The public also has an interest in monitoring how law enforcement responds to criminal behavior. The broadcast was also not aired as a personal attack within an individual dispute. Rather, the high-speed chase was aired during a news program, a fact that also weighs toward a finding that it addressed matters of public concern.

The court in *Rodriguez v. Fox News Network, L.L.C.*, 356 P.3d 322 (Ariz. Ct. App. 2015), addressed identical facts and also concluded that the video of the suicide was a matter of public concern. According to the court,

> "[r]equiring a broadcaster covering a matter of public concern to cut away whenever a violent or disturbing sight may be caught on camera, or to avoid broadcasting such a scene [using] a split-second tape delay, would chill the broadcaster's news coverage to a degree the First Amendment does not permit."

Id. at 327.

2. Privacy Torts

The privacy tort that most closely tracks defamation is the cause of action imposing liability when someone places the plaintiff in a false light. While defamation seeks to remedy damage to reputation, false light claims concern the plaintiff's well-being. The United States Supreme Court imported the actual malice standard into false light claims in *Time, Inc. v. Hill*, 385 U.S. 374 (1967). In that case, a magazine ran a story that depicted an inaccurate portrayal of an ordeal suffered by a private family when they were held hostage by escaped convicts. The *Time v. Hill* Court reversed a damage judgment in the case and remanded to the lower court for determination of whether the plaintiff could prove actual malice. The Court concluded that actual malice was necessary in order to avoid a chilling effect on the media, which may avoid running stories of this kind for fear of being held liable for false light. The Court noted that membership in community required privacy to yield on occasion to the important values of free speech and the press.

Time v. Hill was handed down before the Supreme Court developed the First Amendment principles regarding public figures, limited-purpose public figures, and private persons. The plaintiffs in *Hill* were private persons. One can bring the holding of the case in line with the defamation case law, however, if one characterizes the subject of the story as a matter of public concern.

False light cases are not common. The same holds true for cases asserting privacy torts that concern disclosure of true, private facts. Most of the prominent cases in the area pertain to media stories reporting facts that—though true—are a matter of private and intimate matters. Chapter 15 of this volume discusses the most prominent case in this area, *Florida Star v. B.J.F.*, 491 U.S. 524 (1989), which overturned a damage award against a newspaper for publishing a rape victim's name. In other cases, the Supreme Court has consistently upheld the media's right to publish private information that is a matter of public concern. *See, e.g., Bartnicki v. Vopper*, 532 U.S. 514 (2001) (upholding media's publication of the contents of a wiretap).

Other privacy torts that may touch on First Amendment issues are based on intrusion on seclusion, disclosure of private facts, and appropriation of the name or image of a person without the person's consent. A contemporary constitutional issue pertaining to disclosure of private facts is the issue of regulating revenge porn. Revenge porn is generally defined as publicly distributing sexually explicit images or videos of individuals without their consent. The perpetrator may use this distribution for a variety of purposes: to coerce an individual into performing other sex acts, to coerce them into continuing a romantic relationship, to punish them for ending a relationship, or to silence them.

Nearly all states of the United States have passed statutes criminalizing revenge porn. The state legislature's justification for these statutes is often to protect individuals from public disclosure of private facts and from intentional infliction of emotional distress. Some courts have found these justifications sufficient. *See, e.g., People v. Iniguez*, 247 Cal. Rptr. 3d 237 (2016) (declaring purposes of the California statute compelling for the purpose of strict scrutiny).

Even with these justifications, however, the statutes do not always survive constitutional attack. Overbreadth is a common basis for finding that the statutes violate the First Amendment. For example, the court in *State v. Casillas*, 938 N.W.2d 74 (Minn. Ct. App. 2019), declared the Minnesota statute violated the constitution, finding that the statute's "broad sweep" punished individuals regardless of whether the disseminator knew whether or not the person depicted had consented to the distribution or held a reasonable expectation of privacy. *Id.* at 85, 88-89.

Similarly, the court in *Ex parte Jones*, 2018 Tex. App. LEXIS 3439 (2018), invalidated a Texas statute that penalized the dissemination of visual material of a "person's intimate parts." Applying strict scrutiny, the court determined that not only were the types of images implicated by this statute not inherently obscene, but the conduct that the images depicted did not necessarily make the images "contextually obscene." *Id.* at *8, *9. In determining that the statute did not use the most restrictive means possible for "preventing intolerable invasions of [an individual's] substantial privacy interest," the court held that statute failed strict scrutiny, lacked a requisite intent-to-harm requirement, and was prohibitively broad. *Id.* at *13, *16.

False Speech

This volume covers the topic of false speech in a number of places, most notably in the chapter on commercial speech (Chapter 9) as well as the chapter on defamation and related torts (Chapter 10). The purpose of this chapter is to situate false speech issues within U.S. history of regulating speech, to provide an overview of the inconsistent approaches that the U.S. Supreme Court has taken on the relationship between the First Amendment and false speech, and to provide two contrasting examples of the Court's approach as to whether false speech falls within First Amendment protection: *Illinois ex rel. Madigan v. Telemarketing Associates, Inc.*, 538 U.S. 600 (2003), and *United States v. Alvarez*, 567 U.S. 709 (2012). Understanding how these two examples might be synthesized provides a tool set for confronting new factual disputes bearing on false speech.

A. A BRIEF HISTORY OF U.S. SOCIETY'S APPROACH TO FALSE SPEECH

Although the contemporary constitutional approach to false speech has been inconsistent, the early history to American law's treatment of false speech took a consistently hostile approach. For example, Congress adopted the Alien and Sedition Acts of 1798, which prohibited publication of

> false, scandalous and malicious writing or writings against the government of the United States, or either house of the Congress of the United States, or the

> President of the United States, with intent to defame . . . or to bring them . . .
> into contempt or disrepute; or to excite against them . . . hatred of the good
> people of the United States . . . .

Ch. 74, 1 Stat. 596 (1798).

President John Adams used the law aggressively. Ultimately, however, Thomas Jefferson pardoned those who had been convicted under the law and the law was repealed. Although the U.S. Supreme Court never ruled on the Acts' constitutionality, the Court declared in 1964 that "the attack upon [their] validity has carried the day in the court of history." *New York Times Co. v. Sullivan*, 376 U.S. 254, 276 (1964).

The issue of the legality of false statements nevertheless did not retreat after the Alien and Sedition Acts. Most prominently, the issue came to the fore in the 1890s as the nation became concerned with "yellow journalism," a term used to describe sensational, often fraudulent, news reports. In 1890, Samuel Warren and Louis Brandeis wrote that the sensationalist press ignored the "obvious bounds of propriety and of decency." Samuel D. Warren & Louis D. Brandeis, *The Right to Privacy*, 4 HARV. L. REV. 193, 196 (1890).

In more recent times, the law has taken a more ambivalent tack—sometimes praising the benefits of false speech and other times criticizing or even criminalizing it. False statements of fact can lead to civil liability in defamation and false light tort actions. More than 100 federal criminal statutes punish false statements of concern to the federal government, such as those in the form of perjury and out-of-court lies to government officials. *See United States v. Wells*, 519 U.S. 482, 505-507, & nn.8-10 (1997) (Stevens, J., dissenting) (listing statute citations). Likewise, false statements intended to cause panic or to inspire fear of violence are criminally punishable, such as in the area of true threats made with the requisite criminal intent. *See, e.g., Virginia v. Black*, 538 U.S. 343 (2003).

Within the First Amendment context, the Court has frequently emphasized the limited constitutional value of false speech. The Supreme Court reasoned in *Hustler Magazine, Inc. v. Falwell*, 485 U.S. 46 (1988), that "[f]alse statements of fact are particularly valueless [because] they interfere with the truth-seeking function of the marketplace of ideas . . . ." *Id.* at 52. Similarly, the Court declared in *Virginia State Board of Pharmacy v. Virginia Citizens Consumer Council*, 425 U.S. 748 (1976), that "[u]ntruthful speech, commercial or otherwise, has never been protected for its own sake." *Id.* at 771. Explaining this position, the Court has stated that false statements "are not protected by the First Amendment in the same manner as truthful statements." *Brown v. Hartlage*, 456 U.S. 45, 60 (1982).

More specifically, the Supreme Court has repeatedly emphasized that false and deceptive advertisements are unprotected by the First Amendment. *See Central Hudson Gas & Electric Corp. v. Public Service Comm'n of N.Y.*, 447 U.S. 557,

563 (1980). And, of course, for the purpose of defamation and other civil actions, the Court has declared that "the knowingly false statement and the false statement made with reckless disregard of the truth, do not enjoy constitutional protection." *Garrison v. Louisiana*, 379 U.S. 64, 75 (1964).

Despite these negative statements, the Supreme Court has declined to find that all false statements fall outside of First Amendment protection. In a system built at least in part on the search for truth, why on earth would we want to protect untruth? The U.S. Supreme Court has given us some hints about the virtues of false speech. For example, in *New York Times Co. v. Sullivan*, 376 U.S. 254 (1964), the Court determined that the falsity of a statement does not necessarily deny First Amendment protection for the speech. The Court explained that a false "statement is inevitable in free debate, and [it] must be protected if the freedoms of expression are to have the 'breathing space' that they 'need . . . to survive . . . .'" *Id.* at 271-272. If we want to encourage as much breathing space as is needed, we need to provide peace of mind for speakers so that they will not muzzle themselves for fear that they may encounter some kind of retribution for making a mistake. In terms of other values animating the First Amendment, consider personal autonomy: Do we really want the government to scrutinize theatrical performances for untruths? How about intimate communications whispered at home to a loved one: should that be regulated for truth or falsity? Invoking traditional First Amendment justifications further, a false statement might inspire counter-speech, which together with the initial speech contributes to a robust exchange of ideas.

Characteristic of the dichotomous nature of the First Amendment approach to falsity, the Court in *Gertz v. Welch*, 418 U.S. 323 (1974) stated—on one hand—that the Constitution does not protect false statements of fact, but—on the other hand—that false statements are inevitable in a free debate. The *Gertz* Court quoted James Madison's statement in the Report on the Virginia Resolutions of 1798: "'Some degree of abuse is inseparable from the proper use of every thing; and in no instance is this more true than in that of the press.' 4 J. Elliot, Debates on the Federal Constitution of 1787, p. 571 (1876)." 418 U.S. at 340. Famously, the *Gertz* Court declared, "[u]nder the First Amendment there is no such thing as a false idea. However pernicious an opinion may seem, we depend for its correction not on the conscience of judges and juries but on the competition of other ideas." *Id.* at 339-340.

What accounts for this apparent inconsistency in the attitudes toward false speech emanating from the Supreme Court opinions? Dean Erwin Chemerinsky argues that this is the natural consequence of the competing interests at play:

> On the one hand, false speech can create harms, even great harms. Speech is protected especially because of its importance for the democratic process, but

false speech can distort that process. Speech is safeguarded, too, because of the belief that the marketplace of ideas is the best way for truth to emerge. But false speech can infect that marketplace. . . .

But at the same time, there is great concern about allowing the government to prohibit and punish false speech. . . . [T]he freedoms of expression are to have the "breathing space" that they need . . . [and] allowing the government to prohibit false speech places it in the role of being the arbiter of truth.

Erwin Chemerinsky, *False Speech and the First Amendment*, 71 OKLA. L. REV. 1, 8-10 (2018).

Given these complications, one can see why the United States encounters problems in identifying the proper approach to regulating speech on the Internet (which often contains dubious material in general and "fake news" appearing on and off the Internet). For the moment, however, this is the state of the law and we must understand how to navigate its challenges and inconsistencies. The next section reviews two contrasting approaches to evaluating the First Amendment implications of false speech and provides guidance on understanding and working with the apparent contradictions in this area.

B. CONTRASTING APPROACHES TO FALSE SPEECH

The apparent inconsistency in false speech case law is reflected by two cases arguably in tension with each other: *Illinois ex rel. Madigan v. Telemarketing Associates, Inc.*, 538 U.S. 600 (2003), and *United States v. Alvarez*, 567 U.S. 709 (2012). *Madigan* holds that the First Amendment allows government to punish false speech and *Alvarez* holds that the First Amendment does not allow government to do so.

1. *Madigan v. Telemarketing Associates*

In *Madigan*, for-profit fundraising corporations and their owners were telemarketers that had been retained by a charitable non-profit corporation to solicit donations to aid Vietnam veterans. Under the deal, the telemarketers were allowed to retain a very large percentage of donations. The Illinois Attorney General filed a complaint against the telemarketers, alleging that (1) they represented to donors that a significant amount of each dollar donated would be paid over to the non-profit for specifically identified charitable endeavors and (2) such representations were knowingly deceptive, materially false, and constituted a fraud. The Attorney General included in the complaint detailed descriptions of the fraudulent representations. The telemarketers objected that the state Attorney General's suit was attempting to punish them for exercising their First Amendment rights. The U.S. Supreme Court agreed with the Attorney General.

In rejecting the First Amendment claim, the Supreme Court issued a relatively narrow decision. The *Madigan* Court noted that the First Amendment protects the right to engage in charitable solicitation but does not protect fraud: fraudulent charitable solicitation is unprotected speech. The Court made clear, however, that fraud actions concerning representations made in individual cases are different for the purposes of the First Amendment than for statutes that categorically ban solicitations under circumstances when fundraising costs run high. The Court insisted that allegations in an action against the solicitor of charitable funds must be based more on the percentage of donations the fundraisers would retain. The *Madigan* Court was persuaded that these First Amendment constraints were satisfied under the facts of the case because the Attorney General's allegations included descriptions of specific acts of misleading potential donors. The requirement of specific actions of misrepresentation, the Court reasoned, ensures that the fraud actions do not chill protected speech.

Example 11-1:

A for-profit organization, Donate, Inc., owned and maintained drop-boxes throughout the state for people to donate clothes to charity. In response, one city in the state enacted an ordinance that (1) required organizations to have a permit to maintain drop-boxes, (2) limited issuance of permits to non-profit corporations, and (3) required at least 80 percent of the proceeds from those boxes go to charity. Donate, Inc. filed for a preliminary injunction against the city, claiming that the 80 percent restriction violated the First Amendment principles protecting the freedom to solicit charitable donations under fair terms. The city defends by arguing that the ordinance serves two governmental purposes: preventing deception and ensuring funds acquired through donations actually go to benefit charitable organizations. Should the court grant Donate Inc.'s preliminary injunction?

Explanation:

Because the restriction is not narrowly tailored, the court should grant the preliminary injunction. First Amendment case law in the area of charitable donation regulations generally requires that (1) the government have a sufficient or legitimate interest in enacting the restriction, and (2) the restriction is narrowly tailored to serve that interest. *Riley v. National Federation of the Blind of North Carolina, Inc.*, 487 U.S. 781, 789 (1988); *Secretary of State of Maryland v. Joseph H. Munson Co.*, 467 U.S. 947, 960-961 (1984); *Schaumburg v. Citizens for a Better Environment*, 444 U.S. 620, 636-637 (1980).

In this Example, the city's interests in preventing deception and ensuring funds actually go to benefit charitable organizations are surely substantial. The problem, however, is that — unlike in *Madigan* — the ordinance does not require specific evidence of misrepresentation or fraud. Nor does there appear to be any facts suggesting that Donate, Inc. made any misrepresentations to donors — or anyone else — about the benefits that accrued to charitable organizations as a result of the drop-box donations. For this reason, the restriction is not sufficiently narrowly tailored, particularly in light of the facts in this Example. In the present Example, the ordinance simply works as a prophylactic measure, which is an approach that the *Madigan* Court disapproved. *See Linc-Drop, Inc. v. City of Lincoln*, 996 F. Supp. 2d 845 (D. Neb. 2014).

2. *United States v. Alvarez*

The plurality in *United States v. Alvarez* took a more protective approach to false speech than in the Court in *Madigan*. In *Alvarez*, the Court considered the constitutionality of a federal law, the Stolen Valor Act, which made it a crime for a person to claim falsely to have received military decorations or honors. Writing for a plurality of four, Justice Kennedy concluded that the law imposed a content-based restriction on speech and thus had to meet the most "exacting scrutiny." In the plurality's view, the government did not satisfy this scrutiny because the government failed to prove harm from false claims of military honors and because the government could achieve its goals through less restrictive alternatives.

Most importantly, the plurality expressly rejected the government's argument that false speech is inherently outside the scope of the First Amendment. The plurality declared that the Supreme Court had never recognized a First Amendment exception for false speech. On the contrary, the plurality observed, the Court's decisions reflected "the common understanding that some false statements are inevitable if there is to be an open and vigorous expression of views in public and private conversation, expression the First Amendment seeks to guarantee." 567 U.S. at 718. The plurality opinion further cited with approval the Court's statement in *Garrison v. Louisiana*, 379 U.S. 64, 73 (1964), that "even where the utterance is false, the great principles of the Constitution which secure freedom of expression . . . preclude attaching adverse consequences to any except the knowing or reckless falsehood."

The Court applied these general statements in evaluating the constitutionality of the Stolen Valor Act. Noting that the Act applied to false statements made "at any time, in any place, [and] to any person," without limit on whether the statements provided material advantage to the speaker, the plurality reasoned that upholding this law would leave the government with the power to punish any false discourse without a clear limiting principle. *Id.* at 722.

Justice Breyer, in a separate opinion joined by Justice Kagan, concurred in the judgment, but did so only after evaluating the prohibition under an intermediate scrutiny standard. While Justice Breyer was also concerned about the breadth of the act, his opinion went on to suggest that a similar statute, more finely tailored to situations where a specific harm is likely to occur, could withstand legal challenge.

Example 11-2:

Bo was talking on the phone during a movie in a crowded theater. Patrons around him started complaining and asked him to get off the phone. In response, Bo stood up, yelled that he was a U.S. Marshal on the phone with the government, and flashed a gun and a badge. The patrons found out that Bo was not actually a U.S. Marshal and called the police. Bo was ultimately indicted under a federal statute that made it a crime to impersonate an officer or employee of the United States. In order to be convicted of this offense, the statute requires that (1) the false impersonation must be "coupled with an overt act in conformity with the pretense" and (2) the actor must make the false statements with the intention of deceiving some person into "follow[ing] some course [the deceived individual] would not have pursued but for the deceitful conduct." 18 U.S.C. § 912. The government explains that the purpose of this statute is to protect the integrity of government processes, to ensure public safety, and to maintain the general good reputation and dignity of government service, including the reputation and dignity of law enforcement. Relying on *Alvarez*, Bo argues that that the statute is unconstitutional. Is Bo likely to prevail on this claim?

Explanation:

No, Bo is not likely to prevail. He is correct, however, that *Alvarez* provides appropriate precedent by which to judge the false impersonation statute, but it does not support his position.

Alvarez mandated that a court evaluating the constitutionality of a false speech prohibition must use strict scrutiny: the prohibition must be narrowly tailored to serve a compelling government interest. The government's interests in government integrity and effectiveness as well as public safety in the facts of this Example are compelling interests. The statute is also narrowly drawn. The flaw in the Stolen Valor Act at issue in *Alvarez* was that its plain terms applied to a false statement made at any time, in any place, to any person without regard to whether the lie was made for the purpose of material gain. Section 912 is more narrowly tailored than the Stolen Valor Act because § 912 requires intentional action on the part of the imposter that would cause the deceived person to follow some course that the person would not have pursued in the absence of the deceitful conduct. Unlike the

Stolen Valor Act, the prohibition at issue in this Example prohibits more than a mere lie standing alone and is therefore outside the scope of *Alvarez*. *United States v. Bonin*, 932 F.3d 523 (7th Cir. 2019), *cert. denied*, No. 19-809, 2020 WL 411718 (U.S. Jan. 27, 2020).

Note on the Aftermath of *Alvarez*: In striking down the Stolen Valor Act, the *Alvarez* Court (plurality and concurring justices) showed concern with the lack of an intent requirement in the statute. Congress has amended the Act to require proof of fraud. So far, the Act has withstood challenge. Does this mean that *Alvarez* was truly speech protecting or was it simply stating a rule that applied in the absence of a fraud requirement?

3. How Might a Lawyer Handle the Apparent Inconsistency in the False Speech Cases?

With cases in the false speech area as different as *Alvarez* and *Madigan*, understanding how to use the U.S. Supreme Court's case law on false speech is challenging. Both certainly used different approaches — the plurality in *Alvarez* used what appeared to be strict scrutiny versus what appeared to be an intermediate scrutiny in *Madigan*. The cases clearly embraced different attitudes toward the benefits of false speech and — working from those attitudes — produced decisions that appear inconsistent. While accurate, those observations provide cold comfort for the lawyer seeking to find an authoritative approach for resolving a false speech problem or framing an argument in a new set of facts that involve false speech. Simply declaring "the Supreme Court has taken inconsistent approaches to false speech" is not particularly helpful for those tasks.

What is helpful is for the lawyer (1) to get a handle on how cases such as *Madigan* and *Alvarez* might be distinguished on their facts and reasoning as well as (2) to understand how the conflicting First Amendment values at issue in the false speech cases might play out differently with different disputes. As stated earlier, the First Amendment values particularly most pertinent in the false speech context are (1) to avoid harm, (2) to protect the democratic process from the distortion that may occur from false speech, (3) to prevent false speech from infecting the marketplace of ideas and the ability of that marketplace to serve the search for truth, (4) to ensure that freedom of expression enjoys sufficient breathing space so that individuals do not hesitate to speak, and (5) to avoid undue government control over the exchange of ideas and the search for truth.

How are *Madigan* and *Alvarez* distinguishable on their facts and reasoning? How do these differences implicate the various First Amendment values at play in the false speech cases? The answer to these questions fall into at least three categories:

1. The prohibition in *Alvarez* did not have a distinct individual victim that it was trying to protect. To be sure, the corpus of brave service members, the institution of the military, and society as a whole may be identified as victims. In addition, the Stolen Valor Act was concerned with harm to concepts (e.g., bravery, honor, and patriotism) or to a group of people (e.g., those who actually earn a military honor or medal). But those injuries are only an indirect consequence of the conduct that the Act prohibits. The individual who falsely represents having received the honor or medal is not necessarily seeking to target any particular victim. The law in *Madigan*, however, focused on protecting particular persons who were the victims of fraud or misrepresentation.

The plurality recognized this distinction in *Alvarez* when it dismissed quotes from earlier cases that had condemned false speech and had suggested false speech might be outside First Amendment protection. The plurality said:

> These quotations all derive from cases discussing defamation, fraud, or some other legally cognizable harm associated with a false statement, such as an invasion of privacy or the costs of vexatious litigation. In those decisions the falsity of the speech at issue was not irrelevant to our analysis, but [it was not] determinative. . . . Our prior decisions have not confronted a measure, like the Stolen Valor Act, that targets falsity and nothing more.

Alvarez, 567 U.S. at 719.

Given this distinction between *Alvarez* and *Madigan*, one can see how the laws in the cases had a different impact on the values at play in the false speech area. For example, the law in *Alvarez* more significantly injected the government into the marketplace of ideas with the result that the government was more likely to serve as the arbiter of the truth than would occur under the *Madigan* law. By contrast, the *Madigan* law was more concerned with avoiding identifiable harm to identifiable persons only and thereby gave greater breathing space to expression than the *Alvarez* law.

2. In the First Amendment context, sweeping prohibitions are disfavored. One can see this in the standards of scrutiny mandated in First Amendment doctrine: even for instances in which strict scrutiny is not required, First Amendment doctrine generally requires some tailoring of the prohibition. *Madigan* easily complies with that orientation. The prohibition in that case was confined to specific acts of fraud or misrepresentation within the context of charitable contributions. The *Alvarez* law applied to any false representation regarding a military award or honor.

3. Perhaps most importantly, the *Madigan* law required that the regulated entity act with an element of intent. By specifying that the regulated entity would be liable only for fraud or misrepresentation, the law imported into its requirement the intent element associated with those wrongs. That

intent element generally includes some kind of intent to deceive and/or to make representations that are known to be false or are made recklessly and without regard to whether they are true or not. The *Alvarez* law, however, did not contain such a specific intent requirement. This absence appears quite important given the emphasis on a lack of intent requirements in the *Alvarez* opinions and the apparent staying power of Congress's amendment to the Stolen Valor Act once it added a fraud requirement.

The presence of a specific intent requirement is often a key feature of laws restricting speech deemed acceptable under free speech principles. First, the requirement of intent narrows the prohibited conduct and thus the sweep of the prohibition. Second, a law that prohibits speech only when the regulated entity acts intentionally in violating its prohibitions ensures that those who simply make a mistake are not punished. This in turn minimizes the possibility that the prohibition will chill protected speech, since individuals will be less risk averse as a consequence, knowing that they will not be culpable for a mere error. Both of these factors are important to ensuring that more speech makes its way into the marketplace of ideas, minimizes the government's role in the exchange in ideas, and provides more breathing space for those who wish to express themselves.

Government Property and Speech: Public Forums and Other Types of Forums

Does First Amendment case law provide a unique analysis for speech that occurs on government property? The answer is yes. The law in this area started to develop with the U.S. Supreme Court's recognition of a "public forum doctrine," designed to govern whether and when a citizen may use government property for the purpose of communication. The doctrine has changed over the years and, consistent with the patterns in much of First Amendment law, has become more complicated. As a starting point to appreciating the impetus behind the public forum doctrine, consider the following situation:

Example 12-1:

Oscar runs a movie discussion group that meets twice a month. The group is small and the bi-weekly gathering generally does not exceed six people. The group agrees that the most convenient place to meet is in a public square in the middle of town. The group has never had a difficult time finding a place in the square to meet and discuss political themes in movies. The square is large, and they are never closer to others using the square than 30 feet. They have learned, however, that the government has passed a law prohibiting meetings on property owned by the government. They wish to know whether this law violates their First Amendment rights. What advice would you give?

Explanation:

The city's new law is likely unconstitutional. Since the 1930s, the U.S. Supreme Court has recognized that citizens may use government property for some types of speech under many circumstances. As declared in *Hague v. CIO*, 307 U.S. 496 (1939): "Wherever the title of streets and parks may rest, they have immemorially been held in trust for the use of the public and, time out of mind, have been used for purposes of assembly, communicating thoughts between citizens, and discussing public questions." *Id.* at 515. *See also Schneider v. State of New Jersey*, 308 U.S. 147, 163 (1939) (Roberts, J., concurring) (stating that "streets are natural and proper places for the dissemination of information and opinion"). As will be shown later in this chapter, the location and type of government land where Oscar meets with his group as well as the type of information that they exchange are all of the type to which First Amendment protection extends.

* * *

After the *Hague v. CIO* case, the Supreme Court set to work on developing rules that demarcate the contours for its recognition of the constitutional importance of maintaining open public space for the purpose of dissemination of ideas and information. The Court has not, however, developed a strong theoretical backdrop for this area of law. Legal scholars have suggested some possibilities. One prominent theory is that the United States needs open access to public spaces in order to ensure full and robust exchange of ideas among citizens. Not all speakers have the resources to gain private access — through media or otherwise — to the means to communicate with large numbers of citizens. Another important theory suggests that if governments had the unfettered ability to close public spaces to speakers, governments would be tempted to do so in order to shut down communication of ideas that the governments do not like. This type of content-discrimination is, of course, inimical to basic freedom of speech principles. Both theories are sufficiently grounded in traditional First Amendment analysis as to provide useful and appropriate vehicles for resolving public-forum disputes.

As the U.S. Supreme Court has tooled the contours of its commitment to keeping public spaces open for communication, the Court has settled on four categories of government property relevant to analyzing public speech access questions. The degree of First Amendment restrictions on speech depends on how the property is categorized. The fifth category of location is private property — where no First Amendment restrictions apply:

Traditional public forums: With respect to traditional public forums, the Supreme Court has stated that in areas "such as public streets and parks, 'any restriction based on the content of . . . speech must satisfy strict scrutiny, that is, the restriction must be narrowly tailored to serve a compelling govern-ment interest.'" *Christian Legal Soc'y Chapter of the University of California v. Martinez,* 561 U.S. 661, 679 n.11 (2010).

Designated public forums: Designated public forums occur on government property that has traditionally been closed, but that the government has designated to be opened. Speech restrictions in designated public forums are subject to strict scrutiny.

Limited public forums: Limited public forums occur on government prop-erty opened for "limited . . . use by certain groups or dedicated solely to the discussion of certain subjects. . . . [I]n such a forum, a government entity may impose restriction on speech that are reasonable and viewpoint-neutral." *Christian Legal Soc'y Chapter of the University of California v. Martinez,* 567 U.S. 661, 679 n.11 (2010).

Non-public forums: Non-public forums occur on government prop-erty that the government may properly close and has not opened. This includes public property that "is not by tradition or designation a forum for public communication . . . ." *Perry Education Ass'n v. Perry Local Educators' Ass'n,* 460 U.S. 37, 46 (1983). The Supreme Court has said that the gov-ernment may prohibit speech only if the prohibition is viewpoint neutral and reasonable.

Private property: In a series of cases, the U.S. Supreme Court has ruled that private owners of property could exclude speakers from their property. Although the Court at first determined that privately owned shopping malls could be public forums, the Court changed its mind and determined that the First Amendment does not apply to privately owned malls. *See, e.g., Hudgens v. National Labor Relations Bd.,* 424 U.S. 507 (1976); *Amalgamated Food Employees Union Local 590 v. Logan Valley Plaza,* 391 U.S. 308 (1968).

Each of these categories is explored below.

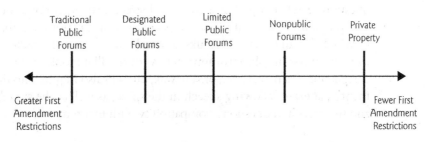

Degree of First Amendment Restrictions on Speech
Regulations in Various Locations

Figure 12-1

A. PUBLIC FORUM ANALYSIS

An initial question to consider before actually launching into public forum analysis is whether the speech restriction concerns only government speech and is therefore not subject to public forum analysis at all. Once one resolves that the speech is not properly characterized as government speech, one might turn to identifying whether the location of the speech qualifies as a public forum and, if so, whether the restriction passes traditional public forum analysis. One must remember, however, that the rules in this area have a few twists. First, public forum analysis must be considered in light of First Amendment principles governing time, place, and manner restrictions as well as licenses and permits. In addition, one should be aware that the U.S. Supreme Court has recognized a subcategory of public forums, so-called designated public forums, which require unique consideration. This section covers each of these matters.

1. Standard Public Forum Analysis

a. What Constitutes a Public Forum?

The standard for a government regulation of speech that occurs in an area designated as a public forum is well settled, the regulation must be content neutral unless it is narrowly tailored to serve a compelling interest.[1] These constraints on government raise the stakes on the question of exactly what qualifies as a public forum.

Streets, sidewalks, and parks clearly fall into the "traditional public forum" category. The U.S. Supreme Court is reluctant to designate other locations as public forums. *See, e.g., International Society for Krishna Consciousness v. Lee,* 505 U.S. 672 (1992) (holding that airport terminals are not public forums); *Arkansas Education Comm'n v. Forbes,* 523 U.S. 666 (1998) (determining that televised political debates are not a traditional public forum). Although this inclination not to recognize "new" forms of public forums simplifies the analysis, the question of when a park is a park, or a street a street, is not always simple. The prevailing test for this issue appears to be a functionalist, objective test in which not all streets, sidewalks and parks are necessarily traditional public forums. Under the objective approach, a court will not only consider a space's designation as a park, street, or sidewalk, but will also inquire into the government's pattern of allowing speech in the space, as well as the space's purpose and the speech in question's compatibility with that purpose.

---

1. The narrowly tailored standard differs from the least restrictive alternative standard in this and other contexts. *See, e.g., Ward v. Rock Against Racism,* 491 U.S. 781 (1989). *See also* Chapter 9 and Figure 9-2 for a discussion of the difference between the two standards.

Example 12-2:

Anton wished to organize a political event on the grounds of a large monument that is dedicated to a President and has been designated as a National Park. He does not want to fill out the extensive permit application for the event and takes the position that all National Parks are traditional public forums. Is he correct?

Explanation:

The United States Court of Appeals for the D.C. Circuit took up this question in *Boardley v. U.S. Department of Interior*, 615 F.3d 508 (D.C. Cir. 2010), concluding that national parks are not per se traditional public forums. In addressing this question, the *Boardley* court stated "[t]he dispositive question is not what the forum is *called*, but what *purpose* it serves, either by tradition or specific designation." *Id.* at 515. That court further explained that "to establish that a national park (in whole or part) is a traditional public forum, [it must be shown] that, like a typical municipal park, it has been held open by the government for the purpose of public discourse." *Id.*

Example 12-3:

Seeking to spur economic revival in its downtown business district, a city converts a shopping street into a pedestrian plaza. The city closed the street to vehicle traffic and installed several public art fixtures. The project successfully drew investment, as business storefronts lined the newly created space and the city licensed portions of the street for vending and other sidewalk performances. Pedestrians continued to use the plaza as a thoroughfare — to get from one location to another.

A political group seeks to hand out leaflets on the plaza but was denied a permit to do so. The political group then brings a First Amendment challenge, arguing that the pedestrian plaza was a traditional public forum. Is the political group correct?

Explanation:

The political group is likely correct. Several factors suggest that the pedestrian plaza is a traditional public forum. Even though the plaza now serves as a place to access entertainment, it continues to serve the original function of a pedestrian thoroughfare. Moreover, the physical characteristics of the current plaza support its traditional public forum status, considering that it is open to the public and is integrated into the rest of the city. Finally, the area had been a traditional public forum before the change.

This conclusion is consistent with the court's decision in *ACLU of Nevada v. City of Las Vegas*, 333 F.3d 1092 (9th Cir. 2003), in which the court held a pedestrian plaza was a traditional public forum. The *ACLU of Nevada* court also noted that courts had recognized that "pedestrian malls and commercial zones," such as Fisherman's Wharf in San Francisco, and Olvera Street and Venice Boardwalk in Los Angeles, had retained their status as traditional public forums. But cf. *H.E.R.E. v. City of New York*, 311 F.3d 534, 550 (2d Cir. 2002) (declining to find a traditional public forum for a public throughway because its status as a "plaza" was "merely an incidental feature of its principal function as the entrance" to an entertainment complex); *Chicago Acorn v. Metropolitan Pier & Exposition Auth.*, 150 F.3d 695 (7th Cir. 1998) (holding that a former downtown Chicago naval facility converted into a pedestrian mall was not a traditional public forum in large part because the city had a strong interest in the continued financial viability of its public space, including collecting rents and other fees).

b. The Neutrality Requirement: Is the Regulation Simply a Time, Place, and Matter Restriction?

Another important component of the standard traditional public forum analysis is the requirement that the government regulation of speech at the public forum be content neutral, unless the requirement satisfies strict scrutiny. For the regulation to be content neutral, the government cannot regulate on the basis of the viewpoint or subject matter of the speech. Some neutral restrictions in a public forum might be time, place, and manner restrictions. If the restrictions are time, place, and manner restrictions, they are subject to intermediate scrutiny, meaning that they must be narrowly tailored to serve a significant state interest and must leave open ample alternative channels for communication.

Example 12-4:

Washington, D.C. had an ordinance that prohibited the display of signs criticizing a foreign government—even if the signs are on the public sidewalk—if the signs are within 500 feet of the foreign government's embassy. Is this ordinance content neutral?

Explanation:

No, the ordinance is not content neutral. It prevents communication that expresses a particular point of view. The ordinance is constitutional only if it passes strict scrutiny. The U.S. Supreme Court held in *Boos v. Berry*, 485 U.S. 312 (1988), that an ordinance like the one in this Example did not pass strict scrutiny. The District of Columbia justified the ordinance by explaining that the protests could embarrass foreign governments, but the *Boos v. Berry* Court was apparently unpersuaded that this amounted to a compelling interest and held the ordinance unconstitutional, stressing that the prohibited speech was classic political speech that took place on a public forum.

* * *

The question whether a regulation is content neutral is often tied to whether a regulation can be characterized as a proper time, place, and manner restriction. Accordingly, issues regarding whether a regulation is a proper time, place, and manner restriction often come up in the public forum context. The usual formulation of a time, place, and manner restriction is somewhat different than the usual formulation of the public forum doctrine. As explained above, case law regarding time, place, and manner restrictions requires that the restrictions on speech must be narrowly tailored to serve a significant government interest and leave open ample alternative channels for communication of the information prevented from being expressed by the restriction. The public forum doctrine does not formally integrate this level of scrutiny for neutral restrictions on speech within the public forum. Nonetheless, if a court characterizes a restriction that applies in a public forum as a time, place, and manner restrictions, then the court will likely follow this level of scrutiny. Time, place, and manner restrictions are covered more fully in Chapter 1 of this volume.

c. Government Speech or Public Forum?

The U.S. Supreme Court has restricted the public forum doctrine to protecting private speech and not instances when government is the speaker. The Court made this clear in *Walker v. Texas Division, Sons of Confederate Veterans, Inc.*, 576 U.S. 200 (2015), in which the Court held that the Texas Department of Motor Vehicles did not violate the First Amendment in refusing to issue a license plate depicting the confederate flag. The *Walker* Court declared that "[w]hen the government speaks, it is not barred by the Free Speech Clause from determining the content of what it says." Id. at 207. Why is it that license plates are properly characterized as government speech? The Court explained that (1) the government has long controlled the content of license plates, (2) license plates are messages perceived by the public as coming from the state, and (3) license plates are government IDs, whose messages are essentially controlled by the state.

These explanations are distilled as a three-factor test for determining whether a particular type of communication is government speech and thus outside the parameters of First Amendment protections for speech in public forums: "(1) whether the government has traditionally used the message or conduct at issue to speak to the public; (2) whether persons would interpret the speech as conveying some message on the government's behalf; and (3) whether the government maintains control over the selection of the message." *Shurtleff v. City of Boston*, 928 F.3d 166, 172 (1st Cir. 2019) (citing *Walker*,

576 U.S., at 209-210). Once it is determined that the challenged communication is government speech, the more rigorous standards of scrutiny that generally govern in the First Amendment context do not apply. In particular, the government need not speak on its own property in a viewpoint-neutral manner, a significant restriction often applied in First Amendment contexts.

Example 12-5:

A city maintains a series of flagpoles immediately outside of city hall. While the city flies the flag for the city, its state flag, and the United States flag, the city has also customarily raised the flags of private, third-party organizations from time to time to acknowledge special events or causes. The city maintains editorial control over which third-party flags it chooses to fly and maintains a public application process whereby an organization can seek permission to raise its flag. A faith-based ministry seeks to fly a flag that espouses a religious message, but the city denies its application.

The ministry brings a First Amendment challenge, arguing that the city engaged in viewpoint discrimination in rejecting their flag application and citing other instances where secular and other religious organizations were granted permission. The city moves to dismiss the suit, arguing that the flagpole constitutes government speech. Should the court dismiss the suit?

Explanation:

Arguments are strong that this Example presents an instance of government speech and that the court should dismiss the case. Applying the first *Walker* factor, one easily concludes from the facts that the city traditionally used the flagpoles to speak (symbolically) to the public. Presumably this also included occasions when the city chose to fly a flag at half-mast. As for the second factor, the location of the flags in such close proximity to city hall suggests that a reasonable observer would attribute to the city any message to be gleaned from a flag raised on one of the flagpoles. Third, although the city has previously flown third-party flags, the facts show that the city had consistently maintained editorial control over which flags it flies, requiring organizations to request to display their flag, and screening such requests using its own judgment. *See Shurtleff v. City of Boston*, 928 F.3d 166 (1st Cir. 2019).

Example 12-6:

For the past two years, a school maintained a practice of allowing community organizations that support its students to hang banners on a fence running alongside the school building, including messaging that contained a commercial advertisement for the organization. (The school has been in existence for over 60 years.) A math tutor who worked privately with many of the school's students asks to hang a banner advertising his services on the fence. Although the school had never been in the position to consider whether to grant permission to an individual private contractor before, the school initially decided to grant the tutor permission. Several parents learned that the math tutor also has a part-time job producing pornography and they complained to the school about his banner. The school responded by taking the tutor's banner down. Up until this dispute, the school had never declined a request to place a banner on its side fence.

The tutor brings a First Amendment suit against the school, arguing that their decision amounted to unlawful viewpoint discrimination. The school maintains that this restriction does not apply because the banner constitutes government speech. Is the school correct?

Explanation:

This Example presents a closer case than Example 12-2, but the school is likely wrong in taking the position that the banners constitute government speech. The first *Walker* factor is missing because the practice of allowing the banner is new, and the school had never had the opportunity to consider whether to allow a banner from a private independent contractor before. As to the second and third factors: although a reasonable observer might associate the school with the message displayed by its sponsors, the school had never before exercised editorial judgment concerning the banners. With two of the three *Walker* factors missing, this is a weak case for concluding that the banners constitute government speech. For a case coming to an opposite conclusion on the basis of slightly different facts, *see Mech v. School Board of Palm Beach County, Fla.*, 806 F.3d 1070 (11th Cir. 2015).

Example 12-7:

A town mayor maintains a social media page where she posts updates about public events, city services, and her political stances. Each of her posts contains a corresponding comments section where members of the public can respond to the mayor and correspond with each other. The interactive comments section also allows the mayor to respond to comments and enter the exchange among members of the public.

After the mayor advocated for a restriction on political canvassing and the town council enacted the restriction as a consequence, an organizer posted several angry comments on the mayor's social media page. The mayor in turn blocked the organizer from accessing her page.

The organizer argues that the mayor's social media page is a public forum and that the mayor *violated* the organizer's First Amendment rights. The mayor, however, argues that her social media page contains only government speech and is therefore exempt from the public forum doctrines. Is the mayor correct?

Explanation:

No, the mayor is not correct. The social media page is not properly characterized as containing only government speech. As an initial matter, one first observes that social media is not a traditional mode for government speech. As a consequence, the first element of the *Walker* test is missing. More fundamentally, however, the interactive component of the media page undermines the second and third *Walker* elements. Neither the mayor nor another government representative is responsible for producing all the content of the social media page. Citizens contribute significant material in the comments section. The mayor also does not exercise all control over the page, as required by the third *Walker* factor. The contents of comments are controlled by the citizens writing the comments and not by the mayor, except to the extent she attempts to do so by blocking the commentator. Although the mayor's contributions to the page might be accurately described as government speech, the contributions of others to the content of the page cannot.

This conclusion is supported by *Knight First Amendment Institute at Columbia University v. Trump*, 928 F.3d 226 (2d Cir. 2019). In that case, the court of appeals held that the comment section of President Trump's twitter page undermined the President's attempt to characterize the page as government speech. The court further held that the President's twitter page was a public forum and thus his blocking of critical users amounted to unconstitutional viewpoint discrimination. Although other courts have agreed with this analysis of government officials' social media pages, at least one court disagreed. In *Morgan v. Bevin*, 298 F. Supp. 3d 1003, 1011-1013 (E.D. Ky. 2018), the U.S. District Court for the Eastern District of Kentucky held that Kentucky Governor Matt Bevin's social media pages constituted his government speech, and thus he was permitted to block users who posted critical comments.

The *Knight* decision supports the organizer's position that the media site is a public forum. This characterization, however, is an expansion of the traditional public forum concept formulated in current U.S. Supreme Court cases. The subsection immediately below explores this case law.

2. Licensing and Permitting

As described in Chapter 4 of this volume, a licensing or permitting requirement is a form of prior restraint, which First Amendment doctrine

strongly discourages. In the context of licensing and permitting requirements for speech that occurs in a public forum, the U.S. Supreme Court
has imposed strict requirements: the regulation must provide clear criteria that leaves little or no discretion in the hands of the licensing or
permitting authority, an important reason must justify the license or permit, and the government must put in place procedural safeguards such
as prompt decisions on applications and judicial review of application
denials.

Example 12-8:

The administrators for the state fair have instituted a license requirement for
groups that would like to hand out literature in the public walkways at the
fairgrounds. The reason for the license is that the administrators are concerned about increasing foot traffic in the public walkways. The administrators show that they are swift in deciding whether to issue licenses, which
they usually issue as requested. If the license is turned down, the groups
may maintain a stationary booth for handing out literature in a portion of
the fairgrounds that are dedicated to booths of this kind. Is this licensing
scheme constitutional?

Explanation:

The licensing scheme is likely constitutional. The goal of reducing foot
traffic as well as controlling the flow of the traffic are important, substantial state interests. One may not readily discern how a licensing system
would reduce foot traffic if most licenses are granted, but the licensing
scheme may influence how the leafletting occurs and thus impact the
actual flow of the crowd. Moreover, the groups have alternative ways of
reaching their audience on the fairgrounds (and off the fairgrounds as
well). Cf. Heffron v. International Society for Krishna Consciousness, Inc., 452 U.S.
640 (1989) (holding that a licensing scheme for the distribution of
printed material at a state fair was a constitutional time, place, and manner restriction).

Example 12-8:

A city had an ordinance that provided that anyone wishing to have a parade
on a public street must obtain a permit. The ordinance provided, however,
that the only reason the government office that processed permit applications could deny an application is that the area was already reserved for a
parade by another entity. Is this scheme constitutional?

Explanation:

Yes, the scheme is likely constitutional. In *Cox v. New Hampshire*, 312 U.S. 569 (1941), the Court determined that making sure an area is used for only one parade at a time is an important goal. In addition, the ordinance in this Example strictly constrained the government office's discretion over the permitting process, thus further reinforcing the constitutionality of the scheme.

3. Designated Public Forums

In some instances, a government may transform a place that a government could close to speech, but choses instead to open to speakers. When that occurs, the U.S. Supreme Court has stated that the government has a created a "designated public forum." Once the government creates a designated public forum, the Court has explained, speech regulations for that location "are subject to the same strict scrutiny as restrictions in a traditional public forum." *Pleasant Grove v. Summum*, 555 U.S. 460, 470 (2009).

The problem with the designated public forum concept is that it blends with the notion of a limited public forum, described immediately below. A government creates a limited public forum in much the same way as a designated public forum—by transforming a space properly closed to speech into one open to speakers. It is often said, however, that the government opens up designated public forums for most speakers but allows only specific speakers and topics in a limited public forum. As a consequence, the constitutional constraints on the two concepts also differ: the government may properly restrict the speech that occurs in a limited public forum without complying with the strict constitutional constraints for traditional public forums, although those constraints do apply for designated public forums. The U.S. Supreme Court has never deployed the concept of a designated public forum within the context of an actual case. The Court has, however, used the limited public forum characterization in many cases.

B. LIMITED PUBLIC FORUM ANALYSIS

A limited public forum is a place that government has opened for speech by a particular group or on a particular topic. Once the government opens the space within the confines of these constraints, the government need not allow all persons to speak there. Nor does the government need to allow speech on every subject. The government restrictions must, however, be "reasonable in light of the purpose served by the forum" and the government must not discriminate against any speech on the basis of viewpoint. *Good News Club v. Milford Central School*, 533 U.S. 98, 106-107 (2001).

As with a traditional public forum, a government does not create a limited public forum by inaction. The government must evince an intent to open up a forum for speech for the location to take on the public forum designation. The government's intent must be viewed objectively. Moreover, the question whether the government intended to create a limited public forum must be measured by reviewing not only the government's stated policy, but also the government's actions and the extent of the public's use of the space. *Cornelius v. NAACP Legal Defense. & Education Fund, Inc.*, 473 U.S. 788, 802 (1985).

Example 12-9:

A city has a limited budget for artwork to be displayed at its newly constructed city hall facility, so it devises a plan to solicit local artists to donate paintings to line the halls of its interior. A longstanding city regulation allows the city to refuse to display any artwork that it deems "controversial," but there is no evidence that the city has ever relied on this rule to decline the display of an artist's work. In fact, several paintings that hung in the city hall facility over a period of several months inspired controversy, but the city did not respond to the controversy by taking down the art.

After the donation program was in place for some time, an artist donated a painting that contained nudity. The artwork remained displayed for several days until city employees complained about it and requested that the city take it down. The city ultimately decided to remove the artwork.

The artist brought a First Amendment challenge to the city's decision to take down her artwork. The artist argued that the city had created a limited public forum for the art, but then discriminated on the basis of viewpoint. The city disputed this characterization of events. According to the city, the city used a standard for taking down the art that was tied to whether it inspired controversy. The city maintains that it did not intend to impose its viewpoint on the decision whether to take down the art. The standard used, the city asserted, was not based on the city's opinion about the merits of the art. The city argued that the standard was pegged only on the reaction of others and the regulatory concern with avoiding unnecessary controversy concerning a building dedicated to fair and evenhanded governance. Which is the better argument—the city's or the artist's?

Explanation:

Given that an objective analysis governs the constitutionality of the city's standard for taking down the art, the artist has the better argument. Under an objective standard, a court evaluates a government's actions as well as its stated policies. Here, the policy of excluding art that is "controversial" does not have definite boundaries. Although the city now claims that the reactions of others are the point of reference in determining controversy, nothing prevents the city from using that standard in any way it sees fit in a particular context. As a consequence, the city can use the "controversy" standard within its own discretion as a subterfuge for censorship. Moreover, given the city's practice of using the regulatory policy inconsistently, the artist makes a credible case that the city is using the city regulation to discriminate against a certain viewpoint, such as disapproval of depicting nudity in public art. Cf. *Matal v. Tam*, 137 S. Ct. 1744 (2017) (observing that government regulation of speech that considers public reaction to the speech is viewpoint-based regulation). The city did not even have a mechanism in place to prescreen proposed donations or evaluate the extent of any controversy about artworks displayed.

In considering limited public forum claims, courts consider whether the government restrictions on speech are consistent with the purpose of the place where access is sought. The city makes a valid claim that the seat of local government might prudently avoid unnecessary controversy. The problem, however, is that a regulation framed only on the judgment of whether expression inspires controversy is sufficiently vague and indistinct as to require that the city should have proceeded in a manner that was far more rigorous and consistent in applying the policy. *See Hopper v. City of Pasco*, 241 F.3d 1067 (9th Cir. 2001).

Example 12-10:

A university erected bulletin boards on its campus: some boards are inside academic buildings and others are outside and located along prominent pedestrian thoroughfares on campus. At the time it put the bulletin boards in place, the university restricted access to using the outside bulletin boards. Any student was permitted to post informational flyers on the bulletin boards located inside the lobby of academic buildings. The university, however, restricted the bulletin boards along pedestrian thoroughfares throughout the campus by permitting only registered student organizations to post flyers there. The university's reason for this distinction was that outside bulletin board space on the university campus was limited. For the purposes of practicality and to convey a professional, competent, and attractive public image, the university wished to keep the appearance of these outside bulletin board neat and to ensure that the notices posted there are readable and up-to-date. For those reasons, the university restricts those who can post on the bulletin boards to groups that it can contact if necessary. (The university has a policy that registered student groups must inform the university of the contact information for the group's leaders at the beginning of each academic year.)

Does the First Amendment allow the university to deny students who are not part of registered student organizations to have access to posting flyers in the outside bulletin boards?

Explanation:

The university's policy complies with the First Amendment. The university was not required to erect outside bulletin boards. When it voluntarily did so, the university created a clear policy restricting the speakers who could use the outside bulletin boards. In so doing, the university created a limited public forum for these boards. The university's standard for who could use the outside bulletin boards was neutral and reasonable. The university had non-discriminatory reasons for wanting to limit the number of flyers on these boards. Moreover, by restricting the bulletin boards to registered student groups, the university ensured that it had contact information in case flyers needed to be taken down because the flyers still in place were out-of-date or causing another problem. See Celletti v. Becherer, No. 12 C 50308, 2013 WL 4759647 (N.D. Ill. Sept. 4, 2013).

Example 12-11:

A county school board maintained a policy restricting public comments at the school board meetings. Individuals seeking to speak at a school board meeting were permitted to speak only on matters that are being voted on by the school board at that meeting. They could not speak on any other matters, including those that were being discussed but for which a vote would not occur. Moreover, individuals seeking to speak at its meetings were required to seek prior approval from the school board by submitting written testimony that outlined what they intended to say and how their statement related to the school board's voting matters. The school board retained the power to edit the testimony and to restrict comments to only those that concerned the community. The school board took the position that a particular comment was not necessarily of concern to the community, even if it related to a matter that would be subject to a vote at that meeting. The guidelines further stated that the comments could not be abusive, defamatory, or disruptive.

A teacher suspected that members of the school board had been engaging in corrupt public acts by approving charter school applications that were submitted by individuals who were also regular donors to the school board members' businesses and campaigns. The teacher sought to confront the school board members during the public comment period of their upcoming meeting. After reviewing her proposed statement, the school board denied the teacher's request to speak.

The teacher brought a First Amendment challenge to the school board's regulation, which prevented her to speak on this suspected corruption. Specifically, the teacher contended that the board had created a public forum at its meetings and had violated the First Amendment by imposing the prior approval requirement for comments and the restrictions on the topics that a comment could cover. Is the teacher likely to prevail?

Explanation:

Yes, the teacher is likely to prevail. The school board had created a limited public forum by limiting discussion of certain topics and creating a system of limited access to the discussion. The school board was engaging in content-based discrimination in doing so, but that is permitted in a limited public forum so long as the restriction is viewpoint neutral and reasonable in light of the forum's purpose. In a limited public forum, a governmental entity has some leeway to conclude that the desired speech is inconsistent with the use or mission of a place.

The board's exercise of its ability to curate the comments made is consistent with the purpose of ensuring that the meeting will focus efficiently on matters bearing directly on running the school system. The problem, however, is that the procedures in place for preclearance review gives the board unbridled discretion to refuse someone the opportunity to speak on these matters and creates an opportunity for the board to censor those comments that may be relevant to school matters to be discussed, but may also make board members uncomfortable. Accordingly, the system does not satisfy the requirement that the restrictions imposed in a limited public forum be neutral. The requirement also suffers because it appears to be a governmentally imposed prior restraint on speech. The prior restraint doctrine is covered in Chapter 4 of this volume. *See Barrett v. Walker County School District*, 872 F.3d 1209, 1225 (11th Cir. 2017).

C. NON-PUBLIC FORUM ANALYSIS

A non-public forum is a space that does not fit into the traditional public forum categories and one in which the government has expressed no intent to open the space up for expressive activities. Within non-public forums, however, the government may regulate speech so long as their restrictions are viewpoint neutral and reasonable.

Example 12-12:

After using a formal selection process, a city social services agency invited ABC Law, a local legal aid agency, to run an informational table in its office waiting room in order to provide clients of the social services agency with information about benefits eligibility and to offer pro bono representational services to the agency's clients. The social services agency made the invitation in order to serve the needs of its clients but adopted a policy of permitting only a single informational table in the waiting room. The agency specifically requested that ABC Law (1) avoid approaching any of the social service agency's clients in the waiting room, (2) provide the social service agency's clients with information only if they requested it, and (3) forbear from soliciting the clients' business. To stay true to its mission, the social services agency wished to maintain its autonomy and believed that it should avoid appearing aligned with or advocating the services of ABC Law. The social services agency was also concerned about avoiding any practices that could aggravate their clients or make them uncomfortable while in the waiting room.

The agency restricted access to the waiting room to individuals who have official business with the agency (and their retained advocates if they have any) as well as ABC Law representatives. In order to maintain an orderly flow of business, to protect some semblance of privacy for its clients, and to ensure that it can monitor whether ABC Law representatives are complying with its restrictions, the social services agency had a policy that only one legal aid agency may provide information in the waiting room.

XYZ Law, a competing legal services provider, sought permission to host a second table in the waiting room. Relying on its policy, the social services agency denied access to XYZ Law.

XYZ Law sued alleging a violation of its First Amendment rights. XYZ Law argued that in light of the importance of the social services agency's mission and its status as a government entity open to all citizens who need its services, the social service agency's waiting room was either a traditional public forum or a limited public forum. They also argued that the social service agency's policy is unreasonable and therefore unconstitutional. Is XYZ Law correct?

Explanation:

No, XYZ Law is not correct. The waiting room is a non-public forum. This status derives from the social services agency's policy of keeping the waiting room closed to all except for one legal services entity and to those who have business with the agency. Moreover, the restrictions align with the mission of the agency, which is to provide confidential services to those who request it. That mission is not consistent with opening its waiting room to anyone who requests admission. The social services agency's decision to extend a well-considered invitation to one legal aid entity to be present in the waiting room does not undermine a non-public forum characterization. The social service agency's decision derived from a desire to serve the specific needs of its clients and was deliberately confined to only one legal aid entity.

Finally, the restrictions satisfy the First Amendment requirements for nonpublic forums. The social service agency's reasons for the allowing only one legal entity to be present in the waiting room—efficiency, ease of monitoring, as well as the privacy and comfort of its clients—were entirely reasonable. The selection of ABC was made after a formal selection process and does not appear to have been discriminatory. Cf. *Make the Road by Walking, Inc. v. Turner*, 378 F.3d 133 (2d Cir. 2004).

Example 12-13:

An advocacy group wished to have airplanes tow aerial banners above a public beach on a resort island. Pointing to a city ordinance prohibiting aerial banners in the area of beaches, the government entity that regulated the beach refused to allow the advocacy group permission to do so. The government entity explained that the purpose of the restriction was to avoid the cost of monitoring the banners and to foster tourism by avoiding distraction from the pristine natural beauty of the area. The advocacy group argued that the air space above a public beach had been traditionally regarded as a public forum. Is the advocacy group correct?

Explanation:

The advocacy group is likely not correct. Perhaps by analogy to a park, a public beach might qualify as a traditional public forum. The space above the beach, however, is physically separate from the ground or the water and requires special equipment to access as well as authorization to do so. Indeed, airspace has been historically subject to strict FAA restriction and its principle purpose has never been viewed as a place for the free exchange of ideas. For those reasons, the airspace does not qualify as a traditional public forum. Because the restriction is absolute, the airspace is also not a limited public forum or a designated public forum: the airspace is a non-public forum.

Since the restriction concerns a non-public forum, the restriction must be neutral and reasonable. The prohibition on banners satisfies these requirements. Because the prohibition is absolute, it does not distinguish between one banner or another and is therefore neutral. Moreover, the reasons for the restriction are reasonable in light of the status of the island as a tourist destination where ambience is particularly important and available public funds for monitoring are likely sparse. See *Center for Bio-Ethical Reform, Inc. v. City & County of Honolulu*, 455 F.3d 910 (9th Cir. 2006).

Example 12-14:

A city prohibits expressive activity in the pedestrian plaza immediately in front of the entrance to a large city-owned sports arena, citing its interest in maintaining efficient pedestrian flow and curtailing harassment of patrons. Under the ordinance, such activities are unrestricted on the adjacent sidewalk. Access to the pedestrian plaza is not physically restricted either: non-patron pedestrians regularly cut through the plaza. Nonetheless, the city has designated a division between the plaza and the sidewalk by placing a series of planters, flag poles, and light posts around the plaza's perimeter. The city's ban for the plaza proscribes most expressive activity within the area of the plaza, including the solicitation of funds and the distribution of handbills. The ban has been in place since the sports arena was built.

Eileen would like to distribute religious handbills and challenges the ordinance as an unduly burdensome regulation on his First Amendment right to free speech in a traditional public forum. The city moves to dismiss the suit, arguing that the plaza constitutes a non-public forum. Should the court grant the motion?

Explanation:

This is a close case, but strong arguments support the position that the plaza constitutes a non-public forum. On one hand, Eileen's argument has foundation because the plaza appears to be physically and functionally similar to any sidewalk that qualifies as a traditional public forum. Yet the attempts by the city to set the plaza apart from the surrounding sidewalk with physical cues such as planters, light posts, and flag poles convey the message that the area is different than a usual sidewalk. The general expectation that the area in front of a large stadium should be kept clear for safe ingress and egress—as well as the fact that the city had the restriction in place since the stadium was built—weigh in favor of characterizing the plaza as a non-public forum. Given that the facts suggest that the plaza has never been used for any expressive activity, a court would be on solid ground in concluding that the area is a non-public forum. Nothing in the facts suggest that the city has enforced the ban in anything but a neutral manner and the concern with avoiding harassment and physical hindrances to access to the stadium suggest that the ban is reasonable. See Ball v. City of Lincoln, 870 F.3d 722 (8th Cir. 2017).

* * *

Restrictions on advertising space in public transit infrastructure occur often in the non-public forum context. In Lehman v. City of Shaker Heights, 418 U.S. 298 (1974), a plurality of the Supreme Court ruled that advertising space within a city-owned bus was a non-public forum and that the city did not violate the First Amendment when it excluded advertising that was political speech. In light of this, consider the following contrasting Example.

Example 12-15:

Over many years, the City of New York followed the practice of featuring advertisements on both buses and subways. The transit system had come to rely on the advertisements as a significant source of income and the riding public had come to expect the buses and subways to be filled with advertisements of all kinds, including political ads, ads with religious themes, and the like. The transit system was in the practice of taking all ads so long as space was available to post them.

The city transit system, however, declined to carry an advertisement from a local magazine that said that the magazine was "Possibly the only good thing in New York Rudy hasn't taken credit for." The magazine took the position that the advertising space is a public forum and that the transit system's refusal to carry their advertisement was content discrimination focused on the mayor, Rudy Giuliani. Is the magazine's assertion valid?

Explanation:

Yes, the magazine's assertion is valid. Most courts take the position that advertising on buses and subways is a non-public forum. But the transit authority's longstanding practice in this Example of allowing all manner of advertisements — including political ads — suggests that the transit authority was willing to accept the possibility of opinion clashes and controversy and to convey to the public a general intent to open a public space for discourse. Excluding one advertisement targeting a particular politician indeed does suggest discrimination on the basis of the content of the speech, rendering the transit system's action unconstitutional. *See New York Magazine v. Metropolitan Transportation Auth.*, 136 F.3d 123 (2d Cir. 1998).

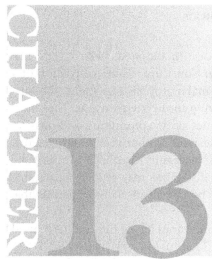

Speech in Government Controlled Contexts: The Military, Prisons, Schools, and Government Employees

As discussed in Chapter 12, the government's ability to restrict speech in a place is significantly affected by the extent to which the place is open to public speech. Similarly, the authoritarian nature of the military, prisons, and schools significantly influences analysis of First Amendment protections within those contexts. The government's role as a custodian in these institutions raises the incentive for government to control expression in order to promote the institutions' missions without disruption. Perhaps unsurprisingly, the Supreme Court tends to defer to institutional decision making in these areas, and approaches First Amendment challenges to restrictions on expression in custodial environments with a great deal of discretion. Although these three contexts each reflect unique qualities, they are joined together in this chapter because governments have strong interests in controlling each of them, an interest which significantly affects the First Amendment analysis. This chapter ends with a discussion of the speech rights of government employees. This topic also appears in this chapter because of government's strong interest in control as well. Each of the four topics in the chapter are loosely related: the tie that binds them is the inclination to loosen First Amendment oversight as a result of the unusual need for government control in the various contexts.

A. RESTRICTIONS ON MILITARY SPEECH

The military context is perhaps the area in which the U.S. Supreme Court extends the most deference when evaluating speech restrictions within government institutions. A key, early case in the area, *Parker v. Levy*, 417 U.S. 733 (1974), set the tone. The *Parker* Court upheld the conviction of a military doctor who was punished for making public statements discouraging Black service members from serving in the Vietnam War. The Court explained that due to the unique qualities of its community and mission the military can infringe on speech that would otherwise be protected if uttered by a civilian: "The fundamental necessity for obedience, and the consequent necessity for imposition of discipline, may render permissible within the military that which would be constitutionally impermissible outside it." *Id.* at 758.

Parker concerned the following provisions that the military used to punish speech under the Uniform Code of Military Justice, 10 U.S.C. §§ 801-946a (2018): (1) section 888, Contempt Toward Officials; (2) sections 890 and 892, which address failure to obey orders from superiors or regulations; (3) section 933, Conduct Unbecoming an Officer and a Gentleman; and (4) section 934, General Article, which punishes "all disorders and neglects to the prejudice of good order and discipline." The *Parker* Court upheld sections 890, 933, and 934 against First Amendment facial vagueness and overbreadth challenges. Invoking strong deference to military decision making, the Court concluded that the military doctor could not have reasonably believed that his statements would be protected under the regulations, and therefore the regulations were not unconstitutionally vague. The Court also ruled that the relevant provisions were not overbroad because although they applied in many circumstances, their interpretations could be sufficiently limited by military courts and military-promulgated guidelines. Finally, the Court concluded that military necessity outweighed the doctor's First Amendment interests in the context of the facial challenges at bar, while preserving the possibility of a successful "as applied" challenge "[lurking] at the fringes" of the law. 417 U.S. at 760-61.

The other major case regarding restrictions on military speech is *Brown v. Glines*, 444 U.S. 348 (1980). Again, invoking military deference, the *Brown* Court upheld an Air Force regulation that required service members to obtain approval from their commanders before circulating petitions on Air Force bases. In *Brown*, an Air Force captain circulated a petition on his base, without seeking prior approval from his commander, urging Congress to amend Air Force grooming standards. The captain brought a First Amendment retaliation claim arising from his resulting punishment, as well as a claim under a federal statute that prohibited, to some extent, the military from interfering with service member communications with members of Congress.

The *Brown* Court determined that the regulations restricted no more speech than "reasonably necessary" to further the military's interest in preventing dangers to maintain order among service members, particularly because a military base is not a public forum and the military necessarily must be able to restrict material determined to hinder troop readiness. *Id.* at 355. The Court reasoned that the regulations were not overbroad because existing Air Force directives limited their scope to material that threatened loyalty, discipline, or morale, and excluded (1) material that was merely critical of the government or its policies and (2) material sent through the U.S. mail or distributed in magazines and newspapers at post-exchange newsstands. Although the preclearance requirement amounted to a prior restraint on speech, the Court nonetheless reasoned that military leaders' "right to command and the [soldiers'] duty to obey ordinarily must go unquestioned," thus deferring to the commanders' choice to review petitions before they are circulated. *Id.* at 357.

Aside from its reinforcement of military deference and tacit endorsement of a prior restraint, Brown is notable for other reasons. First, the Court lowered the evidentiary standard for what constituted unprotected "dangerous speech" in the military context to the "clear and present danger" standard. Cf. *Brandenburg v. Ohio*, 395 U.S. 444, 447 (1969) (requiring a showing of "an intent to incite" and "imminent" danger of "likely" "lawless action," for civilian "dangerous speech").[1] In addition, the Court seemed to imply that a regulation inhibiting a service member's ability to communicate directly to a member of Congress would cover more speech than reasonably necessary and thus potentially violate the First Amendment. The Court's focus was instead on the propriety of preventing a service member from circulating petitions on base and communicating with other service members.

Lower courts have followed the deferential approaches of *Brown* and *Parker* in a variety of free speech conflicts that have appeared in the civilian context as well. In the following Examples, consider how the military context differs from how a court would resolve the conflicts in a civilian setting.

Example 13-1:

During a flag-lowering ceremony, Ned, an Army service member, makes several disparaging comments about Army policies. Once the flag is lowered, he blows his nose on the American flag. Ned is convicted by court martial of "dereliction of duty." Ned takes the position that his act was expressive conduct protected under the First Amendment. Is the conviction a violation of his First Amendment rights?

---

1. Chapter 6 of this volume on incitement of illegal activity explores the clear and present danger and *Brandenburg* tests.

Explanation:

Existing authority supports the conclusion that the conviction does not violate Ned's First Amendment rights. *United States v. Wilson*, 33 M.J. 797 (A.C.M.R. 1991). In the *Wilson* case, the Army Court of Military Review upheld service member's conviction under charges of dereliction of duty and failure to follow orders. The court determined that even assuming the appellant's conduct was expressive, the charges were valid under the O'Brien test: When a regulation prohibits conduct with both an expressive and nonexpressive element, it is constitutional if: (1) the government has the authority to regulate the conduct; (2) the regulation furthers a substantial government interest; (3) the interest is unrelated to the suppression of speech; and (4) the regulation prohibits no more speech than is necessary to further the interest.[2] The court concluded the first element was satisfied because the conviction only incidentally burdened Wilson's symbolic speech, and that the government may validly regulate expressive conduct of soldiers. Next, the court held the regulation furthered the substantial government interest in "promoting an effective military force." *Id.* at 800. In the *Wilson* court's view, the charges were unrelated to the suppression of speech on its face because the relevant law broadly punished insubordination. Last, the restriction touched no more protected speech than necessary to further the government's interest in military discipline and performance. Note the contrast of this decision with the flag-burning case, *Texas v. Johnson*, 491 U.S. 397 (1989), in which the Court concluded that the O'Brien test did not apply because the prohibition against flag-burning was motivated by disapproval of the message conveyed by the expressive speech. In other words, the content-based prohibition in *Johnson* was not entitled to the relatively deferential O'Brien test.

Example 13-2:

The Military Honor and Decency Act prohibits the sale or rental of "sexually explicit materials" at military exchanges, which are mega-retail stores open exclusively to service members, veterans, and their family members. The act prohibits the sale or rental of recordings and periodicals "the dominant theme of which depicts or describes nudity, including sexual or excretory activities or organs, in a lascivious way." 10 U.S.C. § 2495b (2018). Ida is a service member who argues that the law violates her First Amendment free speech rights. Is she correct?

---

2. This test comes from *United States v. O'Brien*, 391 U.S. 367 (1968), discussed in detail in Chapter 11 of this volume.

Explanation:

Ida's position has flaws: the law quite likely may be constitutional. To be sure, several arguments support the position that the law runs counter to First Amendment principles that govern in civilian situations. To begin, although the First Amendment appears to offer protection for indecent speech, *see, e.g., Cohen v. California*, 403 U.S. 15 (1971), it offers no protection to obscenity. The prohibition covers material that is "lascivious," which appears to be a classification that applies to a broader range of expression than material that is obscene (and only obscene speech would fall outside the scope of First Amendment protection). The standard for what constitutes unprotected, obscene speech is detailed, specific, qualities lacking from the restriction in this Example. The government might successfully argue that lascivious speech may be classified together with indecent speech—but most agree that indecent speech enjoys constitutional protection. To the extent that the regulation prohibits obscene speech, no constitutional problem exists. But the scope of the prohibition appears to sweep broader than that.

That does not end the matter: the context here is not mainstream regulation of speech. The regulation of lascivious speech in this Example may meet the standard for upholding a regulation of indecent speech: one can imagine a court might rule that banning lascivious expression among service personnel serves an important or substantial government purpose.[3]

Another complication remains: The Military Honor and Decency Act's prohibition is arguably viewpoint based. This is particularly problematic if the military's mega-retail stores are classified as public forums or limited public forums (which are places where the government may not discriminate on the basis of viewpoint unless the government has a compelling reason for doing so).[4] Nevertheless, the military context—as explained in *Parker* and *Brown*—likely eliminates whatever power these doctrines may have to support Ida's argument that the Act is unconstitutional.

In *General Media Communications, Inc. v. Cohen*, No. 97-6029, 1997 U.S. App. LEXIS 40571 (2d Cir. Nov. 21, 1997), the court of appeals rejected a First Amendment challenge to the Military Honor and Decency Act. The court determined that the military exchanges were non-public forums because they were open only to military personnel, their dependents, orphans, surviving spouses, and certain others. According to the court, the government's rules regarding access to the exchanges made plain that the government did not intend for them to be open for public expression and exchange of ideas. In any event, the court rejected the claim that the military was discriminating

---

3. Chapter 8 of this volume discusses the standard for evaluating obscene and indecent speech.

4. Chapter 12 of this volume reviews the law governing public forums and limited public forums in the civilian context.

on the basis of viewpoint by disqualifying "lascivious" materials. The court opined that "[t]he adjective 'lascivious' is much more plausibly understood as helping to identify more particularly the subject matter (i.e., content) that the Act encompasses: namely, depictions of nudity including sexual or excretory activities or organs, but only those depictions that are also lascivious." Id. at *25.

The *General Media Communications* court also noted that the government was offering the exchanges as a service to military members and therefore enjoyed the prerogative of deciding precisely what items to offer for resale. This prerogative is analogous to the flexibility that governments enjoy in the civilian context to curate libraries and set criteria for public grants. See, e.g., *United States v. American Library Ass'n*, 539 U.S. 194 (2003) (plurality opinion) (emphasizing that libraries enjoy broad latitude in putting together the collections offered to the public); *National Endowment for the Arts v. Finley*, 524 U.S. 569 (1998) (holding that when awarding grants for the arts the government may make aesthetic judgments about artistic quality to determine eligibility).

Finally, the *General Media Communications* court invoked the principle of military deference. Specifically, the court concluded that the restriction on lascivious material was a reasonable means of promoting "military honor, professionalism, proper decorum, and military 'core values.'" 1997 U.S. App. LEXIS 40571, at *33.

For further analysis of the facts of this Example, *see* Example 17-2 of Chapter 17 of this volume, which provides detailed analysis of the interaction of the various strands of First Amendment doctrine presented here.

Example 13-3:

Robby Racist maintained a social media profile in which he identified himself as a "US Army Paratrooper." Robby often posted white supremacist content on his social media page and stated that he would be less likely to follow an order from a non-white superior officer. A local police officer reported his page to the Army, which arranged for an undercover agent to pose as a young woman interested in joining a white supremacist organization and engage Robby via online chat and email. Robby took the bait, admitted responsibility as author of the statements on the post, and offered the woman a chance to join his white supremacist organization. None of Robby's speech occurred while on duty or at a military facility.

Robby was convicted of violating section 934 of the Uniform Code of Military Justice, which prohibits "all disorders and neglects to the prejudice of good order and discipline." 10 U.S.C. § 934. Robby appealed, arguing that his conviction was repugnant to the First Amendment because his online speech was protected. The Army responded that his speech was unprotected because it was "dangerous speech" that could have a detrimental impact on troop discipline. Who has the better argument, Robby or the Army?

Explanation:

If evaluated through the lens of civilian First Amendment doctrine, Robby has the better argument. His speech does not rise to the level of incitement to illegal activity, fighting words, unprotected hate speech, or a true threat. The First Amendment does not allow unfettered regulation of "dangerous speech" that does not instill fear of violent action.[5] If the government cannot prove that Robby's speech was not entitled to full First Amendment protections, then it likely cannot justify his conviction. Yet this analysis fails to recognize the military deference principle and the notion that disturbing speech such as Robby's can undermine military cohesion and morale — not to mention professionalism, honor, and decorum.

The existing precedent is contradictory. In one case, *United States v. Wilcox*, 66 M.J. 442 (C.A.A.F. 2008), the U.S. Court of Appeals for the Armed Forces overturned a service member's conviction under circumstances similar to this Example because the evidence failed to show a sufficient connection between punishing his speech and ensuring military order. According to the court, the First Amendment requires that the military demonstrate "a direct and palpable connection between speech and the military mission" to sustain a conviction of the general prohibition against disorders and neglects that prejudice military good order and discipline. *Id.* at 448.

In another case, however, the U.S. Court of Appeals for the Armed Forces upheld a service member's conviction under section 934 for communicating a threat against President Obama in the wake of the 2012 general election. *United States v. Rapert*, 75 M.J. 164 (C.A.A.F. 2016). In the *Rapert* case, while at a friend's house, a service member criticized and threatened to kill President Obama. He used racial slurs and referenced his affiliation with the KKK. Although the court acknowledged that the statements did not amount to a true threat, the court applied the direction of the Supreme Court in *Brown* to use the clear and present danger test to determine whether the service member's speech was protected by the First Amendment. This test requires a court to consider the gravity of evil posed by the speech, weighed against the likelihood that it will occur. The resulting possible danger is then weighed against the individual's interest in free speech.

The *Rapert* court found that the defendant's statements had a high potential for harm, especially since threats against the President, the Commander in Chief of the Armed Forces, "unquestionably undermine[d] the military's unique interest in ensuring obedience to the chain of command." *Id.* at 171.

---

5. *See* Chapter 7 of this volume for discussion of the categories of violence-inspiring speech for which the First Amendment allows regulation.

The court reasoned that the disregard for chain of command, as well as the possibility that the disobedience might influence the defendant's colleagues, outweighed his interest in expressing his speech.

Rapert had a similar set of facts to *Wilcox*, but the U.S. Court of Appeals for the Armed Forces reached the opposite conclusion. Like in *Wilcox*, the defendant in *Rapert* communicated his statement while he was off-duty, off-base, and without any indication that he intended his statement to reach other service members. But unlike *Wilcox*, the court upheld the conviction despite the lack of any evidence showing the defendant's statements had any effect on order and discipline. What explains the difference between the two cases? Perhaps it was the subject of the *Rapert* defendant's message — violence against the President. Not only does this subject implicate a threat to national security, but in the context of the military speech, violence against the commander in chief undermines the chain of command.

B. RESTRICTIONS ON PRISONER SPEECH

Unsurprisingly, prison inmates also have a curtailed First Amendment right to free speech. The Supreme Court has established that, with narrow exceptions, a prison's speech restriction should be reviewed under a deferential standard. *Turner v. Safley*, 482 U.S. 78 (1987). Under the *Turner v. Safley* test, which applies to all prisoner constitutional rights, a speech restriction will be upheld as long as it is reasonably related to legitimate penological interests. The test calls for a rational basis review standard, which — when applied — will prohibit only those policies that are truly irrational or arbitrary.

As explored further below, despite the approach of *Turner v. Safley*, case law suggests that a court will apply heightened scrutiny when a prison censors a prisoner's outgoing mail. This principle is the product of *Procunier v. Martinez*, 416 U.S. 396 (1974), an earlier case which appears to remain intact. *Procunier* requires that regulations of outgoing prison mail must serve a substantial state interest unrelated to free expression and must be no greater than necessary to ensure prison safety.

The bulk of the inmate free speech issues, however, is governed by the *Turner v. Safley* test, which specifically requires that the prison officials articulate some "valid, rational connection between the prison regulation and the legitimate governmental interest put forward to justify it." 482 U.S. at 89 (internal quotation marks omitted). A court applying the test must (1) determine whether the governmental objective underlying the regulations at issue is "legitimate and neutral" and (2) whether the regulations are rationally related to that objective. *Id.* at 89-90. With regard to neutrality, the prison may punish a prisoner based on the content of her speech so long as the punishment can be justified without reference to the content of the speech. A prison cannot punish an inmate for merely criticizing something about the prison. As to the rational connection element, the prison officials need not show that the speech in question actually interferes, or is even likely to interfere, with the prison's purported interest. The prison officials need establish only that a reasonable prison official might think that the policy advances the interest.

If the court finds the prison failed to establish the first factor, the analysis stops and the policy is deemed unconstitutional. If, as is often the case, the regulation is deemed rationally related to legitimate penological interests, the court will balance three factors: (1) whether alternative means of exercising the right remain open to prison inmates; (2) "the absence of ready alternatives" to the prison's restrictions of constitutional rights; and (3) the impact that accommodating the right would have on guards, other inmates, and prison resources. Id. at 89-91. Cases tend to turn on the threshold step and prisoners rarely prevail on the balancing step.

Example 13-4:

On the twenty-fifth anniversary of a notorious prison riot, a group of journalists petition the prison for access to interview individual prisoners who had participated in the riot and had been detained in particularly restrictive conditions since that time. The prison denied the journalists access, citing their general policy of prohibiting in-person interviews with restricted population members.

The prisoners brought a First Amendment challenge. They argued that the prison's restriction of media access was unreasonably burdensome in

Evaluating Regulations of Inmate Speech under *Turner v. Shaffley*

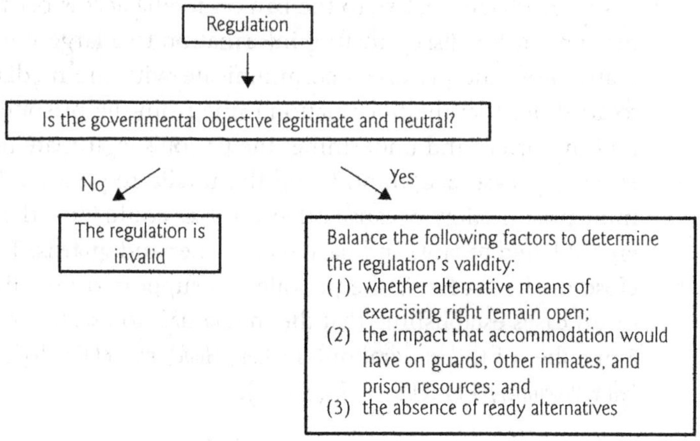

Figure 13-1

213

light of the inherent public service value of the restricted speech: An in-person interview with a journalist on an incident of public interest outweighs the prison's general interest in efficiency and security. The prison officials, on the other hand, justified the restriction by arguing that granting the interviews could potentially impact prison safety by enhancing the influence of the dangerous inmates and glorifying the prison riot. Will the prison prevail?

Explanation:

Yes, the prison officials will likely prevail. Under the *Turner v. Safley* test, the prison officials have a reasonable argument that they are trying to prevent potentially substantial disciplinary problems. This concern is enhanced by the restricted prisoners' participation in the prior riots and apparently persistent disruptive behavior that has kept them in restricted status. In a case similar to this, *Hanrahan v. Mohr*, 905 F.3d 947 (6th Cir. 2018), the court ruled that the restriction on the media was neutral because it was intended to prevent prisoners from gaining influence through media attention, irrespective of the content of any media report. Under *Turner*, a prison may altogether ban a particular form of speech because of its content, so long as the prison can justify the restriction of the speech without reference to its content.

Having concluded that the prohibition was reasonable and neutral, a court confronting the facts of this Example would next balance the three factors: (1) whether prisoners have alternative means of exercising the right; (2) the absence of ready alternatives to the prison's restrictions; and (3) the impact that accommodating the right would have on guards, other inmates, and prison resources. All three factors are met in this case. The prisoners have the ability to tell their story in ways other than through in-person media interviews, such as through outgoing mail or direct phone calls. The prison has no ready alternative to the ban on media access because the media is an instrument for disseminating information to a large number of people. No matter how the prisoners communicate with the media, the media is free to advertise that the information came from the prisoners, which increases their notoriety and undermines the prison's legitimate interest in order and efficiency. Last, accommodating the media request could seriously undermine prison safety because other inmates could view the broadcast, become emboldened to riot, and harm each other and guards. The decision to foreclose media access to the prisoners is supported by a line of U.S. Supreme Court cases establishing that the media has no greater access to prisons than a member of the general public. E.g., *Houchins v. KQED, Inc.*, 438 U.S. 1 (1978); *Pell v. Procunier*, 417 U.S. 817 (1974).

* * *

The cases addressing prisoner speech rights—like the military cases—consistently defer to institutional decision making. But the cases also show special sensitivity to prisoner rights of expression not reflected in the military context. Consider the following:

Example 13-5:

A prisoner is killed in an altercation with prison guards. When his mother sues the prison for wrongful death, another prisoner who witnessed the event submits an affidavit supporting the mother's case. The witness is consequently and repeatedly harassed by prison guards, and otherwise subjected to disparate treatment. The witness brings a First Amendment retaliation claim. The prison counters that the witness's affidavit testimony was not protected speech because it concerned a private dispute and did not touch on a matter of public concern. Is the prison's argument a winning one?

Explanation:

No, the prison's argument is not likely necessarily a winner. In *Bridges v. Gilbert*, 557 F.3d 541 (7th Cir. 2009), the court ruled that prisoner speech is protected by the First Amendment even if it does not concern a public matter. According to the court, prisoners need not even establish that they were attempting to discuss a matter of public concern. The *Bridges* court reasoned:

> Shut off from the outside world, the prisoner's speech would nearly always be speech made "as a prisoner" rather than "as a citizen." To further limit protection to matters of public concern would seem to restrict prisoners' constitutional rights far more than is "justified by the considerations underlying our penal system."

Id. at 550.

In fact, the court reasoned that allowing the speech may actually support penal objectives: "Prisons have an interest in keeping the inmates as safe and secure as possible while imprisoned, and truthful speech that describes possible abuses can actually be quite consistent with that objective." Id. at 551. The Court of Appeals for the Seventh Circuit in *Bridges* found support for this ruling in decisions from other circuits.

* * *

As mentioned above, the U.S. Supreme Court provides more protection to the private, outgoing mail of prisoners than other forms of prison expression. Adding subtlety to this distinction is the case law reflecting arguments that outgoing mail poses less of a threat to prison order and safety than incoming mail. Incoming mail can contain contraband as well instructions for escape and other illegality. Outgoing mail is less likely to include this type of material. Some confusion nevertheless surrounds the matter of protecting prisoner mail from over-intrusive regulation.

In *Thornburgh v. Abbott*, 490 U.S. 401, 414 (1989), the Supreme Court suggested that the heightened scrutiny standard that previously applied to all prisoner First Amendment claims in *Procunier v. Martinez*, 416 U.S. 396 (1974), still applies to censorship of outgoing mail despite the intervening *Turner* decision. *Thornburgh* itself, however, concerned a restriction on incoming mail. For that reason, several courts have treated *Thornburgh*'s statement about outgoing mail as non-binding dicta, and have instead applied the more deferential *Turner* test to restrictions on outgoing mail, rather than the test from *Martinez*.[6] Other courts have not done so.[7] Under the *Martinez* test, a regulation "must further an important or substantial governmental interest unrelated to the suppression of expression" and "must be no greater than is necessary or essential to the protection of the particular governmental interest involved." *Martinez*, 416 U.S. at 413.

Applying the *Martinez* standard to restrictions of outgoing prisoner mail often leads to a judgment for the prisoner, while the *Turner* standard usually ensures a judgment for the prison. However, this is not always the case. Consider the following Examples.

Example 13-6:

A prison routinely inspects all outgoing mail, including correspondence sent to attorneys. A prisoner challenges this regulation, arguing that it does not rationally relate to a legitimate penological interest. The prison officials argue that the policy is necessary to prevent the proliferation of criminal activity, both within and outside the prison, but they concede that they have no evidence that any outgoing legal mail has actually facilitated crime. The prisoner further argues that the prison could adopt an alternative policy of checking for "fakes," by confirming that the letter is addressed to an actual attorney and by checking a state bar list of licensed attorneys as opposed to inspecting each piece of mail. Does the prisoner have a good argument? Does the result differ depending on whether the deferential *Turner* standard or the more rigorous *Martinez* standard applies?

---

6. *See Perry v. Secretary, Florida Dep't of Corr.*, 664 F.3d 1359, 1368 (11th Cir. 2011) (applying *Turner* reasonableness test to outgoing prison mail restriction); *Samford v. Dretke*, 562 F.3d 674, 678-682 (5th Cir. 2009) (same).

7. *See, e.g.*, *Nasir v. Morgan*, 350 F.3d 366, 375 (3d Cir. 2003) (applying the deferential *Turner* test to restrictions on incoming prison mail and the higher-scrutiny *Martinez* test to restrictions on outgoing prisoner mail).

Explanation:

The prisoner does have a good argument and the result may not change whether the Turner standard or the Martinez standard governs. The prisoner's case is strong, even under the deferential Turner approach. While the prison is correct that legal correspondence could facilitate criminal activity, this interest does not merit much weight in considering the constitutionality of the prison's policy because the prison admits that it did not prove that any legal correspondence actually addressed to an attorney contributed to criminal activity. In order for a rational relationship to exist between prison policy and the asserted reasons for the policy, the reasons must be grounded in some evidence. Moreover, the argument that prison authorities could easily use a less intrusive approach by checking whether an outgoing letter is addressed to a member of the bar (rather than, for example, a partner in crime who is merely posing as a lawyer) also suggests that the prison policy is invalid under the deferential approach. Certainly, prison officials could more easily verify the address of an outgoing attorney correspondence with a database of bar-admitted attorneys than review its content. See Nordstrom v. Ryan, 856 F.3d 1256, 1273 (9th Cir. 2017) (holding that "restrictions on outgoing mail must have a closer fit between the regulation and the purpose it serves than incoming mail restrictions," even under a deferential standard applying to all mail). But cf. Altizer v. Deeds, 191 F.3d 540, 548 (4th Cir. 1999) (emphasizing the difference between complete censorship and less intrusive review and preclearance of outgoing inmate mail when evaluating the constitutionality of prison mail policies).

C. RESTRICTIONS ON STUDENT SPEECH

The final custodial context presenting issues regarding government speech regulations — public schools — presents different concerns than prisons and the military. The differences may arise from a number of distinctions: the youth of those restricted in the school context, diminished need for government control in the student context, and support for student exposure to the free flow of ideas and debate. This latter concern focuses on the educational mission of producing citizens that function well in a democratic society. As is often repeated, students do not lose their rights at the school house door. See Tinker v. Des Moines Independent Community School District, 393 U.S. 503, 506 (1969). A successful public school system should promote tolerance, develop critical thinking and communications skills, and empower students to seek knowledge to make informed decisions about public matters. In recent years, the U.S. Supreme Court has treated this concern with diminished importance, and given greater emphasis on school needs in maintaining control. Recent cases highlight the need to give schools latitude to maintain control so as to fulfill their educational mission and to reinforce self-restraint, civil behavior, and moral principles.

Cases in this area generally arise in the context of public high schools. The Court's initial consideration of government control over student speech in public high schools — *Tinker v. Des Moines Independent Community School District*, 393 U.S. 503 (1969) — evinced less tolerance for censorship by school officials than later cases. Evaluating a school restriction on students wearing armbands to protest the Vietnam War, the Court concluded that they constituted a silent protest that did not disturb the work of the school. For a school to justify a speech restriction, the Court determined, the school must show that the restriction is not simply a reaction to an unpopular viewpoint. Restrictions of student speech are constitutional if they ensure against material disruption of schoolwork, substantial disorder, or invasion of others' rights. Courts often focus on the "substantial disruption" component in *Tinker*, but few cases elaborate on the meaning and strength of the "invasion of other rights" component of the *Tinker* approach.

Example 13-7:

City X public high school prohibited Jerome from wearing a tee-shirt that said "homosexuality is shameful." In justifying the prohibition, the high school authorities argued that the tee-shirt disparaged gay students in violation of their rights. The authorities also argued that the tee-shirt could inspire a revolt by gay students and those who supported them. Jerome argues that the school's decision violates his right to free expression. Does he have a viable claim under *Tinker*?

Explanation:

Jerome may have a viable claim under *Tinker*, although the matter is not clear. Although the officials' prediction of an uprising may be overblown, the tee-shirt had strong potential to provide a distraction and to inspire anger. For that reason, it may cause a "substantial disruption" of school business, although more facts may be required to establish that the disruption would in fact be substantial and not simply an opportunity to discuss tolerance and free speech rights. As stated above, little guidance exists on the meaning of *Tinker's* statement that school officials may rightly evaluate whether a student's speech invades other rights. A reasonable reading of the scope of that language, however, might encompasses a homosexual's right not be disparaged by a tee-shirt tolerated by authorities. One could also argue that a disruption in the educational process interferes with the right of all students in the school to a meaningful public education. For a case addressing a claim similar to Jerome's and concluding that the school authorities likely did not violate his First Amendment rights, *see Harper ex rel.*

Harper v. Poway Unified School District, 445 F.3d 1166 (9th Cir. 2006), judgment vacated on mootness grounds, 549 U.S. 1262 (2007).

* * *

The Court increased the deference accorded school officials in *Hazelwood School District v. Kuhlmeier,* 484 U.S. 260 (1988), in upholding a school principal's power to censor a student newspaper. The principal had removed two stories from the paper, one that described a student's experience with pregnancy and another that described the effect of parental divorce on some students. The *Hazelwood* Court distinguished these stories from the student expression in *Tinker. Tinker* involved individual speech that happened to occur on school premises, while this case involved publishing articles with the school's "imprimatur," as part of a student activity "fairly characterized as part of the school curriculum." *Id.* at 271. The Court granted public schools broad authority to regulate student speech under such circumstances. In reaching this decision, the Court established that the school newspaper was only a limited public forum since it was a school-sanctioned, school-supervised publication that did not allow for "indiscriminate use by the general public." *Id.* at 267-268. Accordingly, the Court held that in such limited public forums, school officials are not prohibited from "exercising editorial control over the style and content of student speech in school-sponsored expressive activities so long as their actions are reasonably related to legitimate pedagogical concerns." *Id.* at 273. A school may also censor speech that is "ungrammatical, poorly written, inadequately researched, biased or prejudiced, vulgar or profane, or unsuitable for immature audiences." *Id.* at 271. In allowing the censorship of the articles in *Hazelwood,* the Court looked to several factors, such as: (1) the privacy of individuals mentioned in the article newspaper; (2) whether the censored articles included frank talk about topics inappropriate for the age and maturity of the intended audience; (3) fairness and balance in the school's approach, including the opportunity for relevant parties to respond; (4) adherence to journalistic standards; (5) the immediacy of the school official's decision and whether it would deprive the students of a newspaper; and (6) the faculty advisor's experience with editorial procedures. *See Dean v. Utica Community Schools,* 345 F. Supp. 2d 799, 810 (E.D. Mich. 2004) (summarizing the Supreme Court's analysis in *Hazelwood*). One might explain the Court's deference to the school officials in this case because of the Court's view of the newspaper as a form of school-sponsored speech.

The Supreme Court continued to accord deference to school officials in *Hazelwood* in its most recent decision on student speech, *Morse v. Frederick,* 551 U.S. 393 (2007). In that case, a high school principal allowed students to watch the passing of the Olympic torch in their town. At the event, students unfurled a banner reading "BONG HiTS 4 JESUS." The principal ordered them to take the banner down, one student refused, and the principal suspended the student. The Supreme Court upheld the suspension, with the plurality noting the special concerns relating to the school environment and the government interest in preventing students from drug use.

Taken together these three cases evince a trend of deference toward school officials' decisions to curtail speech. Consider how this deference might impact the outcomes of the following Examples.

Example 13-8:

A high school student recorded a rap song off-campus, after school hours, and without school resources. He posted it on social networking sites intending it to reach the school community. The rap was written in the style of a "diss-track," detailing grievances with particular teachers and coaches, and describing violent acts to be carried out against them. The school board suspended the student, interpreting the language as threatening, harassing, and intimidating to school employees. The student claimed that this discipline violated his First Amendment right to free speech. Did the school board violate the student's rights?

Explanation:

The power of schools to punish student activity wanes when it occurs off-campus, with private equipment, and during non-school hours. The prerogative of school officials to regulate student speech that frustrates the school's mission of teaching discipline, respect, and civil behavior also wanes in such circumstances. Accordingly, the First Amendment is less tolerant of school officials disciplining students whose expression does not occur during school hours or on school property.

The situation is different, however, for speech directed intentionally at the school community and reasonably understood by school officials to be threatening, harassing, and intimidating to staff. Under these circumstances, the punishment falls within the discretion accorded to school officials under the *Morse* and *Hazelwood* decisions. The punishment here also likely satisfies the less deferential *Tinker* approach for evaluating restrictions on student speech because the officials reasonably interpreted the student's speech as foreshadowing substantial disruption in the school community. *See Bell v. Itawamba County School Bd.*, 799 F.3d 379 (2015).

Example 13-9:

Sean kept a diary as a creative writing exercise. Written in the first person, it chronicled the narrator's creation of a pseudo-Nazi group on a high school campus, and detailed the group's plan to commit a mass shooting attack there. Another student told a school official about the substance of Sean's notebook diary, who seized it and ultimately suspended Sean for engaging in "terroristic threats." Sean and his parents maintained that the notebook was a work of fiction, and although violent, did not constitute threats against the school population. They sued, alleging that the suspension infringed on Sean's First Amendment rights. Will they prevail?

Explanation:

Sean and his parents will probably prevail. *Morse* made clear that speech directly threatening the physical safety of the school population is not protected by the First Amendment. Likewise, *Tinker* established that school officials can justify punishment for speech by establishing facts that reasonably led the officials to forecast substantial disruption or interference with school activities. But Sean's writing was simply a work of his imagination and nothing in the facts suggest that it alluded to or was directed to any members of the school community. The dairy may have been distasteful, but it was not actually threatening. *See Ponce v. Socorro Independent School Dist.*, 508 F.3d 765 (2007).

Example 13-10:

A student columnist for a high school newspaper wrote an article entitled "How is Sex Being Taught in Our Health Class?" The columnist sought to publish the article alongside a series of cartoons depicting stick figures in sexually suggestive positions in the next print edition of the newspaper. Upon learning of the stick-figure drawings, the school disallowed the columnist to publish the cartoons. The student columnist sued, arguing that the faculty advisor's decision to censor the stick figure drawings violated the First Amendment. Is the student correct?

Explanation:

The student is likely incorrect. The written critique of the sex education curriculum was allowed and arguably served the pedagogical purpose of providing an opportunity to discuss an important issue. The stick figures, however, were not necessarily related to any pedagogical purpose that the newspaper or the article might serve. Moreover, the school was reasonably concerned that the intended audience was not emotionally developed enough to understand the seriousness of sexual relations, and would view the cartoons as making light of sex. Finally, the school might reasonably be concerned that the stick figures might encourage risky student sexual behavior. *See R.O. v. Ithaca City School Dist.*, 645 F.3d 533 (2nd Cir. 2011).

Example 13-11:

A student newspaper seeks to print an article about a pending lawsuit in which neighbors alleged that the school's practice of idling buses unlawfully exposed them to diesel fumes. The student author attempted to interview school officials, but they all declined, referencing a policy that bars public comment on pending litigation. Undeterred, the student thoroughly researched the topic, accurately reported the facts in the public record of the lawsuit, and submitted a draft of the article to the school before publication. The school superintendent, upon hearing of the article, ordered the school to remove it from the upcoming edition of the newspaper. The student author of the article would like to challenge the school superintendent's censorship of her article as a violation of the First Amendment. Does she have a valid claim?

Explanation:

Considered in light of the *Hazelwood* factors, the censorship likely violated the student's First Amendment rights. Little supports the conclusion that anything in the content or style of the article threatened the school's pedagogical goals. Moreover, the article did not implicate privacy concerns, as it contained only matters of public record. Nor did the article contain unsuitable language for its potential audience. The student author had followed journalistic practices in affording school officials the opportunity to respond. Moreover, no evidence supported the conclusion that the article was biased, poorly researched, contained libel, or was otherwise inaccurate. One can fairly conclude therefore that the school's censorship amounted to impermissible viewpoint-based discrimination based on the content of the article. *See Dean v. Utica Community Schools*, 345 F. Supp. 2d 799 (E.D. Mich. 2004).

Example 13-12:

At a school assembly, Judith nominated another student to serve on the student government. Judith's description of the student was filled with sexual innuendo. As a consequence, the school authorities suspended Judith for two days and prohibited her from delivering the graduation speech for her class. Judith claims that this action violated her First Amendment rights. Is she correct?

Explanation:

No, Judith is not correct. In *Bethal School District No. 403 v. Fraser*, 478 U.S. 675 (1973), the U.S. Supreme Court rejected a claim such as Judith's. Emphasizing the need to give school authorities latitude in determining students' appropriate speech and behavior during school hours, the *Fraser* Court distinguished *Tinker* on the ground that it involved political speech, not sexual speech. The Court asserted that "[a] high school assembly or classroom is no place for a sexually explicit monologue," reasoning that the school acted appropriately in disassociating itself from the student's statement in order "to make the point to the pupils that vulgar speech is wholly inconsistent with fundamental values of public school education." *Id.* at 686-686.

D. RESTRICTIONS ON GOVERNMENT EMPLOYEE SPEECH

Government employees' speech rights are similar to the rights of school students, prisoners, and military members in that they are subject to significant, constitutionally valid restrictions that do not operate when other citizens express themselves. The situation for government employees, however, is much more extreme. In fact, the U.S. Supreme Court has held that the First Amendment does not protect government employee speech while the employee is on the job and speaks within the scope of the employee's duties. *Garcetti v. Ceballos*, 547 U.S. 410 (2006). The Court determined that to hold otherwise "would commit . . . courts to a new, permanent, and intrusive role, mandating judicial oversight of communications between and among government employees and their superiors in the course of official business." *Id.* at 423. To establish a First Amendment violation, the employee must have been "off-duty" when engaging in the challenged speech. Next, the employee must show that the government took an adverse employment action that was motivated by the employee's speech. If that is the case, First Amendment protection attaches to off-duty, unofficial government employee speech if (1) it involves matters of public concern and (2) the employee can prove that the employee's interest in exercising freedom of expression outweighs the government's interests as an employer. *Connick v. Myers*, 461 U.S. 138 (1983); *Pickering v. Board of Education*, 391 U.S. 563 (1968). Accordingly, the *Connick-Pickering* test turns on the question whether the speech is on the job within the scope of employment and also requires that a court engage in balancing government needs and the employee's speech rights.

A significant question in this area concerns whether or not the employee was speaking within the scope of employment or was "off duty." This question is particularly important in the context of whether the government may take negative action against an employee "whistleblower." In this regard, consider the following Example.

Example 13-13:

Rahm was the director of a program at a community college. While he was serving in that capacity, he received a subpoena to testify at the corruption trial of a former program director and provided his testimony without contesting the subpoena or seeking permission from the president of the community college. The president of the community college fired Rahm, claiming that he was not authorized to give the testimony. The president further explained that Rahm's testimony included knowledge that he had gained in his capacity of program director and was therefore within the scope of his employment. Rahm claimed that the firing violated his First Amendment rights and argued that he testified as a citizen only and did not testify within the scope of his usual employment duties. Is Rahm correct?

Explanation:

Yes, Rahm is correct. In *Lane v. Franks*, 573 U.S. 228 (2014), the Supreme Court held that "the First Amendment protects a public employee who provides truthful sworn testimony, compelled by subpoena, outside the scope of his ordinary job responsibilities." *Id.* at 238. The Court reasoned that sworn testimony "is a quintessential example of speech as a citizen" — not as an employee — because one "who testifies in court bears an obligation, to the court and to society, to tell the truth." *Id.* at 249. The fact that the subject of the testimony contained information obtained on the job does not undermine this conclusion. It is also especially clear that the speech was on a subject of public concern because it pertained to corruption in a public institution. It is also clear that the firing occurred in retaliation for the testimony. As for the final, balancing factor, the interest in allowing a person with knowledge about public corruption to testify as a citizen includes both a government interest and personal First Amendment interest. For that reason, it is easy to conclude that these interests outweighed any government interest in preventing Rahm from testifying truthfully about problems concerning the government institution where he worked.

* * *

Issues regarding the First Amendment rights of government employees have arisen frequently in the context of associational freedoms protected by the Amendment. Freedom of association problems arise from loyalty oaths, which require individuals to swear allegiance to the United States as a condition of employment. Often these oaths are accompanied by the government's discretion not to hire individuals who are members of so-called "subversive groups." Although the Court initially upheld these oath requirements in the 1950s, but has since changed course and invalidated loyalty oath requirements. For example, in *Keyishian v. Board of Regents of the State of New York*, 385 U.S. 589 (1967), the Court invalidated an oath law, condemning the law as punishing mere membership in a "subversive" group. Membership might be grounds for dismissal or refusal to hire if the government can also prove that the member knew of the group's illegal objectives, or intended to further those objectives.

Issues regarding the associational rights of government employees are not confined, however, to the loyalty oath context. Consider the following Example.

Example 13-14:

A citizen identified a group of guards from a state prison wearing memorabilia associated with a local chapter of the Rebel Club—a notorious nationwide motorcycle gang—while the guards were off duty and off campus. According to federal law enforcement agencies, the Rebel Club advocates white supremacy and is involved with narcotics trafficking and violent crime. The prison guards were also talking with, touching, and laughing with members of the group. It was clear to the citizen that the gang members and the guards were well acquainted. The citizen recognized some the gang members from news reports about their exploits. She also observed the guards consorting with Rebel Club members on two other occasions.

The citizen reported her observation to prison management. After evaluating the citizen's report, researching the Rebel Club, and interviewing the guards, the prison authorities terminated their employment. The guards filed a First Amendment retaliation claim, arguing that their termination violated their First Amendment rights of free association. The prison officials maintained that they were justified in terminating the officers for their association with the Rebel Club due to concerns with putting prison safety in the hands of guards who may be members of the Rebel Club themselves as well as the strong possibility that the guards would show favoritism for incarcerated members of the Rebel Club. Does the prison management have a winning argument that the guards were properly dismissed?

Explanation:

Yes, the prison management likely has a winning argument. As a threshold matter, the guards' association did not occur in their official capacity at the prison—which would be clearly unprotected—but rather in their free time. The *Pickering-Connick* test applies here because the facts present a conflict between the free association rights of government employees and the government's interest in orderly and fair prison administration. Turning to the first element of the test, the guards will argue that their association with the Rebel Club is expressive conduct on a matter of public concern, and therefore protected. The gang engages in advocacy of white supremacy, and the guards apparently endorsed the nature and character of the organization. This element might be satisfied if the nature and character of the Rebel Club—together with its advocacy of white supremacy—amounts to a matter of public concern.

The next step in the analysis is balancing of the guards' associational and expressive interests against the government interests. The government interests here—prison safety and possible favoritism toward a group of inmates—weigh heavily. The prison officials had a reasonable basis to conclude the guards' association with the Rebel Club could be detrimental to prison operations and reflect negatively on them. The prison officials had a strong interest in proactively reducing the risks to prison safety, and they will argue that dismissing the guards reasonably furthered this interest. Finally, the guards' association could potentially undermine the prison's ability to cooperate with other law enforcement agencies. Considered collectively, these interests appear to substantially outweigh the guards' interest in associating with a group that engages in activities inimical to the mission of their employer: the prison. *Piscottano v. Murphy*, 511 F.3d 247 (2d Cir. 2007).

Conduct that Communicates

The First Amendment speaks in terms of "freedom of speech" and few would question that this protection is designed to promote freedom of expression, particularly freedom to express ideas. To most, "speech" evokes the use of words. To what extent, then, does the First Amendment extend to conduct that expresses an idea, but does not use words? The correct answer is not obvious because expression and action are always interconnected to some extent. As Thomas Emerson said: "Even the clearest manifestations of expression involve some action, as in the case of holding a meeting, publishing a newspaper, or merely talking. At the other extreme, a political assassination includes a substantial mixture of expression." THOMAS EMERSON, THE SYSTEM OF FREEDOM OF EXPRESSION 80 (1970). This quote shows the two poles that must be accommodated in developing an approach that provides some protection of expression through conduct, yet accommodates the occasional need to regulate conduct. At bottom, this accommodation requires tolerating a measure of regulation with an incidental effect on speech.

Whether one concludes that the U.S. Supreme Court has correctly analyzed the extent to which the First Amendment protects conduct that is not accompanied by words, the Court has succeeded in enunciating an approach that has remained stable since 1968. The key case articulating the First Amendment approach for protecting expressive conduct is *United States v. O'Brien*, 391 U.S. 367 (1968). *O'Brien* concerned individuals who protested the Vietnam War by burning a draft card. United States prosecutors charged the individuals with violating a federal statute making it a crime to knowingly mutilate or destroy draft registration certificates.

Recognizing that the burning of a draft card for the purpose of protesting a war has communicative content, the Court nonetheless stated that a regulation such as the federal statute could be justified—even if the statute results in "incidental limitations on First Amendment freedoms"—if "a sufficiently important government interest" supports regulation of the "non-speech element" of a course of conduct. *Id.* at 376. From this starting point, the Court developed a four-part test for evaluating a governmental regulation of a course of conduct that includes speech and non-speech elements. In order for the regulation to steer clear of First Amendment protections, the regulation must satisfy the following conditions:

(1) the regulation is within "the constitutional power of Government;"
(2) the regulation "furthers an important or substantial governmental interest;"
(3) the government interest motivating the regulation "is unrelated to the suppression of free expression;" and
(4) "the incidental restriction on alleged First Amendment freedoms is no greater than is essential to the furtherance of" the governmental interest.

Id. at 377.

Concluding that the federal statute satisfied each of these conditions, the Court confronted the well-founded argument that the reason for the criminal prohibition of draft card burning was to stop individuals from engaging in that practice in order to protest. Dismissing the argument, the Court embraced the constitutional principle of declining to "strike down an otherwise constitutional statute on the basis of an alleged[ly] illicit legislative motive." *Id.* at 383.

Here's an "easy" Example of how the *O'Brien* test plays out.

Example 14-1:

Dinah was deeply disturbed by how the local police recently responded to a peaceful protest against racism that occurred in her city. She is normally a peaceful, law abiding citizen, but was compelled to take dramatic action in order to express her disapproval of the response to the protest. Therefore, to protest the police action, Dinah set off a bomb in the entrance of the police headquarters building.

Dinah was charged with terrorism and arson, and defends these charges by arguing that a prosecution for these crimes would violate her First Amendment rights to express her disapproval of police conduct and would punish her for exercising those rights. Is she correct that the First Amendment prevents the government from pursuing the charges against her?

Explanation:

No, Dinah is not correct that her prosecution amounts to a First Amendment violation. To be sure, she performed the bombing for the purpose of conveying a very specific message bearing on a matter of public concern. A matter of public concern — especially one that can be characterized as a political issue — is the type of expression that the First Amendment generally protects. Nonetheless, the government's pursuit of the prosecution easily passes the *O'Brien* test. First, criminal prosecution for an act of violence is within the power of government. Next, the prosecution serves the important and substantial purpose of punishing individuals for crimes against the public peace and potentially threatening the life and safety of others. Third, the facts do not suggest that the government is motivated by any other purpose than applying a criminal law of general applicability to a situation threatening the life and safety of citizens.

The final *O'Brien* factor is the most difficult to justify in this situation. By subjecting her to potential criminal punishment, Dinah's prosecution does impinge her First Amendment freedom to protest in the manner she deems most appropriate. The prosecution may also impinge others' freedom to protest, since it could have a chilling effect, deterring others from expressing their disdain for the police action for fear that they will be subject to retaliatory prosecution. Yet the government is simply enforcing the criminal law in this instance: Dinah and others have plenty of other, non-criminal avenues for expressing their opinions on this matter.

Example 14-2:

A large city has an ordinance that prohibits panhandling in the city's subway system. The city expressed several reasons for the prohibition. First, panhandlers can sometimes be quite aggressive in their attempt to solicit donations. This can be unpleasant and scary for riders. As a consequence, the presence of panhandlers may discourage citizens from taking the subway. Ridership on the subway is important in order to maintain the financial health of the city's transit authority and to diminish traffic jams. In addition, panhandling can be disruptive and startling to riders. If this inspires a strong reaction from a rider, it can create a hazard in the fast moving and often crowded subway environment.

A public interest group maintains that panhandling is expressive conduct protected by the First Amendment. The group asserts that the government's prohibition on panhandling cannot pass the *O'Brien* test. Is the public interest group correct in these arguments?

Explanation:

Strong arguments support the conclusion that the public interest group is not correct. To be sure, begging implicates expressive conduct or communicative activity for purposes of First Amendment analysis: it is accompanied by speech indicating a need for food, shelter, clothing, medical care, or transportation, and, even without such speech, the presence of what could be an unkempt and disheveled person holding out his hand or cup to receive donations itself conveys a message of the person's need for support. One could also argue that panhandling can carry an implicit political statement about society's failure to care for those in need.

Nonetheless, the law appears to pass the O'Brien test. To begin, the subway law was within the city's constitutional power to regulate transportation in the city. Moreover, the government's interests—avoiding traffic jams, maintaining the financial health of the city's transportation system, and promoting public safety on the subways—all appear to be substantial and important governmental interests advanced by the prohibition. The third O'Brien factor appears satisfied because the government's reasons for the prohibition are not related to the suppression of free expression. The final O'Brien factor is a closer call because the prohibition of panhandling on the subway is absolute and without qualification or nuance. Nonetheless, the possible exigencies created by aggressive begging and panhandling in the subway arguably justify a complete prohibition. Importantly, the prohibition leaves intact other venues around the city where panhandling can occur. See Young v. New York City Transit Authority, 903 F.2d 146 (2d Cir.), cert. denied, 498 U.S. 984 (1990). But cf. Loper v. New York City Police Department, 999 F.2d 699 (2d Cir. 1993) (holding that general, city-wide prohibition on panhandling was an unconstitutional regulation of expressive conduct).

Example 14-3:

A city ordinance made it a summary offense to appear in public completely or almost nude. The preamble to the statute stated that its purpose was to limit "certain lewd, immoral activities carried on in public places for profit [that] are highly detrimental to the public health, safety and welfare . . . ." A local strip club brought suit against the city, claiming that the statute infringed on its First Amendment right to engage in expressive conduct. Should nude dancing be considered "expressive conduct"? If so, does the statute pass the O'Brien four-factor test?

Explanation:

The dancing is expressive conduct and the statute does pass the *O'Brien* test. The Court decided this precise issue in *City of Erie v. Pap's A.M.*, 529 U.S. 277 (2000). In that case, the Court first observed that "[a]lthough being in a state of nudity is not an inherently expressive condition, . . . the nude dancing of the type featured in the case had an expressive message, including artful movement and eroticism."

Having determined that the expressive conduct was regulated, the Court turned to the *O'Brien* test. First, the Court observed, the ordinance was within the city's constitutional power to enact because the city's efforts to protect public health and safety were within its police powers. Second, the ordinance furthered the important government interests of regulating conduct through a public nudity ban and of combating the harmful secondary effects associated with nude dancing. In this regard, the Court noted that the ordinance targeted public nudity as a general matter and did not specifically single out nude dancing. Turning to the third factor, the Court concluded that the city was not motivated by a desire to suppress free expression. Rather, as the preamble explained, the ordinance was premised on the city council's express findings that lewd, immoral activities held publically and for profit damage public health, safety and welfare.

Finally, *Pap's A.M.* Court concluded that the fourth factor—requiring that the restriction is no greater than is essential to the furtherance of the government interest—was satisfied as well. The Court reasoned that the requirement that dancers wear minimal (rather than zero) clothing would not greatly suppress their freedom of expression. According to the Court, the ordinance focused primarily on conduct, and any incidental impact on the expressive element of nude dancing was *de minimis*. The restriction left ample capacity to convey the dancer's erotic and artistic message, while wearing hardly any clothing.

Further discussion of nude dancing regulations appears in Chapter 8, which concerns sexually oriented speech.

* * *

Although the *O'Brien* Court developed a four-part test that has shown staying power, one wonders how seriously we should take the words used. Is the U.S. Supreme Court actually using a more deferential standard than the words of the *O'Brien* test would suggest? Take the nude dancing scenario from Example 14-3: Isn't part of the core essence of the nude dancing's expressive component the fact that the dancers had absolutely no covering on any of their body parts?

In light of how the U.S. Supreme Court has been applying the *O'Brien* test, consider also this hypothetical: assume that an individual is protesting the government's restrictions on expressing political positions opposed to those of the governing authorities. To make a point that these restrictions on expression are a substantial obstacle to the exchange of ideas, the individual throws pamphlets explaining this problem from a roof top. The individual timed this activity to ensure that the pamphlets land on the sidewalk while large numbers of rush-hour commuters are passing by. The individual has made clear that she is using this method of distribution to highlight the difficulty of communicating a message that is at odds with the authorities. Assume further that the authorities arrest and convict the individual for littering. When the individual raises a First Amendment defense, how will the court respond? If the court applies the O'Brien test as deferentially as the Supreme Court did in O'Brien itself and in Pap's nude dancing case, it might easily find the test satisfied, concluding that the littering law has a purpose unrelated to suppressing speech and that the individual has ample alternative avenues for expression. Yet this reasoning would fail to account for the precise expressive reason that the individual used the method of throwing the leaflets from a roof top in order to disseminate her political idea.

This observation about the track record for applying the O'Brien test may not, however, provide the full story. The test still has at least some potential for providing protection for expressive conduct. Consider the following Example.

Example 14-4:

A local county curfew ordinance prohibited teenagers from being in public spaces past 11 p.m. The curfew law did have an exception allowing teenagers to assert an affirmative defense that they were engaging in activities protected by the First Amendment if arrested while they were in public spaces after 11 p.m. A local teenager was arrested driving home from a late-night political rally at 12 a.m.

The government's goal in enacting the curfew was to protect minors and to minimize juvenile crime. Is the teenager driving home from the rally engaging in "expressive conduct" protected by the First Amendment?

Explanation:

The arrest of the teenager violates her First Amendment rights. Literally, driving home is not expressive conduct. Nonetheless, the act of driving home from a political rally is sufficiently connected to expressive conduct as to fall within the ambit of First Amendment protection. Indeed, prohibiting driving home from a rally would discourage individuals from engaging in protected expressive conduct and would be appropriately analyzed under the O'Brien test.

The curfew law is within the local government's constitutional power and thus satisfies the first O'Brien factor. Providing for the safety and well-being of children and combating juvenile crime are important governmental interests, thus satisfying the second factor. Because the government appeared dedicated to these purposes and the purposes are unrelated to the suppression of free expression, the third factor is satisfied.

The problem with the law arises from the fourth factor: whether the incidental restriction on the First Amendment freedoms is no greater than essential to further the government interest. While the curfew law itself does contain an explicit First Amendment exception, the question arises: how is that exception triggered? Once a police officer discovers sufficient facts to establish probable cause that the curfew law was violated (i.e., the presence of an underage person in public after 11:00 pm), the officer has no constitutional obligation to conduct any further investigation for the purpose of discovering exculpatory evidence that would satisfy the exception to the curfew law. Thus, if a police officer stops a 17-year-old on the road at 1:00 a.m. and the teenager informs the officer that she is returning from a midnight political rally, the officer need not take the teenager at her word nor attempt to ascertain whether she is telling the truth.

Because the First Amendment defense under the law imposes no duty of investigation on the arresting officer, as a practical matter it protects only those minors whom the officer has seen actually participating in protected activity. The only way that a minor can avoid this risk is to find a parent or another adult designated by a parent to accompany the teenager to the rally. Yet that alternative itself burdens a minor's expressive rights because adults may be reluctant or unable to accompany the minor to a late-night activity. Thus, even with the affirmative defense based on First Amendment activity, the curfew law is not sufficiently narrowly tailored. *See Hodgkins ex rel. Hodgkins v. Peterson*, 355 F.3d 1048 (7th Cir. 2004).

* * *

Laws prohibiting flag burning and flag desecration have developed into an area in which the U.S. Supreme Court has several times visited the question of expressive conduct. The most recent occasion was *Texas v. Johnson*, 491 U.S. 397 (1989), in which the Court declared unconstitutional a state law making it criminal for a person to "deface, damage, or otherwise physically mistreat" a flag in a way that the actor knows "will serious offend one or more persons likely to observe or discover his action."

In the 5-4 decision, the justices' primary disagreement centered on whether the importance of the flag as a symbol of national unity justifies its special protection. The majority took the view that the flag stands for the civil liberties upon which the United States was founded, arguing that there was no better way to honor the flag than to tolerate those who burn it as an expression of ideas. By contrast, the dissenting justices focused on the special deference owed to the flag that allowed it to take a special place in First Amendment jurisprudence. Interestingly, the dissenting justices' opinions can be read to suggest that the restrictions on flag burning are not only legitimate measures for preventing damage to national loyalty and the national psyche, but actually work to buttress the importance of the flag as a national symbol. In this way, the dissenting justices were identifying a benefit of censorship. *See* Laura E. Little, *Laughing at Censorship*, 28 YALE J. L. & HUMAN. 198-99 (2016).

Recognizing that the act of burning the flag in the case amounted to expressive conduct, the majority grappled with whether the state's prohibition against flag burning could be justified under the *O'Brien* test. The Court easily concluded that prohibition failed the test because the government had clearly intended to suppress the message emanating from the conduct. In other words, the government was attempting to prevent the flag from being used as an instrument of protest. For that reason, the case turned on whether the prohibition (which was clearly content-based) passed strict scrutiny. The Court concluded that it did not.

The decision in *Texas v. Johnson* inspired a good deal of controversy, including proposals to amend the Constitution. Congress ultimately responded by adopting the Flag Protection Act of 1989, which criminalized mutilating, defacing, defiling, burning or trampling the flag. Although the statute did not limit the crime to circumstances where the conduct would offend another (as did the statute in *Texas v. Johnson*), the U.S. Supreme Court nonetheless declared the Flag Protection Act unconstitutional in *United States v. Eichman*, 496 U.S. 310 (1990), concluding that the statute suffered from the same defect as the Texas statute in the *Johnson* case.

Example 14-5:

A state statute makes it a misdemeanor if a person "publicly or privately mutilates, defaces, defiles, or tramples upon or casts contempt in the manner on any [United States] flag." The statute carves out an exception to the prohibition, however, for circumstances when a flag is desecrated in a political or patriotic demonstration. In passing the statute, the state legislature proclaimed that the statute had two purposes: to defend the physical integrity of the United States flag and to protect the symbolic value of the flag.

While in Cary's home to deliver a traffic ticket, a police officer notices that a flag is being used as a doormat. The flag appears dirty and has several pairs of shoes on top of it. The police officer arrests the citizen for desecrating the flag. Later in court, Cary stated that she put the flag there as decoration. She explained that she placed the flag on the floor as an appropriate accent for the off-beat décor in her home. She argues that the prosecution under the statute violates her First Amendment rights.

Is she correct that the prosecution violates her First Amendment rights? Is this statute distinguishable from the statutes in *Texas v. Johnson* and *United States v. Eichman*?

Explanation:

The state statute is distinguishable from the statutes at issue in *Texas v. Johnson* and *United States v. Eichman* because the statute contains an exception for precisely the type of expression that both cases were most concerned about suppressing: political protest. This renders the statute less constitutionally problematic. Nonetheless, the statute still regulates expressive conduct. Indeed, in this case, Cary reputedly employed flag desecration as a form of artistic, not political, expression. Moreover, the statute does not pass the O'Brien test. The interests advanced by the state legislature for regulating the expressive conduct at issue in the case—defending the flag's physical integrity and protecting the flag's symbolic value—are the identical interests that the *Johnson* and *Eichman* Courts explicitly condemned. These interests are related to the suppression of free expression. The third O'Brien factor is therefore not satisfied. For these reasons, the statute is likely unconstitutional under the First Amendment. Cf. *Commonwealth v. Bricker*, 666 A.2d 257 (Pa. 1995).

Issues Related to the Media

Along with its mention of the right to freedom of speech, the First Amendment explicitly provides for freedom "of the press" as well. Does this mean that the Amendment provides special protection for press freedoms? Only one U.S. Supreme Court justice seems to have suggested this,[1] and the notion has not taken hold in the case law. Several specialized doctrines, however, exist to serve press freedoms and to demarcate the contours of press restrictions that the First Amendment tolerates. These complement the more general doctrines covered throughout this volume that bear directly on the ability of the press to do its job: analysis of content-based regulations (Chapter 1), prior restraints (Chapter 4), compelled speech (Chapter 5), commercial speech (Chapter 9), tort actions directed at speech (Chapter 10), and false speech (Chapter 11) all bear routinely on the ability of the mainstream press to do its job of keeping the public informed of current social and political affairs.

This chapter focuses on the categories of special constitutional issues that concern the press. These issues pertain to media access to information and government institutions, media and judicial proceedings, the publication of truthful information, forced access to the press, and the analytical challenges offered by the Internet. The U.S. Supreme Court, however, has given us several general principles by which to evaluate the relationship between the First Amendment and the press. Two of the most important principles are discussed in one of the earlier decisions in this area, *Branzburg v. Hayes*, 408 U.S. 665 (1972). On one hand, *Branzburg* emphasized the necessity of

---

1. Potter Stewart, Or of the Press, 26 HASTINGS L.J. 631 (1975). See also David A. Anderson, The Origins of the Press Clause, 30 UCLA L. REV. 455 (1983).

protecting members of the press as they pursue their job: "[W]ithout some protection for seeking out news, freedom of the press could be eviscerated." *Id.* at 681. On the other hand, however, *Branzburg*, refused to extend special exceptions to the press regarding duties held by all citizens. The Court emphasized: "[V]alid laws serving substantial public interests may be enforced against the press as against others, despite the possible burden that may be imposed [on the press] . . . The publisher of a newspaper has no special immunity from the application of general laws. He has no special privilege to invade the rights and liberties of others." *Id.* at 682. The specific details of *Branzburg* are discussed later in this chapter in connection with issues related to confidential sources. These two statements, however, are useful guides for understanding all of the issues in this chapter because they capture the competing values that courts must balance in resolving First Amendment issues related to the media.

A. MEDIA ACCESS TO INFORMATION AND GOVERNMENT INSTITUTIONS

Questions concerning whether the First Amendment protects the media's ability to gain access to newsworthy information cast the First Amendment in a role differing from the one it takes with most freedom of expression issues. The access to information context evaluates whether the Amendment serves as a "sword" or affirmative tool rather than as a shield protecting entities against government restrictions. Media access issues arise in several contexts, but most decisions in the area concern access to judicial proceedings, a matter covered in the next subsection.

In the context of media access to government-controlled information and institutions, the decisions reflect a need to balance First Amendment interests in the free flow of information and the government's need to run its institutions in a way that ensures safety, privacy, order, and discipline. The U.S. Supreme Court has established that the press enjoys no greater access to government-controlled institutions or information than that enjoyed by the general public. See *Saxbe v. Washington Post Co.*, 417 U.S. 843 (1974) (denying press access to prisons); *Pell v. Procunier*, 417 U.S. 817 (1974) (denying press access to prisons).

In a decision that followed the two earlier prison decisions in *Saxbe* and *Pell*, a splintered (3-1-3) Court determined that the equal access granted to the press and public includes the obligation to afford the press effective access that takes account of the press's special needs, such as use of recording equipment. *Houchins v. KQED, Inc.*, 438 U.S. 1 (1978). Nonetheless, the lead opinion in *Houchins*, which also concerned the media's access to prison, made clear that special measures for the press are not required simply to enhance the press's convenience.

Example 15-1:

Anya works for a news organization and requested permission of the U.S. military to accompany U.S. troops into combat. She desires to become "embedded" with the troops, accompanying them on all their operations. The military denied the request. Anya would like to challenge the denial on First Amendment grounds. Is she likely to succeed?

Explanation:

No, Anya is not likely to succeed. Judged by the standard of *Houchins*, *Saxbe*, and *Pell*, the government has no more obligation to allow the press to accompany troops into combat than the government has for allowing the general public to do so. Although war is certainly a matter of public concern, the government has a panoply of potentially overriding interests that support excluding members of the press from being embedded in the troops: general safety of the journalist, the lack of most journalists' knowledge in military training and technique in conduct of war, the possibility that the journalist's presence may enhance the potential for danger to military members, and concerns with avoiding interference with military efficiency and strategy in the field of combat. The U.S. Supreme Court case law provides no support for Anya's position. *See Flynt v. Rumsfeld*, 355 F.3d 697 (D.C. Cir. 2004).

Example 15-2:

As part of its monitoring of the health and population of wild horses, the United States Bureau of Land Management holds a yearly round-up of the horses. The Bureau provides a public viewing area for those who wish to view the process. Bijoux, a photo-journalist, would like permission to gain closer access to the round-up process to ensure that she can take accurate and compelling photographs. The Bureau has denied Bijoux's request. She takes the position that this violates her First Amendment rights as a member of the press. Is she correct?

Explanation:

Bijoux has a viable claim. Her success in pressing the claim turns on a number of factors, including whether the public viewing site would allow her to take photographs that adequately capture the round-up, the history of access to the horse-gathering process over the years, and the possibility that press access may provide a helpful contribution to the round-up process at the current time and in the future. Importantly, however, Bijoux's success will likely turn on whether the Bureau of Land Management establishes that the restrictions on viewing the round-up serve an overriding purpose that prevent the press access from being any broader than it is.

B. JUDICIAL PROCEEDINGS

The topic of media access to judicial proceedings includes many diverse issues. These include general principles of media access to proceedings that take place in court, special complications that arise in criminal trials by reason of the constitutional protections for the criminally accused, and related issues arising from gag orders.

1. Media Access to Court Proceedings

The U.S. Supreme Court has recognized a right of press access to court proceedings in a series of cases, three of which are particularly illustrative. First, in *Richmond Newspapers, Inc. v. Virginia*, 448 U.S. 555 (1980), a trial court had closed access to a criminal trial, and the Supreme Court declared unconstitutional the trial court's decision to do so. The *Richmond Newspapers* plurality said "[t]he Bill of Rights was enacted against the backdrop of the long history of trials being presumptively open," and reasoned that the right to attend trials gives meaning to the First Amendment guarantees of free speech and a free press. *Id.* at 575. The plurality did not, however, declare this right of access to be absolute, suggesting that an overriding reason might justify closing proceedings.

Later, in *Globe Newspaper Co. v. Superior Court for Norfolk County*, 457 U.S. 596 (1982), the Supreme Court held unconstitutional a statute providing for exclusion of the general public from trials of specified sexual offenses involving a victim under the age of 18. The Court reasoned that the statute could not be justified on the basis of either the state's interest in protecting minor victims of sex crimes from further trauma or its interest in encouraging such victims to come forward and testify in a truthful and credible manner. As compelling as the first interest is, the Court ruled, the interest does not justify a *mandatory* closure rule. According to the Court, the interest could be just as well served by requiring the trial court to determine on a case-by-case basis whether the state's legitimate concern about the specific minor victim's well-being necessitates closure. The Court dismissed the second asserted interest (encouraging victims to testify), maintaining that it is not only speculative in empirical terms, but is also open to serious question as a matter of logic and common sense. *Id.* at 609-610.

In the third case, *Press-Enterprise Co. v. Superior Court*, 464 U.S. 501 (1984), the Court held unconstitutional a trial court order to close jury voir dire proceedings to the press and the public. Recognizing that closure may be appropriate when questioning concerns prospective jurors' personal business, the Court emphasized that closure should be regarded as a matter of last resort given the importance of jury selection to the fairness of the trial.[2]

Example 15-3:

In New Jersey, several public figures were implicated for securities fraud and other related white-collar crimes. The press heavily covered the trial as it was unfolding. After the conclusion of the trial, the court sealed all court transcripts pertaining to the jury, including the transcripts of voir dire and jury instructions given at the close of the trial. One month later, the press requests the transcripts from the court to write an article about the trial. They are given only partial and redacted transcripts. The press argues that they are entitled to receive all of the unredacted transcripts pertaining to the jury and that the court should immediately disclose them. Is the press correct?

Explanation:

The press is not necessarily entitled to everything they want, but they are correct in suggesting that the trial court did not handle the matter properly and they may be entitled to at least some more of the material than they received. The trial court acted prematurely in sealing of the transcripts without adequate notice, without a hearing, and without placing factual findings on the record. Moreover, at the time of sealing, the trial court made no findings of an actual or potential threat either of juror harassment or of facts surrounding the jury's deliberative process that would merit sealing the transcripts. In some situations, a case may be made that the jurors' identities should be concealed in order to protect against tampering, coercion, or threats. If that is the case, a court must carefully articulate specific and tangible reasons for protecting the identities. A court may not simply rely on the possibility of vague and indeterminate threats. *See United States v. Antar*, 38 F.3d 1348 (3d Cir. 1994).

2. In yet another *Press-Enterprise* case, *Press-Enterprise Co. v. Superior Court*, 478 U.S. 1 (1986), the Court ruled in favor of press access to transcripts of a preliminary hearing.

Example 15-4:

A defendant was convicted of robbery. The case did not gather outsized news coverage, and most considered the crime to be a typical and routine burglary. Nevertheless, a local news station wanted to publicly broadcast the trial using cameras and recording devices inside the courtroom pursuant to a state law that allows such coverage. Should the trial court allow the trial to be broadcast? Do the U.S. Supreme Court cases on press access to courtrooms provide guidance on whether the First Amendment supports the broadcast of a criminal trial?

Explanation:

The decisions in *Richmond Newspapers*, *Globe Newspaper*, and *Press-Enterprise* do not answer this question. But the U.S. Supreme Court in *Chandler v. Florida*, 449 U.S. 560 (1981), held that the Constitution does not prohibit a state court system from allowing public broadcast of a criminal trial. In that case, the state had adopted a canon that allowed the broadcast on the theory that operation of the judicial system represents a significant concern to the public and that broadcast of court proceedings would impart a greater confidence and understanding of the system. The *Chandler* Court ruled that although a broadcast poses a risk of prejudice in any trial, that possibility does not demand an absolute constitutional prohibition. The Court reasoned that a defendant may address the potential for undue prejudice by demonstrating that a jury had been inappropriately influenced by media coverage. In any event, the state judicial canon properly provided the additional opportunity for defendants to object to coverage in advance of the trial, and the policy allowing broadcasting is constitutional.

Example 15-5:

The state of California enacted a statute that governs the procedure for involuntary commitment proceedings. The statute dictates that a civil jury trial is to be held to determine whether the individual in question is gravely disabled due to mental illness. The statute also notes that these proceedings are highly specialized and personal. For those reasons, the proceedings are therefore presumptively private.

After two jury trials under the statute, the court determined that a certain individual was not gravely disabled due to mental illness and should not be confined. Eight days later, that individual was arrested and charged with murdering his mother. A local newspaper requested that the court release to them the transcripts from the jury trials on the person's commitment, arguing that the U.S. Constitution requires the court to do so. Will the newspaper prevail?

Explanation:

It is unlikely that the newspaper will prevail. The constitutional presumption in favor of open access applies to civil as well as criminal proceedings. But the presumption is just that: a presumption that can be overcome when overriding factors are present. This situation presents several important factors that are likely to overcome the presumption. The release of the transcript threatens to violate (1) an existing state statute that makes the trials in commitment proceedings presumptively non-public, (2) the disabled individual's right to confidentiality under the statute, (3) the disabled individual's constitutional right to privacy, and (4) the disabled individual's confidentiality rights under the common law psychotherapist-patient privilege. *See Sorenson v. Superior Court*, 161 Cal. Rptr. 3d 794 (2013).

2. Gag Orders

As reflected in the open court principles, an essential part of the United States commitment to a just society is ensuring that legal proceedings remain "in the sunshine." As the aphorism goes: "justice rots in the darkness." Translated to the trial process, this means that closed proceedings allow corruption to flourish and undermine the search for the truth. For that reason, a court order—otherwise known as a gag order—that prevents reports on legal proceedings to the public disrespects constitutional principles of the fair and impartial administration of justice, general freedom of expression principles, as well as the commitment to bringing to the public details about the important government task of conducting a court proceeding. Standing alone, gag orders could be characterized as an unconstitutional prior restraint on speech. To repeat, gag orders are a form of prior restraint, a type of First Amendment that faces high disfavor. Further discussion of prior restraints appear in Chapter 4.

But a strong countervailing constitutional principle is at play in criminal cases when the particular court proceeding pertains to a criminal prosecution: the Sixth Amendment right to a fair trial. This principle has force both in cases when the gag order is focused on the media and in cases when the gag order binds trial participants.

a. Gag Orders Directed at the Media

In the context of a gag order directed at the media, the U.S. Supreme Court provided a framework for negotiating the balance among diverse principles in *Nebraska Press Association v. Stuart*, 427 U.S. 539 (1976). Submerging First Amendment values to the Sixth Amendment (and tipping its hat to the difficulty of trial judges in negotiating this delicate constitutional balance during the pressures of trial), the Court first articulated a strong presumption of constitutionality in favor of a gag order. This presumption makes clear the deference that a reviewing court should give to a trial court's decision to issue a gag order. With this presumption in mind, a reviewing court should weigh the following factors: "(a) the nature and extent of pre-trial news coverage; (b) whether other measures would be likely to mitigate the effects of unrestrained pre-trial publicity; and (c) how effectively a restraining order would operate to prevent the threatened danger." Id. at 562. Possible measures that could mitigate the effects of pretrial publicity include changing the trial venue to a jurisdiction where media scrutiny may have been less intense; postponement of the trial to allow public attention to subside; emphatic warnings to the press and parties about the impropriety of contacting jurors during trial; sequestering the jury, or temporarily closing the proceedings. Id. at 563-565.

Although the Court framed this standard in terms of pretrial publicity, lower courts have readily applied the standard to publicity during the trial. In applying the Nebraska Press factors, a reviewing court should carefully consider the terms of the restraining order. Moreover, one should note that this standard's challenge often arises from the difficulty of establishing that alternative protections will not successfully remove the danger that publicity creates.[3]

Example 15-6:

The problem in this Example arises as a result of two separate jury trial cases that arose in the same jurisdiction: the trials of Bill Banker and Calvin Corporate. Bill Banker was indicted for tampering with subpoenaed evidence. Bill's trial resulted in a hung jury. As Bill awaited his retrial, Calvin Corporate was tried for a high-profile offense. After multiple news outlets disclosed the name of a juror who, they reported, made a hand gesture in open court in support of the Calvin Corporate, the judge in Calvin's case declared a mistrial.

During Bill Banker's second trial after the hung jury trial, the trial court judge read the names of the jurors in open court upon completion of voir dire. (The judge in Bill's case had considered not disclosing the names of the jurors, but concluded that fairness counseled disclosing the names to the trial participants.) Bill's judge then imposed a temporary restraining order prohibiting members of the press from disclosing the names of empaneled jurors, attempting to avoid the same outcome as in Calvin's trial. Is this gag order constitutionally appropriate?

---

3. The Nebraska Press Court created the four-factor test well before the Internet became a pervasive source of communication. The end of this chapter raises the question of how this test might be modified in light of current realities about Internet use.

Explanation:

The gag order is unconstitutional. In fact, the order flunks all three *Nebraska Press* factors. As for the first factor, the order was not motivated by or tailored to exigencies arising from the pretrial publicity in Bill Banker's case. Instead, an unrelated case (Calvin Corporate's case) motivated the trial judge, who made no determinations that the publicity in Bill Banker's case would impair his right to a fair trial. On the second *Nebraska Press* factor, the trial court judge did consider, but ultimately rejected, using an anonymous jury. Yet the judge failed to explore alternative measures to mitigate the potential harm of the gag order, so this factor is not established. Finally, the third factor is woefully deficient. Indeed, the efficacy of the order restraining the press was dubious, since the names of the jurors were read in open court and any member of the public in the courtroom could have disseminated that information notwithstanding the order. *See United States v. Quattrone*, 402 F. 3d 304 (2d Cir. 2005).

Example 15-7:

A 16-year-old is tried for murder as an adult. Many of the witnesses who are expected to testify are also juveniles. Concerned about protecting the safety of the juvenile witnesses, the trial court holds a hearing regarding media access to the trial. After finding that some of the juvenile witnesses were the subject of threats, the judge barred the publication of their names. Is this a constitutional gag order?

Explanation:

This order is likely not constitutional, since it does not meet the second and third *Nebraska Press* factors. As for the second factor, a less heavy-handed measure for protecting the witness would be to give emphatic warning to trial observers, reminding them it is a crime to attempt to influence or intimidate witnesses. Moreover, the order does not satisfy the third *Nebraska Press* factor because it is not an effective method of protecting the threatened juvenile witnesses. Because the perpetrators of the threats already knew the witness's identity, the restraint would not protect the witnesses from these threatening individuals, who would be free to sit in the open courtroom observing the testimony. *See Cheyenne Newspapers, Inc. v. First Judicial District Court*, 358 P.3d 493 (Wyo. 2015).

* * *

As one observes from these Examples, although the *Nebraska Press* Court suggested that an appellate court defer to a trial judge's decision to issue a gag order, when applied from the point of view of a trial court deciding whether to issue a gag order, the *Nebraska Press* nearly always prevents gag orders of the press from occurring. One exception, however, concerns instances when attorney-client communications are involved. Consider the following Example.

Example 15-8:

While awaiting trial for murder with the possibility of receiving the death penalty, a defendant and his attorney are videotaped in a jail visitation room having a privileged conversation about the case. After members of the media obtain access to the tape, the defendant seeks to enjoin them from airing the videotape or characterizing its contents publicly. The trial court issues an ex parte temporary restraining order to that effect and continues the order after a hearing the next day at which several local news outlets had intervened to object.

A local television station would like to air the tape and challenge the order as an unconstitutional prior restraint on free speech. Will the television station prevail?

Explanation:

The television station is not likely to prevail. Since the death penalty hung in the balance, one can imagine that a court would be more careful than usual to avoid damage to the defendant's fair trial rights. In fact, given the possibility of the death penalty in the case, the chances are good that the case had already garnered meaningful media attention, thus satisfying the first *Nebraska Press* factor. The court gag order would effectively curb the videotape's potential prejudicial impact on the case, as it would prevent the jury from learning of the videotape's contents. Moreover, the effects of disclosing the substance of the privileged conversation would be hard to mitigate. Accordingly, the defendant's fair trial right could not have been guaranteed if the tape were made public. *State Record Co., Inc. v. State*, 504 S.E.2d 592 (S.C. 1998).

b. Gag Orders on Trial Participants

In contrast to gag orders focused on the media, the question of when a court's gag order on a trial participant is held as a valid prior restraint is less certain. The U.S. Supreme Court has never ruled directly on the validity of such orders, although the Court in dicta has hinted that they are likely to be viewed as more permissible than gag orders on the media. For example, in *Nebraska Press*, the Court acknowledged that an alternative to the trial gag order on the media in question would have been to "limit what the contending lawyers, the police, and witnesses may say to anyone." 427 U.S. at 564.

Also, the Court in *Gentile v. State Bar of Nevada*, 501 U.S. 1030 (1991), stated that attorney speech is protected by a less demanding standard because lawyers are "officers of the court." Id. at 1074. *Gentile* concerned the constitutionality of disciplining lawyers for speech and was not a gag order case per se. Nonetheless, *Gentile* provided a conception of the special role of lawyers that helps to understand considerations governing whether to subject them to a gag order: lawyers practice under a special moral code, with obligations of trust and confidentiality accompanying their duty to serve their clients as well as the administration of justice. On the other side of the balance, however, one might point out that gagging lawyers and litigants threatens fairness protections under the due process clauses of the Fourteenth and Fifth Amendments of the U.S. Constitution as well as presents an obstacle to a criminal defendant's right to present a defense protected by the Sixth Amendment.

The *Gentile v. State Bar of Nevada* decision is the closest the Court has come to addressing the gag order question. In that case, attorney Gentile sketched out his recently indicted client's defense at a press conference, declaring that his client was a "scapegoat" being prosecuted instead of the "crooked cops" who truly deserved prosecution. The client was ultimately acquitted, and the state bar authorities filed a complaint against Gentile under disciplinary rules prohibiting an attorney from making extrajudicial statements to the press creating a "substantial likelihood of materially prejudicing an adjudicative proceeding." Id. at 1042. The rule provided a number of safe harbors for attorneys to make statements without fear of discipline, such as allowing a defense attorney to state without elaboration the nature of the defense upon which the attorney will rely. The *Gentile* Court upheld this "substantial likelihood" approach, stating that the clear and present danger standard, which the *Nebraska Press* Court had endorsed for reviewing gag orders directed against the press, was not necessary in this context. A majority of the Court, however, found the overall approach of the state disciplinary rule's safe harbor standards void for vagueness and therefore concluded that the rule failed to give attorneys adequate guidance.

Given this somewhat confusing guidance from the *Gentile* Court, lower courts have both upheld and invalidated gag orders on attorneys and other trial participants. A split in the circuits exists on the question of what standard should be used to review such orders. Before *Gentile*, some circuits followed the "clear and present danger" standard from *Nebraska Press. See, e.g., United States v. Ford*, 830 F.2d 596, 598 (6th Cir. 1987). Some circuits have adopted a "substantial likelihood of material prejudice" standard. *See e.g., United States v. Scarfo*, 263 F.3d 80, 94 (3d Cir. 2001). Other circuits have adopted a "reasonable likelihood" of prejudice standard, *see, e.g., In re Russell*, 726 F.2d 1007, 1010 (4th Cir. 1984), which is ostensibly the least strict standard.

Despite these varying standards, the case law makes clear that gag orders directed at trial participants are more likely to survive challenge than similar

247

orders directed at the news media. Consider the following Examples that reflect this more permissive orientation toward trial participant gag orders.

Example 15-9:

In one of several high-profile political corruption cases pending in the same district court, the judge imposed a gag order on the attorneys, parties, and witnesses that restricted what such individuals could discuss with the media. Specifically, the order enjoined statements "intended to influence public opinion regarding the merits of this case . . . ." The order included exceptions whereby individuals could discuss matters of public record or supporting the defendant's innocence, among other things. The trial court rested the orders on the following finding: a high probability that such statements would increase pretrial publicity and thereby taint the district's jury pool, especially in light of the related pending cases.

The defendant, a well-known statewide politician, seeks to vacate the order, arguing that it imposes an unconstitutional prior restraint. Will he succeed?

Explanation:

The defendant will likely fail in this argument. The facts of this Example are similar to those of *United States v. Brown*, 218 F.3d 415 (5th Cir. 2000). In *Brown*, the court upheld a gag order, similar to the one in this Example, as a permissible prior restraint.

The *Brown* court first determined that the "clear and present danger" standard that other circuits had imposed on trial participant gag orders was inappropriate. Citing *Gentile v. State Bar of Nevada*, the court contended that such a high standard "did not consider the distinction . . . between trial participants and the press for purposes of a trial court's ability to restrict the speech of those two groups." *Id.* at 427.

The court then declined to choose between the "substantial likelihood of material prejudice" and the "reasonable likelihood of prejudice," since — the court concluded — the gag order satisfied either standard. The gag order was necessary to avoid the strong likelihood that proscribed statements by trial participants would "increase the volume of pre-trial publicity," and thus lead to the creation of a "carnival atmosphere . . . ." *Id.* at 429. And in light of the presence of two other related trials in the same district, such statements could taint the unsequestered jury.

The *Brown* court also reasoned that the gag order was justified as the parties in the case had already demonstrated that they were prone to making prejudicial statements. As the court put it: "the parties . . . already demonstrated a desire to manipulate media coverage to gain favorable attention." *Id.*

The court did not, however, impose a requirement that courts issuing gag orders must explicitly consider and reject alternatives to a gag order in order to evaluate whether less restrictive means existed to address the threatened harms. The court acknowledged that other circuits had imposed that requirement.

Example 15-10:

In a high-profile public corruption case, the court imposes a gag order at the defendant's request, restricting all extrajudicial statements made by any of the parties or counsel. The order applied to statements directed to the press and statements that a reasonable speaker would anticipate that the press would receive. The order contained exceptions for statements about the general nature of the allegations, information from the public record, or any scheduling matters.

The affected trial participates argue that the gag order on the trial participants is an impermissible prior restraint on speech. Are they likely to prevail?

Explanation:

The trial participants are not likely to prevail. In a case with facts similar to this Example, the court of appeals upheld the gag order. In re Application of Dow Jones & Co., Inc., 842 F.2d 603 (2d Cir. 1988). The Dow Jones court applied the "reasonable likelihood" test, concluding that a reasonable likelihood existed "that pretrial publicity [would] prejudice a fair trial." Id. at 610. Notably, the court placed great emphasis on the fact that the gag order was imposed on the trial participants and not the media—since the media "cannot be haled into court for violating [the order's] terms . . . ." Id. at 608. Moreover, contrary to the Fifth Circuit decision discussed in the previous Example (Brown, 218 F.3d at 429), the Dow Jones court considered less restrictive alternatives to a gag order on trial participants. The court relied on an earlier U.S. Supreme Court pretrial publicity case, Sheppard v. Maxwell, 384 U.S. 333 (1966), and stated that all of the mitigating measures listed in that case "must be explored and ultimately rejected as inadequate—individually and in combination—as a remedy for prejudicial pretrial publicity before a restraining order is entered." Id. at 611.

3. Discovery Protective Orders in Civil Trials

The Supreme Court in Seattle Times Co. v. Reinhart, 467 U.S. 20 (1984), considered the constitutionality of a protective order prohibiting parties to a civil case from disseminating information obtained through discovery before it is made public. Disposing of the case, the *Seattle Times* Court concluded that the order did not amount to "the kind of classic prior restraint that requires exacting First Amendment scrutiny." *Id.* at 33. A Washington state trial court had imposed a protective order in a defamation suit brought by a religious organization against a local newspaper. The protective order barred the newspaper from publishing the identity of the organization's donors and members, which the newspaper had acquired through discovery. The Supreme Court upheld the protective order, noting civil discovery protective orders implicate First Amendment concerns to a "far lesser extent than would restraints on dissemination of information in a different context." *Id.* at 34. The Court observed that information obtained through discovery may ultimately be deemed "unrelated, or only tangentially related" to the public record of the case. *Id.* at 33. In order to serve the government's substantial interest in ensuring the privacy of this information, a court must have "substantial latitude to fashion" such orders to protect the fairness of the litigation process. *Id.* at 36.

Example 15-11:

A small religious congregation brings a defamation action against a local newspaper over several claims that the newspaper made about the organization's recruitment and fundraising practices. During discovery, the religious organization is compelled to send the newspaper lists of all of its congregants and donors. The religious organization delivers the lists, but asks that the court to enter a protective order that prohibits the newspaper from publishing their contents.

The newspaper moves to vacate the discovery protective order, arguing that it is an impermissible prior restraint. Will the newspaper likely succeed in vacating the discovery protective order?

Explanation:

The newspaper will likely not succeed. This case presents a clear example of an instance where private information is handed over as part of litigation, but may ultimately turn out to be irrelevant to the outcome of the case. In light of concerns with fairness and the privacy interests of the congregants and donors, the court acted appropriately in issuing the protective order.

* * *

Although we have all this Supreme Court guidance to work with, one wonders what the effect of social media and the Internet generally has on gag orders in the like. A question for the future: should these changes on widespread availability change the First Amendment rules?

C. PUBLICATION OF TRUTHFUL, LAWFULLY OBTAINED INFORMATION

The U.S. Supreme Court has taken the position that the press has a protected right to publish truthful, lawfully obtained information. The right is not absolute, but a court should strictly scrutinize any restriction on the right. As stated by the Court in *Florida Star v. B.J.F.*, 491 U.S. 524 (1989), a newspaper or other mass-media instrument may be punished for such a publication only when a proscription on publication is "narrowly tailored to a state interest of the highest order." *Id.* at 541.

In *Florida Star*, the newspaper faced civil liability under a negligence per se standard for publishing the identity of a rape victim whose name was mistakenly included in a public document. Although agreeing that protecting the identity of a rape victim was an interest of the highest order, the Court found that the regulation of the disclosure was not sufficiently tailored. For example, the state could have protected the victim's name with safeguards to prevent it from being included in the police report. The *Florida Star* Court further concluded that the newspaper's constitutional right was violated because (1) the negligence per se standard swept too broadly by imposing liability even in circumstances when the victim's name was well known in the community and (2) the restriction was underinclusive because it applied only to the mass media.

The U.S. Supreme Court extended this ruling in *Bartnicki v. Vopper*, 532 U.S. 514 (2001), in which it held that the First Amendment protected publication of truthful information of public concern by a person who lawfully obtained that information, but who knew or should have known that the information had been obtained illegally. The Court acknowledged, however, that the interest in privacy protection could be strong enough to overcome the First Amendment concerns, such as in cases involving disclosure of trade secrets or gossip about private matters.

Example 15-12:

Pursuant to a state's rape shield laws, the contents of an evidentiary hearing in a rape prosecution are sealed and remain confidential until a determination can be made about the materiality and relevancy of the evidence in question. The state justifies excluding the public and the press from such hearings based on the victim's privacy interest as well as the state's interest in encouraging victims to report rape incidents so they can be prosecuted. Not only does the victim's privacy interest include the victim's right to avoid having the public learn of the victim's role in the crime, but also implicates a concern unique to typical defense strategies in criminal rape prosecutions. In such prosecutions, defendants often try to inject irrelevant evidence of the victim's personal sexual conduct into the proceedings. As a consequence, the rape shield statute allows for private "*in camera*" hearings that occur to evaluate the relevancy and materiality of evidence of that personal sexual conduct.

In a widely publicized rape trial, a court reporter accidentally emails the transcript of a private evidentiary hearing to several news outlets. Upon learning of the mistake, the trial judge promptly orders the recipients of the emailed transcripts to destroy the copies of the transcripts and refrain from revealing their contents.

A local news outlet seeks to publish information gleaned from the transcript and challenges the trial court judge's order as an impermissible prior restraint. Will the news outlet prevail in its motion to quash the order?

Explanation:

The news outlet will likely not prevail on its desire to publish the transcript. A decision on this issue starts with the premise — endorsed by the United States Supreme Court — that the transcripts would cause great harm to a state interest of the highest order. The victim has an exceedingly strong privacy interest that would be compromised if the graphic, intrusive testimony were made public and the state has a likewise strong interest in encouraging rape victims to testify.

In order to be constitutional, however, the restraint on publication must also be sufficiently narrowly tailored in the sense that it must pertain to information gleaned from the transcripts and not obtained through independent investigation. For this reason, the portion of the trial court's order requiring the news outlet to destroy the transcript may be overbroad. Although the news outlet may not properly use the transcript as the source of future independent investigation, the outlet may pursue its desire to maintain journalistic integrity and professionalism by using the transcript to confirm information obtained through independent investigation. Accordingly, chances are good that a trial judge would grant the news outlet's motion to quash only to the extent that the order required the outlet to destroy the transcript. *See People v. Bryant*, 94 P.3d 624 (Colo. 2004) (en banc).

* * *

When it comes to protection of truthful information, an important contrast to consider is the law's tolerance for allowing entities to conceal information crucial to economic well-being. Take for example, the trade secret laws. As trade secret is a piece of information that has economic value because it is neither generally known nor readily ascertainable (and is target of efforts to maintain its secrecy). Trademark protection laws provide remedies for the holder of trade secrets under a number of circumstances when the secrets are disclosed. First Amendment concerns have not had much influence in this area. Consider the contrast between the law's protections for trade secrets (an economic interest) and First Amendment treatment of attempts to shield the identity of a rape victim (a personal privacy interest.)

D. PROTECTION OF CONFIDENTIAL SOURCES

Do reporters who are subpoenaed to testify at trials have to comply with the subpoena? Does the media's special role in society justify giving reporters some kind of constitutional protection from being forced to testify? Confidential sources are often crucial to the ability of reporters to get real facts about potential illegality. If reporters must comply with subpoenas requiring them to testify, do First Amendment principles protect them from being forced to disclose the identity of confidential sources?

The U.S. Supreme Court provided guidance in answering these questions in the context of whether a reporter is required to testify as part of a grand jury proceeding in *Branzburg v. Hayes*, 408 U.S. 665 (1972). The news media in *Branzburg* claimed that: (1) if they are required to reveal the identity of or information given by confidential sources, those sources might be deterred from providing information in the future; and (2) such a result would hamper the free flow of information in society. The Court was unconvinced by these assertions, finding the alleged effect on sources speculative. The Court acknowledged that "without some protection for seeking out the news, [the] freedom of the press could be eviscerated." *Id.* at 681. The Court concluded, however, that "the public interest in law enforcement and in ensuring effective grand jury proceedings" is sufficient to override any resulting, but uncertain, burden on news gathering that might result from requiring reporters to honor subpoenas to testify.

A Supreme Court majority joined this opinion in *Branzburg*, which refused to recognize that the First Amendment freedom of press guarantee contained at least a qualified privilege for members of the news media. Justice Powell, however, wrote a concurring opinion advocating a balancing test for courts to use in certain cases that takes account of concerns that the media's forced testimony would jeopardize the ability of journalists to perform effectively. He urged that the media's request for a privilege not to testify in a particular case should be decided "by the striking of proper balance between freedom of the press and the obligation of all citizens to give relevant testimony with respect to criminal conduct." *Id.* at 710 (Powell, J., concurring). Some (not all) lower courts have relied on this opinion in order to recognize a qualified privilege shielding reporters from the obligation to testify. Reinforcing this protection is recognition in some jurisdictions of common law or statutory shield laws that also protect reporters from testifying. *See, e.g.*, *In re Schuman*, 552 A.2d 602 (N.J. 1989) (relying on the balance of factors mentioned in Justice Powell's concurrence and holding that the state shield law protected a reporter from testifying on matters crucial to a murder prosecution).

Example 15-13:

After working as a CIA operative for several years, Mark spoke to a reporter about his experiences. The reporter published a book that included detailed descriptions of what Mark had described about CIA operations. The CIA discovered that the information Mark disclosed in the book contained classified information.

The government initiated a federal court proceeding and indicted Mark for communicating classified information in violation of the Espionage Act. The government subpoenaed the reporter to testify about the information relayed to him by the ex-CIA official. The reporter moved to quash the subpoena. Should the trial court quash the subpoena?

Explanation:

Under the authority of *Branzburg*, the trial court should not quash the order. Because this is a proceeding in federal court, it is unlikely that the trial court would apply state common law principles or a state shield statute that would help the reporter. In a case similar to this, the United States Court of Appeals for the Fourth Circuit refused to quash the subpoena, stating "the Supreme Court in no uncertain terms rejected the existence of [a reporter's] privilege." *United States v. Sterling*, 724 F.3d 482, 492 (4th Cir. 2013) (internal quotations omitted). The *Sterling* court further explained that the *Branzburg* Court declined to treat reporters differently from all other citizens who are compelled to give evidence of criminal activity and that it would not require the government to demonstrate a "compelling interest" for the reporter's testimony or other special showing simply because the reporter was in possession of the evidence needed. *Id.*

E. ACCESS TO THE PRESS

This chapter has thus far focused on various issues relating to the media's ability to access information and communicate that information as it sees fit. This section explores the flip side of those First Amendment issues. Given the importance of the media to the operation of a democratic society, under what circumstances can the government require that the media make available an opportunity for speakers to communicate important messages to the public? This issue implicates general First Amendment values, since allowing access to various communication outlets expands the voices that are available in the marketplace of ideas and fosters public debate about important issues. On the other hand, however, laws requiring access to the media can infringe the media's editorial discretion and autonomy in controlling the content that it makes available.

Although these values apply to all types of media, the Court has handled access to the media issues differently according to which type of media is involved. The Court started first by considering issues related to the broadcast media, then moved to the print media, and finally addressed cable television.

I. Broadcast Media

In *Red Lion Broadcasting Co. v. Federal Communications Commission*, 395 U.S. 367 (1969), the Supreme Court considered the constitutionality of the fairness doctrine and a related doctrine concerning personal attacks. The fairness doctrine required that a broadcast licensee must present balanced discussion of public issues. The personal attack rules provide that when the honesty or character of an individual is attacked on the air, the individual attacked must receive an opportunity to reply. Journalists argued these requirements violated their First Amendment rights by impinging their editorial discretion.

Emphasizing that the rights that were paramount in this context were those of the viewers and listeners, the Court observed that broadcast frequencies are scarce, and the government is justified in regulating their use in order that the public could hear as many viewpoints as possible. The Court therefore upheld the fairness doctrine and personal attack rules, ruling that the government had a proper role in allocating the broadcast frequencies and giving effect to "the legitimate claims of those unable without governmental assistance to gain access to those frequencies for [the] expression of their views." Id. at 400.

Example 15-14:

A political group was devoted to criticizing the President's policies in handling a pandemic that was affecting the nation. A broadcast television station had a blanket policy refusing to sell time segments to entities that advocated that position. The political group sued, arguing that *Red Lion* established their First Amendment right to purchase access to a time segment on the station. Is the political group correct in its reading of *Red Lion*?

Explanation:

No, the political group is wrong. *Red Lion* concerned whether federal regulations infringed the First Amendment rights of broadcasters. This fact pattern presents the question whether the First Amendment affirmatively grants a right of access to the broadcast media held by members of the public. Although the rights of viewers and listeners as well as the editorial rights of broadcasters informed the decision in *Red Lion*, the U.S. Supreme Court ruled in a case similar to this one that recognizing a private right of access would unconstitutionally infringe the editorial judgment of the broadcast media. *See CBS, Inc. v. Democratic National Committee*, 412 U.S. 94 (1973).

2. Print Media

When it took up the issue of access to the print media, the Supreme Court took an entirely different tack than it did with the broadcast media. In *Miami Herald v. Tornillo*, 418 U.S. 241 (1974), the Court declared unconstitutional a statute that required newspapers to print a reply from any candidate for office whose character or official record had been attacked earlier in the newspaper. According to the Court, the statute unconstitutionally imposed a penalty "on the basis of the content of a newspaper . . . taking up space that could be devoted to other material the newspaper may have preferred to print." *Id.* at 256. In the Court's view, the requirement had the potential to chill speech, since the newspaper may avoid printing certain stories in order not to confront a reply demand. The Court also regarded the law as an impermissible restraint on editorial content.

Are *Tornillo* and *Red Lion* inconsistent? Read together, the two decisions hold that the right to reply laws are allowed for broadcaster media, but not for newspapers. Is there a distinction that accounts for the opposite treatment of the two types of media? The differences in the cases appear to rest on the apparent scarcity of broadcast frequencies, a scarcity that makes it more reasonable for the government to regulate access than in the context of newspapers. One wonders, however, in today's world whether the proliferation of radio and television channels and the dwindling numbers of newspapers suggest this analysis is outdated.

Example 15-15:

State X has a statute that grants an individual the right to have a newspaper print a retraction if the newspaper prints a story that is established to be defamatory—that is, the story presented false information that would tend to blacken the individual's reputation in the community. Is this statute invalid after the U.S. Supreme Court's *Tornillo* decision invalidating the right to reply rule?

Explanation:

The retraction statute may still be valid. Justice Brennan, together with Justice Rehnquist, joined the Court's opinion in *Tornillo*, but wrote a concurrence in which he stated that his understanding of the Court's opinion was that it "addresses only 'right of reply' statutes and implies no view upon the constitutionality of 'retraction' statutes affording plaintiffs able to prove defamatory falsehoods a statutory action to require publication of a retraction." *Id.* at 558-559. One wonders why it was necessary for Justice Brennan to write separately to make this point and why the Court's opinion did not simply include the same point out of deference to Justice Brennan. Nonetheless, the Court's opinion does not refute Justice Brennan's understanding. Moreover, statutes requiring retraction of allegedly defamatory material implicate different concerns than right to reply statutes, since retraction statutes seek to avoid harm to an individual rather than opening debate on a particular issue.

3. Cable Television

The Court faced an issue similar to that in *Tornillo* and *Red Lion* in the context of the federal Cable Act, which required cable companies to carry local over-the-air broadcast stations. Cable companies filed suit, arguing this "must-carry" requirement interfered with their First Amendment right to exercise discretion in deciding which channels to carry. In *Turner Broadcasting System, Inc. v. Federal Communications Commission*, 512 U.S. 622 (1994), the Supreme Court ruled that the First Amendment applied to the cable situation, but the principles of *Red Lion* did not control. The Court explained that "[t]he broadcast cases are inapposite in the present context because cable television does not suffer from the inherent limitations that characterize the broadcast medium." *Id.* at 639. A plurality of the Court then explained that the *Tornillo* approach did not govern the must-carry requirement either. Instead, the Court ruled that although any content-based regulation of cable merits strict scrutiny, the must-carry requirement was content neutral and should be reviewed under the test of *United States v. O'Brien*, 391 U.S. 367 (1968). Under the *United States v. O'Brien* test, a court should sustain a content-neutral regulation if it advances important governmental interests unrelated to the suppression of free speech and does not burden substantially more speech than necessary to further those interests.[4] The Supreme Court remanded the case to the lower court in order to determine whether the regulation passed this test.

---

4. Chapter 11 of this volume reviews the *United States v. O'Brien* test in detail.

Example 15-16:

Put yourself in the position of the lower court on remand from the U.S. Supreme Court in the *Turner Broadcasting* case. What do you need to determine in order to follow the U.S. Supreme Court's instructions?

Explanation:

First, you need to evaluate whether the proffered reasons why Congress passed the Cable Act are important. In addition, you need to confirm that these concerns are neutral, meaning that they are not connected to the types of expression that the cable operators feature. In that regard, you might investigate whether evidence supports the neutral, non-content based interests that appeared to motivate Congress to pass the Act, keeping a watchful eye out for any ulterior motives that Congress may have had that relate to the content featured by the cable operators. Finally, you should evaluate whether the Cable Act's must-carry requirement directly serves Congress's interests and does not burden more speech than necessary to serve those interests.

This tracks the precise steps that the U.S. Supreme Court followed in affirming the lower court's decision that the must-carry rule was constitutional. *Turner Broadcasting System, Inc. v. Federal Communications Commission*, 520 U.S. 180 (1997). Specifically, the Court determined the following:

(1) Congress's interests of preserving the benefits of free local broadcast television, promoting widespread dissemination of information from many sources, and promoting fair competition in the television programming market are important governmental interests;

(2) The must-carry provisions of the Act were designed to address real harm. This can be seen in the substantial evidence supporting Congress's determination that significant numbers of broadcast stations would be refused carriage on cable systems if the must-carry requirement were not imposed. As a consequence, the local broadcast stations would be at risk of financial difficulty or failure;

(3) The must-carry requirement served the government's interests directly and effectively; and

(4) The must-carry requirement did not burden substantially more speech than was necessary to further the government's interests.

F. THE FIRST AMENDMENT AND THE INTERNET

The advent of widespread Internet use promises to change dramatically the Supreme Court's interpretation of the freedom of the press clause of the First Amendment. One obvious reason for the likelihood of doctrinal change is that the Internet's works have greater impact around the world than print media, standard broadcast media, and cable TV. The nature of the Internet's unique and pervasive operation means that existing doctrines must be modified. For example, with the Internet, technological limits on such matters as the number of available channels are no longer relevant. What were once important distinctions between print and broadcast media diminish in relevance when members of their audience can access both on their computers.

The required changes in the law are not confined to the consequences of the Internet's capability for wide impact on the world. Indeed, the Internet's ability to provide a means of communication for everyone with access has equally great ramifications. For example, the ability of anyone with access to send messages out on the Internet begs the question of what is "the press" for the purposes of the First Amendment. Should all those who post on the Internet be given the status of "the press" for First Amendment purposes, should that status be confined to the traditional press, or is there another group that should be included? And then questions arise as to the status of social media organizations and service providers. These entities exercise considerable control of what content is available to the information-consuming public. Should they be considered part of the press for the purpose of First Amendment interpretation?

As is the case with any new technology, the Internet also brings with it new legal issues. Poverty or location may prevent a considerable number of people from accessing the Internet. Those realities clearly implicate equality principles. Should they also affect the contours of new First Amendment doctrines? Moreover, existing technology allows broadband providers to control various aspects of their subscribers' Internet access. This control includes such matters as the speed and reliability of different connections and the websites that users are able to access. In this regard, a significant public policy debate rages about whether regulations should stop providers from discriminating among subscribers of their services. To what extent does the First Amendment inform this so-called "net neutrality" debate?

The Internet may also affect gag order issues. With the Internet, disclosure and wide-spread dissemination of sensitive or protected information is much more likely—perhaps often inevitable. Should that change the weight of the *Nebraska Press* factors for courts to consider when deciding whether to issue a gag order? Alternatively, should the *Nebraska Press* test be changed altogether?

The U.S. Supreme Court has evinced a reluctance to reckon with issues pertaining to how the Internet changes the interpretation and application of constitutional issues as a general matter. The Court's approach to Internet issues is the same in the First Amendment context. Noting that electronic media evolves at a rapid pace, members of the Court have suggested that prudence counsels either not reckoning directly with First Amendment Internet issues for a while or developing a flexible approach that permits the law to move with changing technology. *See, e.g., Denver Area Educational Telecomms. Consortium, Inc. v. Federal Communications Commission,* 518 U.S. 727 (1996) (opinions of Breyer, J. and Souter, J.).

Freedom of Association

CHAPTER 16

The final clause of the First Amendment protects "the right of the people peaceably to assemble, and to petition the Government for a redress of grievances." From this language, the U.S. Supreme Court has developed principles designed to protect citizens' right to associate with one another "for the advancement of beliefs and ideas." NAACP v. Alabama ex rel. Patterson, 357 U.S. 449, 460 (1958). Freedom of association also fits well with the free speech clause, since speech is more effective when people band together to express a particular message. Likewise, freedom of association naturally fits together with the clause protecting free exercise of religion, since people often worship in groups. Indeed, First Amendment case law tends to show that the right of free association is strongest when combined with another First Amendment right.

As a result of the natural overlap between freedom of association and other First Amendment rights, earlier parts of this volume touched on freedom of association, particularly in discussing political financing in the chapter on political speech (Chapter 3), the discussion of union fees in the chapter on compelled speech (Chapter 5), and the discussion of the speech rights of government employees (Chapter 13). Chapter 21 will discuss instances when freedom of association overlaps with freedom of religion and freedom of speech. That chapter will provide an overview of strategies for juggling more than one First Amendment freedom when a set of facts presents that challenge.

This chapter covers the U.S. Supreme Court's handling of three additional contexts when freedom of association claims arise: (1) instances when the government prohibits membership in a group; (2) attempts by the government to force disclosure of a group's membership; and (3) the circumstances under which freedom of association protects a group's ability to avoid complying with discrimination laws. This latter context is the focus of the U.S. Supreme Court's most recent freedom of association cases. The end of the chapter explores an important issue that has not yet reached the U.S. Supreme Court: the question of whether a government's stay-at-home orders issued during a pandemic, such as COVID-19, violate the right to free association. As this array of contexts suggests, the freedom of association case law covers a wide span of topics and issues, which are only loosely connected.

The Court has not articulated one "freedom of association" test for all circumstances to which it has attached the freedom of association label. One can speculate about the reason for this. Could it be because the right applies to an especially diverse assortment of contexts? Perhaps various tests emerge because each situation contains a unique blend of expression components (which one would associate with strict scrutiny) and conduct components (which might call for a lessened standard of scrutiny). Or maybe the lack of uniformity results from the freedom of association right's status as an implied right that is only loosely tethered to specific constitutional language.

As a general matter, the Supreme Court has identified a heightened standard of scrutiny applicable to the association right—at least for issues relating to political expression. According to the Court, the government may justify infringement of association rights:

(1) if the regulations are "adopted to serve compelling state interests";

(2) if the regulations are "related to the suppression of ideas";

(3) when the state interests "cannot be achieved through means significantly less restrictive of association freedoms."

Roberts v. United States Jaycees, 468 U.S. 609 (1984). The Court has qualified this approach, however, suggesting that intermediate scrutiny applies in cases when the harm to associational freedoms is not severe. In *Clingman v. Beaver*, 544 U.S. 581 (2005), the Court embraced the view that "[w]hen a state electoral provision places no heavy burden on associational rights, a State's important regulatory interests will usually be enough to justify reasonable, nondiscriminatory restrictions." *Id.* at 589 (internal quotation marks omitted).

A. GOVERNMENT PROHIBITION OF GROUP MEMBERSHIP

Freedom of association is generally synonymous with freedom to be a member of a group. With an eye toward respecting this principle, the U.S. Supreme Court has held that the government may prohibit or punish membership in a group only upon proof that a person is actively affiliated with an unlawful group, knows its illegal objectives, and possesses specific intent to further those objectives. Noto v. United States, 367 U.S. 290 (1961); Scales v. United States, 367 U.S. 203 (1961).

Example 16-1:

The application for a state bar exam contains the following questions:

(1) Are you a member of a group that has the objective of overthrowing the government of the United States by force or violence?

(2) How often do you participate in activities with the group?

(3) Are you willing to take action to further the group's objective of overthrowing the government of the United States by force or violence?

If an exam taker answers the first and third question "yes" and answers the second question "four times a year" or more, the exam taker is prohibited from taking the exam and becoming a lawyer in the state. Is this system constitutional?

Explanation:

Yes, the system is constitutional. The questions are very specific and, if answered as noted, would establish each of the requirements that the Supreme Court has articulated to lawfully punish an individual for group membership. In fact, the Court upheld a system similar to this in Law Students Civil Rights Research Council, Inc. v. Wadmond, 401 U.S. 154 (1971).

B. FORCED DISCLOSURE OF GROUP MEMBERSHIP

Government sometimes requires individuals to disclose their membership in a group, or requires groups to disclose their membership lists. This practice is generally unconstitutional because it violates the privacy of individuals, frustrating their ability to freely associate as well as the goals of their associations. In addition, the practice of forced disclosure implicates freedom of expression concerns about compelled speech, particularly in the context of laws that require individuals to disclose information about their personal identity, or require a group to alter its message. Chapter 5 of this volume covers compelled speech and explores these latter two issues.

The U.S. Supreme Court has held that the government may compel a group to disclose membership lists only when it can satisfy heightened scrutiny. Heralding the important connection between privacy and association, the Court stated in *NAACP v. Alabama ex rel. Patterson*, that "[i]nviolability of privacy in group association may in many circumstances be indispensable to preservation of freedom of association, particularly where a group espouses dissident beliefs." 357 U.S. at 462.

In *NAACP v. Alabama ex rel. Patterson*, the Court declared unconstitutional Alabama's use of an out-of-state corporation disclosure law to require the NAACP to disclose its membership list. Similarly, in *Shelton v. Tucker*, 364 U.S. 479 (1960), the Court struck down a law requiring public school teachers to disclose all their group memberships each year. Concerned that the law contained no provision for keeping the teachers' disclosures private, the Court stated that even if the state did have privacy protection provisions, "the pressure upon [teachers] to avoid any ties which might displease those who control [their] professional destiny would be constant and heavy." *Id.* at 486. The Court's analysis, however, allowed for the possibility that—in an appropriate case—a state might comply with constitutional requirements by advancing a sufficient reason for a narrowly tailored group disclosure requirement.

NAACP v. Alabama ex rel. Patterson suggested that strict scrutiny was the standard of review to be applied in forced membership disclosure cases. Nevertheless, subsequent developments in the U.S. Supreme Court—such as the *Clingman v. Beaver*, 544 U.S. 581 (2005)—suggest that an intermediate level of scrutiny should apply when the infringement of the associational freedoms is not severe. Although *Clingman* did not address forced membership disclosure, lower courts have followed its lead, reasoning that a strict standard of scrutiny does not apply to all forced membership disclosure cases. For example, in *Citizens United v. Schneiderman*, 882 F.3d 374, 381-382 (2d Cir. 2018), the court stated that the strict standard of scrutiny applies only to content-based restrictions and restrictions that discriminate among speakers. From that premise, the *Schneiderman* court reasoned that because forced disclosure cases do not usually fall into those two categories, courts usually should evaluate such disputes with a lower standard of review. *Id.* at 382.

Example 16-2:

A state enacted its own version of a Freedom of Information Act, which mandated that public organizations be transparent and supply individuals with membership information upon request, using proper procedures. The purpose of the statute is to allow voters to trace political donations to their source, facilitating political decision making, preventing fraud and corruption, and fostering trust in government.

A local political group was served with a request for a membership list under the state act and refused to comply. The issuer of the request sued the political group. In response, the political group asserted that requiring it to disclose the names of its members violated its constitutional right to associate anonymously. Are they likely to win their challenge to the request for the membership list?

Explanation:

Significant reasons suggest that the political group will not succeed in the challenge. The government's reasons for the disclosure requirement—to facilitate political decision making, to prevent fraud and corruption, and to foster trust in government—would likely be characterized as compelling if a court used the strict standard of scrutiny. Buttressing this conclusion about the importance of the government's purposes is their connection with integrity of the democratic political process, an overriding value animating all of First Amendment law.

Moreover, at least one lower court determined that under circumstances similar to this case, an intermediate, not a strict, standard of scrutiny would apply. *Disabato v. South Carolina Ass'n of School Administrators*, 404 S.C. 433 (2013). The *Disabato* court relied on the U.S. Supreme Court's *Clingman* decision in concluding that a strict standard of scrutiny applies only when a government regulation severely affects associational rights. If a regulation only incidentally affects associational rights an intermediate standard of review is all that is necessary, and the regulation need only serve an important purpose. In pursuing this course of reasoning, the *Disabato* court upheld the forced group disclosure law, emphasizing that the political group made no showing that the regulation significantly impaired its associational rights.

If the political group in this Example wished to improve its chances of success, it should develop evidence to establish that the state statute negatively restricted its right to free association. Such evidence might demonstrate that: (1) the political group had difficulty recruiting members because of the disclosure requirement; (2) the group members had been subject to harassment or reprisals from strangers who learned who they were; (3) the group would be forced to accept members that it did not wish to accept as a consequence of the regulation; or (4) the government applied the statute to the group because of its dissident views.

C. NON-COMPLIANCE WITH DISCRIMINATION LAWS

The foregoing discussions in this chapter attest to the U.S. Supreme Court's willingness to recognize the constitutional importance of free association. Determining the parameters of associational freedom, however, is more challenging. A particularly knotty issue is presented by federal, state, and local anti-discrimination protections. On occasion, a group expresses its identity by excluding individuals whose beliefs or own identity clashes with the group's self-definition. And sometimes that excluded group is part of a class of individuals protected under discrimination laws. How are those two competing legal protections—anti-discrimination principles and freedom of association—reconciled? The resolution of this clash is often a binary choice. An accommodation of both legal protections may not be possible: only freedom of association or anti-discrimination principles can prevail, not both.

One leading case in this area, *Roberts v. United States Jaycees*, 468 U.S. 609 (1984), concerned local chapters of a men's organization that had been sanctioned by the group's national organization because the chapters admitted women to their chapters in violation of its national bylaws. The national organization sanctioned the offending local chapters, which responded by filing a civil rights complaint under a state anti-discrimination law. The national organization argued that forcing it to admit women would violate its associational rights. In *Roberts*, the Supreme Court disagreed, upholding the anti-discrimination claim and rejecting the freedom of association claim.

In rejecting the national organization's claim, the *Roberts* Court acknowledged that "an intrusion into the internal structure or affairs of an association" by forcing "the group to accept members it does not desire" directly implicated the fundamental right of free association. *Id.* at 623. The Court evaluated the freedom of association claim using a strict scrutiny test, stating that government may limit expressive association rights with regulations that: (1) serve compelling state interests; (2) cannot be served through means that are less restrictive of associational freedoms; and (3) are unrelated to the suppression of ideas. Finding anti-discrimination to be a compelling interest, the *Roberts* Court doubted that admission of women would change the organization's mission or violate its First Amendment freedoms.

In later cases, the Court became more receptive to free association claims in discrimination disputes. In one case, *Hurley v. Irish-American Gay, Lesbian, and Bisexual Group*, 515 U.S. 557 (1995), the Court ruled that requiring the parade organizing group to include a gay and lesbian group in a St. Patrick's Day parade—pursuant to state anti-discrimination law—violated the parade organizers' associational rights. Importantly, the parade organizers were reputedly not troubled by gay and lesbian individuals marching in the parade, but simply objected to including an openly gay and lesbian contingent in the parade. Also, the Court notably avoided any discussion of strict scrutiny or compelling state interests. Finally, the Court explained that freedom of association protects the right to discriminate under limited circumstances, such as gatherings of small, intimate groups and instances when discrimination is integral to a group's expressive activity. Chapter 5 of the volume further discusses *Hurley*.

The Court applied *Hurley* in a subsequent case, *Boy Scouts of America v. Dale*, 530 U.S. 640 (2000). In *Dale*, an openly gay Boy Scout leader was expelled from the organization on the sole basis of his sexual orientation. He sued, arguing that state laws of public accommodation prohibiting such discrimination applied to the Boy Scouts, and ultimately won in the state supreme court. Reversing the state supreme court's decision, the U.S. Supreme Court held that the state violated the Boy Scouts' right to expressive association by prohibiting it from expelling members on the sole basis of sexual orientation. Significantly, the Court found this right to be violated even though the Boy Scouts did not submit evidence proving that admitting gay scout leaders would undermine its mission. The Boy Scouts relied on its internal "Scout Oath," which had members swear to be "morally straight." *Id.* at 649. The Court did not require clarification of the term "morally straight," accepting the Boy Scouts' argument that the Oath proved that exclusion of homosexuals was integral to its mission.

Example 16-3:

A student club at a state university, Students for Restraint, was dedicated to restraint in sexual relations, including abstinence before marriage. The student club sought recognition from the university in order to receive certain financial benefits such as subsidized rent for meeting spaces, and access to certain areas on campus reserved for such groups. In order to receive formal recognition—and the consequent funding benefits—all student groups must provide the university with a copy of its constitution and comply with the state's non-discrimination policy. The non-discrimination policy prohibited discrimination on the basis of gender identity and sexual orientation.

Students for Restraint's constitution stated that homosexual individuals are not permitted to be members or officers. Under the authority of *Hurley* and *Dale,* may the university properly deny recognition and funding to Students for Restraint on the basis of the club's policy against homosexual members?

Explanation:

The university may be able to properly deny recognition and funding to Students for Restraint. First, the university's restriction applies to all groups; it is content neutral. Second, as an institution of higher learning, the university is acting consistently with its mission to ensure that all students can access student groups, particularly those like Students for Restraint that are organized around concepts or ideas. Third, the restriction only incidentally impacts Students for Restraint's associational rights. The group is organized around the concept of restraint in sexual activity, not opposition of homosexual identity per se. The inclusion of a homosexual member who exercised restraint in sexual activities would not necessarily undermine the group's core mission. From this point of view, the restriction is concerned with a student's orientation or self-identification, not conduct that might be irreconcilable with a group's purpose.

Fourth, and perhaps most important for the purpose of distinguishing *Hurley* and *Dale*, the university is not forcing Students for Restraint to admit anyone as a member. Rather, the university is simply conditioning its recognition and grant of funding on the group's agreement not to foreclose certain individuals from joining the group on the sole basis of their homosexuality.

For a case reaching the same conclusion on similar facts, *see Every Nation Campus Ministries at San Diego State University v. Achtenberg*, 597 F. Supp. 2d 1075 (S.D. Cal. 2009).

Example 16-4:

A city passes an ordinance prohibiting employers from discriminating against individuals based on their reproductive decisions or pregnancy. A non-profit corporation in the city provides housing for pregnant, low-income women who agree not to get an abortion. The corporation zealously advocates against abortion and seeks to persuade people not to choose abortion as an option for unwanted pregnancies. The corporation hires only individuals with anti-abortion views. May the city impose the ordinance on the corporation without violating the corporation's freedom of association rights?

Explanation:

Under *Dale* and *Hurley*, the city would likely violate the corporation's freedom of association rights if it applied the prohibition. Doing so would require the corporation to hire someone who holds views irreconcilable with its central mission, impeding its ability to fulfill that mission. *See Our Lady's Inn v. City of St. Louis*, 349 F. Supp. 3d 805 (E.D. Mo. 2018).

D. FREEDOM OF ASSOCIATION DURING A PANDEMIC

The response of state governments to the effects of the COVID-19 pandemic has provided a unique context in which lower courts have explored the current jurisprudence governing the First Amendment freedom of association right. Results have been mixed, as surveyed in the Example below.

Example 16-4:

Assume that you are a lawyer practicing during the time when COVID-19 is infecting people around the globe. Available science shows that close inter-action between humans is the most significant cause of the virus's spread. As a consequence, governors throughout the United States have issued stay-at-home orders that require many businesses to close. The Governor in Western State has issued an order that prohibits (1) indoor dining, (2) social and recreational gathering of more than ten people, and (3) non-essential social and recreational gatherings.

Assume that you represent a restaurant owner that has been forced to close and would like to file suit, challenging the order as a violation of the First Amendment's freedom of association right. The restaurant is located in the downtown area of a small city and the owner is a single individual whose primary concern is keeping the place in business. The owner is concerned that if the stay-at-home order lasts too long she will be forced to close permanently. Advise the restaurant owner of the background legal principles and the possibility that she would succeed on a freedom of association claim challenging the order of Governor of Western State.

Explanation:

You might want to start by explaining to your client that a pandemic presents a unique context in which the ordinary legal rules might not operate as they otherwise would. In *Jacobson v. Commonwealth of Massachusetts*, 197 U.S. 11 (1905), the Court established that states may "institute extraordinary measures to protect public health." Although it is an old case, many courts still look to *Jacobson* and the case appears to remain the governing precedent. (You should also mention that at least two courts did not accept that *Jacobson*'s deferential standard applies to orders issued in connection with the COVID-19 pandemic. *See County of Butler v. Wolf*, 2020 WL 5510690 (W.D. Pa. Sept. 14, 2020); *Bailey's Campground v. Mills*, 2020 WL 2791797 (D. Maine May 29, 2020)).

Jacobson held that "a community has the right to protect itself against an epidemic of disease which threatens the safety of its members," including by "enact[ing] quarantine laws and health laws of every description." *Id.* at 25. Such laws are valid unless it can be shown that they possess "no real or substantial relation to" the public health, morals, or safety or are "beyond all question, a plain, palpable invasion of rights secured by the fundamental law." *Id.* at 31. These are tough requirements to fulfill.

The law governing a freedom of association claim would also be difficult to satisfy in this instance, even without the deference required by *Jacobson*. In *Roberts v. U.S. Jaycees*, 468 U.S. 609 (1984), the Supreme Court explained that freedom of association protects two types of association: (1) "choices to enter into and maintain certain intimate human relationships" and (2) association "for the purpose of engaging in those activities protected by the First Amendment—speech, assembly, petition for the redress of grievances, and the exercise of religion." Id. at 617-618. These are problematic standards for the restaurant owner.

The first type of association mentioned in the *Jaycees* case generally refers to family relationships, which are "distinguished by such attributes as relative smallness, a high degree of selectivity in decisions to begin and maintain the affiliation, and seclusion from others in critical aspects of the relationship." Id. at 619-620. Nothing in the facts of this Example suggests this type of association is implicated. Associations among "a large business enterprise" or "fellow employees" are not constitutionally protected. Id. at 620. *See also City of Dallas v. Stanglin*, 490 U.S. 19, 24 (1989) (stating that "dance-hall patrons, who may number 1,000 on any given night, are not engaged in the sort of 'intimate human relationships' referred to in *Roberts*"); *Michaelidis v. Berry*, 502 F. App'x 94, 96-97 (2d Cir. 2012) (holding that relationships between plaintiffs and "their restaurant customers, and their employees are not sufficiently intimate to implicate [First Amendment] protection").

As for the second kind of association, which is association "for the purpose of engaging in those activities protected by the First Amendment," the restaurant owner would need to show evidence regarding the purpose of associations among those connected with the restaurant in some way—such as friends, customers, or like-minded people are somehow prevented from engaging in First Amendment protected activities that are stifled by the restaurant closure. As the U.S. Supreme Court stated in *Jaycees*, this would include freedom of speech, assembly, petition for the redress of grievances, and the exercise of religion. Again, the facts show nothing that would help establish that those associated with the restaurant are using it for any of those activities.

Viewed through the lens of the *Jacobson* quarantine standard, the restaurant owner would not have a good chance to make a freedom of association claim. Accord *Amato v. Elicker*, 2020 U.S. Dist. LEXIS 87758 (D. Conn. May 19, 2020) (using similar reasoning in finding little likelihood of success in asserting a freedom of association claim to a similar stay-at-home order). Even assuming that *Jacobson* deference is no longer controlling, the claim would encounter significant obstacles to success.

In providing advice to the owner, you could close by explaining that freedom of association is not the only First Amendment claim that could potentially apply to challenge the governor's order. The owner could assert other free-standing First Amendment claims. For example, the owner might claim that the restriction inhibits free speech rights. The problem with this argument, however, is that the order appears content neutral, and would therefore be reviewed under a more deferential intermediate scrutiny standard or under the similar standard for time, place, and manner restrictions. *See* Chapter 1 of this volume for a discussion of evaluating content neutral and time, place, and manner restrictions. A freedom of speech claim would indeed be difficult to assert successfully, particularly if the additional deference required under *Jacobson* is applicable. Freedom of assembly is another possible theory, but that theory would likely fail for the same reasons as the closely related, freedom of association claim. In fact, one court has held that "freedom of assembly claims are largely subsumed" in freedom of association claims, which are more prominent in current case law. *Givens v. Newsom*, 2020 WL 2307224 (E.D. Cal. May 8, 2020), citing *Jaycees*, 468 U.S. at 618. *See, e.g, Geller v. De Blasio*, 20cv3566 (DLC), 2020 U.S. Dist. LEXIS 87405 (S.D.N.Y. May 18, 2020) (rejecting free speech challenge and denying an injunction of government's order under similar circumstances); *Friends of Devito v. Wolf*, 227 A.3d 872 (Pa. 2020) (rejecting free speech and freedom of assembly claims challenging governor's order under similar circumstances). *But see, e.g., County of Butler v. Wolf*, 2020 WL 5510690 (W.D. Pa. Sept. 14, 2020) (holding that governor's order violated freedom of speech, freedom of assembly, and freedom of speech principles).

Finally, to the extent that the stay-at-home order includes prohibitions regarding worship services, a freedom of religion claim might also be pursued, but again might be hard to win given *Jacobson* deference and the availability of virtual, remote worship. Chapter 20 of this volume covers issues related to freedom of religion.

CHAPTER 17

The Multiple Strands of Speech Doctrine

A. THE MESSY PROCESS OF RESOLVING A FREE SPEECH CASE

Human civilization and the lives of individual persons present problems that do not fall into neat packages. Nonetheless, law creates a structure of topics, which attempts to provide a rational mode of analysis and to promote predictability in resolving conflicts and planning affairs. This is particularly true of court-made law — including cases that interpret the broad language of the U.S. Constitution. In adjudicating cases, courts try to ensure fairness and uniformity by treating similarly situated problems similarly. Law's quality of creating rational taxonomies for analyzing human affairs is therefore a trait to be celebrated. That said, the messiness of human affairs never fails to emerge in adjudication, sometimes making it difficult to evaluate how to resolve a controversy using the predetermined analytical structure that law has put in place.

Courts interpreting the Constitution have a guide for their legal categories that comes from the textual structure of the Constitution itself. This, of course, reinforces the inclination of courts to create orderly categories for analysis. But yet again, the complexity of human problems complicates matters. The complex disputes presented in the constitutional context, usually connected with tangled social, cultural, and political realities, ensures that — as in other areas of the law — a court can often decide a particular dispute using one of several strands of constitutional analysis. This is particularly true of the First Amendment. Indeed, we saw this in the last chapter regarding how cases often revolve around both the freedom of association and freedom of speech clauses.

Many would say that this problem infects the First Amendment more than any other portion of constitutional law. This chapter provides a "first stab" at the problem. It does not provide any absolute answer: just simply an idea on how to proceed in dealing with this remarkably important and complicated area of law.

The explanations for why First Amendment issues are particularly prone to analysis under multiple threads of constitutional doctrine are not obvious. Perhaps it concerns the importance of the problems presented or the tendency of the problems to emerge from controversial subjects. Perhaps it is an artifact of history or simply the accident of how parties have framed freedom of expression issues in litigation over the years. One certainty is that the parties in litigation have significant control over which strand of doctrine is used. The influence of parties' litigation-theory choices is amplified in appellate decision making because appellate courts usually dispose of matters using a previously created record from the lower courts, a record largely fashioned by the parties' theory of the case.

As one is beginning to get a handle on First Amendment doctrine, one may find perplexing this quality of First Amendment case law to proceed on multiple—overlapping and sometimes contradictory—lines of doctrine. To provide some guidance on how to reckon with this untidy quality of First Amendment law, this chapter begins by mapping a potential strategy for analyzing a fact pattern that happens to suggest many possible routes for resolution. The chapter then provides some examples that show how to use this strategy. It does not offer a controlling checklist or strategy. As always with the First Amendment, free form may carry the day.

B. STRATEGY FOR ANALYZING A FREE SPEECH FACT PATTERN

Whether on an exam or in another context, you may be asked to resolve a dispute that appears to include so many First Amendment issues that you find the task confounding. The following presents a series of steps that may guide you in organizing your thoughts and choosing the appropriate route for analyzing the facts:

1. Do an inventory of possible First Amendment strands of doctrine for resolving the problem presented to you. If you do not have a list of the various strands of doctrine that exist, make one or use the Table of Contents in this book as a checklist of possibilities.

2. From the inventory of possible strands that might resolve the problem, make a judgment about which strand is a better choice. For this purpose, the following provides you with factors to consider:

*Evaluate the element of each of the possible strands and decide whether the dispute presents each element. If the dispute satisfies all of the elements of only one strand, that strand is likely the best fit for resolution.

*Ask whether one strand appears more accepted in current law than another. If you identify a more accepted strand, that strand of First Amendment doctrine may provide the most solid ground for analyzing and resolving the problem.

*If, after performing these steps, it appears that several options still exist, start with the strand that includes cases with facts that most closely resemble the fact pattern you are analyzing. That factual comparison may be the best route for resolving the dispute. Before making a final decision on this, you might also want to consider the following concerns:

*Sometimes you may find that the fact pattern you are analyzing falls into an overarching (or general) category or methodology of First Amendment doctrine, such as evaluating whether the law is content based, vague, or overbroad. If that is the case, you should consider analyzing the law using these options. But you should also take on the task of evaluating the law using a more specific line of cases—such as true threat jurisprudence, the public forum doctrine, and time, place, and manner restrictions—if the cases in this line appear to be a good fit with the facts that confront you.

*For further assistance in choosing the best strand or strands of doctrine, the First Amendment values listed in the Introduction of this book (promoting self-governance, truth discovery, personal autonomy, and tolerance) may provide guidance as well as fodder for analysis and argument.

*If your analysis takes place in an adversary setting when you are representing the interests of one client (or one side of a dispute), evaluate which of the most promising strands of doctrine best serves your client's interests. Remember that "winning" may not be the only factor to consider: cost of litigation, and intangible factors such as inconvenience, jurisdictional challenges, your client's personal relationships, ethical concerns, your client's mission, and the like may also hang in the balance.

*If your analysis takes place for the purpose of taking an exam, during your own brainstorming in how to frame your litigation strategy, or in a candid interchange with a knowledgeable client, remember to consider and to mention the unfavorable strands that arguably fit the case. This enables you to anticipate (and rebut) the arguments your opponent may use.

*Remember that there is nothing wrong with proposing more than one approach for resolving the dispute, if after your deliberations you conclude that more than one strand of analysis serves your goals well. Whether answering an exam question or counseling a client, do not forget to avoid rabbit holes and look for open doors.

*Remember too that even though the existence of multiple strands of analysis may seem daunting, the existence of these many strands provides you some flexibility in using your creativity, knowledge, and lawyering skills.

* * *

Here's an offensive speech Example demonstrating how you might use all these considerations.

Example 17-1:

A city government passed a declaration that all racial groups should strive to act respectfully toward all other racial groups and should work together to promote harmony and equality. To further the goal of this declaration, the government sponsored a meeting on the topic of promoting racial harmony and equality. The meeting was attended by individuals from various racial groups. At the meeting, a group of individuals were present who identified with a racial group (Group A) that had historically oppressed another racial group (Group B). This group of individuals from Group A gave a presentation that stated that Group B were inferior human beings and that any efforts by Group A members to promote the equal rights of Group B or to try to live in harmony with Group B amounted to supporting a position contrary to the laws of nature.

The city government members who were running the meeting had law enforcement forcibly remove the Group A members giving this presentation from the room before they finished.

The Group A members filed suit against the city, claiming that the actions of the city government violated their First Amendment rights. The group took the position that the city's declaration was viewpoint specific, embracing only one side of the many sides one could take on the issue of racial harmony. The Group A members further maintain that the position they had expressed during the meeting merely presented an alternative point of view on the subject matter that the city chose for the meeting. Group A maintains that not only was the position they had expressed during the meeting directly relevant to the subject matter on the agenda, but their treatment by the city officials discriminated against them on the basis of the position they expressed.

Assume you have been asked to identify the categories of First Amendment doctrine that potentially apply to this case. Discuss these possible categories and evaluate which categories are the closest fit to the facts and circumstances presented.

Explanation:

Tracing the Table of Contents of this volume, here are the categories that arguably are most applicable to the facts, with comments about the advantage and/or disadvantages of each:

1. *Content-Based Analysis:* Although some might say that analyzing whether speech falls into content-based versus non-content-based categories puts you into a particular category for First Amendment purposes, the characterization helps to highlight how much trouble you may encounter. This characterization between content based vs. non-content based focused on analyzing the content of the declaration and content-motivated removal of the plaintiff group from the meeting. Content-based analysis is an apt approach to consider because the group has a cognizable claim that the city chose what it believed to be a preferred point of view and acted on that belief. This category would require meaningful analysis of whether the city had a compelling interest and whether the city's position was under-inclusive or over-inclusive. An added component of this analysis is the important question of whether the statements of the plaintiff group amounted to a particularly privileged category of expression: political speech.

For these reasons, content-based concepts deserve a role in your task of analyzing these facts. Content-based analysis, however, is general. Further inquiry is necessary to determine whether a line of cases exists that is more specifically tailored to the facts here and thus provide a set of close-fitting precedent to dispose of the controversy.

2. *Fighting Words:* The fighting words doctrine is relevant to these facts. The doctrine concerns the meeting itself because the plaintiff group uttered words that could be considered highly inflammatory given the audience and the reason for the meeting. To that extent, the fighting words doctrine is more specific than content-based analysis. (Also-the city might be attracted to this theory because it would mean that the words spoken are unprotected under the First Amendment.)

Nonetheless, limitations to the fighting words doctrine exist, including: (i) the doctrine has become quite restricted and does not appear to be taken seriously in recent U.S. Supreme Court cases; and (ii) the doctrine does not apply to the entire set of facts because it would not answer concerns about the one-sidedness of the city's declaration. Fighting words case law presents a viable, but not a preferred, category of analysis.

3. *Hostile Audience:* The hostile audience doctrine is marginally relevant to these facts because the plaintiff group was expressing views that they knew were contrary to the views of many or most of those in audience. The plaintiff group also would have anticipated that peppering their statements with charged, negative language would be highly insulting to the audience and could prompt a hostile reaction. The hostile audience doctrine, however, is even less viable than the fighting words doctrine as it was not used even once in a U.S. Supreme Court case after the case in which it was announced. Moreover, like the fighting words doctrine, the hostile audience concept covers only the events transpiring in the meeting and not the declaration itself.

4. *Group Defamation:* The concept of group defamation is a perfect fit for the portion of the facts related to the meeting because the doctrine allows punishing defamatory utterances that target a specific group of people. The doctrine suffers from the same limitations, however, as the hostile audience doctrine because it has fallen into disuse, is no longer cited as precedent, and has limited utility in analyzing the constitutionality of the directive itself.

5. *Disparaging and Threatening Speech:* Doctrines governing speech that disparages and threatens others show some promise in providing a specific set of concepts for analyzing the facts here because the statements made during the meeting reflected vitriolic contempt toward a group of people. Interestingly, Supreme Court cases have alluded to—but avoided directly discussing—the main challenge the plaintiff group raises here: the directive and its enforcement against Group A at the meeting distinguished between negative statements (made by Group A) and positive statements on the topic dealing with societal diversity and group identity (made by other individuals who were not forcibly removed from the meeting). Arguably, this set of facts could serve as a vehicle for finally confronting the relationship of such positive/negative distinctions to the principles about disparaging speech. If you are analyzing this set of facts for a court trying to decide to take the case or a public interest litigation group looking to "make law" on particular issues, this could be an important consideration.

As it currently exists in the case law, however, the doctrines governing disparaging speech are not a perfect fit for resolving this controversy. The Court has been parsimonious in recognizing the circumstances when disparaging speech claims are relevant and several reasons suggest that this Example may not present such circumstances. First, the two most recent disparaging speech cases—*R.A.V. v. City of St. Paul* and *Virginia v. Black*—concerned criminal prosecutions and turned on issues of proof and intent that may not directly apply to a civil case such as this. More importantly, the most recent case, *Virginia v. Black*, appeared to restrict disparaging speech regulations to true threats. The facts of the dispute in this Example contain no suggestion that the plaintiff group intended to inspire a fear of violence against another group of people. (For this reason, the more general true threat cases are not applicable here as well.)

All this being said, disparaging speech concepts are worthy of mention in an analysis of the dispute in this Example.

6. *Secondary Effects:* The secondary effects doctrine is arguably an excellent fit for these facts. One can reasonably argue that the city's motivation for passing this directive (and its enforcement by ejecting the plaintiffs from the meeting) did not derive from dislike of the content of any particular communication. The city could make a good showing that it was concerned with many secondary effects of the prohibited speech, including avoiding inter-racial violence, promoting a cooperative society that better meets the needs of its citizens, and supporting the economic vitality that arises from the coordinated and friendly contributions of diverse citizens.

Reasons exist, however, for hesitating to use the secondary effects doctrine. The definition of a valid secondary effect is uncertain. The same is true for identifying the line between a perfectly valid regulation of the secondary effects of speech and a content-based regulation of speech: the distinction between the two is fuzzy. In addition, the U.S. Supreme Court has used the secondary effects doctrine only sporadically—sometimes ignoring the opportunity to use the doctrine when it appears to apply to a particular dispute. On balance, the doctrine would be appropriate for significant mention in the analysis, with the caveat that these qualifications deserve highlighting.

Bottom line: As with much of law, no right answer exists as to the absolutely correct way of analyzing the facts of the controversy here. Certainly, however, content-based analysis deserves detailed treatment in discussing the facts of this Example. The hate speech and secondary effects doctrines are also good candidates for significant discussion. If time and resources allow, the other doctrines mentioned above would also serve as appropriate, albeit limited, talking points during the discussion.

Example 17-2:

For the purpose of this Example, consider the facts of an earlier Example, Example 13-2:

> The Military Honor and Decency Act prohibits the sale or rental of "sexually explicit materials" at military exchanges, and mega-retail stores open exclusively to service members, veterans, and their family members. The Act prohibits the "sale or rental of recordings and periodicals the dominant theme of which depicts or describes nudity, including sexual or excretory activities or organs, in a lascivious way." Ida is a service member who challenges the law, claiming that it violates her First Amendment free speech rights.

For the purpose of this Example 17-2, assume that you represent Ida. You need to identify the multiple strands of First Amendment doctrine arising from Ida's dispute, but you also need to evaluate which doctrine or doctrines would be best to emphasize in order to best serve Ida's interests. What categories of First Amendment doctrine are presented in this fact pattern? What are the merits and demerits of each for Ida's claim?

Explanation:

1. *Military Speech:* The overriding character of this set of facts is the military context. The hard-wired deference that First Amendment doctrine accords military decisions affects every free expression principle presented in Ida's claim. This means that Ida will find it difficult to prevail: the military has a thumb on the scale of justice when it comes to the expressive rights of service members. But the military context is inescapable, so the best approach is to consider whether any free expression theories actually could be most effective given the inescapable presence of the military deference principle.

For challenging cases such as this, keeping an open mind is an especially good idea. Maybe . . . just maybe . . . there exists an unexpected benefit of an apparently detrimental doctrine. For example, could it be possible that analytical synergy exists between the military deference orientation and one of the other doctrinal strands that could actually *benefit* Ida? In the event that none of the general free expression approaches can garner any benefit from the military deference principle, then prudence counsels evaluating which free expression theory might be least analytically damaged by the military deference principle. At bottom, however, candor would suggest telling Ida that the military context makes this a long-shot case for Ida.

2. *Offensive Speech:* Obscene speech does not receive constitutional protection. Thus, the military might argue that the lascivious material prohibition does not violate the Constitution because it prohibits obscene speech. Yet the definition of the material prohibited appears to extend to much more material than that which meets the formal definition of obscene speech. This helps Ida, but she should be mindful that the lascivious material may be indecent speech, which some believe has a lower standard of scrutiny requiring only a substantial or important government interest. One can imagine a court deciding that a substantial or important government interest justifies keeping lascivious material away from service personnel. The military could reasonably argue that military members agreed to a reduced right of privacy and special responsibilities when the joined. This observation plays into an impulse to give full force to the military deference principle, since one might reasonably argue that banning lascivious material serves military discipline.

3. *Public Forum Analysis:* Because the military exchange is not open to the public and because there is nothing about the history of such exchange suggesting that the government uses it to inspire discourse, the exchange is not a traditional public forum or a limited public forum. In that event, the exchange is properly categorized as a non-public forum. This characterization does not help an attempt to avoid the military deference principle.

Nonetheless, even in non-public forums, government restrictions must be viewpoint neutral. The non-public forum analysis thus presents at least a glimmer of hope for Ida.

4. *Viewpoint Discrimination:* Non-public forum analysis allows viewpoint discrimination only if it is justified by strict scrutiny. One might argue that enjoyment of lascivious material is not wholesome and carries with it a taboo quality that may deteriorate decorum, professionalism, and honor as well as encourage defiance to orders and lack of discipline. But is the connection between lascivious material and defiance, discipline, professionalism, honor, and decorum close enough to rise to a compelling reason for government to ban the material? Is not the consumption of lascivious material usually something that is not freely disclosed and takes place after hours in private? How then would there be significant derogation of decorum, honor, professionalism, defiance, and discipline that results in having the material available?

These observations may provide some ground for Ida to frame an attack on the restrictions. Yet, as discussed in Chapter 13, at least one court has held that the restriction does not discriminate on the basis of viewpoint, but merely describes the content of the material. *General Media Commc'n, Inc. v. Cohen*, 131 F.3d 273 (2d Cir. 1997). Ida could challenge this characterization of the restriction as "non-viewpoint based" by pointing out that the government's prohibition clearly shows the restriction communicates disapproval of any notion that lascivious material has merit. As persuasive as this may sound, this argument is likely not sufficient to overcome the extreme deference due the military's judgment on the undesirability of lascivious material.

Bottom line: Ida does not have encouraging prospects for success. Her arguments based on viewpoint discrimination have the greatest promise. Nonetheless, none of the strands of the free expression doctrine appear to overcome the military deference principles that will likely provide an effective obstacle to her winning her challenge.

* * *

With so many different options in First Amendment doctrines, the possibilities of how various doctrines might be joined in one dispute are vast. Some pairings are more common than others. The offensive speech area — illustrated in Example 17-1 and 17-2 — is a particularly common area that is paired with other strands of First Amendment analysis. The same is true for the military speech area, illustrated in Example 17-2.[1] One might note, however, that the reason why military speech often presents multitude

---

1. *See, e.g., Am. Freedom Def. Initiative v. King County*, 904 F.3d 1126 (9th Cir. 2018) (evaluating a case combining non-public forum analysis and disparaging speech); *Kalman v. Cortes*, 723 F. Supp. 2d 766 (E.D. Pa. 2010) (analyzing a case joining the commercial speech doctrine and principles relating to regulation of profanity); *Wiegand v. Motiva Enters., LLC*, 295 F. Supp. 2d 465 (D.N.J. 2003) (evaluating a dispute combining doctrines governing commercial speech, fighting words, and speech within the employment context).

of doctrinal strands is different from the reasons why offensive speech can include many alternative threads of analysis. The category "offensive speech" is largely a creation of legal analysis. Yet speech that the law brands as offensive can easily implicate other legally created approaches to analysis, since many types of speech can be offensive. The area known as military speech is demarcated by forces outside of legal principles—militaries act as unique and almost independent social organizations that can give rise to almost all of the same disputes as emerge among humans outside the military context. Hence the term "military speech" merely describes a micro-society in which nearly all of the free speech doctrines are potentially implicated. The same is true for the categories of cases that arise in the prison and school contexts.

Whether the cases presenting multiple potential strands of free expression include only legally created categories of issues (as in the offensive speech Example above) or include a micro-society such as the military, prisons, or schools, an effective approach to analyzing these two situations is the same: start by listing the particular doctrines that appear relevant to the facts presented and ultimately settle on the doctrine or doctrines that best fit the facts of the dispute and best serve your goals.

As emphasized above, you are best advised to regard this complexity in free speech doctrine as an opportunity for good lawyering and creativity. That mindset can help prepare you to accept yet another complexity in First Amendment law: an additional set of principles regarding the role of religion in U.S. society. Because religion is entangled with expression and human associations, First Amendment religion clause issues often join with free expression and freedom of association issues. The last chapter of this volume, Chapter 21, discusses strategies for handling those entanglements. In the meantime, however, we turn to the basics of the religion clauses.

Religion

Although many U.S. citizens do not identify as religious, few would challenge the notion that religion plays a key role in U.S. society. For many citizens, religious values inform their views on "lightening rod" social issues such as the rights of LGBTQ+ individuals, abortion, and euthanasia. These controversial issues have made their way into constitutional jurisprudence, expanding the already prominent role of the First Amendment's religion clauses.

The First Amendment's religion clauses are the free exercise clause and the establishment clause. Sometimes referred to as the "antiestablishment clause," the establishment clause aims to ensure that the government remains separate from religion and, through that separation, is prevented from "establishing" religion. The free exercise clause protects individuals' right to practice the religion of their choice free from government interference. The two clauses are sometimes grouped together as the "freedom of religion clauses." The notion behind this moniker is that prohibiting government meddling in religious matters protects the free exercise thereof.

Although the case law for the two religion clauses generally proceeds on separate tracks, the clauses are intertwined and often cannot be untangled.

II. Religion

In some ways, they complement each other and, in others, they conflict. The current trend in the U.S. Supreme Court is to enhance the power of the freedom of religion clause and diminish the power of the establishment clause. What does this mean? It means that government may be on firm ground in preferring free exercise over the establishment clause. But the tension between the two clauses still remains and requires serious study.

Chapter 18 explores this tension and also considers the knotty question: What counts as religion for the purpose of interpreting the scope of the clauses' protections? Chapters 19 and 20 then investigate the free exercise and establishment clauses separately (as much as the two lines of deeply interwoven case law allows). The final chapter in this volume — Chapter 21 — brings together the three major components of the First Amendment (expression, association, and religion), exploring why on Earth the Framers of the Constitution would yoke these two concepts together in one constitutional amendment.

Introduction to the Religion Clauses: Understanding the Tension Between the Two Clauses and Defining Religion

Courts frequently invoke the Framers' original understanding of the religion clauses to guide their interpretation. As with many parts of the Constitution, however, competing, largely inconsistent accounts have emerged regarding just what that original understanding was. This arises in substantial part from the abstract nature of the Framers' debate on religion as well as their clear lack of consensus on the policies and philosophies underlying the religion clauses.

The difficulty of interpreting the religion clauses is compounded by demographic and institutional changes that the Framers could not have anticipated. For example, at the time the First Amendment was drafted, America's population was more religiously homogenous and lacked a public education system. The Framers may not have contemplated these historical developments, and many thinkers therefore argue that their original understanding of the religion clauses is of dubious value.

While sobering, this background is essential to understanding the apparently chaotic jurisprudence of the religion clauses. But one can find help in understanding from the definitional and analytical building blocks that inform the "big picture" an overview of the cases presents. A beacon for starting to piece together that big picture is to look to fundamental concepts. The Introduction to this volume—which you may want to reread now—provides a beginning glimpse at the animating values behind religion clauses. This chapter dives deeper into two basic questions: (1) what is the relationship between the two religion clauses? and (2) what amounts to a "religion" within the meaning of the clauses? Later chapters directly confront how the U.S. Supreme Court has ruled on free exercise and establishment clause challenges individually.

A. THE TENSION BETWEEN THE FREE EXERCISE CLAUSE AND THE ESTABLISHMENT CLAUSE

The two religion clauses of the Constitution state (1) "Congress shall make no law respecting an establishment of religion," and (2) Congress shall make no law "prohibiting the free exercise thereof." One might assume that the two clauses work in isolation, but they do not. When Congress makes a law designed to ensure that a religion flourishes — so as to eliminate any legal impediment to "the free exercise thereof" — Congress runs the risk of endorsing — and thus establishing — the religion. Here lies the uneasy balance between the two clauses. The dilemma is exacerbated by the Supreme Court's incorporation of the religion clauses through the Fourteenth Amendment to bind the states. *See Everson v. Board of Education*, 330 U.S. 1 (1947) (incorporating the establishment clause); *Cantwell v. Connecticut*, 310 U.S. 296 (1940) (incorporating the free exercise clause). Accordingly, both the state and federal governments are bound to ensure religious non-discrimination while avoiding establishment of religion.

Making matters even more complicated, an argument can be made that the establishment clause does not actually conflict with the free exercise clause. In the long run, separating church and state keeps government from favoring a particular religion, and thus allows other religions to develop and to flourish. From this perspective, the establishment clause supports and reinforces the free exercise clause. However, most litigation concerning the U.S. Constitution's religion clauses focuses on the tension between them. Consider the following Examples.

Example 18-1:

A state made public funds available to private universities so long as the universities met certain requirements, including promising that the institution would not use the funds for sectarian (non-secular) purposes. According to the state funding regime, once the state forwarded the funding to the university, the institution could place the money in its general fund to use at its discretion. The state simply forwarded the money and did not have a system to monitor its use.

A religiously affiliated private university, Holy Trinity University, applied for the funds and was rejected when the state concluded that the university was pervasively sectarian. The state based its decision primarily on four observations about Holy Trinity University: (1) All students there were required to attend religious services twice a week; (2) the admissions policy strongly favored students who were affiliated with the same religion as the school itself; (3) the school curriculum included six courses on religious doctrine that were required for graduation (as well as many other courses on topics directly related to the school's official religion); and (4) 8 percent of the full-time faculty shared the same religion as the affiliation of the school. As a university, Holy Trinity offered students a full array of secular, research-based programs in the sciences, social sciences, and humanities. Holy Trinity argued that despite its religious affiliation, it served the secular purposes of any other university—the preservation, development, and teaching of general knowledge.

Holy Trinity filed a lawsuit, arguing that the state had discriminated against it in denying funds because of university's religious orientation. Holy Trinity took the position that it was entitled to public funds because it was similarly situated with other secular institutions offering a broad range of subjects for students seeking higher education. The state defended its decision to deny funding by arguing that doing so was necessary to avoid violating the establishment clause. Holy Trinity sought a determination that the state violated the free exercise clause. Will Holy Trinity prevail?

Explanation:

Holy Trinity University may prevail, particularly in light of the current direction of the U.S. Supreme Court's establishment clause and freedom of religion clause jurisprudence. But be mindful that the law is in flux, so the outcome is not certain.

This Example illustrates a classic presentation of the clash between the two religion clauses of the First Amendment. That Holy Trinity offers a full panoply of courses and generally serves the role of other secular universities suggests that the denial of public funds was a free exercise violation. However, Holy Trinity's (1) admissions policy, (2) faculty religion orientation, (3) curriculum requirements, and (4) student worship requirements indicate its strong orientation toward religion. This weighs heavily toward the conclusion that the state correctly denied funding to comply with the establishment clause. Importantly, since the government allows the university to place public funding in the university's general fund and does not monitor its actual use, one can conclude that at least some state funding would be channeled to support religion in the institution. All those considerations taken together reasonably tip the balance away from the suggestion that the state is discriminating against Holy Trinity because of its religious orientation, but is instead motivated by reasonable concern that providing the funding would foster religion and therefore "establish" religion contrary to the First Amendment's goal of erecting a wall between church and state. This conclusion would be consistent with prior case law in the lower courts. *See, e.g., Columbia Union College v. Clarke*, 159 F.3d 151 (4th Cir. 1998).

One must take account, however, of a series of cases handed down by the U.S. Supreme Court suggesting that the establishment clause should not weigh so heavily when also evaluating a free exercise concern. As will be illustrated in this chapter and the next, the Court's majority opinions are following a now well-established trend of diminishing the importance of establishment clause concerns and increasing the importance of free exercise concerns. *See, e.g., Little Sisters of the Poor v. Pennsylvania*, 140 S. Ct. 2367 (2020) (contraception coverage under the Affordable Care Act); *American Legion v. American Humanist Association*, 130 S. Ct. 2067 (2019) (40-foot cross on war memorial on state property); *Town of Greece v. Galloway*, 572 U.S. 565 (2014) (government practice of commissioning ministers to offer prayers at town council meetings); *Zelman v. Simmons-Harris*, 536 U.S. 639 (2002) (school vouchers); *Mitchell v. Helms*, 530 U.S. 793 (2000) (loans to religious schools); *Agostini v. Felton*, 521 U.S. 203 (1997) (state-sponsored education initiative to allow public school teachers to instruct at religious schools); *Mueller v. Allen*, 463 U.S. 388 (1983) (parental tax deductions for parochial school related expenses). This suggests that what was a winning case for the state in this Example at one time, may now be a winning case for Holy Trinity.

Example 18-2:

A fountain in a public location outside a church for a well-recognized religion fell into disrepair. The church asked the city for permission to use parishioners' donations for renovations. The city agreed because the church's request to renovate a fountain in a public place was consistent with contemporaneous municipal improvement efforts. The church sponsored a fundraiser to collect parishioners' private donations specifically for this project. Although the fountain was located on public property and regarded as a lovely addition to the neighborhood ambience, the repairs were funded exclusively by the church's parishioners. Parishioners happily donated to this church fundraiser because the fountain was long-considered a hazard and an eyesore.

As a condition of their offer to coordinate and fund the renovation, the church requested permission to place a plaque on the fountain that "honored children." The city approved the use of some general religious language on the plaque. The church then created and displayed the plaque without asking the city for final approval of its design and message, which specifically honored the death of the unborn through legalization of abortion. In other words, the church used the plaque to convey an anti-abortion message. The plaque was created and put in place without asking the city for its final approval of the plaque's design and message—and the city did not insist on prior approval.

After the renovation was complete and the plaque installed, a dedication ceremony occurred at the fountain location and included many mentions honoring unborn children. At the dedication ceremony, a clergy member led a prayer for the unborn who were victims of "the abomination of abortion," a practice that the clergy member stated was against Gospel teachings. The clergy member also extended a hearty thanks to the government for allowing the plaque to be installed on public property.

A group of concerned citizens filed a lawsuit challenging the government approval for the renovation that included an anti-abortion message. They argued that the government authorization for the fountain and funding violated the establishment clause and demanded that the city remove the plaque. The church argued that accepting the notions that the city should have refused the renovation and the placement of the plaque, and that the church should now be required to remove the plaque, would violate its religious freedom to spend funds in accordance with its religious beliefs.

Explanation:

This is a closer call than the previous Example. The analogous, although not identical, case of *Fausto v. Diamond*, 589 F. Supp. 451 (D.R.I. 1984), suggests that the fountain renovation described in this Example complies with the free exercise clause and does not run afoul of the establishment clause. Nevertheless, that result is not guaranteed by *Fausto*, in which the court considered many arguments on either side of the question.

On one hand, the church can argue that the renovation served the public interest of revitalizing and beautifying the city, and therefore complied with the establishment clause. The use of private funds to accomplish this task strengthens its case to the extent that it shows citizens' commitment to the *secular* purposes behind the renovation—making the city more beautiful, honoring the history of the area, and providing an attractive venue for tourists. Furthermore, the city decision makers were unaware of the church's plan to use the plaque to make a statement about religious opposition to abortion, undermining any argument that the government permit endorsed religion. The church will argue that since the renovation project did not violate the establishment clause, compelling it to remove the plaque will violate its free exercise rights.

On the other hand, plaintiffs will argue that the renovation project did violate the establishment clause. The church clearly viewed the fountain as a vehicle to advertise its mission since it used church resources to sponsor a campaign to raise a large amount of funds for its renovation, applied for permission to renovate the fountain, and organized the creation and installation of the plaque. Moreover, the dedication ceremony was quite problematic. The ceremony might have appealed to the deeply held, First-Amendment-protected religious inclinations of the parishioners in attendance. Yet it also sent a message that the permission to renovate the fountain and place the plaque on public property was religiously motivated and then approved by the government, which appears to be a clear violation of the establishment clause. The "hearty thanks" of the clergy member for the government's permission to place the plaque on public property suggested that the government endorsed the plaque's religious message.

Finally, plaintiffs will argue that the less-than-full disclosure on the part of the church in negotiating what it wanted to do certainly did not help matters: it suggested the church may have wanted to sneak in a religious message under the radar — only to turn around and create an innuendo that the city endorsed the message. This behavior suggests the church knew the plaque's text would not be allowed by the city government, thus undermining arguments in favor of a free exercise violation that might arise were the city to remove the plaque. On the other hand, the city did not help matters by not insisting on giving prior approval of the plaque.

The final judgment on the establishment clause component of this Example must be considered in light of recent U.S. Supreme Court establishment clause jurisprudence, which shows an inclination to indulge religious symbols if situated in a context that suggests wider societal meaning. Take the U.S. Supreme Court's statements in *American Legion v. American Humanist*, 139 S. Ct. 2067 (2019), in which the Supreme Court upheld a city's decision to maintain a 40-foot Latin cross on public land as part of a war memorial. Objectors argued that a cross is a Christian symbol, not meaningful to many who wish to honor the dead who fought in the war. The full *American Legion* opinion was splintered, with several justices troubled by the cross's association with one religion rather than another. Nonetheless, a majority of the U.S. Supreme Court agreed that the cross had "acquired historical importance" and had "become part of the community." *Id.* at 2089. A Court majority also joined a statement saying that "[i]t is natural and appropriate for those seeking to honor the deceased to invoke the symbols that signify what death meant for those who were memorialized." *Id.* In this instance, the symbol was a cross.

In light of these statements from the *American Legion* Supreme Court, the court in this Example may simply conclude that the city needed an uplift — the fountain was a lovely part of the cityscape — and no one should bother with its religious meaning, because the fountain contributes to city renewal.

But then one must reckon with the constitutional question of what to make of the plaque's anti-abortion message. For the church, of course, the message merely expressed its religious beliefs. From the point of view of the city government — which is a "state actor" for constitutional purposes — the message not only touched on the establishment clause, but other constitutional provisions protecting abortion rights. By permitting the expression of a controversial religious belief on public property, the city government risked the appearance of endorsing religion. Taken together, the close relationship between the anti-abortion message and the church's tenets suggest that the religious context for this dispute is sufficient to find a constitutional violation on the basis of the establishment clause alone. But yet again, the city's negligence in not requiring approval of the plaque will negatively affect the city's possibilities of success.

* * *

The U.S. Supreme Court does not always see the tension between the two clauses as an inconvenient complication. In a series of cases, starting with *Walz v. Tax Commission*, 397 U.S. 664, 669 (1970), the Court has referred to the "play in the joints" between the two clauses as an opportunity for neutrality toward religion. The Court stated:

> The general principle deducible from the First Amendment and all that has been said by the Court is this: that we will not tolerate either governmentally established religion or governmental interference with religion. Short of those expressly proscribed governmental acts there is room for play in the joints productive of a benevolent neutrality which will permit religious exercise to exist without sponsorship and without interference.

Id.

As the cases in Chapters 19 and 20 demonstrate, the Court has waffled on the extent of that "play in the joints." Some argue that the Court has recently tended toward construing that "play" narrowly by favoring free exercise rights over establishment clause protections. This argument derives, however, from observation of the reasoning and holding of each decision, and not from any explicit statement that the U.S. Supreme Court has made.

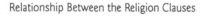
Relationship Between the Religion Clauses

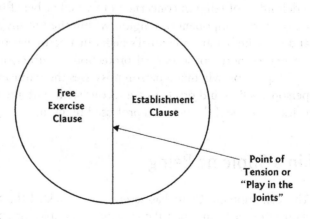

Figure 18-1

For the purpose of navigating the relationship between the clauses, the best advice is:

1. Evaluate every fact pattern implicating religion in light of both clauses, looking for how both clauses could be relevant to resolving a controversy;
2. Fully analyze the facts in light of case law interpreting each clause;
3. Recognize and note that the two clauses are often in tension;
4. Understand that a particular government action or regulation could comply with both clauses;
5. When the government action or regulation is problematic in light of both clauses — and each clause considered alone suggests a different result than the other, choose the result that favors the party most harmed by the government action or regulation; and
6. In the unusual case when both clauses are violated, conclude that the government action or regulation is unconstitutional.

B. WHAT IS RELIGION?

Defining religion serves precision and consistency in interpreting the religion clauses of the Constitution and — of course — answers a profoundly important question of human existence. Actually settling on a definition, however, turns out to also be quite difficult. One might think that the definitional issue is crucial, given that it implicates the protection of important constitution protections that may govern to resolve a given controversy. Nonetheless, oddly (and perhaps fortunately) the task of evaluating whether a belief system qualifies as a religion does not occur much in litigation. The U.S. Supreme Court has confronted the definitional task on only a handful of occasions. The two main contexts in which the Court has grappled with a definition of religion concerned (1) whether belief in a superior being is a necessary component of religion within the meaning of the Constitution and (2) whether an individual's belief in a particular religion is sufficiently sincere to merit constitutional protection. A subset of the second inquiry is the question whether a person possesses the requisite sincerity when the person's beliefs and practices are inconsistent with the dominant characteristics or views of the person's professed religion.

I. Belief in a Supreme Being

The U.S. Supreme Court has several times tackled the task of defining religion in order to interpret the conscientious objector exemption set forth in the Universal Military Training and Service Act (UMTSA), 50 U.S.C. § 456(j) (known as § 6(j) and currently codified under 50 U.S.C.S. § 3806(j)). This section provides the conscientious objector exemption to the military draft only upon a showing of an individual's training and belief "in a relation to a Supreme Being." In *United States v. Seeger*, 380 U.S. 163, 165 (1965), the Court held that the term "Supreme Being" in section 6(j) showed Congress's intent to clarify that all religions are to be accepted, so long as the individual passes "the test of belief." This test assesses whether the belief "occupies a place in the life of its possessor parallel to that filled by the orthodox belief in God." *Id.* at 166. Applying this standard to the lead petitioner in the case—Seeger—the Court observed that although he was agnostic, Seeger had a "belief in and devotion to goodness and virtue for their own sakes." *Id.* The Court determined that Seeger's research in religion and culture constituted individual training and that his belief in "goodness and virtue" amounted to belief in a "Supreme Being." Based on its interpretation of Congress's intent, the Court concluded that the statute was facially neutral and thus avoided constitutional infirmity.

Seeger provided the foundation for the current approach to defining religion for the purpose of the First Amendment. In a subsequent case, *Welsh v. United States*, 398 U.S. 333 (1970), the Court again interpreted the conscientious objector language in section 6(j), expounding on (and perhaps expanding) *Seeger's* approach to defining religion. Specifically, even though section 6(j) excluded objections that stem from a "merely personal moral code," the *Welsh* Court stated that the law still allowed an exemption when an objector's "opposition to war stem[s] from . . . moral, ethical, or religious beliefs about what is right and wrong [so long as] these beliefs be held with the strength of traditional religious convictions." *Id.* at 340. The Court later held that a conscientious objector's opposition to war must be an opposition to all wars. *Gillette v. United States*, 401 U.S. 437 (1971).

Interestingly, *Welsh* exemplifies the conflicting incentives that exist in defining religion for the purposes of the free exercise clause as compared with the establishment clause. In both *Seeger* and *Welsh*, the Court defined religion broadly to show neutral tolerance for a range of belief systems and avoid violating the free exercise rights of believers. Yet in so doing, one might argue that the Court talked its way into problems with the establishment clause's prohibition.

In his *Welsh* dissent, Justice White discusses this dilemma in defining religion for the purpose of the two clauses by examining government tolerance for Sabbatarians—those who maintain they cannot work on their Sabbath as a result of religious compulsion. If the government accommodates that religious belief, one may argue that government is taking on the job of protecting (and hence endorsing) certain beliefs because they are religious. This is especially true when the government would not accept many other, non-religious reasons for refusing to work on that same day of the week—such as a desire to watch sports on that day or to attend a weekly family tailgate. Justice White did not accept the proposition that the government would actually be violating the establishment clause in that situation. He was only emphasizing that when the government rejects a non-religious reason for an exemption, yet endorses a religious reason for the same exemption in order to comply with the free exercise clause, the government could be said to engage in "establishment" or endorsement of religion. From this reasoning, one might argue that the desire to avoid violating the free exercise clause may suggest the prudence of using a broad definition of religion and, by contrast, the desire to avoid violating the establishment clause may suggest using a narrow definition.

Example 18-3:

Assume that a public school system has concluded that mindful meditation is beneficial to learning and discipline in the schools. The parents of a child in the school believe that meditation is consistent with their religion because it promotes reflection on the necessity of being in full harmony with God. They have no problem with their child meditating with the other children. In order for their child to stay true to their religious tenets, however, they have asked that the child be given five minutes before each group mediation session to perform individual, non-disruptive religious rituals.

In order to accommodate these religious beliefs, the school authorities approve the parents' request. Does the school district's approval highlight the same tension between the free exercise and establishment clauses that Justice White highlighted in his *Welsh* dissent?

Explanation:

No. The school's decision to allow the child to engage in private religious rituals before group mediation was clearly motivated by the its desire not to violate the family's religious freedom. But the risk of violating the establishment clause was lower in this Example than in the Sabbatarian situation noted in Justice White's dissent. In this Example, the government was not excluding any other student from doing what the religious child was allowed to do: engage in an individualized pre-mediation activity. Thus, the school authorities were not discriminating between approved "religious" activity and unapproved non-religious activity.

2. Sincerely Held Beliefs

The *Seeger* Court's definition of religion required that the foundational belief at issue in the dispute must be "sincere and meaningful." *Seeger*,

380 U.S. at 166. This statement prompted the Supreme Court to elaborate on what these words mean. In *United States v. Ballard*, 322 U.S. 78 (1944), the Court made clear that in evaluating professed religious beliefs, courts were not to determine whether the beliefs were true or false. Instead, courts were only to evaluate whether the beliefs were held "honestly and in good faith." *Id.* at 81. Two justices dissented, expressing concern that the well-meaning approach to honoring a professed belief—however unorthodox or unpopular—might allow fraudsters to exploit the free expression clause. The *Ballard* majority, however, apparently believed that a searching inquiry into the sincerity of the professed beliefs was sufficient to protect against manipulations of the First Amendment religious protections.

The Supreme Court revisited the sincerity question in two cases concerning an individual's conduct that deviated from the mandates of his or her professed religion in which the individual demonstrated meaningful and sincere belief. In *Thomas v. Review Board of the Indiana Employment Security Division* 450 U.S. 707 (1981), the Court allowed a religious exemption for a member of the Jehovah's Witnesses faith who quit his job rather than manufacture turrets for military tanks. Even though the Jehovah's Witnesses faith did not prohibit an individual from working in an armaments plant, the Court said that all members of a particular faith should enjoy the guarantee of free exercise. The Court explained "it is not within the judicial function and judicial competence to inquire whether the petitioner . . . correctly perceived the commands of [his] faith. Courts are not arbiters of scriptural interpretation." *Id.* at 716. The Court took a similar approach in allowing an exemption for someone who refused to work on a Sunday even though his faith did not require the refusal. *Frazee v. Illinois Department of Employment Security*, 489 U.S. 829 (1989).

Example 18-4:

Jessica is employed at a local medical center. The center implemented a new policy requiring a flu vaccine of all staff members. Jessica, being morally and ethically against vaccines, refused to get one. The medical center had exempted some employees from the policy for religious and medical reasons, but required these employees to wear a mask instead.

Jessica submits to a letter to her employer in support of her decision not to get a vaccine, and includes in the letter the following description:

I am not a member of an organized religion and thus cannot obtain a signature from Clergy to support my request to be exempt as required by my religion. I have my own personal belief system, which I call "My Conscience." My Conscience dictates what I must do to live in harmony with it. Not to do so, to act against it, to violate it, would be to commit a crime against oneself. Not to do so would entail a rejection of one's autonomy and a surrendering of one's body to others for their self-interest.

My body belongs to me and from this fact it follows that the right to make a medical risk decision belongs to me alone. This is why the ethical practice of medicine has as its foundation the concept of "informed consent" which is voluntary by definition as opposed to mandatory consent imposed after information is provided.

Jessica's employer does not grant the exemption and fires her. She sues for wrongful termination, claiming that her moral opposition to vaccines should be considered "religious." Is she protected under the First Amendment?

Explanation:

Jessica is likely not protected under the First Amendment. In a case similar to this, *Fallon v. Mercy Catholic Medical Center*, 877 F.3d 487 (3d Cir. 2017), the United States Court of Appeals for the Third Circuit affirmed the dismissal of a medical center employee under similar circumstances. The court of appeals stated that three factors guide the determination whether a belief is religious and therefore entitled to First Amendment protection: "First, a religion addresses fundamental and ultimate questions [about] deep and imponderable matters. Second, a religion is comprehensive in nature [consisting] of a belief system as opposed to an isolated teaching. Third, a religion often can be recognized by the presence of certain formal and external signs." Id. at 491 (quoting *Africa v. Pennsylvania*, 662 F.2d 1025, 1032 (3d Cir. 1981)). Although these factors were developed in the Third Circuit, they have had influence elsewhere.

The medical worker in *Fallon* made similar representations as Jessica did in this Example. The *Fallon* court determined, however, that the medical worker satisfied none of the three factors. First, the court observed that the main thrust of the worker's concern turned on worries about the health effects of the flu vaccine. The court concluded that this is an isolated, medical concern that does not involve a comprehensive approach to deep and imponderable matters. Like Jessica, the medical worker in *Fallon* manifested no "formal and external signs" of a religion, such as "formal services, ceremonial functions, the existence of clergy, structure and organization, efforts at propagation, observation of holidays and other similar manifestations associated with the traditional religions." Id. at 492. For all these reasons, the *Fallon* court concluded that the medical worker enjoyed no First Amendment protections and the result would likely be the same for Jessica.

Example 18-5:

A recognized church starts recommending custom-made bracelets, designed for use during an "auditing session" to "diagnose the mental and spiritual condition of the subject." The Church sells these bracelets, as well as an informational pamphlet on how to use them. The government brought an action against the Church, alleging that the bracelets and their pamphlets require approval by the federal Food and Drug Administration. Can the Church claim the products as religious objects, therefore barring the government from assessing their truth or falsity?

Explanation:

The church will probably succeed with its argument. In a case similar to this, *Founding Church of Scientology v. United States*, 409 F.2d 1146 (D.C. Cir. 1969), the court of appeals found that bracelets used for a religious ritual and supporting pamphlets were protected under the First Amendment. The government had argued that the use of the bracelets and supporting pamphlets represented action, and that under *Ballard*, the First Amendment did not protect religious action. The *Founding Church* court determined that the government's interpretation of *Ballard* was incorrect, since the litigants in that case embraced religious belief and took fundraising action to support that belief. The Scientologist use of bracelets in specialized religious rituals was thus protected religious action. The *Founding Church* court concluded by emphasizing *Ballard*'s holding that judicial questioning of the truth or falsity of a religion is improper. The court *added*, however, that "we make no holding concerning the power of Congress to deal generally with the making of false claims by religions deemed injurious to the public health or welfare." Id.at 1162.

Looking to the future, one wonders how courts might react to circumstances when religious freedoms collide with overwhelming public health emergencies. In this area, the United States Supreme Court has not decided any cases on point, but lower courts have been generally uninterested in embracing religious freedom in the face of public health concerns. *See, e.g., Morningside Church, Inc. v. Rutledge*, 2020 WL 4333539 (W.D. Mo. 2020).

CHAPTER 19

The Establishment Clause

Few writings on the First Amendment's establishment clause begin without stating that the jurisprudence interpreting the clause is confused. That observation, of course, is not helpful for anyone trying to get a handle on the basics of the case law interpreting the clause. Part of the problem emerges because cases interpreting the clause reflect different tests for determining its meaning. Enhancing the confusion that arises from using different tests is the evolving nature of the establishment clause jurisprudence: the Supreme Court appears to be in the process of changing the law in the area. Another part of the problem arises because establishment clause issues appear in myriad contexts, many of which have little to do with each other. Finally, as discussed in Chapters 18, 20, and 21, the establishment clause often clashes with the clauses of the Constitution guaranteeing free exercise of religion as well as freedom of speech. For that reason, it is three, not one, clauses of the First Amendment that one must often consider in evaluating the constitutionality of a particular government scheme with religious implications. Predictably, you may find it particularly helpful to review this chapter together with Chapter 20 (pertaining to the substance of the free exercise clause) and Chapter 1 (pertaining to content-based restrictions on speech). Although the two religion clauses sometimes clash, the Supreme Court has often said that there exists "play in the joints" between the two clauses—such that a particular regulation may comply with both clauses. Identifying the current parameters of that "play," however, can be tricky.

To organize the diverse materials and provide an antidote for some of the confusion, this chapter begins with an overview of competing establishment clause tests. Understanding that cases come out different ways because the justices are deploying different tests to resolve them adds at least some coherence to this otherwise chaotic area of First Amendment jurisprudence. This chapter then moves on to organize the materials according to what government was doing that gave rise to establishment clause litigation. Indeed, every establishment clause dispute starts with the question: "What has government done to have caused the allegation that its action diminished the wall between church and state?" Using this approach to cover the material, this chapter reviews: (1) government aid to religion; (2) government-run public schools and religion; (3) government acknowledgement of religion.

A. COMPETING TESTS

As the expression goes, "there are many ways to slice a pie." This is particularly true with the constructions of the establishment clause, which is a highly contested issue among the justices. One is not surprised, therefore, to discover that those who study establishment clause jurisprudence identify varying ways for describing and organizing the legal tests that arise from the diverse cases. One common approach—presented below—is to organize the tests into the following three categories: (1) the "*Lemon*" Test; (2) the Endorsement/Neutrality Test; and (3) the Coercion Test. The *Lemon* test is routinely criticized, but is continually called back into service. As in the past, the current Supreme Court has referred to some combination of all the tests, thus the necessity of being familiar with each.

I. The "*Lemon*" Test

Named after *Lemon v. Kurtzman*, 403 U.S. 602 (1971), the *Lemon* test is the most well-known and perhaps the longest lasting test in establishment clause jurisprudence. Under the test, a government action is constitutional if: (1) the government action has a secular legislative purpose; (2) the action neither advantages nor inhibits religion; and (3) the action does not foster an excessive government entanglement with religion. An obvious problem with the test is the abstract terms it features. Unlike some other abstract tests in the law, this one has not inspired many precise rules. Another problem with the test is the routine condemnation of its terms by various Supreme Court justices. For that reason, the precedential value of the test is not certain. Yet the test has not gone away and courts often state that it sets forth a general rule for resolving establishment clause problems.

An analysis of the case law suggests that the third prong, entanglement, is no longer a strong concern. Two major problems accompanying government entanglement with religion is promotion of political divisiveness and problems arising from government supervision of religion. Yet recent case law suggests less concern with these matters. The first or "purpose" prong of the Lemon test still has influence, since the bottom line of the cases often focuses on whether the government's purpose in regulating is unrelated to promotion of religion. Likewise the second prong — asking whether the action advantages or inhibits religion — also animates current cases, which often evaluate the effect of the government's action on the religion. (For that reason, the second prong is sometimes called the "effect" prong.) Importantly, one can see vestiges of the purpose and effect prongs in tests that developed after the Lemon test. Thus, even though the opinions of the Supreme Court and other courts criticize the test, the purpose and effect of a government action is a safe point of discussion in resolving establishment clause challenges. One should proceed cautiously before heavily relying on discussion of entanglement in finding an establishment clause violation. Yet an entanglement problem still weighs against constitutional compliance and one may legitimately mention such a problem in analyzing an establishment clause dispute.

Example 19-1:

A state government allows parents to deduct certain expenses for their children's education from their state income taxes. The tax law capped the deductions at low amounts. The tax law allows this deduction for both public and parochial school expenses. Is this law constitutional under the Lemon test?

Explanation:

Yes, the law passes the Lemon test. In Mueller v. Allen, 463 U.S. 388 (1983), the Court applied the Lemon test to a law of this kind and concluded the law was constitutional. Here is a rundown of the Mueller Court's application of Lemon's tripartite test:

(1) Purpose: The law's application to both public and parochial schools shows that the state had a secular purpose in passing the law: it was trying to defray educational expenses for all children.

(2) Effect: The limit on the size of the deduction and the existence of many other deductions supports the conclusion that the deduction did not advantage or inhibit religion. Supporting this conclusion is

the availability of the deduction to all parents: it does not provide a benefit available only to those who seek to have their children obtain religious knowledge and values as part of their education.

(3) *Entanglement:* The law did not require the government to oversee or to monitor any aspect of parochial schools. Thus, the law did not entangle the state in religious affairs.

Further discussion regarding aid to parents of parochial school children appears later in this chapter.

2. The Endorsement/Neutrality Test

Justice O'Connor is credited with developing the endorsement/neutrality test, announcing it for the first time in a concurring opinion in Lynch v. Donnelly, 465 U.S. 668 (1984). Lynch dealt with a city's inclusion of a crèche in a holiday display on public land. In that case, she stated:

> The Establishment Clause prohibits government from making adherence to a religion relevant in any way to a person's standing in the political community . . . . Endorsement sends a message to nonadherents that they are outsiders, not full members of the political community, and an accompanying message to adherents that they are insiders, favored members of the political community. Disapproval sends the opposite message.

Id. at 687-88 (O'Connor, J., concurring). Justice O'Connor's point here is that endorsement—even symbolic endorsement—undermines citizens' belief that the government is neutral on religious matters. (Presumably symbolic endorsement comes from government's use of symbols and express endorsements come from words.) Government neutrality is tied to a key purpose of the establishment clause: preventing government from suggesting to those who do not embrace a favored religion that they are not welcome. Although the justices differ on precisely how to measure whether citizens perceive that the government is endorsing a particular religion, the "reasonable person" standard is often invoked for the purpose of evaluating what message citizens are likely to glean from a particular government action.

Those justices who favor the endorsement/neutrality test have not clarified its relation to the Lemon test. Lower courts take different views on the matter. Some treat the two tests as different from each other. Others see the two tests are related and emboss the reasonable person standard on Lemon's purpose and effect inquiries. Express endorsement is obviously more problematic than symbolic endorsement.

Example 19-2:

A white supremacist group wanted to erect a cross in a public park across from a state house. The government allowed the group to erect the cross, but placed a government sign near the cross stating that the cross was erected by a private group exercising its right to freedom of expression and disclaiming any government sponsorship or support for the cross. An establishment clause challenge results from the government granting permission to erect the cross on public land. How would a court resolve this challenge using the endorsement test?

Explanation:

The government's action in this case likely passes the endorsement test. A reasonable observer would not interpret the cross's presence in the public park as a government endorsement of the cross or any religion. In a case similar to this Example, *Capitol Square Review and Advisory Board v. Pinette*, 515 U.S. 753 (1995), three justices joined a concurrence stating that the presence of the sign near the cross "remove[d] doubt about state approval of [any] religious message." *Id.* at 776 (O'Connor, J., concurring). Further discussion of crosses placed on government land appears later in this chapter.

3. The Coercion Test

Perhaps least restrictive of all the tests is one that focuses on whether the government coerces citizens to support or participate in a religion. What that means is that this test might qualify as the "lowest common denominator"—everyone thinks that a law that coerces is unconstitutional.

While including coercion in the list of government acts that could violate the establishment clause is uncontroversial as a general matter, the justices disagree whether lack of coercion by itself is sufficient to save a government measure from a successful establishment clause challenge. All say that coercion is sufficient to satisfy the standard. Some say that coercion is the only condition that will satisfy the standard. Others emphasize that the establishment clause is designed to protect matters other than coercion, such as government funding or other support for religion. In addition, the justices have not agreed on what constitutes coercion. For example, Justice Scalia narrowly defined coercion to include only legal restrictions and punishment. One of the main proponents of the coercion test, Justice Kennedy, had a broader definition. He included in the coercion concept economic incentives, psychological pressure, and even symbolic governmental actions that appear to recognize or accommodate religious faith. He also agreed that the establishment clause included an independent prohibition on "direct benefits to religion in such a degree that it in fact establishes a religion or religious faith, or tends to do so." *County of Allegheny v. ACLU*, 492 U.S. 573, 659 (1989) (Kennedy, J., concurring) (internal quotation marks omitted).

Example 19-3:

Each year at high school graduation, a state-run school district had a member of the local clergy deliver prayers during the ceremony. The parents of one of the graduating students filed suit, arguing that this tradition violated the establishment clause because it amounted to coercion to engage in a religious practice. Do they have a valid claim?

Explanation:

Yes, they will likely win their establishment clause challenge. In a case similar to this Example, *Lee v. Weisman*, 505 U.S. 577 (1992), Justice Kennedy wrote the majority opinion and reasoned that the pressure on students to attend their graduation and refrain from walking out during the prayers amounted to government coercion. Although other justices agreed that the tradition was unconstitutional, they maintained that coercion was not the only way that the government could violate the establishment clause. The dissenting justices espoused a narrower approach to coercion, confining coercion to instances when the government uses "law and [the] threat of penalty" to ensure compliance with religious thought and practices. *Id.* at 640 (Scalia, J., dissenting).

* * *

Further discussion of government inclusion of prayers during public ceremonies and events appears later in this chapter. Also later in this chapter are discussions of government aid to religion, government aid to parochial schools, tax exemption issues, government-run public schools and religious rights, as well as government acknowledgement of religion. In evaluating the cases discussed below, consider all three tests described: the *Lemon* test, the coercion test, and the endorsement/neutrality test. Be mindful that these tests are only a point of reference. Often the Court deploys an approach that shows markings of some combination of each.

B. GOVERNMENT AID TO RELIGION

In his 1785 polemic, "Memorial and Remonstrance Against Religious Assessments," James Madison wrote against requiring citizens to fund religion, connecting this practice to the derogation of free will and respect for personal conscience that freedom of religion promotes. Only in the last century, however, has the Court grappled directly with the propriety of government aid to religion. Three areas in which this topic commonly emerges are: (1) instances when the government provides some form of aid to parochial schools and other religious entities; (2) government tax exemptions for religious organizations; and (3) religious group access to public school facilities.

I. Aid to Parochial Schools and Other Religious Entities

The Court's first full-scale reckoning with government aid to religion came in *Everson v. Board of Education*, 330 U.S. 1 (1947). In *Everson*, the Supreme Court considered whether New Jersey violated the establishment clause by reimbursing parents, including parents of children in religious schools, for the cost of busing their child to school. The Court concluded that the establishment clause prohibits federal and state governments from doing the following:

- Set up a church
- Pass laws that aid one religion, aid all religions, or prefer one religion over another
- Force anyone to attend a church or not attend a church, or punish church attendance or non-attendance
- Force anyone to profess religious beliefs or disbeliefs, or punish anyone for professing religious beliefs or disbeliefs
- Tax any amount to support religious activities or institutions
- Participate in the affairs of any religious organization
- Allow religious organizations to participate in government
- Exclude individual members of a religion to receive a public benefit due to their faith or lack thereof

After determining the outer limits for government action allowed under the establishment clause, the Court held that the state is permitted to provide reimbursement for transportation to parochial schools, though it is not required to do so. Why did the state reimbursement (which appeared to come from tax money) not violate the prohibition against taxing an amount to support religious activities? First observing that the scheme did not discriminate against any particular religion, the Court determined that supporting school transportation was a public benefit that could be available to all—whether it be parents of a public school student or a parochial school student. Moreover, the *Everson* holding reflects an important theme in cases adjudicating public financial aid to religious institutions: the Court is sensitive to the identity of the recipient of the funds. A scheme designed to provide financial help to parochial school parents or students is more likely to survive an establishment clause attack than a scheme providing financial assistance directly to the religious institution itself. Although much of the *Everson* rhetoric suggests that the establishment clause requires strict separation of public money from religion, some reasoning as well as the holding of the case suggests that the Court concluded that the scheme was constitutional because it was neutral: neutral among all citizens and neutral among all religions.

Fast forwarding many years, the Court in *Mueller v. Allen*, 463 U.S. 388 (1983), embraced the notion that establishment clause problems could be avoided if government funds were filtered to religiously-affiliated schools through the parents of children who attend the schools. The Court viewed the parents as buffers insulating government from direct influence over the schools.

Two decades later, the next major case in the lineup was *Mitchell v. Helms*, 530 U.S. 793 (2000), in which the Court evaluated a federal program distributing funds to state and local governmental agencies that lend school materials and equipment to both public and private schools, regardless of any religious affiliation of the latter. Although the program required the materials to be "secular, neutral, and nonideological," many schools receiving the funds were religiously affiliated. The case had no majority opinion, but a majority of the Court upheld the program, with some justices in this majority emphasizing that a scheme in which the school could divert government funds to religious education would violate the establishment clause.

Two years later, in *Zelman v. Simmons-Harris*, 536 U.S. 639 (2002), the Supreme Court considered whether an Ohio voucher program was constitutional under the establishment clause. The State's program provided grants to low-income families to offset the cost of private school, if they chose to

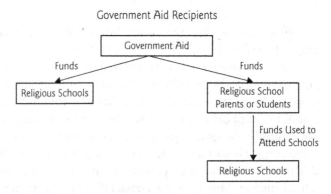

Government Aid Recipients

Figure 19-1

send their children there. The Court determined that, due to the government aid being religiously neutral on the question of voucher qualification, and because the scheme included no financial incentives for parents to choose a religious school over a non-religious one, no establishment clause violation existed. After *Zelman*, government can comply with the establishment clause using a parent-subsidy approach so long as (1) the subsidies are neutral in the sense that parents of secular school students also have access to them and (2) the parents use their own private, independent choice in deciding to direct the subsidies to a religiously affiliated school.

Example 19-4:

To address a crisis in local funding of public schools, a state provided for an across-the-board grant to the parents of all private school students to assist them with financial assistance for all tuition and books. The conditions for these grants were (1) that all students had to remain in the private school where they were enrolled for at least three years after receiving a grant and (2) that the students use the grants for school tuition and books. This meant that if parents accepted the grant, the students had to continue attending the school where they had been attending for at least three years, whether the school was religiously affiliated or secular. The grants had no other conditions, so the money could be used to buy religious books for courses at the religious schools, such as Bibles and texts on theological doctrine. Is this scheme constitutional?

Explanation:

Judged by the establishment clause jurisprudence, this scheme appears to run into constitutional trouble for two reasons: (1) it conditions the grant on the parent's agreement to use the grant on tuition and books and to keeping their child in parochial school if the child already attended there; and (2) it contains no restriction on using the money on religious books. Accordingly, the grant runs into problems under both *Zelman* and *Mitchell v. Helms*.

The question remains, however, whether omitting children attending parochial schools from the grant program would violate the free exercise clause of the First Amendment. In 2020, the U.S. Supreme Court held that a voucher program similar—but not identical—to the program in this Example violated the free exercise rights of the parents and students who were omitted from benefitting from a scheme that involved tax credits for third parties. *Espinoza v. Montana Department of Revenue*, 140 S. Ct. 2246 (2020). The *Espinoza* Court did not provide guidance on the establishment clause ramifications of the scheme, but its emphasis on the strength of the free exercise rights that hung in the balance suggests that the Supreme Court would emphasize those rights over establishment clause difficulties in similar situations. Chapter 20 discusses the *Espinoza* case further.

Example 19-4:

A town had a program where it outsourced secondary education of students to other, nearby towns that were equipped to handle them. If it could be demonstrated that a student had an educational need that could not be satisfied in public schools, the student could apply to receive funds in order to attend a private school. The town granted the funds to students who qualified, with the condition that students could not use the funds to attend religious schools.

The town structured the funding arrangement in this way in an attempt to avoid establishment clause problems. Nevertheless, a family from the town who wished to send their child to a private, religious school filed suit, arguing that the scheme violated the establishment clause. Are the parents likely to prevail?

Explanation:

No, the parents are not likely to prevail. The scheme does not violate the establishment clause: the scheme does not involve the government in religion and it does not coerce citizens to be involved in religion. Moreover, the town was motivated to structure the program this way for a secular purpose: to avoid establishment clause problems. (It should be noted that the purpose of avoiding establishment clause problems now does not amount to a compelling interest, but it a secular purpose nonetheless). In a way, the scheme in this Example is the inverse of that endorsed in *Zelman v. Simmons-Harris*. To the extent that *Zelman* suggests that the town's program would not violate the establishment clause if it allowed students to use the subsidy for religious schools, it does not follow that the town's actual arrangement here violates the clause. The town had the prerogative of attempting to avoid potential establishment clause problems if it wished, so long as doing so did not violate the free exercise clause.

Thus is the dilemma illustrated in this Example: the tension between the establishment clause and the free exercise clause of the First Amendment. Does the scheme interfere with the parents' exercise of their religion? For detailed reasons covered in Chapter 20, the answer is probably not. Parents could be motivated by any number of factors that fueled their desire for their child to attend a religious school. The scheme here does not appear to burden the parents' or the children's religious rituals or other conduct integral to their exercise of religion. Nor is there any showing that the failure to fund religious education interfered with the parents' or the child's religious beliefs. Cf. *Eulitt v. Maine Department of Education*, 386 F.3d 344 (1st Cir. 2004). Of course, if such a showing were made, the case discussed in the previous Example and in Chapter 20 would support changing the scheme in order to protect the parents' and child's free exercise rights.

* * *

An example of the dynamic nature of this line of cases is a related case-duo that addresses whether public school teachers could be shared with private religious schools. In 1985, the Court ruled in *Aguilar v. Felton*, 473 U.S. 402 (1985), that the establishment clause prohibited such a scheme. But in 1997 the Court overruled this holding, ruling in *Agostini v. Felton*, 521 U.S. 203, that public school teachers could provide remedial education to parochial school students.

Example 19-5:

The religious schools in the Town of Recession are suffering from lack of funds. These schools educate a significant number of school-age students in the town. In order to assist the religious schools in their educational mission, the Town of Recession is considering whether it may pay the salaries of all the parochial schoolteachers consistently with the establishment clause. The Town of Recession is interested only in assisting the parochial schools with their mission of providing a general education, although the town also knows that these schools include religious education in their mission.

Explanation:

The establishment clause likely prohibits the Town of Recession from paying all the salaries of parochial school system teachers. The *Agostini v. Felton* ruling in 1997 was confined to lending public school teachers for remedial education in religiously affiliated schools. Remedial education does not generally address religious matters. In upholding the scheme in that case, the *Agostini* Court noted a significant difference between programs where aid to parochial schools resulted in "indirect, remote, or incidental" effect on religious education (which does not present establishment clause problems) and programs where the aid resulted in "a direct and substantial advancement of the sectarian enterprise" (which does present establishment clause problems). The scheme that the Town of Recession developed appears to be so broad that it could assist in supporting religious education in the schools. For this reason, the establishment clause likely prohibits the award of unrestricted government aid.

Example 19-6:

Due to budget issues, a public school board had to end its alternative school services and close the alternative public school. Since the state required some of these services to be available, the school board contracted with a private organization to provide an alternative school. The private organization was religiously affiliated, but ran a secular program for the state that provided the required alternative services. As part of the private organization's program, students experienced some minor religious exposure. The state monitored the organization's program to ensure that it satisfied state requirements for alternative education.

Former employees of the closed public alternative school filed a lawsuit: they believed that the school board had violated the establishment clause. Are they correct?

Explanation:

The former employees will likely not win their establishment clause challenge. The private organization's program was secular, geared to state requirements, and the student's exposure to religion was minor. All of these factors suggest that the state was not endorsing religion, but instead was simply responding to a budget crisis. Moreover, the state involvement in the program focused on ensuring its compliance with general state alternative services education requirements and thus ensured the essentially secular nature of the program. This guarded against state entanglement with religion and complied with *Agostini's* concern that the religious education affected in any way by the state actions was "indirect, remote, or incidental" to the basic education provided to students. Cf. *Smith v. Jefferson County Bd. of School Comm'rs*, 788 F.3d 580 (6th Cir. 2015)

* * *

Much of the case law in this area focuses on vouchers and other forms of subsidies for school tuition and the like. Similar concerns arise, however, in other, more diverse contexts—as illustrated in the following Examples.

Example 19-7:

Sporty City contains various public schools and private religious schools. Every autumn, each school applies to the city for a permit to use a particular athletic field for soccer and football practices and games. Sporty City employs an informal, holistic permitting process, generally giving preference to high schools over junior high schools, and public schools over private schools.

A public high school is denied its first choice for athletic field three years in a row. The first two years the favored athletic field was awarded to a private Catholic high school, and the last year it was awarded to a public junior high school. As a result, the public high school had been denied the permit all three years and had to use a less convenient field, which led to some practice cancellations and game reschedules. Other schools in the city were also denied their first choices during this time, including private Catholic schools.

Taxpayers sue the city alleging the permitting scheme violates the establishment clause. Since the permitting process awarded the private Catholic high school first choice over the public high school, they argue that Sporty City endorsed Catholicism. The city argues that the permit denial to the public high school was the result of a neutral, secular permitting process. Has Sporty City violated the establishment clause?

Explanation:

Under recent establishment clause case law, Sporty City's actions were constitutional. According to *Agostini*, a government's action does not constitute excessive entanglement with religion for the purpose of the establishment clause if the action concerns ministerial or mechanical tasks unrelated to religious matters. That is the case here: the activity concerns only secular sporting activity. Moreover, the city's actions do not involve monitoring or surveillance of religious activity, which might entangle the city with religion. Finally, the city is simply implementing a system to allocate sports fields and is not attempting to benefit religion in general or Catholicism in particular. To be sure, the Catholic schools have benefitted over the last few years, but the benefit is wholly secular: the religious institutions are using athletic fields for athletics, and not for engaging in any religious practice.

Example 19-8:

A state created an economic development corporation that provided funding for local building and improvement projects. A religious school applied for funds to renovate those buildings on its campus that were dedicated to a secular, educational purpose. The economic development corporation approved the funds.

A taxpayer filed a lawsuit, arguing that by funding the school's project, the economic development corporation had violated the establishment clause. Will the taxpayer prevail?

Explanation:

No, the taxpayer is not likely to prevail. To begin, the reason for the initiative is secular: economic development. Second, the initiative applies to religious and non-religious institutions, so it is neutral. Most significantly, the funds were directed only to secular, educational buildings, thus they did not support buildings dedicated to religious activities. Whatever effect the funding had on the school's ability to provide religious education or other religious activity was likely both indirect and de minimis. *See Johnson v. Economic Development Corp. of County of Oakland*, 241 F.3d 501 (6th Cir. 2001). For an example showing why free exercise rights would likely not be violated if the state has specifically exempted the funds from use for renovating church sanctuaries where worship takes place, see Example 20-9 in Chapter 20.

2. Tax Exemptions for Religious Organizations

Exemptions from taxation are similar to direct payments to religious institutions or to those who use religious institutions, although tax exemptions are arguably a more indirect form of support. Under what circumstances do the exemptions comply with the establishment clause? The answer, it appears, depends on the details of the exemption scheme.

In *Walz v. Tax Commission of New York*, 397 U.S. 664 (1970), the Supreme Court evaluated the constitutionality of a taxing scheme that gave a tax exemption to religious groups for properties used solely for religious worship. Upholding the scheme in the face of establishment clause attack, the Court was convinced that the scheme was sufficiently neutral because it "granted exemption to all houses of worship within a broad class of property owned by nonprofit, quasi-public corporations that include hospitals, libraries, playgrounds, scientific, professional, historical and patriotic groups." Id. at 673. The Court determined that the legislative purpose of the tax exemption was not religious, but motivated instead by a desire to enhance life in the community. For that reason, the Court analogized the tax exemption to similar exemptions for hospitals, playgrounds, and other non-profits that positively interact with the community at large. As such, the Court determined that the scheme did not advance religion, inhibit it, sponsor it, or show hostility to it. The Court was also persuaded that tax exemptions involve government less in religious institutions than the practice of imposing a tax on them.

Example 19-9:

A state law provided an exemption from state taxes for periodicals that a religious faith organization wrote and published as well as for books published by religious organizations that are exclusively comprised of writings deemed religiously sacred. Is this scheme constitutionally allowable?

Explanation:

No, the scheme violates the establishment clause. In *Texas Monthly, Inc. v. Bullock*, 489 U.S. 1 (1989), a majority of the U.S. Supreme Court concluded that the scheme was unconstitutional. Three justices joined an opinion emphasizing that this scheme is unlike the scheme in *Walz* because it lacked breadth comparable to the scheme in *Walz*. Instead, the *Texas Monthly* plurality reasoned, the scheme targeted only writings that promulgated the teachings of religious faith and therefore lacked a secular objective. The plurality noted that a taxing scheme that sought to promote discussion of what constitutes a meaningful life would be constitutional because the exemption would be available to a broad category of organizations. In concurrence, Justices Blackmun and O'Connor found the scheme unconstitutional because it amounted to providing a preference to writings with religious messages.

3. Religious Groups Access to Public School Facilities

The U.S. Supreme Court cases in the area of religious groups access to facilities largely concern government efforts to avoid establishment clause problems by restricting religious groups' use of school facilities. For example, in *Widmar v. Vincent*, 454 U.S. 263 (1981), a state university implemented a policy of allowing registered student groups to use its facilities but prevented groups from using the facilities for worship or religious discussion. The Supreme Court held this policy unconstitutional, observing that the school had created a public forum by opening up facilities for discussion, but discriminated against the religious groups by depriving them of their freedom of speech and association. (See Chapter 12 for discussion of the public forum doctrine.)

Over a decade later, the Court applied this reasoning in *Lamb's Chapel v. Center Moriches Union Free School District*, 508 U.S. 384 (1993). In that case, the state opened a school facility to community groups in the evening and on weekends but denied this privilege to groups that would use the facility for religious purposes. Applying the *Lemon* test, the Court concluded that allowing the religious groups to use a school facility would not violate the establishment clause because the state policy had a secular purpose, did not have the primary effect of advancing or inhibiting religion, and did not promote excessive entanglement with religion.

The Court came to a similar conclusion in *Good News Club v. Milford Central School*, 533 U.S. 98 (2001), holding that an elementary school could not exclude a religious group from using school facilities after school. Holding that the school had created a limited public forum in the school, the Court concluded that the exclusion of religious groups constituted viewpoint discrimination under the First Amendment's free speech clause. Invoking a neutrality concept, the Court added that including the religious groups would not violate the establishment clause because the school made the facility available to secular organizations as well.

Example 19-10:

A school had a policy of allowing religious groups access to its facilities when school was not in session. The school did not extend this privilege to other types of groups and evaluated any application for after-hours use of the facilities to ensure that the groups that applied were primarily devoted to religious matters. Is this policy consistent with the establishment clause?

Explanation:

The policy in this Example is inconsistent with the establishment clause for several reasons. First, contrary to the policy in the *Good News Club* case, the policy here is open only to religious groups and is therefore not neutral. Moreover, contradicting the *Lemon* test applied in *Lamb's Chapel*, the exclusive access accorded to religious groups belies a secular purpose for the policy. Also contrary to *Lamb's Chapel*, the school's scrutiny of whether a group is—in the school's judgment—primarily devoted to religious matters at least raises concern about whether the school has become entangled with religion through the process of evaluating what is and what is not religion. Various courts have, however, concluded that the decision is necessary for government to comply with establishment clause requirements and should not be interpreted as unconstitutional entanglement. Accordingly, the school's approach arguably triggers a problem with the entanglement prong of the *Lemon* test. For further discussion of a similar entanglement issue, see Example 19-12 below.

Example 19-11:

One day a year, a public school would allow a diverse array of outside organizations to come in and distribute literature to its students during the school day. After the U.S. Supreme Court's decisions in *Lamb's Chapel* and *Good News Club*, a school board determined that it did not need to continue its ban which prevented religious organizations from distributing religious materials during school hours. The board determined that with one restriction in place—not allowing any persons or signage to encourage students to take the religious materials—religious groups could attend and display religious materials. Under the policy, the school allowed a religious organization to attend and to place Bibles on their table with the following sign: "Free Bibles. Please Feel Free to Take One." Non-religious groups were allowed to distribute literature without any restrictions.

A group filed a lawsuit to prevent the distribution of religious material. They argue that it would violate the establishment clause to allow this distribution to occur at the school during school hours. Is the group's argument correct?

Explanation:

The group's argument is probably wrong. This case is different from *Lamb's Chapel* and *Good News Club* because the religiously oriented actions in question occurred during the school day and not after hours. This difference creates a stronger impression that the school may be endorsing religion as part of the school curriculum or mission, which the establishment clause prohibits. Nonetheless, the school board and the school likely did not violate the establishment clause. The act of lifting the earlier prohibition against religious groups participating did not show favoritism to religion. The board was simply reacting to legal developments and attempting to put the religious groups on the same plane as secular groups.

Although the timing of the arguably religious activity makes this case different from *Lamb's Chapel* and *Good News Club*, the event took place during a non-instructional time and included a diverse assortment of organizations. This lowers the concern that students may get the impression that the school was endorsing any particular message promoted by the groups participating. In addition, the board's or school's actions did not appear to coerce students to participate in a religious activity or compel students to hear a religious message.

From a First Amendment point of view, however, this Example does raise some concern because the school board's policy is not entirely neutral. Conditions were placed on religious groups that were not placed on other groups. In this regard, this Example presents a freedom of speech question as well. As illustrated in this chapter and in Chapter 21, establishment clause cases often include free speech claims as well. In this Example, the free speech claim arises because the board discriminated on the basis of the identity of the speakers: conditions were placed on religious organizations that were not imposed on secular organizations. This differential treatment may suggest that the board and the school were engaged in content-based regulation of speech, for which free speech doctrine generally requires strict scrutiny.

Some uncertainty exists as to whether the board would satisfy the strict scrutiny standard in this case because the board appeared motivated to make the distinction in order to comply with the establishment clause. Under Supreme Court precedent interpreting the establishment and speech clauses of the First Amendment, the Court has suggested that avoiding an establishment clause violation amounts to a compelling state interest for the purpose of the free speech clause. In *Widmar v. Vincent*, 454 U.S. 263 (1981), the Court stated that the interest of the state in avoiding an establishment clause violation may provide a compelling reason to justify abridging free speech protected by the First Amendment. Nonetheless, in a later case dealing with a state counterpart to the federal establishment clause, the Supreme Court stated that compliance with separation of church and state principles did not amount to a compelling state interest for the purpose of evaluating a free exercise challenge. *See Espinoza v. Montana Dep't of Revenue*, 140 S. Ct. 2246 (2020) (analyzing a state "no aid" to religious institutions requirement).

Example 19-12:

A school board allows organizations to rent public school buildings for private events when class is not in session. However, the board refuses to grant applications "for the purpose of holding religious worship services, or otherwise using a school as a house of worship." Although the board's policy is not to challenge the purported use as stated on the application, the board does review publicly available information about each applicant. If it finds a discrepancy—for example, an organization's website indicates that the organization exists to conduct religious worship—it asks the applicant for an explanation.

A local church has a congregation, but no physical location. The school board denies its application to reserve a school building because it reports the intended use as "religious worship" on the application. The local church sues to enjoin the enforcement of the board policy, alleging that the policy violates the establishment clause. How should the court decide?

Explanation:

The court has a difficult decision to make: this case presents a close call. Several factors indicate an establishment clause problem. The likelihood that the religious organization will be using the school for religious worship heightens concern with an establishment clause violation than the situations in *Lamb's Chapel* and *Good News Club*. Under the facts of this Example, the availability of school facilities may actually facilitate and make possible religious worship, since the organization may have no other place to offer worship services. This gives the appearance that the school board is endorsing or fostering religious worship. In addition, the board policy is not entirely neutral, since it has a condition for religious organizations that it does not impose on secular organizations. Finally, the inquiry that the school board makes after finding reason to believe that the organization may worship in school space could inject the school board into the business of figuring out what does and what does not constitute worship. This raises the specter of possible entanglement with religious practices.

In a case similar to this, the Court of Appeals for the Second Circuit disagreed with a conclusion that the school board was violating the establishment clause. Noting that various obligations of a public school system require governments to engage in at least some inquiry about the details of a group's mission and activities when inviting the group to enter school premises, the *Bronx Household of Faith v. Board of Education*, 750 F.3d 184 (2d Cir. 2014), court upheld the school board's approach. The *Bronx Household* court emphasized that the school board did not second guess any organization's own characterization of the activity that was to take place in the school facility. In this regard, the court concluded that consulting information not listed on the application did "not represent a deviation from the policy of using only an applicant's own characterization." *Id.* at 202. The court emphasized that government must always exercise some amount of judgment to ensure compliance with the establishment clause.

Unlike the plaintiffs in this Example, the plaintiffs in *Bronx Household* brought a freedom of speech claim as well as an establishment clause claim. This likely prompted the court to tread especially cautiously in finding an establishment clause violation. When considered in light of potential free speech problems, the school board was in an untenable position: either grant permits for religious worship and risk violating the establishment clause, or prohibit religious worship and risk violating free expression. Given that the school board uniformly restricted "religious worship services" without particular preference for any religion, and permitted other types of religious expression (such as individual prayer or bible study), the *Bronx Household* court determined the rule to be a good faith and reasonable attempt to comply with the establishment clause.

* * *

C. GOVERNMENT-RUN PUBLIC SCHOOLS AND RELIGION

Establishment clause issues also arise from the interaction of government and public schools. The two major contexts in which this occurs are issues related to religion in the public school curriculum and government endorsement of prayer and other religious traditions in public schools.

1. Religion in the Public School Curriculum

The Supreme Court has taken a dim view of public school decisions about curriculum that are motivated by religious goals. In *Epperson v. Arkansas*, 393 U.S. 97 (1968), the Court invalidated an Arkansas law that criminalized the teaching of evolution in public schools. The *Epperson* Court accepted as fact that "Arkansas' law selects from the [vast] body of knowledge a particular segment which it proscribes for the sole reason that it is deemed to conflict . . . with a particular interpretation of the Book of Genesis by a particular religious group." *Id.* at 103. Articulating a neutrality approach to interpreting the establishment clause, the Court concluded that the Arkansas statute impermissibly promoted a religious theory of human origin.

Almost two decades later, the Court used a similar approach in *Edwards v. Aguillard*, 482 U.S. 578 (1987), finding unconstitutional a Louisiana law requiring schools to teach "creation science" whenever "evolution science" was part of a biology curriculum. Louisiana argued that it passed the law with the secular purpose of promoting academic freedom, not to promote or disparage any religion. The Supreme Court rejected this argument. Applying the *Lemon* test, the Court concluded that the legislative history for the law showed that it was passed with a religious, non-secular purpose. Moreover, the Court determined that the Louisiana law was clearly intended to endorse religion because it effectively promoted the teaching of creationism without providing similar incentives or protections to teachers of evolution.

The Court spoke with a degree of clarity and agreement in these creationism cases that is unusual for cases interpreting the religion clauses. The question arises, however, concerning the meaning of these cases for other circumstances in which curricular decisions implicate religious beliefs and practices. The following Example illustrates one circumstance among many. Nonetheless, the approach to resolving the dispute in the Example provides guidance for other contexts as well.

Example 19-13:

A school district plans to roll out a new health education curriculum focusing on human sexuality. The curriculum requires teachers to distribute materials expressing tolerance for homosexuality. The materials explicitly identify the Baptist church as particularly intolerant of homosexuality and link that intolerance to the church's earlier support for racial segregation. The materials contain the following statement:

> Religion has often been misused to justify hatred and oppression. Less than a half a century ago, Baptist churches (among others) in this country defended racial segregation on the basis that it was condoned by the Bible. Early Christians were not hostile to homosexuals. Intolerance became the dominant attitude only after the Twelfth Century . . . . Fortunately, many within organized religions are beginning to address the homophobia of the church. The Nation [sic] Council of Churches of Christ, the Union of American Hebrew Congregations, the Unitarian Universalist Association, the Society of Friends (Quakers), and the Universal Fellowship of Metropolitan Community Churches support full civil rights for gay men and lesbians, as they do for everyone else.

Students, parents, and religious advocacy groups challenge the use of materials that include this statement in the human sexuality curriculum. They argue that the statement violates the establishment clause? Are they correct?

Explanation:

Those who challenge the statement are correct that it violates the establishment clause. The curriculum is problematic because it appears to endorse one religion over another. As a result, one might reasonably conclude that the proposed curriculum had the principal effect of advancing religions that approved of homosexuality over those that did not. Indeed, one might come to this same conclusion even if the language of the proposed curriculum did not specifically identify by name the sects, denominations, or entire religions that are labeled as tolerant or intolerant of homosexuality. Significantly, the materials in this Example are even more problematic than the practice of naming names because the materials appear to discriminate against specific religions in favor of others. This adds to the establishment clause violation, especially because an important purpose of the clause is to avoid government promotion of one religion over another. *See Citizens for a Responsible Curriculum v. Montgomery County Public Schools*, No. AW-05-1194, 2005 U.S. Dist. LEXIS 8130 (D. Md. May 5, 2005).

2. Prayer and Other Religious Traditions in Public Schools

Like issues related to government attempts to limit the teaching of mainstream science on religious grounds, cases related to prayer in public schools evince a uniformity that is unusual for establishment clause jurisprudence. The U.S. Supreme Court has issued several opinions on the school prayer issue over the last few decades with a majority of the Court holding unconstitutional the practice of prayer in schools. Accordingly, the Court's guidance to lower courts and school districts on the issue of prayer itself has been uncharacteristically clear.

More uncertainty has arisen, however, on whether public schools violate the establishment clause by allowing or inviting religious exercise similar to prayer or other religious traditions as part of school activities. For example, the issue has emerged whether a moment of silence may constitutionally be included in the school day. In *Wallace v. Jaffree*, 472 U.S. 38 (1985), the Supreme Court struck down a state statute providing the following requirement for public school teachers:

At the commencement of the first class each day in the first through the sixth grades in all public schools, the teacher in charge of the room in which each such class is held shall announce that a period of silence, not to exceed one minute in duration, shall be observed for meditation, and during any such period silence shall be maintained and no activities engaged in.

Id. at 40 n.1 (citation omitted).

Example 19-14:

A school district had a policy that at the beginning of each school day, teachers must lead students in the classroom in a moment of silence. The policy specifically states that teachers may not mention the word "prayer" in connection with this exercise. Is this policy constitutional?

Explanation:

Strong arguments support the policy's constitutionality because the policy specifically prohibits mention of prayer. Considered independently, silent meditation is not necessarily religious and need not be associated with any religious practice. From this perspective, the major problem with the *Wallace* requirement was that it made an association between the moment of silence requirement and prayer. In this way, one might interpret the *Wallace* approach as a subterfuge for encouraging prayer, yet appearing not to endorse prayer or require students to pray.

Justice O'Connor made an argument similar to this in her concurring opinion in *Wallace*. Lower courts have tended to follow her reasoning and upheld moment of silence practices free from any mention of prayer. *See, e.g.,* Brown v. Gilmore, 258 F.3d 265 (4th Cir. 2001), *cert denied,* 534 U.S. 996 (2001).

One should be mindful, however, of other cases. For example, in *Lee v. Weisman,* 505 U.S. 577 (1992), the Court held unconstitutional as clergy-delivered school prayers at a public school graduation. *Lee* is significant for at least two reasons. First, *Lee* is an example of the coercion approach to establishment clause jurisprudence. Second, *Lee* concerned a moment of silence, which is a close cousin of prayer. To put a point on the matter, prayers in this context tend to be Christian in orientation.

* * *

The Court provided at least some guidance on a matter related to beginning public school days with prayer in *Santa Fe Independent School District v. Doe,* 530 U.S. 290 (2000). In that case, a school had conducted prayers over the public address system through a student chaplain before school football games. Fearing an establishment clause violation, the school had conducted a student election to determine (1) if students wanted to continue pre-game prayers, and if so (2) to elect student chaplains. The U.S. Supreme Court determined that this election process did not insulate the student-led prayer from official state endorsement, and held the practice unconstitutional.

Example 19-15:

An elementary school conducts an annual talent show, after school hours, for the entire community where the school is located. Most participants are students in grades K-8, but some adults also perform at the talent show. Participation is completely voluntary. Those who wish to participate must submit any lyrics or spoken lines to the show for the school's coordinator to approve and may not modify their act thereafter. All performances must be "G-rated."

Alma is an 11-year-old student at the elementary school. She submits the lyrics for her prospective performance, which features a devotional, religious song called "Awesome God." After review, the coordinator denies her permission to perform the song, suggesting Alma choose something with less overtly religious themes. Alma's parents object to the decision. The coordinator raises the issue with the school board and counsel, which affirm the coordinator's decision not to allow the performance of "Awesome God," for fear of violating the establishment clause.

Alma's family files suit on her behalf, alleging the school's refusal to allow the performance violated the First Amendment. Is that claim valid?

Explanation:

Yes, Alma's family asserts a valid claim. The school's concern with violating the establishment clause is likely unfounded because allowing Alma to perform the song during the talent show would not have the appearance of a government establishment of religion. Indeed, no reasonable observer with knowledge of the circumstances surrounding the talent show would interpret Alma's performance to constitute any official endorsement of the song's religious message. In particular, the number and independence of the performers would suggest to any observer that the school is not at all endorsing the performances' content, but is simply giving the students and other members of the community an opportunity to participate in a social gathering and to showcase their own preferences and talents.

Further supporting this conclusion is the school's minimal interference in any of the acts prepared by the volunteer participants. This Example is different from the Supreme Court's *Santa Fe* decision because the school in that case was much more involved in crafting the objectionable message as well as designing and administering the process of selecting the student chaplains. Finally, Alma's case is made even stronger by the possibility that the school violated any free speech rights she might enjoy as an elementary school student. *See O.T. v. Frenchtown Elementary School District Bd. of Educ.*, 465 F. Supp. 2d 369 (D.N.J. 2006).

* * *

Some of the situations in which the endorsement issue arises concern school tolerance for religious traditions within the context of school celebrations. These issues present concerns unique to schools, since they implicate possible school-endorsed religious messages conveyed to young people at an impressionable age. The following two Examples explore the establishment clause ramifications of these particular situations. The issues in these Examples, however, are also a subset of another line of cases addressed in the next subsection of this chapter, which analyzes government acknowledgement of religion by allowing religious displays on public property.

Example 19-16:

A public elementary school has an annual graduation ceremony each year, but does not have a room in its own facilities that fits all the people who wish to attend. A nearby private Christian university has offered to lend its chapel for the event and the elementary school accepted the invitation. The chapel prominently features a cross on the podium as well as other Christian symbols that appear throughout the stained-glass windows in the chapel sanctuary. This religious imagery is clearly visible to all graduation attendees. The university is not involved in the graduation ceremony other than providing the venue. Conversely, the public school has complete control over the organization and administration of the graduation ceremony.

Parents of a student at the school argue that the graduation ceremony violates the establishment clause by subjecting public school students to religious iconography in a religious venue during a meaningful rite of passage in their lives that is unrelated to religious matters. The school board argues that the graduation ceremony does not violate the establishment clause. Which side has the most persuasive argument?

Explanation:

The school board probably has the better argument. The Court's opinion in *Agostini v. Felton*, 521 U.S. 203 (1997), regarding aid to parochial schools provides some guidance for this Example. In order to find an establishment clause violation, the *Agostini* Court required that entanglement between the public school and religion must be "excessive," since some contact between church and state is inevitable. In this Example, the presence of religious symbols during the ceremony appears only to be a happenstance: the consequence of a purely ministerial decision to use a convenient, free, and adequate facility for the ceremony. The religious institution merely provided the venue for the event. The religious institution's lack of control or input over the secular graduation ceremony is significant to avoiding an establishment clause problem. The conclusion may have been different if the religious institution were to take a more active role in planning and executing the ceremony. *See American Humanist Ass'n v. South Carolina Dep't of Educ.*, No. 6:13-cv-02471-BHH, 2015 U.S. Dist. LEXIS 35179 (D.S.C. Feb. 18, 2015), *adopted by*, No. 6:13-2471-BHH, 2015 U.S. Dist. LEXIS 34002 (D.S.C. Mar. 19, 2015).

Example 19-17:

The Department of Education of a large, diverse public school system issues the following guidance to its employees regarding holiday displays on school property:

1. The display of secular holiday symbol decorations is permitted. Such symbols include, but are not limited to, Christmas trees, Santa Claus, Menorahs, and the Star and Crescent.
2. Holiday displays shall not appear to promote or celebrate any single religion or holiday. Therefore, any one symbol or decoration that may be used must be displayed simultaneously with other symbols or decorations reflecting different beliefs or customs.
3. All holiday displays should be temporary in nature.
4. The primary purpose of all displays shall be to promote the goal of fostering understanding and respect for the rights of all individuals regarding their beliefs, values, and customs.

A Catholic mother in the city sent her two children to local public schools. Over the course of two years, at three schools, the children experienced holiday displays that included kinaras, menorahs, star and crescents, Christmas trees, Santa Claus, Rudolph the Red Nosed Reindeer, and wreaths. The Department of Education refused to allow display of nativity scenes on school property, believing such displays would violate its internal guidelines and the establishment clause.

The mother sued the Department of Education for violating the establishment clause by promoting non-Christian religions, or alternatively, denigrating Christianity. More specifically, the mother alleged that by requiring school employees to judge which symbols are "secular" or "religious," the Department of Education was excessively entangling itself with religion. Is she likely to win the suit?

Explanation:

Several reasons suggest that the mother will likely lose. To begin, the Department of Education's distinctions among the holiday symbols is consistent with U.S. Supreme Court case law on holiday displays in town squares and other public property, explored in the subsection of this chapter immediately below. Moreover, the Department of Education's motivations for its distinctions were (1) avoiding an establishment clause problem and (2) promoting understanding of pluralism within a diverse student body. These motivations show that the Department of Education did not make judgments about religious dogma. These motivations also do not support the mother's allegation that the Department was taking sides in a dispute among religions or preferring one religion over another. Finally, the mother's arguments about entanglement are misplaced. The Department's guidelines did not target a private citizen or religious institution. Rather the guidelines regulated only government speech and had no effect on individual and religious institutions' judgments about the religiosity of particular symbols. The government is not prohibited from monitoring itself to ensure compliance with the establishment clause. *Skoros v. City of New York*, 437 F.3d 1 (2d Cir. 2006).

D. GOVERNMENT ACKNOWLEDGEMENT OF RELIGION

Establishment clause issues related to government acknowledgement of religion arise in a number of contexts. The most prominent contexts, however, concern religious symbols on government property and religious practices that are included in government activities.

1. Religious Symbols on Government Property

a. Nativity Scenes and Menorahs

Around the December holidays, towns and cities often decorate public lands with symbols of the season. In evaluating the establishment clause restrictions on these displays, the Court (quite reasonably) has focused on whether or not the displays convey a symbolic government endorsement of religion. In the process of doing this, however, the Court has resorted to what some characterize as a reindeer-counting endeavor: the idea of this characterization being that if a display has enough secular images, those images could be sufficient to counterbalance a symbol that most individuals would associate with religious celebration. Whether one believes this approach to enforcing the establishment clause's prohibitions is reasonable, silly, or just plain bizarre, one must accept it as the approach that we have.

In Lynch v. Donnelly, 465 U.S. 668 (1984), the U.S. Supreme Court held that the depiction of a Nativity scene as part of a Christmas display erected by government on public grounds did not violate the establishment clause. Noting that the display included secular images such as a Santa Claus, reindeer pulling a sleigh, and a Christmas tree, the Court found that the inclusion of the depiction of the birth of Christ in the form of a Nativity scene was not wholly motivated by religious considerations. In the Court's view, the Nativity scene joined the other symbols in promoting legitimate secular purposes, such as celebrating and depicting the origins of Christmas. The Court also noted a lack of political divisiveness about including the Nativity scene in the Christmas display throughout "the 40-year history of [the city's] Christmas celebration." Id. at 684. Critics argue that while appearing to "tolerate" a religious symbol, the Lynch Court's approach actually denigrates the religious meaning of the Nativity scene.

Five years later, the Court took a different tack. In County of Allegheny v. ACLU, 492 U.S. 573 (1989), a majority of the Court writing in separate opinions held that the establishment clause did not allow the government's inclusion of a Nativity scene on the grand staircase of a county courthouse, even though the government had displayed a Chanukah menorah just outside a building jointly owned by a major city and a county in the state. The majority ruled that the menorah display did comply with the establishment clause. The case did not have a majority opinion, but at least two justices concluded that the distinction between the crèche and the menorah display was appropriate because (1) the crèche stood alone on the steps of a courthouse, a place of honor, and (2) the menorah was accompanied by a Christmas tree and a sign proclaiming liberty.

Example 19-18:

A town has sought your advice about whether its intended holiday display complies with the establishment clause. The town officials explain that they understand they need to include purely secular images in the display if they also want to include images that have religious connotations. Their plan is to put a crèche and a cross at the top of the sweeping staircase leading up to the town hall and to put large wrapped presents, a family of snowmen, and a Christmas tree in the park immediately across the street from the town hall. Advise them on how to proceed.

Explanation:

The town should know that their plan may run afoul of the establishment clause. First, as represented by the result in *ACLU v. Allegheny County*, the placement of the crèche in a place of honor right by the front door of the town hall is problematic, given its separation from the purely secular symbols. The cross is possibly problematic as well because it is not specially associated with the holiday season. The case law suggests that the crèche — a symbol of the birth of Jesus Christ — is acceptable only because it is associated with the season and in that way loses some of its religious connotation. Nonetheless, the United States Supreme Court has decided two cases that involved a cross placed on public lands, but the splintered opinions in both cases did not give any definitive guidance on whether a cross on public land — without any historical explanation for the presence of the cross — is properly interpreted as a government endorsement of religion and is therefore an establishment clause violation. *See Capitol Square Review & Advisory Bd. v. Pinette*, 515 U.S. 753 (1995); *Salazar v. Buono*, 559 U.S. 700 (2010).

You would be wise to advise the town that if it wished to avoid establishment clause problems altogether it should consider eliminating the cross, although the law is not clear that the town must do so. Nonetheless, the law does strongly suggest that they should definitely move all of the symbols closer together.

b. The Ten Commandments

In 2005, the Supreme Court decided two cases regarding Ten Commandment displays on government property. As in the holiday display cases, the Court came to opposite conclusions in the two cases, with filigreed reasoning that may appear baffling to a non-lawyer. In *McCreary County, Kentucky v. ACLU*, 545 U.S. 844 (2005), the Court determined that the government had the impermissible purpose of advancing religion in placing Ten Commandment displays in county courthouses. The Court considered three displays — which had evolved over time — and ruled as follows:

(1) The Court ruled the first display unconstitutional because it was isolated without other documents. In this way, the Court noted, the display suffered for the same reasons as the isolated Nativity scene on display at the top of the courthouse steps in *County of Allegheny*.

(2) Although the second Ten Commandments display appeared together with additional documents, the Court ruled that this display violated the establishment clause because the additional documents highlighted their religious aspects such that the entire display had the effect of advancing religion.

(3) The third display (appearing later) also included other documents. The Court nevertheless concluded that this display was also unconstitutional because it contained even more religious language from the Ten Commandments and the additional documents did not sufficiently conceal the government's overt religious purpose of displaying the Ten Commandments.

Noteworthy: the government never renounced the religious roots of the displays.

In the companion case, *Van Orden v. Perry*, 545 U.S. 677 (2005), the Court came to the opposite conclusion. The *Van Orden* Court ruled, in a 5-4 decision without a majority opinion, that a six-foot high, three-foot wide Ten Commandments monument placed between the state capitol building and the state supreme court, did not violate the establishment clause. The plurality opinion for four justices stated that the government may place religious symbols on government property. An opinion concurring in the judgment reasoned that the presence of the monument on the location for over 40 years, the surrounding secular displays and monuments, and the monument's donation by the Fraternal Order of Eagles all supported the conclusion that the government was not impermissibly endorsing religion. The concurring opinion (by Justice Breyer) emphasized that the 40-year lineage was significant because no one had complained during that time, suggesting that its presence was not divisive.

These two contrasting opinions caused confusion over whether the Lemon test should govern religious symbol cases. For example, in *Green v. Haskell County Board of Commissioners*, 568 F.3d 784 (10th Cir. 2009), the Court of Appeals applied the Lemon test as the U.S. Supreme Court had done in *McCreary County*, and invalidated a Ten Commandment display surrounded by secular monuments outside a county courthouse. However, in *ACLU v. City of Plattsmouth*, 419 F.3d 772 (8th Cir. 2005), the Court of Appeals held that the display of the Ten Commandments was "passive" like in *Van Orden* and refused to apply the Lemon test. Consider these two contrasting Examples:

Example 19-19:

In the center of the courtyard of the local high school, an area where students sit during their lunch break every day, stands a large granite monument containing the text of the Ten Commandments. The monument also has an etching of two tablets (which resemble Moses' tablets of law), the Greek letters Chi and Rho (which represent Christ), and two Stars of David (which are symbols of the Jewish faith). The monument had been located on school grounds without any legal challenges for over 50 years. No other monuments are located on the courtyard. Recently a few students sued the school in attempts to have the monument removed. Will the students prevail?

Explanation:

According to the district court in *Freedom from Religion Foundation, Inc. v. Connellsville Area School District*, 127 F. Supp. 3d 283 (W. D. Pa. 2015), the students should not prevail. In evaluating how to resolve the case, the court first evaluated whether it should be decided pursuant to the analysis of *McCreary County* or *Van Orden*. To make this determination, the court evaluated whether the case shared similarities with either of the cases, and looked to the following factors (1) the display's context and physical setting, (2) the length of time the display has been in place, and (3) previous legal challenges of the display. *Id.* at 308-309. Applying these factors, the court distinguished the facts of the case from *Van Orden*, finding that the context of the two displays differed. The monument in *Van Orden* was displayed in a park with 17 other monuments and reflected secular purposes for its display whereas the monument at issue stood alone on public school grounds where impressionable young students attend. The *Freedom from Religion Foundation* court further concluded that the fact that the monument had been unchallenged for quite some time is not "dispositive" of the constitutional inquiry in this instance because the context in which the *Van Orden* monument was displayed was very different from the high school memorial. Turning to the *Lemon* test used in *McCreary County*, the court determined that the decision to keep the display of the Ten Commandment in place showed a predominantly religious purpose and had the effect of conveying government endorsement of the Christian religion.

Example 19-20:

In the aftermath of the explosion of a library in City X, rescue workers discovered an object that resembled a cross. The explosion trapped hundreds of children in the rubble and the rescue workers viewed the cross as a sign of hope for the future. City X created a museum to commemorate the lives lost in the explosion and to recognize the efforts of rescue workers. As part of the exhibit, the city included the cross that had been discovered at the site of the explosion. A group of atheist residents who had lost family and friends in the explosion argued that the display of the cross violated the establishment clause. Are they correct?

Explanation:

No, the atheists do not have a good claim. The cross obviously has religious connotations, but in the context of the museum exhibit, it does not convey a message that the government supports Christianity. Rather, the symbol is one of many artifacts found in the rubble and is part of the historical events that took place surrounding the library explosion. The museum included the mission of honoring the rescue workers who found the discovery of the cross meaningful. As such, the cross was part of the entire historical narrative surrounding the explosions.

If the display of the Ten Commandments to show the development of secular law or the inclusion of a Nativity Scene as part of Christmas celebration can be constitutional, then, without fearing a constitutional violation, City X can display a cross, found in the aftermath of a tragic explosion, in a museum along with many other artifacts intended to honor and memorialize a historical event. In this way, the cross is akin to the Ten Commandment memorial in *Van Orden*, which was displayed along with 17 other monuments. This result is also consistent with the Supreme Court's earlier cross-display cases, mentioned in Example 19-18. *See, e.g., Capitol Square Review & Advisory Bd. v. Pinette*, 515 U.S. 753 (1995) (finding in splintered opinions that the display of a cross in a public park did not violate the establishment clause because the origin of the cross was private—a fact announced by a plaque that appeared next to the cross).

2. Religion as Part of Government Activities

Governments include religious practices and references in many government activities, tangible items that the government produces, and intangible government practices. Consider "In God We Trust" on U.S. currency, religious references on government buildings, and the reference to "under God" in the pledge of allegiance. Two particularly prominent contexts in which the U.S. Supreme Court has evaluated the propriety of the government activities are prayers before legislative sessions and various religious practices within the U.S. military.

a. Prayers Before Legislative Session

In *Marsh v. Chambers*, 463 U.S. 783 (1983), the Supreme Court considered whether a state violated the Constitution by employing a Presbyterian minister for 18 years to begin each day of a legislative session with a prayer.

The Court upheld the practice, observing that it is "deeply embedded in the history and tradition" of the United States and that the practice has existed since the nation was founded "with the principles of disestablishment and religious freedom." Id. at 786. The Court found no problem with the state's practice of paying the minister with public funds.

Example 19-21:

A town has followed the practice for a ten-year period of opening every town board meeting with a prayer. A group of citizens object that this practice is unconstitutional under the establishment clause because it prefers one religion over others. The citizens point out that the prayers are delivered exclusively by Christian ministers and argue that the prayers should be delivered by those who do not represent any particular religion or sect. Are the citizens correct that this failure raises constitutional problems under the establishment clause?

Explanation:

No, the citizens are not correct. The town's practice does not raise an establishment clause problem. In *Town of Greece v. Calloway*, 572 U.S. 565 (2014), the Court addressed this issue and dismissed any claim that the practice of using only Christian clergy was unconstitutional. In fact, the Court reasoned that any requirement of non-sectarian prayers would actually heighten constitutional problems: "To hold that invocations must be nonsectarian would force the legislatures sponsoring prayers and the courts [that are asked to decide these] cases to act as supervisors and censors of religious speech . . . ." Id. at 581. According to the Court, this would put government and the courts in a position of monitoring the prayers by creating "a rule that would involve the government in religious matters to a far greater degree" than would exist under the town's approach "of neither editing or approving prayers in advance nor criticizing their content after the fact." Id.

b. Military Activities

Even without the Religious Freedom Restoration Act (RFRA),[1] service members have routinely prevailed on establishment clause challenges to military regulations, particularly where the military is regulating the members' quality-of-life issues as opposed to regulations that focus on matters related to military operations, strategy, and tactics. As for quality-of-life matters, courts have not extended the deference in evaluating quality-of-life

---

1. Chapter 20 has an extensive discussion of RFRA.

regulations that they usually extend in many other matters related to the U.S. military.

Military chaplaincy programs that show preference for chaplains of particular religious sects have inspired frequent establishment clause challenges. Courts have generally upheld government-established chaplaincy programs against First Amendment establishment clause challenges, particularly on the issue of military branch chaplaincy programs. Despite these rulings, many have challenged on establishment clause grounds the manner in which the military selects and promotes chaplains to provide religious and spiritual guidance to service members. The U.S. Supreme Court has not provided much input on the intersection of the establishment clause and the military, although some guidance comes from the Court's opinion in *Goldman v. Weinberger*, 475 U.S. 503 (1986), a free exercise case concerning the military's refusal to allow an orthodox Jewish doctor to wear a yarmulke, discussed in Chapter 20. For the most part, however, the matter has stayed in the lower courts. *See, e.g., Heap v. Carter*, 112 F. Supp. 3d 402 (E.D. Va. 2015); *Larsen v. U.S. Navy*, 486 F. Supp. 2d 11, 25-36 (D.D.C. 2007); *Adair v. England*, 183 F. Supp. 2d 31 (D.D.C. 2002).

CHAPTER 20

The Free Exercise Clause

By providing that "Congress shall make no law . . . prohibiting the free exercise" of religion, the First Amendment appears to single out religion for special protection. Why did the Framers do that? One answer is that religion is deeply tied to personal autonomy — the freedom to live one's life in the manner one believes is best. Another answer comes from James Madison's concern with the potential tyranny of factions in a democracy. Madison apparently believed that religious freedom would encourage religious groups to fragment and that the resulting diversity among the groups would encourage competition, preventing one religious group from dominating over and oppressing others. Finally emerged the concern that the relationship between believers and non-believers may become fraught (and lead to societal discord), since the concepts that are deeply held as truth by believers may seem baffling or wrong to non-believers (and vice versa).

Whatever the theoretical foundation for the free exercise clause, it has remained consistently important to First Amendment jurisprudence, although the U.S. Supreme Court has changed course on several key features of the clause over the years. Recent cases lean heavily toward protecting freedom of religion rather than protecting against government establishment of religion. One should expect that the law may change considerably. At present, the theoretical changes that are most prominent concern whether the freedom of religion clause protects religious conduct in addition to belief, and the applicable standard of reviewing government regulations of religion, particularly for religious exemptions. This chapter begins with these two issues. This chapter next examines a particularly pointed interaction between the U.S. Supreme Court and Congress regarding free exercise protections. Finally, the chapter addresses issues related to government involvement in employment disputes within the church.

A. THE SPEECH/CONDUCT DISTINCTION

The language of the First Amendment refers to the free *exercise* of religion. One would think that the word "exercise" suggests that the clause protects religious conduct in addition to belief. Yet early cases took a different view, construing the clause to apply only to belief and not to conduct. The U.S. Supreme Court held in *Reynolds v. United States*, 98 U.S. (8 Otto) 145 (1879), that the First Amendment used the conduct characterization to allow government to outlaw the practice of polygamy. The *Reynolds* Court reasoned that "[l]aws are made for the government of actions, and while they cannot interfere with mere religious belief and opinions, they may with practices." *Id.* at 166. The Court did not explain how one wholly separates a religion's beliefs from its liturgy.

The Court later rejected this dichotomy between belief and conduct, recognizing that the First Amendment protected religiously motivated conduct. In connection with this shift, the Court instituted a strict standard of reviewing governmental regulation of religion. The next section addresses the standard of scrutiny issue. In the meantime, however, consider the following Example highlighting the difficulty of separating belief from conduct—and identifying conduct that is not religiously motivated enough to fall under First Amendment protection.

Example 20-1:

Elizabeth belongs to a religion that condemns any use of violence between humans. Elizabeth was hired for a government job and was asked to sign an oath affirming the duty of all citizens to defend the U.S. Constitution, even if doing so requires use of weapons that are capable of killing a human being. The government made clear that she could not take the position if she refused to sign the oath.

Elizabeth argues that this requirement violates her free exercise rights. The government argues that the act of signing an oath—or not signing an oath—is mere conduct that the government may regulate consistent with First Amendment restrictions. Is the government correct?

Explanation:

The government is probably not correct. The crux of the government's regulation is not aimed at the act of signing the oath. Rather, the government is concerned with the substance of the oath, which directly contradicts Elizabeth's religious belief. Accordingly, the government's requirement is likely unconstitutional, even under the older case law embracing a strict dichotomy between conduct and belief.

* * *

A key case recognizing that the free exercise clause protects religious conduct is *Sherbert v. Verner*, 374 U.S. 398 (1963). *Sherbert* required government to exempt religious conduct from neutral laws that applied to all conduct (now known as "neutral laws of general applicability"). The case is also well known for establishing a strict standard of scrutiny for government regulation of religious exercise, a matter discussed in the section immediately below.

B. THE STANDARD OF SCRUTINY FOR GOVERNMENT EXEMPTIONS FOR RELIGION: *EMPLOYMENT DIVISION v. SMITH*

Take note: the (currently prevailing) iconic case on the level of scrutiny for evaluating the constitutionality of government accommodation of religion is *Employment Division v. Smith*, 494 U.S. 872 (1990). This section will describe and explain *Smith* in short order. As is usually the case with Supreme Court precedent, *Smith* is a reaction to what came before it. That means, full understanding of *Smith* requires an understanding of the cases that preceded it.

The *Sherbert* case, mentioned in the section of this chapter immediately above, provides the appropriate starting place. In *Sherbert*, the U.S. Supreme Court established that government action that substantially burdened religious practice was valid only if it was narrowly tailored to serve a compelling government interest. *Sherbert* concerned a member of the Seventh-day Adventist Church who quit her job rather than work on her Sabbath, which was Saturday. The state denied her unemployment benefits, and her appeals eventually reached the Supreme Court. Upon review, the *Sherbert* Court declared that the denial of benefits violated the free exercise clause because applying the unemployment eligibility provisions and denying the benefits did not serve a compelling state interest.

The Court subsequently applied this strict scrutiny with rigor in two or more contexts. One context concerned similar instances when the state denied unemployment benefits to an individual exercising religious beliefs. The other context involved the application of compulsory school attendance laws to Amish youth. In *Wisconsin v. Yoder*, 406 U.S. 205 (1972), the Court concluded that requiring Amish children over the age of 13 to attend public school violated both the free exercise clause and the right of parents to control their children's upbringing. The Amish objected to their children attending high school on the ground that secondary school education impermissibly exposed them to "a 'worldly' influence in conflict with their beliefs." *Id.* at 211. The Court concluded that compulsory high school attendance would severely impact the Amish way of life and would compel students "to perform acts undeniably at odds with . . . their religious beliefs." *Id.* at 218. The Court ruled that although the power of a State to control educational requirements is high, that power is not absolute. In light of the impact on the Amish religion resulting from compelling high school attendance with a criminal sanction, the Court held that "[a] regulation neutral on its face may, in its application, nonetheless offend the constitutional requirement for governmental neutrality if it unduly burdens the free exercise of religion" *Id.* at 220.

In some but not all of the following cases, however, the Court was reluctant to use strict scrutiny to strike down government regulation. Indeed, many commentators described this period as one in which strict scrutiny existed in name only. A particularly telling example is *Lyng v. Northwest Indian Cemetery Protective Association*, 485 U.S. 439 (1988), in which a Native American group challenged the federal government's decision to build a road and allow timber cutting in an area containing burial grounds. Recognizing that the road would "virtually destroy the Indians' ability to practice their religion," the Court nonetheless refused to find a free exercise clause violation. *Id.* at 451-452. The Court reasoned that the clause should not be read to "afford an individual a right to dictate the conduct of the Government's internal procedures." *Id.* at 448 (quoting *Bowen v. Roy*, 476 U.S. 693, 699-700 (1986).

Example 20-2:

An Orthodox Jewish doctor serving in the U.S. Air Force challenged the military dress code preventing him from wearing a yarmulke as required by his religious faith. Will the doctor win his claim that the requirement violates his free exercise rights?

Explanation:

Under established U.S. Supreme Court precedent, the doctor will not prevail. In a case emblematic of the U.S. Supreme Court's disinclination to apply strict scrutiny with rigor, *Goldman v. Weinberger*, 475 U.S. 503 (1986), the Supreme Court rejected a free exercise challenge identical to the one in this Example. In so holding, the Court emphasized deference owed to the military:

> The considered professional judgment of the Air Force is that the traditional outfitting of personnel in standardized uniforms encourages the subordination of personal preferences and identities in favor of the overall group mission. Uniforms encourage a sense of hierarchical unity by tending to eliminate outward individual distinctions except for those of rank. . . . The Air Force has drawn the line essentially between religious apparel that is visible and that which is not, and we hold that those portions of the regulations challenged here reasonably and evenhandedly regulate dress in the interest of the military's perceived need for uniformity.

Id. at 508, 510.

Given the dynamic nature of the law in this area, one wonders whether this approach may change. In 1986, a majority of the Court found that military discipline far outweighed any free exercise concerns. In light of the recent trend in the Court toward elevating the free exercise of religion, one wonders whether the result would be the same today.

* * *

The U.S. Supreme Court made official its inclination not to probe too deeply into government regulation of religion in *Employment Division v. Smith*, 494 U.S. 872 (1990). *Smith* involved Native Americans who participated in religiously required peyote use in the State of Oregon where peyote is a controlled substance and its use is a crime. The Native Americans were fired from their jobs for drug use, and because their terminations were classified as "misconduct," they could not qualify for unemployment compensation. They sued arguing that the denial of unemployment compensation stemming from their participation in a religious ritual violated their free expression rights.

Rejecting the challenge, the Court minimized the reach of *Sherbert*. The Court said that *Sherbert*'s strict scrutiny standard applied only in the context of employment benefit denials and did not create a test for evaluating criminal law. As for *Yoder* and similar cases, the Court noted that the application of strict scrutiny was justified by the presence of constitutional concerns in addition to free religious exercise—the rights of parents to dictate their children's upbringing.

At bottom, the Court ruled that strict scrutiny did not apply to challenges to neutral laws of general applicability that effectively burden religion. Reminiscent of the reasoning in *Goldman v. Weinberger*—discussed in Example 20-2—the Court stated that because "we are a cosmopolitan nation made of . . . almost every conceivable religious preference . . . we cannot afford the luxury of deeming *presumptively invalid*, as applied to [a] religious objector, every regulation of conduct that does not protect an interest of the highest order." *Id.* at 888 (emphasis in original) (internal quotation marks omitted). *Smith* stands for the proposition that a neutral law of general applicability is valid—even if that law had the effect of prohibiting a religious practice—unless the case also presents infringement of another fundamental right. In such a hybrid case, strict scrutiny applies.

Lower courts have clarified *Smith*'s scope by expounding on the meaning of "neutral" and "general applicability." Case law states that a law lacks neutrality if it reflects faith-based discrimination, which would include laws that are motivated by animus directed toward a particular religion or constituents thereof. A law does not have "general applicability" if it regulates only religious activity. *See, e.g., Roberts v. Neace*, 958 F.3d 409 (6th Cir. 2020).

Based on this elaboration, *Smith* can be understood as mandating the analysis reflected in Figure 20-1:

Example 20-3:

A state law specifies vaccination requirements for public and private schools, requiring all children of a certain age to be vaccinated against certain illnesses. The law has three possible exemptions from the vaccination requirement: (1) medical evidence suggesting a vaccination would be dangerous to the child; (2) the child is educated in an at-home independent study

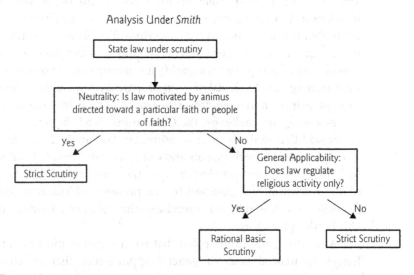

Figure 20-1

program; or (3) the child qualifies for an individualized education program that separates the child from other children. A group of parents challenges this law because it does not provide an exemption for those individuals whose religious teachings prohibit vaccination. Would the challenge be successful under the *Smith* approach?

Explanation:

No, the challenge will not be successful under *Smith*. The reasoning in *Smith* disposes of any claim here that the religious preferences of the parents should be satisfied at the expense of the public health concerns that motivate the vaccination law. In the language of *Smith*, a court need not "afford the luxury of deeming presumptively invalid" a law that negatively impacts religious preferences, but also protects an entire community from a communicable disease that could result in serious illness or death. Indeed, in *Smith* itself, the Court rejected the notion that a strict standard of scrutiny should apply in a case like this:

> The [compelling interest approach opens] the prospect of constitutionally required religious exemptions from civic obligations of almost every conceivable kind — ranging from compulsory military service, to the payment of taxes, to health and safety regulation such as manslaughter and child neglect laws, compulsory vaccination laws, drug laws, and traffic laws . . . . The First Amendment's protection of religious liberty does not require this.

Id. at 888-889 (internal citations omitted).

Finally, the three secular exemptions in the law do not change the result, as they bear no indication that the vaccination law is targeting religion or that it suggests hostility to any particular religion. *See, e.g., Whitlow v. California Department of Education*, 203 F. Supp. 3d 1079 (S.D. Cal. 2016).

Example 20-4:

Two sets of parents in a state challenged a school district's refusal to exempt their children from using instruction materials that depict same-sex relationships. Both families established that they held religious beliefs that condemned any recognition of LGBTQ+ rights. One family objected to a book being sent home with their child for optional reading, which depicted a same-sex couple. The other family objected to their child being read a book in class that described a gay wedding.

The parents claimed several violations of their constitutional rights, including the right that they and their children enjoy free exercise of religion protections. They did not challenge the school's use of the books, but rather the school district's refusal to provide notice of proposed exposure to these materials, and an exemption for their children. The state where this occurred did have a law requiring that parents be given notice and the option to exempt their children from education on human sexual education or sexuality issues. Nonetheless, the courts in the state took the position that books that simply depict same-sex relationships or celebrations are not education on human sexuality within the meaning this state law.

Will the parents win their constitutional challenge?

Explanation:

The parents will not win on the basis of *Smith*, but they possibly could prevail on other theories. *Smith* is no help since the school district was applying generally applicable policies that do not single out religion. Nothing suggested that its choice of books and refusal to tailor curriculum to the preferences of individual families was irrational. The parents might still prevail because this Example presents a hybrid case: in addition to the free exercise issue, the case implicates parental control over a child's upbringing. In this way, this Example resembles *Yoder*, which appears to have survived *Smith*'s change on when to apply the scrutiny standard.

However, the parents in this Example have a weaker claim than those in *Yoder* because the state intrusion into parental control over a child's upbringing is relatively mild. The *Yoder* Court concluded that compulsory high school attendance would severely interfere with Amish religious convictions and daily way of living. This Example involves only ephemeral exposure to images that did not target religious beliefs or even appear as part of human sexuality education. Moreover, nothing stopped the parents from home-schooling their children if that was their preference. Although the state interference with the parents' right to raise their children preserves their claim in light of *Smith*, the modest nature of that interference makes their claim unlikely to succeed. That said, it remains unclear whether the Court truly intended for there to be a hybrid claim exception to *Smith*, or whether the *Smith* Court was merely adroitly trying to distinguish inconvenient case law such as *Yoder* without expressly overruling it.

For a slightly different approach to facts such as those that appear in this Example, *see Parker v. Hurley*, 514 F.3d 87 (1st Cir. 2008).

Example 20-5:

During a worldwide viral pandemic, a state governor issued two separate orders prohibiting mass gatherings and closing down organizations that are not "life-sustaining." The orders exempted some businesses from the shutdown order, such as landscaping, laundromats, dry cleaners, liquor stores, shopping malls, and grocery stores. The order also prohibited certain mass gatherings, such as crowded airports, provided that social distancing practices were maintained at all times. The orders did not exempt faith-based gatherings, like church services.

The orders extended through the Christian celebration of Easter in the spring, which meant that congregants of the local Baptist Church would not be able to attend either in-person or drive-in worship services. Several congregants chose to violate the order and attend Easter services. Despite complying with the state's social distancing and hygiene requirements, congregants were notified that violation of the order amounts to a criminal act and that all people in attendance would have to self-quarantine for 14 days or be subject to sanctions.

Some of the congregants sued the governor and other state officials, seeking to enjoin enforcement of the orders, which they argued violate their right to free exercise of religion under the First Amendment. Do the congregants have a viable free exercise challenge to the orders?

Explanation:

Yes, the congregants have a viable challenge, although the challenge may depend on ever-changing scientific and empirical evidence. As interpreted by lower courts, *Employment Division v. Smith*, 494 U.S. 872 (1990), requires an inquiry into whether the orders targeted faith-based practices and whether they were prompted by anti-religious animus. Nothing in this Example suggests that is the case. Nonetheless, in order for *Smith's* rational basis standard to apply, the mandates must be neutral and generally applied. The orders are arguably not generally applicable because they include so many exceptions for secular activities. Accordingly, the rational basis standard may not apply, prompting a strict scrutiny analysis. Despite the state's compelling interest in public safety, a strong argument can be made that the state could have used less restrictive means to further the state's goal — such as limiting the number of people who may attend religious services — rather than imposing an outright ban and requiring the church to adhere to social distancing practices. *See Roberts v. Neace*, 958 F.3d 409 (6th Cir. 2020).

The dynamic nature of this situation makes this a particularly challenging case. What does the court make of scientific evidence of the lethal nature of aerosols? Should we be concerned that religious services often involve singing, which is a particularly potent way of spraying aerosol particles of virus? What do we do with the reality that people who know each other well and share their personal spiritual life tend to take fewer precautions than those interacting with others who do not share the same bonds? The questions could go on. At bottom, however, the Governor should know that she could refashion the order in order to try to steer clear of the free exercise problems.

* * *

Courts and scholars regard *Smith* as a dramatic change in the law. The impact and scope of the decision, however, is yet to be determined. The Court provided some guidance on *Smith's* scope in *Church of Lukumi Babalu Aye v. City of Hialeah*, 508 U.S. 520 (1993). The dispute in that case concerned the Santeria religion's practice of animal sacrifice as one of its principal forms of devotion. The animals are killed by cutting an artery and are then cooked and eaten following Santeria rituals. After the church leased land in a city and announced plans to establish a house of worship and other facilities there, the city council held an emergency public session. It passed a resolution noting city residents' "concern" over religious practices inconsistent with public morals, peace, and safety, and declared the city's "commitment" to prohibiting such practices. *Id.* at 527. The city then passed an ordinance incorporating state animal cruelty laws broadly punishing "[w]hoever . . . unnecessarily or cruelly . . . kills any animal." *Id.* at 526. The ordinance was interpreted to reach religious animal sacrifice.

Reaffirming *Smith*, the U.S. Supreme Court reasoned that under the free exercise clause, a law that burdens religious practice need not be justified by a compelling governmental interest if it is neutral and generally applicable. The Court added that where a law burdening religion is not neutral or not of general application, the law is subject to strict scrutiny — requiring that the law be narrowly tailored to advance a compelling governmental interest. The ordinance here was not neutral because it appeared to target religion. Nor did the law satisfy the strict scrutiny standard because it was not narrowly tailored to further the city's legitimate interests in promoting public health and preventing animal cruelty. The Court concluded that the ordinance suppressed much more religious conduct than necessary to achieve the city's stated ends and the city could have addressed the legitimate governmental interests in protecting the public health and preventing cruelty to animals by restrictions stopping far short of a flat prohibition of all Santeria sacrificial practice, such as general regulations on the disposal of organic garbage, on the general care of animals, or on slaughter methods.

Example 20-6:

The City of Caution had an ordinance on the books specifying that only those individuals who had city-sponsored training in the use of a certain cleaning agent could use the agent while in the city. This law applied to all entities in the city, whom the city could fine for non-compliance. Any individual or organization in the city using the cleaning agent without proper certification could be fined.

The Church of Purity had a specially designated cleric who followed certain cleaning rituals after each service. The church appointed the designated cleric by vote of the parishioners. The cleaning task was a great honor for the cleric and an important sacrament. Although those who are not members of the Church of Purity would not understand, religious teachings make it impossible for the cleric to subject herself to the possible veto that the city's training mechanism sets up. The cleric who performed this job at the local Church of Purity used the regulated cleaning agent without the mandated city training. The city found out and imposed a fine. The church argued that the fine violated its free exercise rights. Is the church correct?

Explanation:

The church may have a viable free exercise claim, but not on the basis of *Smith* or *Hialeah*. The ordinance appears to be neutral because it applies to everyone using the cleaning agent while engaged in any activity, religious or secular.

The problem for the city arises from the ordinance's interference with the church's essential faith and mission. In *Hosea-Tabor Evangelical Lutheran Church & School v. Equal Employment Opportunity Comm'n*, 565 U.S. 171 (2012), the Court found a free exercise violation for a neutral law of general applicability because the law interfered with a similar internal church decision. This is arguably an exception to the *Smith* test, although the Court did not couch its reasoning in those terms and merely distinguished *Smith*. Whether a formal exception to *Smith* or not, the *Hosanna-Tabor* Court emphasized the need to protect the autonomy of internal church decision making against government interference. This presents difficulty for the city in this Example, especially because the facts suggest that the church evaluates, considers, and votes on the qualifications of the cleric who cleans the church as part of its procedures, belief structure, and liturgy. Further discussion of *Hosanna-Tabor* and the ministerial exception appear later in this chapter in connection with employment claims against religious institutions by employees of the institutions.

Example 20-7:

State X has an anti-discrimination law that prevents all individuals and businesses in the state from discriminating against individuals on the basis of sexual orientation. This law applies to all entities in the state. A wedding cake shop turned down a gay couple's request to bake a cake for their wedding. The owner of the shop explained that it is against his religious belief for two individuals of the same sex to marry. The couple filed a complaint with the state X anti-discrimination commission against the bake shop owner. The owner defended by arguing it would violate his free exercise rights to require him to bake the cake or pay a fine. Does he have a winning free exercise claim under *Smith*?

Explanation:

Based on the facts in the Example, the bake shop owner likely does not have a winning claim under *Smith* because the discrimination prohibition would probably be viewed as neutral and generally applicable. The facts of this Example are nearly identical to *Masterpiece Cakeshop, Ltd. v. Colorado Civil Rights Commission*, 138 S. Ct. 1719 (2018). The *Masterpiece Cakeshop* Court agreed that a free exercise violation had taken place in that case, but it did not reach the claim on the basis of the constitutional principles laid out in *Smith*. Instead, the Court based its free exercise decision on a more fact-specific basis: the Court focused on the comments made by the Colorado Civil Rights Commission that were impermissibly hostile toward religion. The Court did, however, suggest that *Smith* would foreclose a successful free exercise claim in the absence of the authorities' expression of hostility to religion. Specifically, the Court said that as a general rule, religious "objections do not allow business owners and other actors in the economy and in society to deny protected persons equal access to goods and services under a neutral and generally applicable public accommodations law." *Id.* at 1727.

Example 20-8:

Arlene runs a florist shop and refuses to provide floral wedding arrangements for a same-sex couple, citing her religious belief that marriage should be an institution solely available to opposite-sex couples. Arlene turns away a same-sex couple from her shop and they file suit under the state's anti-discrimination statute, which prohibits discrimination in the provision of goods and services on the basis of sexual orientation.

Arlene defends her refusal to serve the same-sex couple on the grounds that the anti-discrimination ordinance cannot be enforced without contravening her First Amendment free exercise right. Her sole argument is that contributing flowers to a same-sex marriage is repulsive to her religious beliefs.

Explanation:

As was the case for the wedding cake baker in Example 20-6, Arlene is unlikely to prevail on a free exercise claim based solely on the application of a general anti-discrimination law to her business. *Smith* simply does not allow this claim to proceed. Moreover, Arlene further weakens her position by alleging that the injury to her religious rights arises solely from the thought that her artistic creation would be used in a certain ceremony. She is not claiming that she regards the sale of her flowers to the same-sex couple to represent her endorsement of their marriage or the wedding ceremony.

This Example is based on *State v. Arlene's Flowers, Inc.*, 441 P.3d 1203 (Wash. 2019). The U.S. Supreme Court vacated and remanded the Washington Supreme Court's decision in that case in light of *Masterpiece Cakeshop*. Thereafter, the Washington Supreme Court upheld enforcement of the Washington state anti-discrimination statute against the florist who refused to provide floral arrangements for a same-sex couple's wedding ceremony.

The *Arlene's Flowers* case is instructive because the Washington Supreme Court rejected First Amendment claims related — but not identical — to a free exercise claim. Specifically, the court rejected the florist's freedom of expression arguments that her arrangements "encompass[ed] her 'unique expression,' crafted in 'petal, leaf, and loam,'" and that the non-discrimination statute compelled her to adopt a viewpoint at odds with her religious values. *Id.* at 1225. The Court held that the arrangements were merely flowers and not expressive speech, and therefore the state did not compel her speech. In connection with this argument, the *Arlene's Flowers* Court refused to identify what is an artistic endeavor protected by the First Amendment, stating it could not get into "the business of deciding which businesses are sufficiently artistic to warrant exemptions from antidiscrimination laws." *Id.* at 1228 (internal quotation marks omitted).

Although nominally not changing the law, the Court injected uncertainty into the scope of the *Employment Division v. Smith* deferential approach to freedom of religion claims in *Roman Catholic Diocese of Brooklyn v. Cuomo*, No. 20A87, 2020 WL 6948354 (11/25/2020). That case confronted an order by the Governor of the State of New York that imposed occupancy limits on services held by religious institutions during the COVID-19 pandemic. Five justices joined the per curiam opinion in the case, which issued a judgment enjoining the enforcement of the Governor's order. Four dissenting justices wrote separately from the per curiam opinion, explaining that the injunction was premature at best: at the time of the Court's judgment, the New York Governor's order no longer actually applied to the parties who had sought injunctive relief before the U.S. Supreme Court. In the majority per curiam opinion, the Court determined that the Governor's order did not qualify as a neutral edict of general applicability — and thus merited strict scrutiny. Although the Court viewed curtailing infections from COVID-19 to constitute a compelling interest, the Court further determined that the regulation was not narrowly tailored, as required by the strict scrutiny test.

The precise reach of the *Cuomo* decision is not clear given its procedural posture: the Supreme Court evaluated the constitutionality of the Governor's order through the lens of the procedure requirements for issuing an injunction, which require only a likelihood of success on the merits, not actual success on the merits. By imposing the strict scrutiny test only after determining that the Governor's order was not "neutral," the Court did not upset the *Smith* approach to free exercise claims. Nonetheless, observers of this November 2020 *Cuomo* decision pointed to a change in direction for the

Court's readiness to find a First Amendment free exercise violation. Why would this decision be interpreted as a change in direction? The case arose in a context that generally calls for significant judicial restraint: a change in direction generally required because the case concerned a request for the extraordinary remedy of an injunction and because the particular complainants were not adversely affected by the order.

C. Funding for Religious Education

The U.S. Supreme Court has decided three major cases addressing the circumstances under which a state's decision to deny funding to parochial schools or parochial school students violates the free exercise clause. The cases lie on a spectrum in terms of the power their holdings grant to state governments to restrict individual free exercise rights. In the first case, *Locke v. Davey*, 540 U.S. 712 (2004), the Court considered whether Washington State could constitutionally deny state scholarship funds to individuals pursuing a theology degree. The Court rejected the challenge, concluding that the exclusion had at most a *de minimis* impact on free exercise rights. In reaching this conclusion, the Court observed that although the state would not allow those pursuing a theology degree to apply for the scholarship, the state allowed religious individuals to apply, and allowed the individuals to use awarded scholarship money at religious, private universities at which the students could take devotional theology courses. This case lies at the most deferential extreme of the spectrum, allowing a state to exclude individuals from a public program on the basis of their religious motivation.

The second case in the lineup, *Trinity Lutheran Church of Columbia, Inc. v. Comer*, 137 S. Ct. 2012 (2017), rests at the other end of the free-exercise-impact spectrum. *Trinity Lutheran* concerned a Missouri program that granted recycled tires to schools and daycare centers to use as playground materials. The Court held this policy violated the free exercise clause because it automatically excluded religiously affiliated schools from even applying for the grant, even though the schools would not be using the grants for religious education, but rather were motivated by a secular purpose of providing safe playground equipment for all children.

Finally, the Court most recently found a free exercise violation in *Espinoza v. Montana Department of Revenue*, 140 S. Ct. 2246 (2020). *Espinoza* falls in the middle of the spectrum between *Trinity Lutheran* and *Locke*. That case concerned a Montana state program granting tax credits for donations to organizations that award private school tuition scholarships. To reconcile the program with a provision of the Montana Constitution that bars government aid to any school "controlled in whole or in part by any church, sect, or denomination," Montana Constitution Article X, § 6(1), the Montana Department of Revenue promulgated a rule prohibiting families from using the scholarships at religious schools. Challengers claimed that the rule discriminated on the basis of their religious views and the religious nature of the school they had chosen, and the U.S. Supreme Court agreed.

Citing *Trinity Lutheran*, the *Espinoza* Court evaluated Montana's no-aid provision using strict scrutiny because it was not neutral: Montana excluded schools from public benefits solely because of religious status. Importantly, the Court concluded that Montana's interest in separating church and state is not compelling in this instance. The Court distinguished *Locke v. Davey*, stating that the plaintiff in *Locke* was denied a scholarship because he proposed to use the funds to prepare for the ministry, which is an essentially religious endeavor. By contrast, the Court observed that Montana's no-aid provision did not focus on whether a religious school offered an essentially religious course of instruction, but instead barred aid to a religious school simply because it was affiliated with religion. The Court also noted that *Locke* had invoked a "historic and substantial" state interest in not funding the training of clergy, but that Montana was not relying on a comparable tradition in disqualifying religious schools from receiving government aid. *Espinoza*, 140 S. Ct. at 2259 (quoting *Locke* at 725).

Espinoza falls in the middle of the spectrum between *Locke* and *Trinity Lutheran*. *Locke* allowed discrimination against religious schools engaged in an overwhelmingly religious purpose—training ministers—while *Trinity Lutheran* disallowed discrimination against religious schools engaged in an overwhelmingly secular purpose—providing playground equipment. *Espinoza* dealt with a situation where the purpose of the religious schools was not clearly religious or secular. Without that clarification, the state could not possibly prove that its refusal to award scholarship funds to religious schools was narrowly tailored to achieve a compelling purpose, and thus pass strict scrutiny. The distinction between the cases is important for evaluating the scope of the First Amendment free exercise provision because the distinction suggests that the Court accepts the tradition of limiting state funding to promote essentially religious instruction. At the same time, the Court permits states to fund secular activities at religious schools.

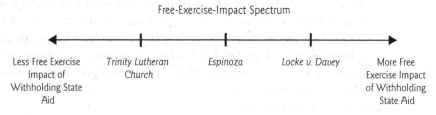

Free-Exercise-Impact Spectrum

| Less Free Exercise Impact of Withholding State Aid | Trinity Lutheran Church | Espinoza | Locke v. Davey | More Free Exercise Impact of Withholding State Aid |

Figure 20-2

Significantly, the Court in both *Trinity Lutheran* and *Espinoza* also made clear that compliance with the state's version of the establishment clause (so-called "no-aid" provisions, which are part of the constitutions in more than half the states) could not amount to a compelling interest under the facts of those two cases. Although the Court has apparently sought to elevate freedom of religion values, the thrust of the three decisions considered together — *Trinity Lutheran, Locke,* and *Espinoza* — may be that the government now has more latitude to restrict the expression of religious institutions by denying public funds when those funds are used to further a core religious mission of the institution. In other words, expression facilitated by government aid is less protected as it becomes more overtly religious. One explanation for that result is the recognition of the tension between the Constitution's establishment clause and free exercise clause, a tension covered in Chapter 18 above. Indeed, the *Locke* Court reiterated what is now a common mantra in this area: "[The two Religion Clauses] are frequently in tension. Yet we have long said that 'there is room for play in the joints between them.' In other words, there are some state actions permitted by the Establishment Clause but not required by the Free Exercise Clause." 540 U.S. at 718-719 (internal citations omitted).

One wonders whether the trend in this case law takes away most of that "play in the joints" between the clauses. State policymakers have always struggled to develop constitutional education funding policies that accord deference to parental choice concerning private schools — whether religious or secular. Policymakers know that being too generous with state funds to religious schools may violate the establishment clause. But now more than ever they face the heightened challenge of evaluating whether their funding to religious schools is sufficiently similar to funding granted to public schools so as to avoid running afoul of the free exercise clause.

Example 20-9:

All religious and secular private schools in State ABC use computer facilities for all academic classes — math, English, social science, and the like. State ABC created a fund to help secular — and not religious — private schools upgrade their computer capabilities. St. Bridget's School provides basic education to elementary school students. The school does teach some religious doctrine (without the use of computers), but the bulk of its curriculum is devoted to basic elementary school subjects taught in all schools. St. Bridget's School applies for funding to upgrade its computer lab and is denied because of its religious affiliation. St. Bridget's sues, arguing that the religious exception violates its free exercise rights. Is State ABC's religious exception constitutional?

Explanation:

No, the religious exception violates the free exercise clause. The facts of this Example are closest to *Trinity Lutheran* (the playground case) because the computer activities affected by the exemption are not overwhelmingly religious (such as the program devoted to training clergy in *Locke*). Rather, the exception discriminates against St. Bridget's and similar schools simply because of what they are—religiously affiliated—and not what they do—which is primarily to provide a general elementary education. The school's practice of not using computers to teach religious doctrine reinforces this conclusion.

Example 20-10:

A city instituted a program to promote urban renewal. As part of this program, organizations and building owners may apply for public funds to renovate their building in the city. The program allows religious institutions to apply for the funds and provides grants to renovate building exteriors as well as some parts of the interior. The program, however, forbids the use of public funds to renovate interior sanctuaries where religious services are held. Is this exclusion constitutional or is it a violation of the free exercise clause?

Explanation:

The exclusion of grants to renovate sanctuaries is likely constitutional. The scheme targets for exclusion a core religious activity (worship in a sanctuary), but otherwise allows funding to renovate the church building. By confining the exception in this way, the scheme in this Example most resembles the scheme in *Locke*, which the Court upheld because it targeted a core religious activity—training clerics. Importantly, the scheme does not categorically deny aid to churches because of their religious status. Cf. *Freedom From Religion Foundation v. Morris County Bd. of Chosen Freeholders*, 232 N.J. 543 (2018). For analysis of the establishment clause implications of a similar scheme, see Example 19-8 in Chapter 19.

D. INTERACTION BETWEEN CONGRESS AND THE U.S. SUPREME COURT

1. The Religious Freedom Restoration Act

Lawmakers and religious groups reacted negatively to the U.S. Supreme Court's change of the standard of scrutiny in *Employment Division v. Smith*.

Not long after *Smith*, Congress passed (almost unanimously) the Religious Freedom Restoration Act (RFRA), which sought to return to the strict scrutiny standard in *Sherbert v. Verner*. RFRA provided that this standard of scrutiny should apply to all federal and state laws. The portion of RFRA that applied to state law, however, did not last very long. In what was arguably a jealous act to maintain its own power,[1] the U.S. Supreme Court ruled in *City of Boerne v. Flores*, 521 U.S. 507 (1997), that Congress had exceeded its power under section 5 of the Fourteenth Amendment when it changed the standard of scrutiny. Specifically, the Court ruled that Congress did not have the prerogative to make the standard of scrutiny more protective of religious expression than the U.S. Supreme Court had established in *Smith*.

Importantly, later cases confirmed that RFRA is not wholly invalid and remains in effect for evaluating whether federal law contravenes the First Amendment's protection of religious liberty. Although the Supreme Court has never explained why RFRA is constitutional as applied to the federal government, several of the Court's decisions assume that is the case. Scholars have proposed several theories as to why the federal government is treated differently than the states. The most obvious factor is that Congress passed RFRA pursuant to the Fourteenth Amendment, which governs the relationship between state and federal governments. Even if Congress's power to regulate states under the Fourteenth Amendment is limited, the same does not follow for Congress's power to regulate the extent to which federal laws might impinge on religious rights.

Maintaining the validity of RFRA for federal laws and regulations of religion has turned out to be significant. In *Burwell v. Hobby Lobby Stores, Inc.*, 573 U.S. 682 (2014), the Court evaluated a federal law that exempted religious institutions and non-profit corporations affiliated with religious institutions from including contraception coverage in employer health care plans. The Supreme Court held that this exemption violated the RFRA because it did not also exempt closely-held, for-profit corporations whose owners had religious objections to providing contraceptive coverage. The Court applied RFRA's strict scrutiny standard and concluded both that corporations have religious rights and that the contraception mandate substantially burdened the religious beliefs of closely-held corporations' owners. Although the Court accepted the government's compelling interest in ensuring the availability of contraceptives, the Court identified less restrictive alternatives to the requirement, such as paying for contraception with federal dollars.

---

1. *See* Laura E. Little, *Jealousy, Envy, and Separation of Powers*, 52 HASTINGS L.J. (2000).

Example 20-11:

Abortion Alternatives is a non-profit anti-abortion organization without any religious affiliation. Its purpose is to provide alternatives to abortion services, such as pregnancy and parenting support, and abstinence education. Abortion Alternatives and its employees do not support contraceptive use because they consider it to be morally wrong. In 2015, Abortion Alternatives excluded contraception care from the health insurance plan it offers its employees.

Because it was not religiously affiliated, Abortion Alternatives was not exempt from a federal mandate that all employer health insurance plans provide contraception coverage for employees. Several employees at Abortion Alternatives deeply embraced a religion that condemned the use of contraceptives and filed suit, arguing that the contraception mandate violated their religious rights under RFRA. Will they win this claim under the Supreme Court's *Hobby Lobby* case?

Explanation:

No, the employees are not likely to win the case under *Hobby Lobby*. In *Hobby Lobby*, it was the employer who challenged the contraception mandate. In this Example, it is the employees bringing the challenge. The mandate imposes different burdens on employers—who may be compelled to provide contraception in violation of their religious beliefs—and employees—who are free to refuse contraceptive services. The law has a process in place that institutes the health coverage. The employees, by their own volition, submit a form to become eligible for employer-provided health insurance. The employees are not, however, required to take any other action relating to contraception coverage. Once enrolled, the employees may choose not to use contraceptive services. Since the employees can decline to use contraception, they are not substantially burdened by the mandate, because simply signing up for insurance that might provide contraception to others is too attenuated to truly hinder their free exercise rights. Accordingly, the employees cannot successfully claim to have been compelled to endorse, advocate, or participate in facilitating that care. *See Real Alternatives, Inc. v. Secretary of Health and Human Servs.*, 867 F.3d 338 (3d Cir. 2017).

Note, however, the outcome of this Example might change as a result of the administrative changes to and other legal developments regarding the Affordable Care Act and the U.S. Supreme Court's statements about RFRA in the 2020 decision in *Little Sisters of the Poor v. Pennsylvania*, 140 S. Ct. 2367 (2020).

* * *

In 2017, the Trump administration created new "conscience exemptions" to the Affordable Care Act for private entities and organizations that had either moral or religious objections to contraceptives. Pennsylvania and New Jersey challenged the exemptions for employers that refuse to provide contraception to female employees, arguing that such opt-outs impose undue burdens on states that must provide alternate funding. Little Sisters of the Poor Saints Peter and Paul Home, a Catholic non-profit organization offering services to the poor and elderly, sued to force compliance with the expanded federal rules.

The Supreme Court ruled in favor of the Little Sisters of the Poor. The Court did not explicitly rely on the Constitution's free exercise clause in upholding the 2017 administrative changes to the Affordable Care Act and emphasizing the relevance of RFRA to the exemption issue. Nonetheless, many view the result as consistent with a trend in the U.S. Supreme Court to strengthen free exercise protections over establishment clause protections.

Example 20-12:

A religious organization known as Devoted Worshipers of the Heart of God holds the purity of the human heart as core to its belief system. The Devoted Worshipers believe that any medical treatment that affects the functioning of the human heart is contrary to its religious tenets. As a consequence, the Devoted Worshipers refuse to provide any health insurance to its employees that covers heart-related conditions. Several states bring suit, claiming that this position is illegal and arguing that the refusal to fund coverage for such common ailments as high blood pressure, congestive heart failure, and irregular heartbeats, would substantially burden state budgets. The Devoted Worshipers maintain that their refusal is lawful under the Supreme Court's decision in *Little Sisters of the Poor*.[2]

Explanation:

The Devoted Worshipers may win their case, although that result is uncertain. The *Little Sisters of the Poor* decision addressed a commonly held religious objection to contraception use, while this Example addresses an unusual objection to medical treatments for heart-associated maladies. That difference may trigger an inquiry into whether the objection of the Devoted Worshipers is indeed based on "religion" as interpreted in Supreme Court cases. Chapter 18 of this volume, as well as Example 20-13

---

2. This Example is inspired by the following newspaper column: Gail Collins, Opinion, *Sex, Sisters, and Dr. Donald*, N.Y. Times, July 8, 2020, at A22, available at, https://www.nytimes.com/2020/07/08/opinion/birth-control-supreme-court.html

below, explore the issue of what constitutes a religious belief for the purpose of free exercise protections. The new federal law in this Example provides for conscience exemptions in addition to religious ones. The Devoted Worshippers may find it easier to establish that treatments of heart-associated illness violate their consciences rather than their legally-recognized religious beliefs. With that approach, however, the organization may have a harder time invoking the protections of RFRA — which pertain to religious freedom. Nonetheless, the *Little Sisters of the Poor* Court relied primarily on its construction of the Affordable Care Act in reaching its decision. Assuming that interpretation would also apply in this Example, the Devoted Worshipers will win their case.

* * *

Although contraception coverage under federal law has served as a frequent subject for the application of RFRA to the federal government, other issues have emerged as well. The U.S. Supreme Court has not clarified whether any limits exist on RFRA's scope of coverage of federal law and federal activities.

Example 20-13:

The federal government hired a contractor to build an oil pipeline that would pump more than half a million gallons of oil through four states every day. Part of the proposed pipeline would run underneath a lake. In order to build that part of the pipeline, the contractor had to secure an easement from the federal government to use the land underneath the lake. A nearby Native American Tribe routinely used the lake water to perform religious rites. The Tribe believes that having clean, pure water is critical to perform the religious rites. Invoking RFRA, the Tribe sued to stop the federal government from granting the easement. Is the Tribe likely to succeed on this claim?

Explanation:

The chances are not good that the Tribe will succeed. In *Standing Rock Sioux Tribe v. U.S. Army Corps of Engineers*, 239 F. Supp. 3d 77 (D.D.C. 2017), the court entertained a similar RFRA challenge. The *Standing Rock* court assumed that RFRA controlled the challenge. The court noted that a person who brings a challenge under RFRA bears the burden of proving that: (1) the government's policy or action implicates her religious exercise; (2) the relevant religious exercise is grounded in a sincerely held religious belief; and (3) the policy or action substantially burdens that exercise. The court analyzed each of these prongs individually.

Considering these factors, the court noted that the religious exercise at issue focused on water-based ceremonies. The Tribe believed that water is sacred and that clean, pure water was an essential part of their way of life. Water also played a specific role in several of the Tribe's ceremonies. Observing that the sincere-belief inquiry is handled "with a light touch, or 'judicial shyness'" because it is almost exclusively a credibility assessment, the *Standing Rock* court determined that the Tribe established its sincerely held belief that the pipeline would interfere with its members' religious ceremonies. *Id.* at 90-91.

The court nevertheless took a strict view of RFRA's "substantial burden" standard. (Not all courts take a strict view and the Supreme Court has not articulated a precise definition.) The *Standing Rock* court reasoned that the government action here — granting the easement — did not sanction the Tribe members for exercising their religious beliefs. Nor did it pressure them to choose between religious exercise and the receipt of government benefits. Accordingly, the court cabined its inquiry to the government's precise action, and not the immediate consequences of that action.

Finally, the decision in *Lyng v. Northwest Indian Cemetery Protective Association*, 485 U.S. 439 (1988), which was decided under the strict scrutiny standard of *Employment Division v. Smith*, did not help the Tribe. The *Lyng* Court held that the incidental effect on religious exercise — even if extreme — from government action undertaken in furtherance of the management and use of government land is insufficient to give rise to a valid free exercise claim.

* * *

The U.S. Supreme Court has not addressed whether military service members enjoy protections under RFRA as federal employees, given the limitations imposed under *City of Boerne v. Flores*. Lower courts, however, have assumed that military personnel are protected by RFRA. As such, service members enjoy a substantially stronger right to free religious exercise under RFRA than they did under *Goldman v. Weinberger*, 475 U.S. 503 (1986), discussed in Example 20-2. This is true even though *Goldman* was decided under the strict scrutiny analysis established by *Sherbert v. Verner*, before the Supreme Court lowered the standard of scrutiny in *Employment Division v. Smith*. That said, the legislative history to RFRA makes clear that Congress expected courts to apply lower scrutiny to military regulations.

Example 20-14:

Harpreet is a university student seeking to join his school's Army ROTC program. The program requires that students who enroll in the program abide by the Army grooming standards while on duty which, among other things, prohibit service members from growing beards and wearing non-uniform headwear. The ROTC program allows enrollees to petition for exemptions from the grooming standards for medical reasons, and has granted exceptions to students with religious reasons for growing beards. Harpreet is a practicing Sikh and believes that he must be permitted to grow a beard and wear a turban at all times as part of his religious practice. He applies for an exemption from the grooming standards, but did not receive approval. The Army ROTC program denied Harpreet's exemption request for two reasons: (1) his proposed deviation from the grooming standard would adversely impact Army unit good order, morale, discipline, and cohesion; and (2) he would be unable to wear Army gas masks if he had a beard. The gas masks are used in optional Army ROTC drills, and although Harpreet could opt out of the drills, he could be required to report to active duty on short notice where he could be required to wear a mask as part of an Army operation.

Harpreet challenges the ROTC's denial of his exemption on grounds that his inability to wear a turban and grow a beard would infringe on his religious exercise in violation of the Religious Freedom Restoration Act. Is Harpreet likely to succeed in his suit?

Explanation:

Even given the RFRA legislative history and First Amendment case law regarding the high level of deference to military decision making, Harpreet is likely to succeed with his claim. As in *Goldman*, the government is arguing about the need for uniform dress and appearance in order to promote good order, morale, discipline, and cohesion. Assuming these are compelling state interests as required under RFRA's strict scrutiny analysis, it is not clear that those interests would be served by denying Harpreet's request. His fellow ROTC unit members would likely interpret Harpreet's deviation from the usual rules as an understandable and reasonable approach to his sincerely held religious beliefs. As for the gas mask issue, the Army could use less restrictive means for meeting this concern. Since the plaintiff would not need to wear a gas mask during his ROTC training, a temporary accommodation until military necessity actually required gas-mask wearing would both further the military's proffered interest and provide some accommodation for Harpreet's religious practice. If Harpreet were called to active duty, the army might constitutionally require him to shave in order to safely wear a gas mask or provide a non-standard issue mask that works with bearded operators. *See Singh v. McHugh*, 109 F. Supp. 3d 72 (D.D.C. 2016).

2. The Religious Land Use and Institutionalized Persons Act

After the Supreme Court's decisions in *Employment Division v. Smith* and *City of Boerne v. Flores*, Congress enacted the Religious Land Use and Institutionalized

Persons Act (RLUIPA). Like RFRA, the act revived *Sherbert v. Verner's* strict scrutiny standard for analyzing alleged violations of the First Amendment's free exercise protections. Unlike RFRA, which faced constitutional difficulties because it was enacted pursuant to the Fourteenth Amendment, Congress passed RLUIPA pursuant to the spending clause. Congress requires states to comply with RLUIPA's requirements as a condition for receiving certain federal funding, and each state has done so. RLUIPA is confined, however, to laws governing land use (such as zoning laws) and laws governing institutionalized persons (such as criminally convicted prisoners).

The U.S. Supreme Court has addressed RLUIPA twice, though only in cases concerning prison regulations. First, in *Cutter v. Wilkinson*, 544 U.S. 709 (2005), the Court upheld RLUIPA against a First Amendment establishment clause challenge. Several current and former Ohio inmates, including a Satanist and a Wiccan, sued the state under RLUIPA alleging that the state failed to accommodate their exercise of minority religions. The state responded by arguing that RLUIPA was unconstitutional because it provided protections only to religious individuals and not non-religious individuals. The Court unanimously upheld the statute as a permissible prophylactic measure that did not violate the establishment clause, emphasizing that the statute applies to all religions. The Court rejected Ohio's argument, stating that "[r]eligious accommodations . . . need not come packaged with benefits to secular entities." *Id.* at 724 (internal quotation marks omitted).

RLUIPA litigation presents the persistent issue of federal-court deference to prison administration. Yet the Court seems less deferential to prison administration in RLUIPA litigation than in other prison regulation contexts. This reduced deference is reflected in the Court's decision in *Holt v. Hobbs*, 574 U.S. 352 (2015). In that case, the Court struck down a prison policy prohibiting most prisoners from growing a beard longer than a quarter-inch. A Muslim inmate sued under RLUIPA after his request for permission to grow a half-inch beard—as part of his religious exercise—was denied. The Court held that, even assuming the prison had compelling interests in preventing individuals from using beards to conceal their identity from prison guards and to hide contraband, the prison failed to establish that its beard restriction was the least restrictive means of furthering those interests.

Example 20-15:

A Muslim inmate believes that he is bound by his faith to watch a weekly prayer television broadcast. The broadcast is generally available to inmates via cable television. The inmate is in solitary confinement, however, because of his significant history of disciplinary infractions and fights within the prison. As part of the prison's good-behavior incentive program, an inmate in solitary confinement is deprived of several amenities, including all television access. He can regain his access through the program if he demonstrates good behavior and remorse.

The inmate argues that, putting the good behavior program aside, the prison's denial of his television access amounts to a violation of RLUIPA. He argues that the prison could accommodate his request by bringing a television to his cell or escorting him to a separate room with a television to watch the program once a week. The prison did not dispute the sincerity of the inmate's belief. The prison instead argues that these accommodations would undermine its ability to incentivize good behavior through conditional privileges. Is the inmate likely to succeed in his claim?

Explanation:

Yes, the inmate is likely to succeed. The prison's refusal to allow him to watch the prayers significantly burdens his religious exercise, and the prison does not doubt the sincerity of his beliefs. The prison's reasons for withholding television privileges for prisoners with behavioral infractions are no doubt compelling: the privileges provide an incentive to improve behavior, and withholding them would promote prison discipline and safety. Yet the inmate is correct that the prison had less restrictive means to maintain the incentive program and accommodate the prisoner's religious need to view the weekly prayer without providing him unfettered television access: it could have either wheeled a television into the prisoner's cell, or it could have escorted the prisoner to a community television room to watch the broadcast. *See Greenhill v. Clarke*, 944 F.3d 243 (4th Cir. 2019).

E. EMPLOYMENT DISPUTES

The courts try to avoid entanglement in disputes between religious institutions and their employees, citing U.S. Supreme Court cases recognizing the so-called "ministerial exception" to government regulation of church labor practices. *See, e.g., Kedroff v. Saint Nicholas Cathedral of Russian Orthodox Church*, 344 U.S. 94, 116 (1952) (holding that the First Amendment protects the church's freedom to select clergy members against government interference); *Serbian Eastern Orthodox Diocese v. Milivojevich*, 426 U.S. 696 (1976) (holding that religious organizations can create their own rules and regulations for internal discipline and government, and tribunals for adjudicating internal disputes).

The Court elaborated on this concept more recently in *Hosanna-Tabor Evangelical Lutheran Church & School v. Equal Employment Opportunity Comm'n*, 565 U.S. 171 (2012). In that case, a religious school hired a teacher and commissioned her as a minister after she completed a theological course of study. The commission came with certain tenure benefits as well as the formal title "Minister of Religion, Commissioned." Id. at 177. In her role, the teacher led chapel services, student prayer, and taught a religion class. She sued the school under the Americans with Disability Act (ADA) when she was fired due to an employment dispute stemming from her narcolepsy. The Hosanna-Tabor Court determined that holding the school liable under the ADA for its choice about who could serve as a minister would violate the free exercise clause (and the establishment clause). The Court arguably could have disposed of the case under Employment Division v. Smith because the ADA is a neutral law of general applicability. But the Court distinguished Smith, observing that Smith concerned government regulation of personal conduct (ingesting peyote), while this case involved government interference with the internal decision making of a religious institution.

Hosanna-Tabor elaborated on the scope of this ministerial exception, making clear that religious schools are not liable for violations of employment discrimination laws with respect to their ministers, including elementary school teachers ordained as ministers. The Court outlined four factors to consider when analyzing if the exception applies: (1) whether the employee possessed the formal religious title of minister; (2) whether ministerial substance was reflected in the employee's title; (3) whether the employee proclaimed himself or herself a minister; and (4) whether the employee performed religious functions. The Court explained that the inquiry involves balancing and looks at "all the circumstances of [one's] employment" rather than a "rigid formula." Id. at 190. In this case, the teacher was exempted from traditional labor protections because all four factors were satisfied.

The Court more recently expanded this exception in Our Lady of Guadalupe School v. Morrissey-Berru, 140 S. Ct. 2049 (2020), determining that teachers in a Catholic elementary school could not bring claims against the school under the federal Age Discrimination Act or the Americans with Disabilities Act, although the teachers did not bear the title of "minister." According to the Court, an employee's title is not determinative of whether they merit the ministerial exception. What matters is whether the teacher played an important role in educating students in the school's faith, such that the teacher could be said to be an important part of school's religious mission.

Example 20-16:

Adrian was the music director at a Catholic parochial school for over ten years. As the music director, he was responsible for overseeing the music department's budget and expenditure, maintaining and managing the sound equipment and instruments in the music room, and accompanying members of the student choir on the piano during weekly mass held at the school.

Because Adrian was not Catholic himself and lacked the requisite knowledge and education, he could not handle all the liturgical responsibilities required to ensure that the music program included proper and accurate religious education. For that reason, the church hired a part-time employee to assist Adrian in those matters.

The school ultimately fired Adrian and replaced him with a young woman to serve as music director. Adrian sued the church under the federal Age Discrimination Act, claiming that the church fired him because of his age. The school argues that Adrian's lawsuit is barred by the ministerial exception because Adrian classifies as a ministerial employee. According to the school, Adrian's role was integral to the school's religious mission by providing students with education in and exposure to various aspects of Catholicism as expressed through music.

Should Adrian's lawsuit be barred by the ministerial exception as expanded in *Our Lady of Guadalupe School*?

Explanation:

Adrian's lawsuit is likely barred. The *Our Lady of Guadalupe School* Court ruled that a determination of whether the ministerial exception applies to an employee of a religious institution should be guided by his or her job responsibilities. Adrian's job appears to touch the religious mission of the school in one way—playing the piano at weekly Mass. But the Court also stated that in evaluating whether an employee's duties are key to the mission of a religious institution, courts should defer to the judgment of the religious institution. Here, the religious institution alleged that Adrian's duties were indeed integral to the school's religious mission. Given the deference to a religious employer emphasized in *Our Lady of Guadalupe School*, that allegation should be sufficient to trigger the ministerial exception for Adrian's lawsuit.

Communication, Association, and Religion Intersect

This chapter embraces the admittedly impossible task of providing a guide forward in reckoning with the First Amendment. What follows is a series of thoughts, not a set-in-stone formula or roadmap—simply a series of thoughts or a list of considerations as one wonders what to make of the chaos that emerges from First Amendment case law.

Whether a practitioner dispensing legal advice directly to a client, an associate, or a law student, using subject matter as one's guide, one could divide the First Amendment in a number of ways. One useful split in the subject area is communication, association, and religion. One can easily see how communication and association go together, as humans often express themselves in groups. Freedom of association protects groups and, therefore, protects expression. Freedom of association goes easily with religion too. Humans often worship in groups, and freedom of association helps to ensure that a group can worship together and remain intact.

The joinder of communication and religion is a little more baffling. Of course, one often practices religious rituals using words and expressive conduct, but almost everything in life occurs while words are used and meaningful conduct occurs. Moreover, religious worship is in many cases (not all) a deeply solitary endeavor. One wonders, then, whether the Framers had more in mind when they joined communication with religion in one document. With just a little research, one discovers that they did indeed have a more meaningful connection in mind than arises because groups use words and meaningful ritual (conduct) when they worship.

And what is the additional connection? One promising idea is freedom of conscience. One can see this emphasis on freedom of conscience in the initial draft of the First Amendment, which was presented by James Madison to the First Congress of the United States as a proposed amendment to the new national constitution. Madison's draft stated as follows: "[T]he civil rights of none shall be abridged on account of religious belief or worship, nor shall any national religion be established, nor shall the full and equal rights of conscience be in any manner, or on any pretext, infringed." *Lee v. Weisman*, 505 U.S. 577, 612 (1992) (Souter, J., concurring). Madison's draft failed and the word "conscience" does not appear in the ultimate First Amendment, but the insight is helpful (so long as it does not take over the analysis).

What is freedom of conscience? Conscience is that inner voice or feeling that helps one understand right and wrong so as to develop a personal moral code. Freedom of conscience is the liberty that one possesses in order to follow that voice. It is freedom to explore the world of thought, to believe what one wants, and to express that belief as one sees fit. The Founders likely spoke so extensively about the liberty of conscience because their own conscience had been oppressed by imperial leaders and overbearing established religion in Europe and in the American colonies.

Religion can guide individuals to understand the distinction between right and wrong and to develop a personal moral code. The freedom of conscience allows citizens to exercise religious beliefs and protects against government interference with religion. Accordingly, the liberty of conscience allows citizens to exercise or not exercise whatever religion they choose without heavy handed government control or endorsement of one religion over another.

Likewise, liberty of conscience also includes freedom to express ideas, thoughts, prayers, and opinions whether they are religious or secular in nature. Whether an individual expresses these matters alone or in association with others, the expression can inspire useful debate and conversation that assists all citizens in their search for truth and in their quest to define their personal moral code.

While the concept of freedom of conscience provides an analytic bridge between religion and communication, the concept does little to instruct on how to deploy the different categories of the First Amendment to frame a demand, to plead a cause of action, or to resolve a dispute. One must reckon with the language of the Amendment as well as the multiple strands of constitutional precedent to take on those tasks.

If you are called on to resolve a set of facts that potentially implicate more than one of the general categories of First Amendment rights, the approach reflected in the checklist presented in Chapter 17 serves as a useful starting point. Here is a summary of how the checklist applies in the context of a dispute that presents issues pertaining to more than one of the general First Amendment categories for protections for communication, association, and religion:

1. Identify which general category might apply to the dispute. One might easily find that more than one category applies.
2. Analyze each general category separately. Within each general category, use the Chapter 17 checklist to evaluate whether more than one strand of doctrine applies. That is, make a judgment about which strand of cases is the better choice and about whether prudence allows pursuing more than one strand. This process is outlined in the Chapter 17 checklist.
3. Once you have performed this task within each general category of First Amendment protections, you then need to evaluate whether one general category presents the best choice. You may conclude that more than one category works, or you might identify a reason why a particular category is weak or presents unwanted complications in the way it interacts with other categories. Many of the factors to consider in making these judgments are similar to those mentioned in Chapter 17. Some, however, are unique to the more global considerations bearing on which general category of First Amendment doctrine best fits the dispute you are analyzing. In this regard, here are some factors to consider:

*One general category may appear more accepted in current law than others. If you identify one category that is much more current than the others, that category of First Amendment doctrine may provide the most solid ground for analyzing and resolving the problem.

*If, after performing these steps, it appears that several general categories appear relevant and viable, identify the category that includes case law with facts that most closely resemble the fact pattern you are analyzing. That factual comparison may be the best route for resolving the dispute. To further evaluate the best choice, you might also want to consider the following:

*Evaluate which choice would best implicate the First Amendment values listed in the Introduction of this book (promoting self-governance, truth-seeking, personal autonomy, and tolerance). These can help you identify the strength of a particular category and may provide grist for framing effective arguments.

*If your analysis occurs in an adversary setting when you are representing the interests of one client (or one side of a dispute), evaluate which of the most promising strands of doctrine best serves your client's interests. Remember that "winning" may not be the only factor to consider: cost of litigation, and intangible factors such as inconvenience, jurisdictional challenges, your client's personal relationships, ethical concerns, your client's mission, and the like may also hang in the balance.

*Whether your analysis takes place when you are taking an exam, during your own brainstorming in how to frame your litigation strategy, or in a candid interchange with a knowledgeable client, remember to consider and to mention the unfavorable categories that arguably fit the case. It is quite possible that more than one First Amendment category is relevant, but one of the categories contains unfavorable case law for you. The process of identifying and discussing this unfavorable category will ensure that you can anticipate (and rebut) the arguments your opponent may use.

*Remember that there is nothing wrong with proposing more than one approach for resolving the dispute, if after your deliberations you conclude that more than one general category serves your goals well. In this regard, remember the following important caveat:

*Be on the lookout for negative ways in which the general categories intersect: emphasis on one category can create difficulties in using another. You cannot avoid this negative interaction as it is "baked" into the law. You can, however, avoid exacerbating, enhancing, or drawing attention to the negative effect by framing your arguments in a certain way or avoiding reliance on both categories.

Example 21-1:

You represent a group of public high school students who belong to a religious organization that engages in group worship that includes collective recitation of complicated verses referring to God and a series of vigorous physical movements. The movements are a form of ritual designed to symbolically demonstrate the religious participants' supplication to the will of God as well as to reinforce the participants' shared beliefs and sense of collective fellowship as members of the religious group.

The students would like to hold meetings at lunch hour during school days somewhere on the school property. In their meetings, they plan to assist each other in memorizing the lengthy verses used in worship, to discuss the meaning of the verses, and to practice the various movements used during worship.

The school refused the request. In justifying its refusal, the school explained that it has two main concerns. First, the school officials concluded that the practice of movements could create distracting noise, create a potentially dangerous environment to the participants, and disrupt others in the school. Second, the school officials explained that by allowing the group to use school facilities, it would be accused of endorsing or facilitating the practice of religion in violation of the Constitution's establishment clause.

The students have come to you for your help in enabling them to use school facilities for their meetings. As part of their description of the problem, the students inform you that the school allows three other student groups to meet during lunch hour, including the Young Democrats Club, the Environmental Advocacy Club, and the Gymnastic Club. In addition, they explain that the entire school takes lunch during the same hour.

Outline the advice that you would give the religious students, including a consideration of the best arguments concerning the categories of First Amendment protections that may serve them as well as practical concerns that they should consider.

Explanation:

This Example presents an opportunity to analyze a number of matters, including practical concerns and advocacy techniques, many of the legal principles covered in this book, and strategies for juggling the interaction among the general categories of First Amendment protections, as well as the various strands of doctrinal analysis.

1. Practical Concerns and Advocacy Techniques

As an initial matter, you would be advised to explore with the students the wisdom of avoiding a hostile confrontation or full-on adversary approach with the school administrators. The students are confronting an unequal power dynamic: the administrators have far more authority and resources than they do. Moreover, the administrators have the ability to affect their lives in ways unrelated to club meeting issues, whether by direct retaliation or micro-aggressions directed at the group or the members individually. Other details that would inform your advice include the group's size, general social status, ethnic affiliation, sexual orientation, gender identity, immigrant status, racial identity, and the like.

You might counsel the students to also consider whether an aggressive, adversary approach would be consistent with their belief system and group mission. They might also consider how the approach would affect the public relations image of their particular group and the larger religious organization. They should also be apprised of the possible monetary and emotional costs of an adversary approach to resolution.

At bottom, prudence suggests starting with a friendly, low-key approach with the school administrators: laying out for them the legal ramifications of their outright denial of the religious students' request. In pursuing this approach, you may conclude that all would benefit if the students were closely involved in meetings and planning. By participating, the students are more likely to be happy with the ultimate resolution, to understand the reasons for and details of the resolution, to comply with the terms of the resolution, and generally to take ownership of it.

Finally, in discussing the students' participation with the administrators, you might point out that including the students in the entire process would serve an educational function. They would be able to observe an attempt at dispute resolution, learn the benefit of controlling emotional impulses, and become acquainted with principles of constitutional law. This may not only be appealing to the administrators' sense of the school's pedagogical mission, but may also inspire them to adopt a conciliatory attitude.

2. Evaluating the General Categories of First Amendment Protections

First Amendment case law shows that a First Amendment challenge is usually more likely to succeed by establishing that a regulator (such as the school administrators here) violated more than one First Amendment protection. Doing so enhances the impression that the regulator either intentionally or recklessly disregarded the effect of its actions on precious constitutional protections enjoyed by citizens of the United States. Moreover, relying on more than one general category increases the possible grounds for success, particularly where—as here—the decision maker need only choose one of the grounds for challenge in order for the challenger to prevail completely.

In following this approach, however, you should be mindful of potential pitfalls, looking for negative consequences of joining two or more First Amendment categories. Do any doctrinal details make one general category more problematic when joined with another general category? For example, by urging a freedom of religion problem, are you talking yourself into an establishment clause problem? From a rhetorical point of view, does including arguments about more than one general category suggest that you are "overplaying your hand?" (In the First Amendment area, as elsewhere in the law—it is usually a successful approach to pursue more than one legal theory.) Also, be sure to look out for instances of appearing as though you are "piling on," or unfairly portraying the regulators in a nefarious light. ("Piling on" is less problematic in an exam situation than in another context: in an exam situation, one is usually throwing out ideas to get points, but in a litigation situation one runs the risk of annoying the decision maker with more than necessary arguments.)

These admonitions do not, of course, suggest that that you should not carefully consider all the possible First Amendment protections or leave open the possibility that all the general First Amendment categories may provide a potent source for challenge.

(a) Freedom of Communication

Two strands of the freedom of communication doctrine appear particularly relevant to the school administration's decision here. First, the administration's outright refusal to the religious students and permission granted to other groups suggests unconstitutional content-based discrimination against speech (covered in Chapter 1 of this volume). Second, the administrators' decision may violate the students' rights to engage in expressive conduct (covered in Chapter 11 of this volume).

(1) Free Speech

To begin with a challenge based on speech, you might start by observing the U.S. Supreme Court has held that religious worship and discussion are a form of speech protected by the First Amendment. *Widmar v. Vincent*, 454 U.S. 263 (1981). Moreover, by their own admission, the school administrators established that they refused your client's request because of the religious content of the activity that they planned for their meetings.

One could also point out that the religious students planned to discuss ideas embodied in religious verses during their meetings. Presumably, the Democratic students and the environmental advocacy students would do the same. Discussion and debate of ideas linked closely with many of the First Amendment's core values: self-governance, personal autonomy, and truth discovery. The school officials may attempt to minimize this argument by pointing out that the Democratic students and environmental advocacy students concentrate on political matters, a crown jewel of First Amendment concerns. While it is true that debate about political matters is often deemed the most crucial component of freedom of speech protections (see Chapter 3 of this volume), that fact does not diminish the status of religious worship and discussion as speech or permit the school administrators' discriminatory treatment of religious speech.

In order to survive constitutional attack against that kind of discriminatory, content-based exercise of authority, the administrators must satisfy the strict scrutiny standard of review. This requires them to demonstrate that their decision is narrowly tailored to serve a compelling purpose. Considered in a vacuum, the administrators' proffered concerns with avoiding disturbance to others in the school building and ensuring the safety of the religious students may be compelling. One wonders, however, whether the disturbance concern is lessened during lunch hour when most of the building is not engaged in formal instruction. More importantly, one might reasonably doubt that the proffered safety concern is sincere, since that same concern would presumably arise for the Gymnastic Club for which the administrators have granted permission.

The administrators' establishment clause concern deserves more serious evaluation. A look at the U.S. Supreme Court case law, however, suggests several cases potentially undermine the concern. Most importantly, the Supreme Court has held in three cases that a school does not violate the establishment clause when it provides a religious group access to school facilities.

One relevant case, *Widmar v. Vincent*, 454 U.S. 263 (1981), concerned a university. The school administrators might argue that *Widmar* does not present a close analogy because universities operate in a much less restricted manner than secondary schools, opening their facilities to a larger range of individuals and groups than secondary schools (which need to keep tighter reins on discipline and safety). Moreover, establishment clause concerns are heightened in the secondary school context because high school students are more impressionable than the adult students at universities. One would guess that mature university students are more likely to make their own independent judgment about religious matters than teenagers, whether or not it appears that school authorities endorse or approve those religious matters.

The two other most pertinent cases, *Lamb's Chapel v. Center Moriches Union Free School District*, 508 U.S. 384 (1993), and *Good News Club v. Milford Central School*, 533 U.S. 98 (2001), are discussed in Chapter 19 of this volume. *Lamb's Chapel* concerned an entire public-school district policy and *Good News Club* concerned an elementary school, thus providing an arguably closer analogy to this Example. One salient distinction, however, is that both cases found no establishment clause problem with a school allowing religious groups to use school facilities *after school hours*. This after school timing suggests to any observer that the school administrators are less removed from events occurring on school property than they would be for events allowed during school hours. One mitigating factor in this Example is that the religious group would be meeting during non-instructional time for nearly everyone in the school. This separates the group meeting from the school-endorsed and school-implemented curriculum.

Yet another line of recent religion cases adds strength to the conclusion that the school's establishment clause concern is not a viable obstacle. As discussed in Chapter 19, recent U.S. Supreme Court cases have expressly held that the concern with avoiding establishment clause challenges does not amount to a compelling reason for infringing on a First Amendment right. The Court made this statement in the context of free exercise of religion challenges, not free speech challenges. The Court, however, has labeled both speech and religious freedoms as fundamental rights, thus suggesting that a justification that is not compelling in one context would not be compelling in the other context.

Assuming the students do not succeed in showing that any of these obstacles to challenging the school administrators' establishment clause concerns are insurmountable, the administrators would still need to show that their decision regarding the religious club is narrowly tailored. Given that the decision took the form of a blanket refusal to provide access to school facilities, this would be difficult to establish. The school would need to show why lesser restrictions, such as moving the meetings to after school hours or moving the location of the meetings to the gym where the gymnastic group meets, would not sufficiently satisfy their concerns.

(2) Expressive Conduct

The religious students plan to practice the movement portion of their religious worship ceremonies in their group meetings. These movements unquestionably have an expressive purpose: they communicate beliefs in a human's relationship with God and celebrate group membership. The administrators' decision to prevent students from meeting to practice these movements thus prevents them from engaging in expressive conduct. For conduct that has a religious component, the law does not have a clear answer. Free expression law does have an approach to help, which could (or could not) provide an answer. *See United States v. O'Brien*, 391 U.S. 367 (1968), which concerned a test for an entirely different expressive conduct context: draft card burning during the Vietnam War. Chapter 11 of this volume covers *O'Brien* and issues related to expressive conduct.

O'Brien articulated a four-part test for evaluating whether restrictions of expressive conduct are constitutional. Three of those parts are relevant here: (1) the restriction must further "an important or substantial governmental interest;" (2) the interest must be "unrelated to the suppression of free expression; and" (3) the "incidental restriction on alleged First Amendment freedoms [must be] no greater than is essential to the furtherance of that interest." *Id.* at 377. The *O'Brien* Court joined the various parts of the test with the conjunction "and"—thus making clear that the government authorities must satisfy all parts of the test.

Given the dearth of Supreme Court guidance on the particular issues presented in this problem, *O'Brien* could potentially provide a guide. If that is the case, school administrators in this Example run into potential problems with these three parts of the *O'Brien* test quoted above:

(a) Important or substantial government interest: While the above discussion provides strong grounds for concluding that the administration's concern with avoiding problems with the establishment clause is not compelling, it is not clear whether the concern amounts to a substantial or important interest.

(b) As established above, the purpose of the restriction is decidedly targeting on suppressing expression—at least in context of a meeting on school property during the school day.

(c) Also established above, the school administrators' decision is an absolute denial of access and they have not provided a rationale for why less intrusive restrictions may not suffice to serve their proffered reasons for the restrictions.

In conclusion, both the freedom of speech and freedom of expressive conduct theories provide solid grounds for challenging the administrators' decision.

(b) Freedom of Association

Freedom of group expression and freedom of association generally go hand-in-hand. This Example is no exception. The students belong to a religious group defined by group worship and celebrating the benefits of group cohesion. Providing an obstacle for students to engage in group activities that reinforce those goals thus interferes with the students' freedom of association.

This type of interference is far less complicated or nuanced than the types of regulation discussed in detail in this volume's chapter on freedom of association (Chapter 16), such as prohibitions or punishment of group membership and forced disclosure of group membership. Like freedom of communication, freedom of association is a fundamental right requiring strict scrutiny of government decisions that restrict the right. Thus, the freedom of association approach to evaluating the constitutionality of the school administration's restriction on access is nearly the same as the approach for evaluating the intrusion on freedom of speech. Accordingly, as was the case with the conclusion regarding a challenge based on the students' religious speech rights, a challenge based on their associational rights has a firm foundation.

(c) Religion Clauses

The only religion clause that would serve as an affirmative basis for challenge to the administrators' decision is the free exercise clause. While relevant to this Example, the establishment clause would serve only as a possible defense to the students' claims that other First Amendment privileges were violated by the access denial. For the reasons surveyed above, the school administrators are unlikely to prevail with an establishment clause defense.

As explained in Chapter 20 of this volume, a free exercise claim is difficult to raise successfully given the current constitutional test articulated in *Employment Division v. Smith*, 494 U.S. 872 (1990). Nonetheless, three other closely analogous U.S. Supreme Court cases provide strong support for the students' free exercise claim. The establishment clause discussion immediately above covers each of these cases: *Widmar v. Vincent; Lamb's Chapel v. Center Moriches Union Free School District;* and *Good News Club v. Milford Central School.*

All three of the cases stand for the proposition that depriving a student religious club of access to school facilities violates the students' free exercise rights. The school administrators in this Example might argue that the first case, *Widmar*, is no longer good law after the Court's 1990 decision in

Employment Division v. Smith. This argument does not work for the other two decisions, which postdated the *Employment Division* case. For the reasons stated above, these latter two cases are marginally distinguishable from the facts of this Example because of the students' ages, but this distinction is likely not fatal. Accordingly, the students' free exercise claim has strong precedential support.

2. Ultimate Conclusion on the Major Categories of First Amendment Protections and Probability of Success

All of the major categories present a strong basis for challenging the school administrators' decision to deny the religious students' request. Each category has current precedent to support the students' challenge. The various categories generally work together synergistically in these facts and do not appear to raise the possibility of complications. Nor does the prospect of joining them together raise the possibility that pressing a challenge based on one category would highlight an unfavorable aspect of another challenge. In short, the best strategy is likely to raise challenges based on all categories.

The existing precedent suggests that the students are in a good position to persuade the administrators to change their mind. If nothing else, the administrators may very well be willing to compromise by allowing the students to meet on school property after the school day is finished or on weekends.

* * *

The lengthy and meandering nature of the explanation to Example 21-1 is emblematic of First Amendment analysis and advocacy. But no need to despair at the various complications that arise in the First Amendment area! This quality provides you with the opportunity for success and intellectual satisfaction by giving you a rich occasion to deploy your creativity, knowledge, and lawyering skills in service of refining and understanding some of the most important rights in U.S. democracy.

Table of Cases

Table of Cases

Table of Cases

Table of Cases

Table of Cases

Index

Index

Index

Index